S0-DTH-695

TEACHING
ELEMENTARY SCHOOL
MATHEMATICS FOR
UNDERSTANDING

QA
135.5
T397

TEACHING ELEMENTARY SCHOOL MATHEMATICS FOR UNDERSTANDING

Fourth Edition

John L. Marks
Professor of Mathematics
and Education
San Jose State College
San Jose, California

C. Richard Purdy
Formerly Professor
of Mathematics
California State College
Hayward, California

Lucien B. Kinney
Formerly Professor
of Education Emeritus
Stanford University
Standford, California

Arthur A. Hiatt
Mathematics Coordinator
California State University
Fresno, California

McGraw-Hill Book Company

New York   St. Louis   San Francisco   Auckland   Düsseldorf
Johannesburg   Kuala Lumpur   London   Mexico   Montreal   New Delhi
Panama   Paris   São Paulo   Singapore   Sydney   Tokyo   Toronto

WITHDRAWN
LIBRARY
Pacific College M. B. Seminary
Fresno, 93702

42656

Library of Congress Cataloging in Publication Data
Main entry under title:

Teaching elementary school mathematics for understanding.

   First ed. published in 1958 under title: Teaching arithmetic
for understanding. Previous editions by J. L. Marks, C. R. Purdy,
and L. B. Kinney.
     1. Mathematics—Study and teaching (Elementary) I. Marks,
John L. Teaching elementary school mathematics for understanding.
QA135.5.T397   1975   372.7   74-12122
ISBN 0-07-040422-4

Teaching Elementary School Mathematics for Understanding

Copyright © 1958, 1965, 1970, 1975 by McGraw-Hill, Inc. All rights reserved.
Printed in the United States of America. No part of this publication may
be reproduced, stored in a retrieval system, or transmitted in any form or by
any means, electronic, mechanical, photocopying, recording, or otherwise,
without the prior written permission of the publisher.

1 2 3 4 5 6 7 8 9 0 V H V H 7 9 8 7 6 5 4

This book was set in Univers by Publications Development Corporation.
The editor was Stephen D. Dragin; the designer was Publications Development
Corporation; the production supervisor was Milton J. Heiberg
Von Hoffmann Press, Inc., was printer and binder.

CONTENTS

PREFACE

As the demand for competence in mathematics for both personal and professional life continues to increase, constant reexamination and revision of the school mathematics program is required. Hence, the mathematics teacher today must keep up with new developments in an ever-changing curriculum.

Mastering the essential mathematics is a first step toward effective teaching; however, what pupils learn depends upon what the teacher has them do. The teacher must provide classroom experiences which reinforce basic concepts for each pupil, as well as stimulate his interest and meet his individual needs. Thus the second step toward effective teaching is the acquisition of a fund of such experiences.

A fourth edition of this book was undertaken because of the belief that its basic approach to teaching elementary school mathematics, that of providing the teacher with classroom experiences for pupils, was still a useful and effective one. At the same time, the need was recognized for a revision to update the content by incorporating the most recent curricular changes.

Research into how children learn verifies the premise that learning proceeds from the concrete to the abstract. Hence, in this fourth edition, even more than in the first three, the pattern has been to provide the pupil first with a concrete model for a mathematical idea, then with the verbal language required to describe the model, and finally with the symbolic language to express the idea in written form. Consistent with this emphasis, the mathematical content has been presented not for its own sake but as a means through which pupils can learn mathematical processes.

This edition, like the previous ones, relies on activities with demonstrated value for helping pupils understand, use, and enjoy mathematics. There is particular stress on:

● *Intuitive experiences* as well as experiences emphasizing the formal and structural aspects of mathematics.

● *Experiences* through which the teacher can prepare, motivate, and guide pupils in their study of new topics.

● *Organizing experiences* into lessons.

● *Techniques* for appraising progress with specific examples of diagnosing difficulties and prescribing experiences to overcome these difficulties.

● *Procedures* for attacking mathematical problems.

The number and variety of experiences for pupils provided in this book is unusually extensive. No one teaching method is exclusively recommended, except where its superiority has been well established. Lists of suggested experiences supply ready references as the teacher plans lessons. From them, exercises specially suited to certain classes or pupils can readily be selected.

But a variety of experiences in itself is not sufficient to ensure effective learning; a proper sequence is equally essential. The teacher planning such a sequence will find practical suggestions for guiding the pupil step-by-step from the initial readiness for learning to the application of the matured skill or concept in new situations. Several new features highlight this fourth edition:

● The last section of Chapters 3-12 contains a sample list of experiments expected to accomplish one or more objectives. Each experiment can be given to an individual pupil or group of pupils.

● Appendices contain games, activities, a supplementary bibliography and directions for making inexpensive teaching materials.

● The role of the mathematics laboratory as an added source of effective learning and discovery by pupils is discussed in detail in Chapter 2 and emphasized in each succeeding chapter with examples of class-tested experiments.

● Chapter 10 has been expanded to include the concepts of number pairs and functions, two ideas basic to the elementary school mathematics program which pervade the entire curriculum through graduate mathematics.

● Metric units are used almost exclusively.

● References to sources and research have been kept to a minimum, however, a selected sample is included in the up-to-date Bibliography at the end of each chapter.

● The student will also find questions and exercises and a list of projects at the end of each chapter. They are designed to lead the teacher-in-training to translate ideas into action in the classroom.

This fourth edition is dedicated to the memory of the late C. Richard Purdy and Lucien B. Kinney who gave great thought, energy, and time to preparing the first three editions of this text. Their insights into how children learn mathematics have been retained in this edition.

We would like to thank Professor Donald A. Buckeye of Eastern Michigan University who assisted in the early planning of this book.

John L. Marks
Arthur A. Hiatt

TEACHING ELEMENTARY SCHOOL MATHEMATICS FOR UNDERSTANDING

1
SCOPE, SEQUENCE, AIMS, AND TRENDS

In addition to the primary task of selecting and directing experiences for pupils in his own classes, the teacher has a responsibility to work with other teachers, administrators, and the public in planning a mathematics program oriented toward well-defined goals for each grade level and each child. This chapter provides a background for understanding the essentials of effective programs and experiences for pupils by:

● Reviewing and discussing the recent history of elementary school mathematics curricula development.

● Suggesting the scope and typical sequence for contemporary school mathematics.

● Outlining the primary aims for school mathematics instruction.

● Illustrating some of the apparent trends in school mathematics instruction.

● Summarizing concerns about the mathematics curriculum especially those influencing the development of a pupil regardless of his ability and background.

RECENT HISTORICAL BACKGROUND

The history of teaching mathematics over the centuries reveals many examples of different emphases, each having its effect on curricula of the period. At various times stress was placed on skills, applications, or the mathematical aspects and their understanding by the learner. While details of this earlier history are interesting and enlightening, their current significance is slight, and attention here will be focused on more recent developments.

Dramatic modifications in mathematics curricula since the mid-1950s may be viewed as a rapid acceleration and change in emphasis of the *meaningful arithmetic* program that emerged during the thirties, forties, and fifties.

Brownell presented a comprehensive discussion of what has generally been called *meaningful arithmetic* in 1935. His point of view may be illustrated by some typical statements: "Arithmetic is best viewed as a system of quantitative thinking...."[1] "The meaning theory conceives of arithmetic as a closely knit system of understandable ideas, principles and processes."[2] "The basic tenet in the proposed instructional reorganization is to make arithmetic less a challenge to the pupil's memory and more a challenge to his intelligence."[3]

The meanings approach stressed understanding of computation procedures through applications of properties of the Hindu-Arabic numeration system. This was accompanied by increased attention to types of experiences appropriate for meeting individual differences among pupils, greater use of manipulative materials for promoting learning from the concrete *to the abstract,* and shift from reliance on a "tell-do" method of teaching to greater use of methods such as discovery of relations and generalizations by pupils.

The many changes brought about by applying the meaning theory resulted in an improved curriculum. Actually, however, the basic purposes of meaningful arithmetic were never fully realized. Because insufficient attention was given to basic properties of the operations on various sets of numbers, and because some meanings were taught in such a way that they had to be unlearned at a later date, understanding was not complete.

The main emphasis, therefore, during the decade from about 1957 to 1967 was on retaining advances made under the meanings approach, while eliminating ineffective procedures and incorporating more mathematical ideas and effective methods for teaching them. These changes are in accord with the modern needs of everyday life and are designed to broaden the understanding of mathematics. Some educators believe that a major direction of contemporary curricula may properly be interpreted as an extension of the meaningful arithmetic of the 1930s and 1940s; others feel that contemporary programs constitute a trend only slightly related to meaningful arithmetic.

Regardless of the interpretation, major alterations in content, sequence, and emphases of elementary school mathematics took place through the mid-1960s. Special attention was focused on teaching mathematical concepts, structure of mathematics, and na-

[1] W. A. Brownell, "Psychological Considerations in the Learning and the Teaching of Arithmetic," *The Teaching of Arithmetic*, Tenth Yearbook of the National Council of Teachers of Mathematics, Washington, D.C., 1935, p. 10.
[2] *Ibid.,* p. 19.
[3] *Ibid.,* p. 31.

ture of proof; there were refinements in the vocabulary with a stress on precision of expression. This program could be generally characterized as oriented toward mathematics itself rather than its social uses.

Many of the changes that took place during this period are included in present programs. In addition there now seems to be a trend toward making the curriculum more "relevant" with special consideration to outlining objectives. There is also at present a renewed interest in individualizing instruction with a special emphasis on the use of a mathematics laboratory where individuals or groups work with materials, perform experiments, and discover ideas and algorithms. Thus the coming decade should be a fertile period for experimenting with teaching methods and classroom management systems.

TYPICAL SCOPE AND SEQUENCE

The summary in the following seven sections is intended to provide a broad comprehensive view of the elementary school mathematics program by outlining major concepts and topics that are introduced and a general sequence for their introduction. Many of these concepts will be explored in later chapters. Specific information in grade placement and more detailed information on content may be obtained through an examination of up-to-date textbook series.

Sets and Numbers

The concept of *set* is usually studied early in the program. Pupils identify and name sets of children, school supplies, and other objects in the classroom. They find that some pairs of sets can be placed in one-to-one correspondence and some cannot. They form subsets of a set, join them, and separate them. Later they learn to count members of sets and identify a number with a set such as four with the first set and two with the second as in Fig. 1-1. Pupils begin very early to concentrate on studying sets of numbers and geometric figures, as in Fig. 1-2. In the middle grades they study sets of fractional numbers, prime numbers, and names for the same number, and formalization of operations on sets, such as union and intersection. Suitable notation is introduced as it contributes to understanding.

Computation

Addition of whole numbers is introduced soon after joining sets is objectified. Addition facts (Fig. 1-3a), column addition (Fig. 1-3b), and algorithms (Fig. 1-3c) are studied in a more or less specific order by the end of grade two. Subtraction of whole numbers is

Figure 1-1
A set of four members and a set of two members.

Figure 1-2
Sets of numbers and geometric figures.

{1, 2, 3, 4}

{5, 10, 15, 20}

{□, ⬭, △}

Figure 1-3

(a)	6 + 1	8 + 4	9 + 8	3 + 7

(b)	3 1 + 4	4 5 + 8	9 5 + 6

(c)	31 + 46	127 + 548

related to addition, and skills associated with these two operations are learned concurrently. The concepts of multiplication and division of whole numbers are begun at about grade two, and the facts and algorithms constitute an important part of the curriculum through grade five. The operations with fractional numbers are taught in grades three through six, and those for decimals are taught in grades four through six.

Numeration

The pupil learns to use a symbol to represent a number as he finds it necessary to record data from experiments with sets. The properties of our numeration system, such as base ten and place value, are gradually developed by concrete experiences with bundles of cards or sticks and other devices. Numerals for fractions, decimals, and percents are learned in the middle grades. Numeration systems in other bases and those of ancient peoples may be studied in grades five through eight as an enrichment.

Measurement

In the first grade pupils learn that the pencil is longer than the paper clip, the book heavier than the pencil, and the floor warmer than the window. Later they tell that the desk is about seven pieces of chalk wide or that the rock weighs about the same as four tablets. Subsequently they make scales and are able to assign numbers, together with units, to describe the measurement of things (Fig. 1-4). After they discover that a unit which covers a region can be used to measure its size, they begin the study of area. In grades four through eight, formulas for areas of the interiors of such figures, as rectangles, triangles, trapezoids, and circles are developed, and formulas for the areas of surfaces and volumes of interiors of prisms, pyramids, and cylinders are discovered and applied.

Geometry

The environment of the child furnishes the basis for his first geometric experiences. He identifies spheres (balls), prisms (boxes), triangles, squares, and so on, and observes and describes their properties. The idea of geometric figures as sets of points is introduced in the middle grades. The concepts of union and intersection of these sets are used to define figures such as angles, parallel lines, and polygons. Simple construction, using a straight edge and compass, is learned in grades four through eight. While the study of figures and their properties is essentially nonmetric (no measurement) geometry, it is introduced along with ideas of measurement for maximum effectiveness.

Figure 1-4

"This kitten weighs about 2 pounds"

"This jar holds about 4 pints"

"This fence is about 10 feet long"

Applications

The study of applications of mathematics—numerical and geometric problems from the life of the child and from the textbook—continues to be of major importance in the mathematics curriculum. Even before pupils can read, they solve problems encountered in the classroom or given orally by the teacher; then they "make up" their own problems. The program continues with more complex problems—some with too much data, some with insufficient data, some stated without numbers, some that cannot be solved, and other variations. In every grade the pupil studies many of these *word* problems, which are applications of the content of that grade.

Structure

The word *structure* is used with many different meanings. In a broad sense, it refers to ideas that help tie together the study of mathematics. We may illustrate briefly here the structure dealing with the properties of numeration and number systems, with their applications to understanding various algorithms.

By understanding the properties of our numeration system, the pupil can comprehend the meaning of numerals. Very early in school he learns to recognize the properties of the numeration system that permit him to name 47 as

$$40 + 7 \text{ or } 30 + 17 \text{ or } 50 - 3 \text{ or as } (3)\,(15) + 2$$

Later he thinks of 8,000 as

$$8,000 \text{ ones, } 800 \text{ tens, } 80 \text{ hundreds, or } 8 \text{ thousands}$$

Figure 1-5

These various forms for recording numbers are one aspect of the properties of the system of numeration which the pupil must understand in order to comprehend the steps in algorithms for adding, subtracting, multiplying, and dividing whole numbers. In the middle grades and beyond, he applies these properties to greater numbers and uses exponents to simplify his symbolism.

Studying properties of number systems is also begun early in school. For the whole-number system the pupil discovers many illustrations of the commutative laws: first, that

$$1 + 2 = 2 + 1 \text{ and } 3 \times 4 = 4 \times 3$$

and, later, that

$$83 + 17 = 17 + 83 \text{ and } 31 \times 48 = 48 \times 31$$

finding the easier of the two multiplications (Fig. 1-5). Still later, he may generalize:

$$\text{If } a \text{ and } b \text{ are whole numbers, then } a + b = b + a$$

"I need to find the cost of 382 tickets at $0.75 each"

It's easier to do
382   0.75
×0.75 than ×382

and

$$\text{If } r \text{ and } s \text{ are whole numbers, then } r \cdot s = s \cdot r$$

The pupil senses early, too, that the sum of two whole numbers and product of two whole numbers are always whole numbers (closure). He applies the associative property for addition in adding a column of numbers. He uses the identity elements first in learning addition facts with one addend 0 such as $0 + 3 = 3 + 0 = 3$ and multiplication facts with a factor of 1 such as $5 \times 1 = 1 \times 5 = 5$. The properties are studied again as fractional numbers are introduced, and in the upper grades pupils find they apply also to the system of integers (Fig. 1-6) and arithmetic on a clock (Fig. 1-7). These and other properties for operations on numbers, together with the properties of numeration systems, provide justification for various algorithms, such as those for addition, subtraction, multiplication, and division. For example, the *invert and multiply* algorithm for division with fractional numbers is rationalized when properties for operations on this set are established. In the upper grades similar properties provide justification for procedures in algebra. The pupil more fully realizes and isolates the significance of these properties as he finds operations such as subtraction and division for which they do not hold.

With this very brief preview of content and its order, a preliminary look at the nature of outcomes sought from the study of mathematics provides additional perspective for more careful study of experiences for pupils in contemporary programs.

AIMS FOR ELEMENTARY SCHOOL MATHEMATICS

The major purposes of the mathematics curriculum for the elementary school are closely interrelated. Any lesson contributes to more than one major aim, but, for convenience, five major goals for the K-8 mathematics program may be distinguished. Each of these goals is illustrated below by typical behavior that would be expected if the goal were realized. When aims are stated in this form, progress of the pupil can be evaluated readily; also, the aims serve as a guide in the selection of content.

The overall purpose of contemporary education is to equip people to function effectively in our technological age. Mathematics is a key to this preparation because of its unique role in every facet of common life. For example, understanding concepts and having well-developed skills are necessary, but not sufficient, for the scientists who develop new mathematics or who apply it to new situations. Such persons must also have the ability to discover, create, verify, and generalize. Development of these abilities, which

Figure 1-6
Zero for addition and 1 for multiplication are identities for integers.

$$0 + {}^-3 = {}^-3 + 0 = {}^-3$$

$${}^-7 \times 1 = 1 \times {}^-7 = {}^-7$$

Figure 1-7

"On these clockfaces
$4 + 2 = 1$ and $2 + 4 = 1$.
So $4 + 2 = 2 + 4 = 1$."

are needed by the average citizen as well, is a product of the methods of learning employed rather than the specific content studied.

This list of aims is not presented as a complete description the mathematics program. The subtopics under each major ding are merely illustrations which will be expanded in more ail in subsequent chapters.

I Development of concepts

    A The concept of a number such as five

        1 Uses symbol 5 to represent the number in sets such as in Fig. 1-8.

        2 Thinks of five as one more than four, two less than seven, or half of ten.

        3 Knows that 5 divides, with no remainder, any whole number named with a 5 or 0 in the 1s place.

    B The concept of a fraction such as 3/4

        1 Pictures 3/4 as in Fig. 1-9.

        2 Uses 3/4 as equal to three 1/4s or 1/2 and 1/4, or six 1/8s, or as 1/4 less than 1.

        3 Knows 3/4 is greater than 2/3, 1/2, or 3/5 but less than 8/10, 7/8, or 5/6.

        4 Writes different names for 3/4 and recognizes that there is an infinite set of such names.

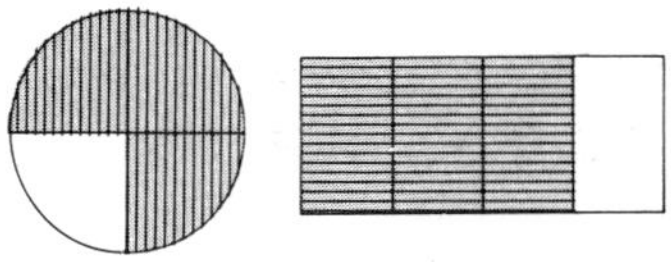

    C The concept of a triangle

        1 Understands a triangle such as ABC (Fig. 1-10) as a set of points that is the union of line segments AB, BC, and CA.

        2 Draws pictures of triangles that have three congruent or two congruent sides.

        3 Distinguishes among points on the triangle, in its interior, and in its exterior.

II Development of mathematical understanding

    A Kinds of numbers

        1 Knows sets of numbers, as in Fig. 1-11.

        2 Knows that the set of fractional numbers can be expressed in the form x/y, where x may represent any whole number and y may represent any counting number (Fig. 1-12).

    B Properties of numbers under addition and multiplication

        1 Knows that the sum of any two whole numbers is unchanged if the order of adding is changed.

Figure 1-8
Sets of five members.

0
0000

Figure 1-9
Picturing 3/4.

Figure 1-10
$\triangle ABC$ is the union of $\overline{AB}$, $\overline{BC}$, and $\overline{CA}$.

Figure 1-11
Sets of numbers.

Counting   {1, 2, 3, 4, . . .}

Prime   {2, 3, 5, 7, 11, 13, . . .}

Integers {. . .⁻3, ⁻2, ⁻1, 0, 1, 2, 3. . .}

Figure 1-12

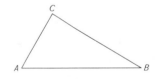

Fractional numbers expressed as

Fractions $\frac{2}{3}$, $\frac{17}{8}$, $6\frac{3}{8}$, $\frac{0}{9}$, $\frac{12}{2}$

Decimals   0.3, 0.68, 1.79

Percents   8%, 127%, 8.34%

C Properties of the Hindu-Arabic numeration system

1 Understands 105 as 105 ones, 10 tens and 5 ones, or 1 hundred and 5 ones.

2 Recognizes that the symbols 1 and 5 in 105 represent, respectively, 1 hundred and 5 ones.

3 Understands names for 105 as in Fig. 1-13 and that, in 105, 0 means no tens left after 1 hundred has been grouped.

4 Can explain that, for 2,222, each digit represents a number 10 times that represented by the digit immediately to its right.

Figure 1-13
Names for 105.

$105 = 100 + 5$

$105 = (1 \times 10 \times 10) + (5 \times 1)$

$105 = (1 \times 10^2) + (0 \times 10^1) + (5 \times 10^0)$

D Mathematical rationale of the operations

1 Understands that addition of whole numbers may be illustrated by the union of two disjoint sets.

2 Explains what actually takes place as he regroups in addition and subtraction.

3 Explains for division what each digit in the quotient means and how division is related to subtraction.

4 Describes why, when denominators are the same, addition with fractions is accomplished by adding the numerators but not the denominators.

E Relationships, such as between multiplication and division

1 Represents four 3s, as shown in Fig. 1-14, and uses the same array to show that 3s in 12 are four.

2 Senses that for three numbers, such as 3, 4, and 12, there are four relationships:
$4 \times 3 = 12,\ 3 \times 4 = 12,\ 12 \div 4 = 3,$ and $12 \div 3 = 4.$

Figure 1-14
Four 3s are 12 or 3s in 12 are 4.

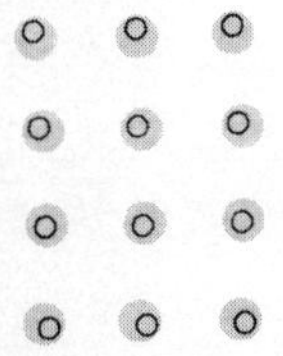

III Development of skills

A Computation

1 Knows the basic facts for addition, subtraction, multiplication, and division (Fig. 1-15).

2 Knows accepted algorithms (forms for recording computations, as shown for division in Fig. 1-16).

3 Performs formal checks for computations.

4 Estimates answers to avoid unreasonable results.

Figure 1-15
Illustrations of basic facts.

Addition	$1 + 7,\ 3 + 8,\ 9 + 4$
Subtraction	$9 - 2,\ 13 - 7,\ 2 - 1$
Multiplication	$2 \times 7,\ 8 \times 5,\ 9 \times 1$
Division	$8 \div 2,\ 15 \div 3,\ 72 \div 9$

Figure 1-16
Algorithms for division.

```
                                        8 }
      28           28                  20 }
 17)476      17)476 | 10          17)476
     34          170 |                340
    ---          --- |                ---
    136          306 | 10             136
    136          170 |                136
    ---          --- |                ---
      0          136 |  8               0
                 136 |
                 ---
                   0
```

B Measuring and constructing

1 Uses measuring instruments, such as ruler, scales, liquid containers, thermometer, protractor, and compass.

2 Measures to the nearest meter, centimeter, millimeter, etc., according to the needs of the situation and subdivision of the measuring instrument.

      3   Draws models for line segments of required length, perpendicular or parallel to lines, and bisectors of segments or angles.

      4   Constructs or sketches pictures of geometric figures, such as triangles, rectangles, cones, and cylinders.

IV   Ability to solve problems

   A   Problems with data from the environment

      1   Uses correctly, in normal conversation, numbers and mathematical terms, such as *ratio, average, interest rate, volume, decimal, angle,* and *perpendicular.*

      2   Interprets data represented in graphic or tabular form.

      3   Solves problems arising from his role as a consumer.

      4   Rejects data unnecessary or inappropriate to a problem, or decides what further data are necessary to solve it.

      5   Draws conclusions from available data.

      6   Checks and verifies conclusions.

   B   Textbook problems needed for continued study in technical vocations and for applications beyond the immediate environment

      1   Draws sketches of problems to bring out relations among data.

      2   Associates mathematical sentences with numerical situations described.

      3   Formulates general laws from available data.

   C   Nonroutine problems

      1   Solves problems merely to "climb an intellectual mountain."

      2   Alters the conditions of a problem to make it easier.

      3   Uses proof when guessed conclusions are of doubtful validity.

      4   Generalizes solutions.

V   Development of appreciation and favorable attitudes

   A   Recognizes elementary school mathematics as a basis for further study in high school and college.

   B   Recognizes the power of expressing quantitative ideas with symbols.

   C   Understands the power of numbers in the affairs of man.

   D   Understands the development of mathematics as paralleling the development of civilization.

   E   Enjoys the logic of arithmetic and geometry.

   F   Takes pleasure in recreation with numbers.

G   Recognizes the metric system as a logical and convenient means of measuring.

The values of mathematics exist in the school only as they are attained by pupils. Achievement of aims depends on guidance by teachers with a clear understanding of the subject of mathematics and its place in the curriculum, insight into the problem of how children learn, and familiarity with the order and nature of experiences for effective learning.

TRENDS IN THE MATHEMATICS PROGRAM

Among the many different aspects of mathematics instruction that are receiving increasing attention today, a few show promise of being important forces in the coming years. These include the laboratory approach to learning mathematics, renewed and greater consideration of *relevant* content and experiences, development of programs for low achievers, preparation of graphic materials to convey concepts and information without high verbal requirements, and the "systems" approach to experiences for promoting mathematics learning. There is the promise, too, of accelerated programs for more capable pupils, under which considerably more mathematics will be mastered by the end of grade eight. While these trends obviously are interrelated, for convenience they are considered separately here.

Experimental Programs

The drive for an improved mathematics curriculum during the 1960s was guided by a number of experimental programs supported by the federal government, various foundations, school districts, colleges and universities, and publishing companies. Programs were conducted by groups ranging from nationwide teams to committees in school districts and by individual investigators.

In some projects, writers prepared more or less complete texts and teacher's commentaries for all grades; while in others the concentration was on only a few grades. Experimental texts for specific fields such as graphing, logic, statistics, or functional relations grew out of some programs. Some projects developed materials for the general student, others for faster or slower students only. Model lessons, designed to achieve more effective learning of specific concepts and techniques were also developed. Some of the topics included measuring, graphing on the number line and in the coordinate plane, concepts and operations with negative numbers, and properties of numbers under various operations.

Varieties of learning aids developed in experimental projects included programmed books and units, projection materials such as slides, overlays, and films, diagrams and charts for conveying information nonverbally, games, manipulative and demonstration aids, and laboratory discovery experiences.

The number of large national experimental programs has now decreased dramatically. Yet there is still experimental activity at the individual school and school district level and even in some places at the state level. Most of this is aimed at individualizing the mathematics program. The variety and worth of such programs presently available is huge, thus making the choice of a program to meet the needs of given pupils extremely difficult. Programs range in sophistication from a pupil working alone with teacher help as needed on paper and pencil tasks to computer-assisted learning where every response of the pupil is recorded and studied. Most activity, however, lies somewhere between these two extremes, with a basic program augmented with laboratory activities and supplementary materials.

It does seem that major changes in the curriculum may be made in the near future because of the impact of modern electronic technology. Industries working alone or in conjunction with universities are producing powerful and flexible digital computing equipment and "teaching machine" hardware, and are continually reducing the cost.

Laboratory Experiences

The importance of learning mathematics through experimentation and *doing* has been recognized and has been given sporadic attention since the work of Pestalozzi (about 1800) and even earlier.

Today throughout the school mathematics community, particularly in England, organized attempts are being made to develop coordinated laboratory experiments from which pupils discover most of the mathematical ideas in the curriculum for the first five or six years of school. Through activities such as weighing and other measuring, manipulating materials, folding paper, and making observations concerned with realistic mathematical situations pupils are guided to sensing and formulating conclusions. It is hoped that such a program will develop in them a feeling that mathematics is a way of thinking and dealing with certain aspects of life. In this respect the learning of the metric system, which will soon be used extensively in all areas of our life, can be facilitated with experiments in the mathematics laboratory.

The great enthusiasm of many teachers and pupils for this expansion and organization of the laboratory approach to learning mathematics gives promise that there will be considerably more of this emphasis in all school mathematics programs in the years ahead.

Relevant Experiences

The fact that structure and content have received major attention in the school mathematics curriculum reforms of the last decade has been pointed out previously. This tended to correct the overemphasis on unorganized social experiences and the undue stress on skills as the end product of instruction. Yet teachers actually working day by day with pupils were quick to recognize that exclusive emphasis on the mathematical aspects, although it proved fruitful with faster pupils, very often failed to achieve desired ends with average pupils and was generally ineffective with slower pupils.

In recent years there has been a trend toward renewed concern regarding the selection of learning activities so that they have real relevance for all pupils. The laboratory experiments mentioned in the previous section are a part of this movement. Beyond this, however, there are numerous attempts to select experiences related to the mathematics being developed but taken from relevant situations in pupils' environments. For example, mathematics is correlated with problems and activities in studies such as art, science, social science, geography, music, and reading. Also, greater attention is given to problems arising from pupils' daily lives in and out of school, for example, concerning paper routes, scouting, sports, and daily classroom affairs such as roll-taking, distribution of materials, bulletin board layouts, and health reports.

The difference between this approach and the emphasis during the time frequently called *the social arithmetic period* (about 1925 to 1940) lies in the current attempts to relate laboratory experiences to mathematical topics being studied in a systematic order. These experiences are used either to motivate pupils, to introduce mathematical ideas, or to provide applications of mathematics topics.

Since the desirability of using more learning activities relevant to pupils' interests is recognized and is proving effective, it is likely that mathematics curricula will expand in this direction in the years ahead. This is specifically indicated by a growing awareness of urban problems and the symptoms of urban blight which have called attention to the special learning requirements of the underprivileged, especially those in minority groups and in lower-income brackets. Several special problems need to be solved in order to progress in this area. For example:

● The home and neighborhood environments of these pupils are lacking in intellectual stimulus.
● Underprivileged pupils probably lack vocational plans that create a drive for learning.
● Some of these pupils come from minority groups that have a language handicap.

- The experiences of underprivileged pupils may be so different from those of the majority of the class that discussions have little interest for them.
- Their school attendance is probably irregular.
- The schools they have attended previously may have been inferior.

All of these factors would have special influence in retarding the learning of mathematics for these pupils. Steps are being taken, with such programs as Head Start, to bring underprivileged pupils into the mainstream of education. But it is necessary to get them into good schools at an early age, with specially trained teachers using specially adapted materials and methods, in order to begin to solve these problems.

Systems Approach

The development of materials and programs to provide coordinated experiences through use of a wide variety of educational media presents an exciting and promising outlook for the future. During the past few years, publishers have been producing manipulative materials, filmstrips, overlays, films, flannel board cutouts, games, and workbooks to accompany their textbooks. Other publishers have produced booklets accompanied by movies or TV programs, progammed materials, and tapes. Research usually has been restricted to comparing outcomes from exclusive use of textbooks and *one* of the other media, such as programmed texts.

Currently there appears to be a trend toward examination of the total job required for guiding pupils to learn mathematics, leading to preparation of a coordinated set of materials from which teachers may select to provide a many-faceted program of experiences. When this approach is fully developed, it is envisioned that the textbook will become only one incomplete resource.

Some minor beginnings of this *systems approach* to learning mathematics have taken place. Impetus to this development is promised as some textbook publishing companies have been absorbed by major communications companies, other communications companies have started educational sections, and new organizations promoting this approach have been established. Hopefully they may take a broad communications point of view. The development, however, must be based very carefully on studies to determine which media are most effective in furthering various specific objectives. Above all, care must be exercised in coordinating *total systems*. Producing more unrelated or poorly related materials is of doubtful value.

Recognition of Differing Backgrounds and Abilities

Mathematics programs of the past decade have been characterized by increased concern for experiences that challenge the more capable pupils. Today the pendulum is swinging back. As indicated previously, realistic programs and experiences are being developed that are designed especially for underprivileged, culturally deprived, and underachieving pupils. Included among the materials are *tracked* textbooks, special syllabi, and technical instructional aids.

The problem of providing for individual differences in background and ability has long been recognized, and many approaches have been tried with varying degrees of success. Now that advances in technology have produced so many supplementary aids for the mathematics curriculum, it is hoped that more impact may be made on this problem. It must be remembered, however, that in the long run it is the teacher who is the greatest factor in determining the effectiveness of the mathematics program, not the physical materials available.

In general, a broad view of contemporary mathematics programs—their nature and directions—serves as background for study of specific techniques for directing learning:

● Present-day curricula are designed to reveal the varied systematic, logical, and, at the same time, useful nature of the subject.
● Curricula provide for progressive development from kindergarten through grade eight, with content interwoven from numeration, number systems, skills, applications, measurement, geometry, number theory, logic, mathematical sentences, and the like.
● Purposes stated in terms of observable pupil behavior give direction in planning and selecting experiences and appraising the outcomes. Important categories include understanding, skill, ability for application, ability to solve problems, and possession of favorable attitudes.
● Curricular emphases giving promise of increased attention in the years ahead include continued development of special methods and materials for culturally deprived, slow, or retarded pupils and special acceleration for highly capable pupils. At the same time, stress on improving teaching-learning experiences for all pupils should be continued; particularly promising are programs which make maximum use of coordinated teaching media.

Continuous examination of the mathematics curriculum is necessary because of the many new developments both in modern society and in mathematics; this is indicated by the concern of the public as well as professional educators. Because there is more to learn in less time, we must delete from mathematics programs all that is not essential for effective citizenship and replace it with what is essential. Further, it is necessary to experiment with new methods and new materials to find improved ways to promote learning.

QUESTIONS AND EXERCISES

1 What features stressed in present-day curricula were also emphasized in meaningful arithmetic?

2 In what ways did curricula developed from about 1957 to 1967 differ from those of the meaningful arithmetic emphases?

3 Describe the seven major concepts and topics which compose the elementary school mathematics program.

4 Beyond the concepts described under Aims, give *another* concept developed in elementary school mathematics and describe typical behavior that a pupil should evidence if he has mastered that concept.

5 Give some specific behavior that a pupil should exhibit if he possesses an understanding of the relation between addition and subtraction.

6 Why might slower pupils have more success with geometric topics than with topics related to numbers?

7 What is meant by the statement: *"Pupils should have relevant experiences while learning mathematics"* ?

8 Describe a *relevant* situation that might arise in the pupils' environment that would require each of the following: (a) for whole numbers, addition or subtraction; (b) measuring weight or area.

9 What are the most important reasons for utilizing laboratory experiences in studying mathematics?

10 If a systems approach is completely implemented in the elementary grades, what will be the role of the textbook?

11 One medium of the systems approach is demonstration materials, such as flannel board with cutouts; textbooks are another. Name as many different media as possible that might be used.

12 What are some procedures for providing for individual differences in the mathematics classroom?

PROJECTS

1 Examine an up-to-date mathematics textbook for a grade level of your interest and find examples of experiences for developing a concept or skill in *each* of the seven categories described on pages 3-6. Place bookmarks for each and prepare to describe them to the class.

2 In a teacher's manual for an up-to-date mathematics text at a grade level of your choice, locate and summarize briefly a lesson or lessons that use laboratory experiments to promote learning of a topic.

3 In an elementary school textbook select three pages and write aims for the study of them. State aims in terms of a measurable pupil behavior.

4 Contrast an up-to-date mathematics textbook for a given grade with one published prior to 1960. Identify key differences such as emphasis on concepts, understanding, and experiences for developing skills.

5 Choose important words from the chapter such as *concept, algorithm, akill, attitude,* and so on. Define each, illustrate with examples and pictures, and report to the class.

6 From a grade-placement chart, syllabus or contemporary textbook, give a skeleton outline of the major topics to be covered in mathematics for a grade of your choice. Be sure to include "how far" each topic is carried at that grade.

Bibliography

1 Begle, E. G.: "Curriculum Research in Mathematics," *The Journal of Experimental Education*, vol. 37, pp. 44-48, Fall 1968. Points out the importance of research in effecting substantial improvements in mathematics education.

2 Cruikshank D. E., and C. de Flandre: "There Always Are More Questions," *The Arithmetic Teacher*, vol. 18, pp. 443-447, November, 1971. An affirmative answer to thirteen questions would mean an excellent mathematics program.

3 Davis, R. B.: *The Changing Curriculum: Mathematics*, Association for Supervision and Curriculum Development, NEA, Washington, D.C., 1967. The new mathematics so far is an inadequate response to the complexities of our scientific age.

4 Fehr, H. F.: "Sense and Nonsense in a Modern School Mathematics Program," *The Arithmetic Teacher*, vol. 13, pp. 83-91, February, 1966. A discussion of nonsense in school mathematics and the characteristics of a sensible program.

5 Kramer, K.: *Problems in Teaching of Elementary School Mathematics*, Allyn and Bacon, Inc., Rockleigh, N.J., 1970. A book of readings concerned with the improvement of instruction in elementary school mathematics.

6 Lockhard, J. D.: *Seventh Report of the International Clearing House on Science and Mathematics Curricular Developments*, Science Teaching Center, University of Maryland, College Park, Md., 1970. Information on experimental projects.

7 National Council of Teachers of Mathematics: *The Teaching of Arithmetic*, Tenth Yearbook, Bureau of Publications, Teachers College, Columbia University, New York, 1935. Chapter 1 is Brownell's exposition of the *meaning theory* for teaching arithmetic.

8 National Council of Teachers of Mathematics: "Status Report: Mathematics Curriculum-development Projects Today," *The Arithmetic Teacher*, vol. 19, pp. 391-395, May, 1972. An overview of the developments of the late sixties with a discussion of experimental projects.

9 The Schools Council: *Mathematics in the Primary Grades*, Selective Educational Equipment, Inc., Newton, Mass., 1969. A classroom environment with activities that help pupils discover concepts.

10 Stern, C., and M. B. Stern: *Children Discover Arithmetic*, Harper and Row, New York, 1971. An excellent book with a multitude of suggestions for an effective curriculum.

11 Watson, L. W.: "Stating Broad Goals of Mathematics Education," *School Science and Mathematics*, vol. 72, pp. 535-538, June, 1972. A statement of goals in terms of student behavior for mathematics education.

12 Weaver, F. J., and J. Kilpatrick (Editors): *The Place of Meaning in Mathematics Instruction: Selected Theoretical Papers of William A. Brownell*, School Mathematics Study Group. Studies in Mathematics, vol. 21, Stanford, 1972. The best research of the best researcher in elementary school mathematics in the last fifty years.

13 Willoughby, S. S.: "Issues on the Teaching of Mathematics," in *Mathematics Education*, National Society for the Study of Education, Sixty-ninth Yearbook, pp. 260-281, NSSE, Chicago, Ill., 1970. Illustrates extremes in our philosophy of mathematics education.

2
PLANNING EFFECTIVE LEARNING ACTIVITIES

Learning is something the pupil does, not something that is done to him. It is an active, purposeful process, not a passive one. It is most likely to be effective when suitable instructional materials are utilized and when the pupil is directed into suitable activities at the proper time. Effective teaching, then, consists in establishing a setting that will be conducive to learning and the activities that will result therefrom. In order that planning and execution may be successful, the teacher needs to understand the nature of the learning process and the conditions under which it is most likely to occur. This chapter emphasizes practical ways of planning effective learning activities by:

● Summarizing the essential principles of present knowledge about how children learn mathematics.

● Describing and illustrating ways in which pupils discover mathematical ideas.

● Outlining procedures for establishing and operating a mathematics laboratory.

● Describing a learning sequence by means of which a teacher may plan effective lessons.

WHAT LEARNING ACTIVITIES ARE EFFECTIVE?

Under what conditions can pupils learn most effectively? How can the teacher provide these conditions? Classroom teachers, as well as experts in learning theory, have studied these and similar questions for many years. One important fact that has emerged is that learning conditions must be related to the desired outcomes. If information and simple mastery of operations are all that are desired from the mathematics class, then the mechanical learning process is wholly satisfactory:

Memorize   Drill   Test

The outcomes sought in mathematics classes today are much broader and more significant than mere mechanical mastery. An important new responsibility of the mathematics teacher today is to encourage creativity by helping pupils discover the basic ideas, laws, and principles of mathematics. As a result of this focus on understanding as well as mastery of skills, many pupils discover that the most interesting thing in the study of mathematics is mathematics itself. One of the most striking features in the teaching of mathematics today is the increasing attention given to development of ability to discover, verify, and generalize in the systematic study of mathematics. If the pupil is to acquire these abilities, it is necessary for him to devote more attention to the development of concepts, together with that precision in vocabulary without which there can be no precision in concepts.

ESSENTIALS IN THE LEARNING PROCESS

Anyone who studies the many theories of learning that have been developed, accepted, and abandoned over the years will be impressed by their apparent conflicts, contradictions, and continued modifications. Actually, however, many of these inconsistencies are more apparent than real, and it is readily possible to find basic principles that are common to all of them and at the same time wholly in accord with the practices of successful teachers. In these principles one can find more useful guidance to effective classroom practices than is available in any one theory. These principles will be listed and described here as essentials of the learning process. They will be illustrated in the following chapters with classroom activities in elementary mathematics.

Readiness to Learn

Readiness to learn has two aspects. One is *subject-matter readiness,* which includes the mastery of prerequisite skills, concepts, and vocabulary. The other is *motivational readiness,* which is the basis for active pupil interest in what is to be learned and purposeful activity in learning it.

Subject-matter readiness is especially important in mathematics because of the sequential nature of the content. Each new topic is built upon mastery of skills and understanding previously acquired. Learning the multiplication algorithm requires knowledge of place value, ability to perform addition, and knowledge of the basic multiplication facts. For any new topic or new step in a topic, the teacher must verify the mastery of the skills and understanding that are prerequisite to its successful learning.

The importance of motivational readiness becomes evident when we realize that learning is a participation activity, not a spectator sport. The motives and goals of the learners are of primary importance in all learning activities. Among other things they determine:

> What the pupil learns.
> How permanently he retains what he learned.
> How intelligently he applies it.
> The persistence and intensity of his efforts to learn.
> The attitudes he develops during the learning activity.

Exploration and Discovery

The effective teacher encourages pupils to explore a process and discover rules, rather than explaining it to them. The value of such exploration and discovery by pupils has been recognized for a long time by expert teachers as well as by scholars in learning theory, and is receiving wider attention today for several reasons. Perhaps the most important of these is recognition of the fact that the attitudes and abilities required for exploration, discovery, and generalization are required in our present-day scientific age. Thus, the greatest value of mathematics will be derived from its application to new and unsolved problems in science, economics, and technology. The real test of his understanding will come when the pupil is confronted with a difficult problem situation which requires new ways of finding a solution.

Emphasis on the Mathematical Structure

It is easier to memorize words than nonsense syllables. It is easier to memorize numbers expressed with digits in a systematic pattern than in a random sequence. In like manner, learning in mathematics is accomplished most economically and effectively when the emphasis is on structure, organization, and relationships in what is learned.

Through attention to structure, it is possible in successive reviews of concepts and operations to make the approach progressively more mature. This not only maintains pupil interest and promotes understanding, but provides for individual differences by making it possible for each pupil to learn at his level of capability.

Repetitive Practice

All teachers and all psychologists agree on the need for practice in learning a skill such as is required in playing a piano, operating a typewriter, playing golf, or mastering the facts of addition and multiplication. They also agree, however, that mere meaningless repetition will not necessarily lead to mastery of the skill. Repetitive practice needs expert guidance. The development of meaning does not eliminate the necessity for practice, but it is a necessary prerequisite for learning through practice. Understanding should precede drill, so that the pupil may comprehend not only what it is that he is to learn, but why he should learn it. To place primary emphasis on understanding, then, does not preclude the necessity for practice; it merely changes the position of drill in the learning sequence, with consequent changes in its nature.

Practice sessions are most effective when the teacher recognizes certain principles that have been established as essential to learning through repetitive practice.

Understanding precedes practice The pupil does not practice to fix a skill until after he has explored the process to discover why and how he is to perform it, and has participated in formulating appropriate generalizations or accepted algorithms. When these steps have been completed, he sees the importance of facility in using the process and realizes that he must memorize basic facts and working patterns in order to acquire this facility.

Spaced practice The quantity of practice at any one sitting is adjusted to avoid fatigue and to maintain interest.

Supervision of practice It is essential that the pupil practice correct procedures. If the practice is premature, he may flounder and not benefit from the time and effort expended. Proper guidance, therefore, is essential.

Variety in activity Variety increases the effectiveness of practice. While workbooks, duplicated material, and textbooks are the basic practice material, teachers also find that games, puzzles, and other specialized activities such as oral exercises are useful in providing variety and helping to maintain interest.

Practice should be rational Practice should always retain an exploratory character, with guidance from the teacher to help pupils rationalize answers by objectifying a solution or describing the *why* of an algorithm. This procedure keeps them aware of fundamental ideas, reveals the possible source of their mistakes, and may help them later on to reason out forgotten steps of an algorithm.

Effective Learning Facilitates Transfer

Transfer of training is not automatic. The extent to which a pupil may apply a principle or process to a new situation depends largely upon how he has learned it. Ability to recognize and identify situations in which application of a process would be appropriate can be acquired by the pupil with proper guidance once the fact is accepted that it cannot be left to chance.

Research evidence as well as classroom experience supports the idea that learning mathematical principles, relations, and rationales for algorithms strengthens the possibility of transfer.

However, while all effective teaching is planned to promote transfer, the final step in any carefully planned sequence is designed directly for the purpose. Usually this takes the form of an exploration of the occurrence and use of the concept or process in a variety of situations. Attention has shifted from the mathematical properties and relationships of the process and is now directed to use of the concept or process, with special attention to the kinds of situations that call for applications of what has been learned.

Modification of Behavior

Learning is not a process of filling a container, but rather one of modifying what is already there. That this is true of pupil interest has been noted previously. Knowing the present interests and the new interests required to make learning effective, the teacher has a defined starting point, and, thus, he can plan his procedure for developing pupil growth in a given direction.

This *developmental* characteristic of learning is manifest in a variety of ways that are familiar to the teacher. For example, it is well known that both learning and interest start where the pupil is, and are guided by the teacher toward a predetermined end. The pupil proceeds from the known to the related unknown, preferably mastering one difficulty at a time. The development of concepts and the mastery of operations starts with manipulation of objects and develops toward abstract mathematical symbolism. In short, the acquisition of mathematical abilities involves developmental sequences and a continuous reorganization of behavior. When this occurs, more mature responses replace less mature but nevertheless essential and useful stages of understanding and skill. The fact that mathematics is highly interrelated and structured requires that we recognize developmental characteristics in planning learning activities.

DISCOVERY BY PUPILS

The current concern with the pupil's discovery of concepts and procedures has great potential for improving the mathematics curriculum.

While the exact meaning of the word *discover* may vary somewhat with the context and the situation, it generally has to do with invention or uncovering new ideas. Thus, the word can be applied quite aptly to mathematicians who throughout recorded history have invented new branches of mathematics such as calculus or new algebras or created new theorems and their proofs. The concept of pupil discovery in a learning situation is somewhat different, and there is some disparity of opinion as to its exact definition; however, sufficient agreement exists to permit its use in describing a method of teaching.

Teaching For Discovery

Discovery will be understood in this discussion to mean the producing of something new. What is new here is a mathematical idea, rule, or method of attacking a problem. The chances are that the unknown which is new to the producer or discoverer is not new to other people. Teaching for discovery, then, is the establishment of an atmosphere or means through which the learner may explore and find something that is new *to him*.

Two very simple examples illustrate discovery by pupils:

A young pupil knows that $6 + 6 = 12$. He does not know the result for $6 + 7$. He reasons, "Because $6 + 6 = 12$, then $6 + 7$ is one more than 12 because 7 is 1 more than 6." This pupil has produced a new idea from a known one. He has discovered a result.

Figure 2-1

Number	Number of factors
2	2
4	3
8	4
16	5

An upper-grade pupil in studying factors found that 2 had factors of 1 and 2 and that 4 had factors of 1, 2, and 4. He determined the number of factors for 8 and 16, collecting his data as in Fig. 2-1. He guessed, "32 has 6 factors." and verified his answer by writing the factors of 32. He rewrote $2 = 2^1$, $4 = 2^2$, $8 = 2^3$, $16 = 2^4$, and $32 = 2^5$, Then he said, "For each of these numbers, the number of factors is ___ more than the exponent." (Can you fill in the blank and discover what he did?)

Examples of Teaching For Discovery

The following examples of teaching for discovery have been used successfully in the classroom. Each is relatively short and could be extended if time permits or continued on the following day. Further examples will appear in following chapters.

Discovering the Unknown Addend Experiences in the first grade of finding an unknown addend can emphasize individual or group discovery. For example, pupils are told, "Take out your box of materials. You may work alone or with your partner. Invent a way to find $\square$ if $2 + \square = 5$." (The teacher writes $2 + \square = 5$ on the board.) When pupils are ready, they come to the overhead projector and show their experiments.

Barbara put down two paper clips, said, "Two and some more make five," then put down three more paper clips.

Jim held up two poker chips in one hand and three in the other. He said, "Two and three are five."

Boris simply said, "That means two plus what is five. So the answer is three."

These pupils knew that $2 + 3 = 5$ but they did not know how to solve $2 + \square = 5$. Their understanding of the relationship of union of sets to addition of numbers allowed them to discover a solution to the problem. It should be recognized that most pupils need extensive experience in relating mathematical symbolism to a physical act before they can interpret that symbolism without reference to the corresponding physical act.

Discovering generalizations about adding even and odd numbers Individual pupils or small groups were given sets of cards, with holes punched in them (Fig. 2-2). They first determined that the characteristic shape for even numbers was rectangular and that for odd numbers the shape was "one hole short of rectangular." Next, they were asked to choose two cards showing odd numbers and fit them together. As various pupils did this, they were asked to show their results (Fig. 2-3). In every case the shape showed an even number and the equation with numerals verified this. Later pupils checked their experiment using larger numbers such as $23 + 19 = 42$. (For an extension of this experience for fast learners see page 336.)

Here, pupils actively using concrete representations of numbers verified a generalization. Some pupils may have sensed this idea prior to the experiment as they performed a number of additions, for others it was probably a "new idea."

Making up Problems Pupils enjoy problems such as matching names for the same number from two lists and drawing a mark between them as shown for 19 and $12 + 7$ in Fig. 2-4. They attack the problem more vigorously when they make up part of it, and they can invent interesting problems if given the opportunity. The teacher may say, "Make up one name for each of 19, 39, 9, 28, and 1. Give your list to your partner to solve." A typical fourth grader's list is shown in Fig. 2-5. Older pupils may invent more ingenious matching problems, as in Fig. 2-6.

Investigating diagonals For mathematics laboratory Ms. Rawl's class was divided into sets of four pupils. She gave each set a card on which was written the objective for the experiment, the apparatus needed, and the details for performing it. Such instructions are referred to as Activities throughout this book.

ACTIVITY I

Apparatus needed: geoboard, dot paper

Objective: To find the number of diagonals of a polygon and to define diagonal.

Figure 2-2
Cards for even and odd numbers.

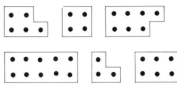

Figure 2-3
Odd + odd = even.

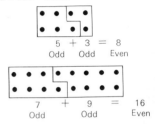

5	+	3	=	8
Odd		Odd		Even

7	+	9	=	16
Odd		Odd		Even

Figure 2-4

19	5 + 4
39	12 + 7
9	8 – 7
28	31 – 3
1	30 + 9

Figure 2-5

19	13 × 3
39	57 ÷ 3
9	7 × 4
28	1 × 1 × 1
1	15 – 6

Figure 2-6

19	exactly 4 factors
39	a perfect square
9	a factor of every number
28	a prime
1	3 less than a prime

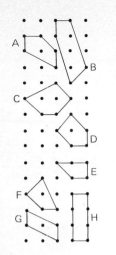

1 Use a blue elastic to make on your geoboard[1] the polygons to the left.
2 Show all diagonals for each polygon with red elastics.
3 Draw pictures of each figure and its diagonals on your dot paper.
4 Fill in the chart with the results of your experiment.
5 (a) Four-sided polygons seem to have _____ diagonals.
  (b) Five-sided polygons seem to have _____ diagonals.
6 Make six sided polygons on your geoboard. How many diagonals for each?
7 A diagonal of a polygon is a _____.
8 *Brainbuster*: How many diagonals from one vertex for a polygon of *n* sides?

Figure	Number of diagonals
A	
B	
C	
D	
E	
F	
G	
H	

Figure 2-7
25-peg geoboard.

Soon after the cards were handed to the pupils a boy said, "Ms. Rawl, what's a polygon?" Her reply was, "Where could you find the answer to your question?" She gave the same response to "What's a diagonal?" Pupils located the meaning of each in their textbooks.

In this lesson there was the opportunity for each set of pupils to do something besides listen. Some learned how to find answers to their questions. They also had experiences with diagonals on various figures and from those experiences attempted to define a diagonal.

Promoting Discovery

Some educators maintain that there must be fundamental changes in the way schools are organized if they are to foster creativity, inquiring minds, and the ability to attack problems. While this may be true, there are certain "common sense" directives that every teacher can follow.

Remember that *how* a pupil learns is as important as *what* he learns. The pupil who puts together sets of ten cards can learn more about place value than the pupil who is told about sets of tens. The pupil who examines data such as

$$1 = 1$$
$$1 + 3 = 4$$
$$1 + 3 + 5 = 9$$
$$1 + 3 + 5 + 7 = 16$$

guesses that the next sum is 25, and then tests his results is learning how to attack problems.

[1] A geoboard is a piece of plastic with 9, 16, 25 or 36 pegs in a square arrangement (Fig. 2-7). Plans for its construction are in Appendix A.

Secure the involvement of pupils. Learning is a participation activity, not a spectator sport. Pupils who are lectured to about ideas and algorithms by a teacher cannot discover them for themselves. However, by manipulating objects that illustrate mathematical concepts and by collecting and studying data, they can create their own algorithms and with teacher guidance can develop them into those most generally used.

Give pupils a chance to experiment and explore problems. For many pupils discussing and attempting to solve a problem in a small group can be more profitable than doing another page of textbook practice.

The Danger of Inhibiting Discovery

Teachers must constantly guard against inhibiting discovery. Some teaching techniques to be avoided are:

- A traditional pattern for a lesson: assign, read, recite.
- Insistence on always doing things "the teacher's way".
- Teacher talk that dominates the day.
- A learning theory based on memorization, drill, and test.
- Inflexibility of daily schedules.
- Assigning practice exercises as a disciplinary tactic.

THE MATHEMATICS LABORATORY

The mathematics laboratory has been referred to as a place and a procedure. It is a place in that it is space set aside for an experimental approach to mathematics, and it is a procedure because in that space pupils work in an informal manner, discuss experiments, collect data, and often discover mathematical concepts. The space itself may be a separate room, specifically designated stations in the regular classroom, three or four chairs pushed together, or even a rug on the floor. At times the playground or a field trip may become "the lab."

Whatever its physical arrangement, the mathematics laboratory is the basis for an activity-centered program that helps to promote the objectives of a carefully developed mathematics curriculum. It is not a replacement for well-planned instruction, but one of a number of effective teaching methods designed to stimulate individuals or small groups of pupils to perform experiments, record data, and draw conclusions to discover mathematical ideas. Pupils can do a number of prescribed experiments, or they can choose from a variety of available activities. Experiments are often conducted with concrete materials, commercial and homemade. The teacher gives the instructions orally or writes them on the chalkboard, or pupils are given cards listing instructions and apparatus to be used. In some experiments pupils study sets of numbers or geometric figures to discover a pattern; in some they examine and interpret arrangements of materials, pictures, or symbols; and in others they explore techniques for solving problems.

Organizing and Introducing a Laboratory

The most effective mathematics laboratories are those that are incorporated into the curriculum and used whenever an experience in the lab is the best way to achieve an objective. Laboratory lessons may serve to introduce a topic. Children beginning the study of triangles, for example, may sort models of triangles into subsets with all sides the same length, two sides the same length, or no two sides the same length, and also observe other characteristics of triangles. The laboratory is also an effective follow-up to class discussion. Small groups may, for instance, after participating in a class demonstration of the union of sets, form the union of various sets of materials stored in their arithmetic boxes. Similarly, topics can be reviewed with experiments in the laboratory. Sometimes the laboratory is separated from the regular program with pupils attending it one or more periods a week. In this arrangement, it provides a change of pace and is a means for supplementing work from the textbook. Regardless of the framework in which they are used, laboratory experiences are designed to promote discovery of concepts by pupils and individualize instruction. Although there is much yet to be learned about their use, their value is evident: pupils progress through the thrill of discovery, slow pupils often succeed for the first time, and many concepts are more completely understood.

Introducing the mathematics laboratory There are many problems associated with beginning a mathematics laboratory. First, the teacher must be willing to try. This is a formidable step to take because of the many plans that must be made and implemented, and because for many teachers it is a step into the unknown. While the separate-room approach requires the cooperation of an entire school or district, the individual teacher can make a start in his classroom. Some suggestions for instituting the laboratory approach are the following:

Begin gradually. The teacher may use a lab setup once a week. He will study the mathematics program for that week, decide what objectives can be best attained in the lab, and organize the activities to accomplish it. He can write experiments on cards (these are also available commercially), which he will give to the pupils. As the number of experiments increases, those of less value can be discarded.

It is also possible for a teacher to outline lab experiences for one topic. If the idea of remainders in division is to be introduced, for example, experiments can be planned, utilizing the physical apparatus available, that help pupils discover and understand this concept.

Think about grouping the class. There are many ways of grouping a class with many important considerations such as how many in each group and whether or not each group needs a leader. Some teachers may want to start by involving the pupils in planning and completing class experiments before breaking them into groups.

Have pupils assume responsibilities. Chaos may result unless pupils assume responsibilities such as returning materials and keeping the work area neat. In addition, recorded results of completed experiments must be kept up-to-date by each pupil.

Explore the many available materials. There is presently an abundance of commercial apparatus with a wide range of quality, so the selection of materials is difficult. Many teachers prefer to start their mathematics laboratories with homemade materials. (Many are described in the following chapters and in Appendix A.)

Remember that teachers plan and observe, while pupils experience and discover.

One of the biggest problems teachers face in setting up a laboratory is coordinating it with the textbook. It must not be forgotten that while an experimental approach to many mathematical topics is necessary, so is a textbook. In the beginning the teacher may mark each experiment with a code number indicating the concept it reinforces. These can be updated and filed for use when the concept is studied again. This also permits some individualization. If a pupil needs remediation in the idea of place value, for example, experiments filed under its code may be brought out for his use. The code number may also be written on the appropriate page in the teacher's manual.

Samples of Experiments

Laboratory activities are found in many forms. Often, as we have seen, pupils are given cards on which are instructions for completing an experiment. (Instructions for non-readers may be given verbally or put on tape.) In some cases the instructions may be merely to plan an experiment such as: "Here are 16 toothpicks. Find the polygon of greatest area you can form with them."

Below is one experiment that can be written on an Activity Card for use by pupils. It is understood that pupils working on this experiment know about triangles and have had some background with intersection of geometric figures.

ACTIVITY II

Apparatus needed: scissors   *Objective:* To find all possible intersections of two triangles.

1 Cut out the two triangles.
2 If you place them like this you can see two points of intersection.

3 Place your triangles to show these intersections:
(a) 0 points   (d) 4 points   (f) 6 points
(b) 1 point   (e) 5 points   (g) 7 points (be careful)
(c) 3 points
4 Draw a picture of each intersection.
5 *Brainbuster:* Place your triangles to show these intersections and draw pictures: (*a*) one line segment (*b*) one line segment and a point not on the segment.
6 *Superbrainbuster:* Try to find a different intersection of your two triangles.

Building a Set of Experiments A laboratory experience can be developed to help pupils understand most concepts of mathematics. Examples which illustrate this are listed below with little detail. Most are discussed again in the following chapters.

Objective: To learn to measure lengths. Pupils measure the lengths of small objects at their desks and longer objects as they move about the room. Still longer distances are measured on the playground.

Objective: To find the volume of odd-shaped containers. Pupils fill small paper cups with beans and determine the number of full cups required to fill each container.

Objective: To use mathematics in physical education classes. With a stop watch pupils time members of the class as they hop, walk, run, and skip around the playground. They make bar graphs of this data and calculate average speed of a pupil in meters per second for each way of moving.

Objective: To practice using the idea of a factor. Pupils know the factors of 6 are 1, 2, 3, and 6. Now the factors of 6, except 6 itself, add to 6: $1 + 2 + 3 = 6$. Because it had this property the Greeks called 6 a perfect number. Find another perfect number less than 30.

Discovery And The Mathematics Laboratory

On the previous pages some of the purposes of the mathematics laboratory have been brought into focus. Many lists of such purposes have been compiled. Nearly all would include the following in one form or another. The mathematics laboratory:

● Promotes discovery of concepts.

- Provides effective experiences for pupils with varying rates of learning.
- Helps pupils discover procedures and strategies for solving problems.
- Motivates pupils to study mathematics.
- Gives slower pupils an opportunity for success at a task.
- Enriches the program of more capable pupils.

The mathematics laboratory should be a part of every mathematics program. Every teacher should utilize it. However, it is not a panacea. There are huge benefits from its effective utilization, but there is danger in using it excessively or incorrectly. In a similar vein, teaching for discovery has its place in the mathematics curriculum. There is no better way to learn some concepts, and the thrill of the learner who has discovered for himself is immense. Yet there are dangers from excess here too. A few words of caution are necessary to avoid the idea that the perfect mathematics curriculum can be achieved through the discovery and laboratory approaches alone.

- Discovery and laboratory approaches are effective methods of teaching, not the only method of teaching.
- Mathematics is learned in many ways. One is in the laboratory, and another is with paper and pencil. Experiences in both are necessary.
- All mathematics cannot be discovered; and even if it could, there would not be enough time to use the discovery approach exclusively. Less than 180 hours of an average school year are released to study mathematics.
- Sometimes the physical activity obscures the mathematical idea or the experiment is not designed properly for the pupil to discover. Also, it should be evident that without proper guidance pupils can learn to play as easily as to learn mathematics in the lab.
- Evaluation of results of laboratory experiences is difficult.

There are many objectives best achieved through laboratory activities. Other objectives are best achieved through a class or small group discussion, individual work with paper and pencil, or a combination of these and other experiences. Hence, the activities of the mathematics laboratory must be coordinated with a well planned sequential program of instruction. It is the teacher's responsibility to determine those lab experiences within the framework of his curriculum which maximize learning.

Commonly, the learning sequence with which the individual teacher is concerned is for a topic extending over a few days or a week or two. The developmental nature of learning provides a framework of planning instruction for a topic and establishing the direction—from the concrete to the abstract and symbolic, from current interests to broader ones in the desired direction, from the known to the related unknown. Within this framework, it is possible to set up a general sequence of activities to incorporate the characteristics desirable in effective learning. In this sequence the attention of the pupil is directed first to the problem situation as such. It is gradually shifted from the concrete situation to the process for solving the problem aspects of the situation, and then to the applications of the process. The specific outcomes defined by the teacher and the characteristics of the classroom activities change accordingly. For this reason, it is useful to consider the steps in the learning sequence. These are outlined in the flow chart (Table 2-1), together with the immediate objectives and kinds of activities and learning materials that are useful for each step.

PLANNING FOR THE STEPS

The flow chart is useful as a framework for planning the classroom

TABLE 2-1   FLOW CHART OF THE LEARNING SEQUENCE

Step	Purpose	Activities	Materials
1 Preparation	To provide readiness: both subject-matter—including prerequisite skills, vocabulary, and concepts—and interest.	A checkup—formal or informal—on prerequisite skills and vocabulary.	Tests, if necessary, teacher-made or commercial. Models, real objects, and other learning aids as necessary.
2 Exploration and discovery	To lead the pupil to develop the concept (or operation) as a solution to a problem situation.	Presenting a stimulating problem situation requiring improvisation of the process, concept, or operation as a means of solution.	Learning aids as needed to provide the setting. Materials as required for manipulation in exploratory activities.
3 Abstraction and organization	To develop an understanding of the nature of the operation (or concept) and its interrelationship with other operations.	Development of generalizations about the operation (or concept) and its interrelationships to others.	Textbooks and semisymbolic manipulative materials.
4 Maintaining and extending skills and concepts	To make manipulation of the operation automatic and to provide overlearning to assure retention.	Memorization of facts, organization and memorization of tables, and repetitive practice with the operation.	Textbooks, practice materials, and tests.
5 Application	To promote transfer of training by developing ability to recognize the typical situations calling for use of the operation (or concept).	Experience in application to a variety of situations, with emphasis on identifying the appropriate situations.	Life and simulated problem situations; models, visual aids, textbooks, and bulletin boards.

activities, giving proper recognition to the immediate objectives in each step. At any given time it is useful for the teacher to plan in terms of a given step, while recognizing that pupils vary widely in the rates at which they move to the abstract level. A variety of activities is suitable for use at each step. The teacher must be responsible for guiding the pupils from one step to the next and seeing to it that the experiences at each step are appropriate and effective for their purposes. To achieve this, three considerations must be kept clearly in mind:

- The special outcome that is desired at each step.
- The kinds of activities that are suitable.
- How to tell when the pupils are ready for the next step.

To illustrate the kinds of activities characteristic of each of these steps and how the teacher proceeds from one to the next, we will follow the experiences of Ms. Archer's third-grade class as they undertook the study of division with remainder.

The teacher's general aims were to help her pupils:

- Reinforce the concept of remainder in division with concrete materials and pictures.
- Represent the idea of remainder with symbols.
- Use and understand the specialized vocabulary related to remainder and quotient.
- Perform the algorithm for division with remainder.
- Become skillful in using algorithms for division with a remainder.
- Locate and recognize applications of division with a remainder.

Preparation

Ms. Archer's class had already encountered real situations that required partitioning a set into disjoint subsets of two, three, or four objects. Sometimes these situations involved remainders, but in each case pupils, working with concrete materials, found answers by improvisation. For example, when members of the class were going to walk to the library with partners, such questions were raised as "Will everyone have a partner?" and "How many pairs will there be?" The pupils paired themselves, counted by twos, and found the number of sets and whether each pupil had a partner. At another time, when they saw a turtle in their aquarium, the pupils settled the questions "How many sets of three can view the turtle?" and "How many will be in the last set?" by similiar methods.

Ms. Archer made a careful analysis of the background skills and concepts that are prerequisite to success in dividing with remainders. In preparation for study of the topic, she made certain that each pupil could:

- Illustrate "even" division, such as 6 ÷ 3, by means of objects or pictures: xxx
  xxx

- Verbalize division problems, such as 12 ÷ 4 = 3, as "In a set of 12 there are three sets of 4." or "4s in 12 are three."

- Check division problems by relating them to subtraction (6 ÷ 2 is seen as the number of 2s subtracted from 6) (Fig. 2-8).

- Relate multiplication and division (five 2s are 10; therefore, 2s in 10 are five).

- Multiply, with 2 as one factor (2 × 4, 2 × 9, 3 × 2, 8 × 2, and so on).

- Out of the numbers from 1 to 19, pick those divisible exactly by 2.

The ability of each pupil was checked on each skill and concept, and remedial experiences were provided as needed.

Figure 2-8
Relating 6 ÷ 2 to subtraction.

$$\begin{array}{r} 6 \\ -2 \\ \hline 4 \\ -2 \\ \hline 2 \\ -2 \\ \hline 0 \end{array}$$

Exploration

Ms. Archer selected a real situation within the interests of the pupils to focus attention on the use of the process which was to be learned—the idea of *remainder* in division. In this instance, members of the class were going to folk dance with partners. Questions were raised such as "Will everyone in our section of 15 pupils have a partner?" The pupils improvised solutions; some paired plastic disks, tongue depressors, or bottle caps, while others counted by twos. More abstract representations such as tallies or pictures were used by a few pupils. In each instance attention was focused on the idea of *remainder*.

Additional situations with the same elements were then explored. The pupils in the class were planning to make a mural on the bulletin board. This presented the following problems: "How many pieces of newsprint 2 feet long are required for a mural on our bulletin board which is 13 feet long?" and "If we do not cut a piece, how many feet will be left for margins?" In regard to a Christmas party, pupils wondered, "The eight windows of our classroom are to be decorated. If two children can work at each window, can all 17 pupils in the first section of the class work in the windows at the same time?"

The pupils, working in groups, improvised answers for these and other real problems with remainders in division. Following each solution, they compared their results and how they had been obtained. Ms. Archer's purpose in this step was to get each pupil to recognize remainders in the variety of situations in which they occur and to develop confidence in his ability to improvise a solution.

Abstraction and Organization

When she knew that her pupils were familiar with the typical problem situation—remainders in division—Ms. Archer guided them in discovering the common mathematical elements. In each situation the question arose: How many disjoint (the use of the word *disjoint* is not forced at this time) sets of two could be found in a given set with a remainder of one? The pupils and teacher agreed that it would be useful to study the process of *division* where remainders occur. A variety of activities was then used to focus attention on the process itself.

Class dramatization   A set of three children was brought to the front of the room and separated into one set of two with one left over. Similar groupings showed five as two 2s with one extra and seven as three 2s with a remainder of one. As the "uneven" division facts were dramatized, different pupils stated the number story represented in each situation. The remainder idea was presented, using a variety of socially significant objects: groupings and remainders were illustrated with piles of books, boxes of crayons, erasers, and pencils.

Ms. Archer continued to emphasize the relation between division and subtraction by having pairs of children step away from the original set, illustrating the taking-away idea. The number of pairs removed was indicated as the answer, and the one or none left over showed an "uneven" or "even" division, respectively.

Individual objectification   Each pupil was given 20 strips of colored paper, and the class experimented with arranging various numbers of strips in sets of 2 to illustrate odd and even numbers and remainders. Similar groupings were studied using other materials such as bottle caps, toothpicks, and disks.

Individual picturing of the facts   The pupils drew pictures to illustrate partition of chairs or other objects into sets of 2. The separation of nine chairs into sets of 2 each was depicted as shown in Fig. 2-9a. Other, more abstract, illustrations were used, as shown in Fig. 2-9b and c.

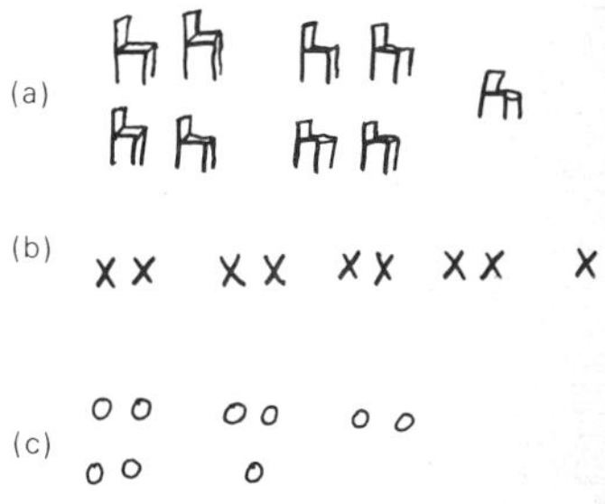

Symbolic representation   Here the purpose was to have pupils represent the object and pictorial expressions symbolically. For example, the real or pictured groupings of materials were stated as "11 books is the same as 5 sets of 2 books each and 1 book left over," or "13 circles is the same as 6 sets of 2 circles and 1 circle left over." The expression "remainder of one" was introduced at this stage for "the one left over."

Figure 2-9
Nine objects into sets of two.

After the pupils had stated and written statements for a variety of experiences, their attention was turned to the similarity of the representation of the same fact independent of the material used. They came to the important conclusion that when seven of anything is separated in three sets of 2 each, 1 will be left over. Similar generalizations were developed for the other divisions that were carried out. Accordingly, labels were dropped, and the statements were expressed in the following form: 7 contains three 2s with a remainder of 1.

Expressing the abstract facts As pupils gained understanding of the abstract concepts, they were encouraged to think about the process abstracted from the situation. Pupils were led to the generalization that the quotient for each odd dividend is the same as that for the even dividend "just below it." For example, for $2\overline{)13}$, one can think, "2 × ? gives a number one less than 13." This generalization grew out of experiences such as working problems in which it was necessary to think of the number which immediately precedes 5, 7, 11, 17, and so on, and which can be "evenly" divided by 2. Also there was oral practice with questions such as, "Which is greater, five 2s or 11?"

Through experimentation with objects or pictures used as needed to derive or verify results, the pupils made charts showing the quotients and remainders upon division by 2. These were in the following form:

- 2 divided by 2 gives 1 with remainder 0.
- 3 divided by 2 gives 1 with remainder 1.
- 4 divided by 2 gives 2 with remainder 0.

Attention to notation, symbolism, and verbalization As pupils dealt with the abstract process, important details emerged. Examining the division algorithm, some groups of pupils found, for example, that the 6 represented three 2s. When these were subtracted from 7, there was 1 left over; the 3, 7, 6, and 1 were placed directly under each other because each expresses a number of ones (Fig. 2-10). This was reported to the class and recognized as a quicker method than subtracting three times (in the form $7 - 2 = 5$, $5 - 2 = 3$, $3 - 2 = 1$).

Pupils had previously checked division facts by multiplication. Now they discovered that if the divisor were multiplied by the quotient, adding the remainder to the product yielded the dividend.

The new and old vocabulary (*odd, even, uneven, remainder, compare,* and *quotient*) was used continually as it applied. Each word was given special and frequent attention during these lessons: "How does the remainder compare in size to the divisor? Is there a

Figure 2-10
Dividing 7 by 2 and checking.

$$2\overline{)7}^{\,3\ r\ 1}$$
$$\underline{6}$$
$$1$$

check $7 = (3 \times 2) + 1$

remainder when you divide an odd number by 2? Which number is the quotient?"

Maintaining and Extending Skills and Concepts

To master the algorithm, it is necessary to know the facts rather than rediscover them each time they are required. This became clear to the pupils as they solved problems. In order to develop mastery, pupils organized and practiced facts in many different ways.

They first showed the relationship of division and multiplication by writing equations:

$$3 = (1 \times 2) + 1 \quad 5 = (2 \times 2) + 1 \quad 7 = (3 \times 2) + 1$$

and so on. They thought of these in such terms as "3 is one 2 and a remainder of 1." and "5 is two 2s and a remainder of 1." They also organized the divisions in another systematic way:

$$2 \overline{)5}^{\;2r1} , \quad 2 \overline{)7}^{\;3r1} , \quad 2 \overline{)9}^{\;4r1} , \text{ and so on.}$$

With the answers covered, they then tried to see how many they could recall. Next random arrangements were practiced, and, finally, problems with remainders were intermixed with previously learned facts without remainders. Pairs of pupils of equal ability tested each other with practice cards. As difficulties were encountered, Ms. Archer had pupils return to manipulation of objects, paralleling the work using the algorithm.

The class also played a variation of a Bingo game that had been introduced while studying another topic earlier in the year. Each child was given a card, as in Fig. 2-11, and small squares of paper which would cover each numeral on the card. As Ms. Archer asked various questions and wrote them on the board, each pupil covered the numeral representing the correct answer. Some of these questions were:

● The quotient for 19 ÷ 2 is ____?
● The remainder for 16 ÷ 2 is ____?
● The number for the blank in 15 = 2 × (____) + 1 is ____?

Figure 2-11
Card for a Bingo game.

Free	9	0	1	6
1	Free	5	0	2
8	1	Free	3	0
4	0	1	Free	1
2	1	7	0	Free

Application

As pupils began to demonstrate automatic mastery, they turned to their daily experiences to find applications of division with remainder. It was important that each pupil learn to recognize the typical situation in which the process applied. New examples were examined, problems were formulated and solved, and the examples were added to a list of applications that was kept on the bulletin board.

Pupils were encouraged to look for key ideas or elements that called for division. The characteristics of the division situation were highlighted by verbalizing the typical process that it called for: "Find the number of sets. What is the cost of each? How many in each?"

Several features of Ms. Archer's organization and treatment of the topic are worth noting.

While she gave continued attention to the general aims of the topic, her immediate aims changed as the class moved from one level to another. On the other hand, there was no sharp distinction between levels, but rather an easy transition, marked by a shift in attention from one aspect of the topic to another.

The degree of emphasis placed on any one step varied according to the kind of topic being studied. If the purpose of the topic had been to master an algorithm (as in long division), attention would have been directed to fixing skills until the algorithm became automatic. However, the purpose was to develop concepts and vocabulary rather than skills. The mastery of vocabulary requires less time than mastery of a skill, though it may be *equally important*. The degree of emphasis may vary, too, in the final step where experiences are designed to secure transfer. In a study of long division this step would be extended to ensure recognition of more complex division situations and a broader understanding of the meaning of the algorithm. Here the purpose was to recognize and apply the concepts in a variety of problems.

The preparation step could be called *checking for readiness* or *review*. Some educators may refer to it as one way of achieving some "diagnosis and prescription." The diagnosis is illustrated by the activities of the class in reviewing essential material from which Ms. Archer determined the readiness of each child for the topic. The prescription was provided by Ms. Archer in the form of needed remedial experiences.

The stage in the unit designed to maintain and extend skills and concepts is another place in the learning sequence for the teacher to diagnose difficulties and prescribe remedial experiences. It was possible for Ms. Archer to identify some pupils as needing more concrete experiences, some needing more activities wherein they could record results of experiments with symbols, others needing practice in writing abstract statements about remainders, and so on.

Throughout the lessons as described, pupils were actively involved, making individual discoveries and comparing them with the discoveries of other pupils.

Most of the experiences described evolved through a class working together under teacher guidance. It was presented here in this form for purposes of clarity of narration. Many of the foregoing experiences, however, could and should occur in a laboratory situation.

The teacher who is to be successful must understand the mathematical ideas he is to teach. Beyond this, however, he will strive for expertness in providing a setting in which each pupil can learn mathematics to the maximum of his capacity. This demands a continuous study of how each pupil learns and a continuous search for experiences that promote effective learning.

QUESTIONS AND EXERCISES

1 Assuming that learning is an active rather than a passive process ("We learn through experience." "Learning is by doing"), explain the conditions under which each of the following could be an active learning experience: (a) the teacher explains the division algorithm on the board; (b) the pupils read an explanation in the textbook.

2 What are methods in teaching mathematics that increase transfer?

3 What activities are performed by pupils in a mathematics laboratory?

4 Outline problems associated with introducing a mathematics laboratory.

5 Why must the experiences of the mathematics laboratory be coordinated with work in the textbook?

6 In Activity II on page 28, explain why seven distinct points of intersection are impossible. Answer the superbrainbuster.

7 Explain why teaching for discovery in the mathematics laboratory does not constitute a panacea.

8 Describe characteristics of the mathematics classroom that tend to promote and those that tend to inhibit discovery by pupils.

9 What are some methods that every teacher may use to help pupils discover mathematical ideas?

10 Referring to the Ms. Archer example in this chapter: (a) identify different specific principles of learning as they were recognized; (b) list experiences that gave pupils the opportunity to discover and explore.

11 What are arguments to support the procedure of introducing the physical situation before the abstract mathematical idea it represents?

12 It is said that teaching which relies wholly on the textbook is deficient in that it starts at step 3 of the flow chart (Table 2-1). Explain why this is true. What characteristics of desirable learning does such teaching ignore?

PROJECTS

1 Examine a series of elementary school mathematics texts and teachers' manuals. Locate and report to the class examples of experiences that (a) help pupils discover ideas or procedures; (b) can be performed in the laboratory; (c) are drill exercises but are on the "thinking level."

2 Choose a grade of an elementary school mathematics text. Locate and describe examples of manipulative materials that are both homemade and commercially made.

3 Choose one of the four experiments briefly described on page 28. Write the experiment in the form of Activity I on page 23 so it may be given to pupils to complete.

4 Write a paragraph describing how activities in the mathematics laboratory might help achieve each major purpose of the mathematics program listed on page 6-10.

5 Do the experiment on diagonals in Activity I on page 23. After doing the brainbuster try this superbrainbuster: How many diagonals for a polygon of n sides? Describe to a friend how you discovered the answer.

6 Develop a topic such as learning the idea of place value for two-digit numerals or learning the meaning of 1/2 using the flow chart sequence.

7 Argue the affirmative of "Subject matter readiness is more important in mathematics than in other studies."

Bibliography

1 Biggs, E. E., and J. R. MacLean: *Freedom to Learn*, Addison-Wesley (Canada) Ltd., Don Mills, Ontario, 1969. Reports the successful laboratory approaches to learning mathematics used in England.

2 Brousseau, A. R.: "Mathematics Laboratories: Should We or Should We Not?," *School Science and Mathematics*, vol. 73, pp. 99-105, February, 1973. Results of research on the effectiveness of discovery and laboratory methods.

3 Bruner, J. S.: "On Learning Mathematics," *Mathematics Teacher*, vol. 63, pp. 610-619, December, 1960. A discussion of the place of discovery and intuition in the learning of mathematics.

4 Copeland, R.: *How Children Learn Mathematics, Teaching Implications of Piaget's Research*, The Macmillan Company, New York, 1974. Puts the theories of Piaget into understandable language in terms of classroom situations and makes the role of the mathematics laboratory clear.

5 Fawcett, H., and K. Cummins: *The Teaching of Mathematics from Counting to Calculus*, Charles E. Merrill Publishing Co., Columbus, Ohio, 1970. Chapter 3 is a fine description of discovery approaches to learning.

6 Laycock, M. and G. Watson: *The Fabric of Mathematics*, Activity Resources Co., Hayward, CA., 1971. A "must" book for teachers desiring to develop a laboratory approach to mathematics.

7 National Council of Teachers of Mathematics: *The Growth of Mathematical Ideas*, Twenty-fourth Yearbook, Washington, D.C., 1959. Chapter 10 contains many practical suggestions for teaching mathematics based on a modern psychology of learning.

8 National Council of Teachers of Mathematics: *The Learning of Mathematics, Its Theory and Practice*, Twenty-first Yearbook, Washington, D.C., 1953. Chapters 2, 3, and 6 contain many examples of good practices in learning mathematics.

9 National Council of Teachers of Mathematics: *Mathematical Thinking*, N.C.T.M. Unit Six of Experience in Mathematical Discovery, Washington, D.C., 1971. Helps the teacher put activity experiences into perspective in terms of mathematical thinking.

10 Shulman, L. S.: "Psychology and Mathematics Education," in *Mathematics Education*, National Society for the Study of Education, Sixty-ninth Yearbook, pp. 23-71, NSSE, Chicago, Ill., 1970. Strategies for instruction based on the psychology of learning of Bruner, Piaget, and others.

11 Weaver, F. J.: "Seductive Shibboleths," *Arithmetic Teacher*, vol. 18, pp. 263-264, April, 1971. A strong plea to look carefully at experiences in the mathematics laboratory to make sure they are appropriate and not merely interesting activities.

3

THE MATHEMATICS PROGRAM FOR THE PRIMARY GRADES

Long before he enters school, the child must compare, describe, and think about size, shape, position, quantity, set, time, and money. "How long?" "How many?" "When?" "How much?" These questions are posed for him or by him wherever he turns. His answers are first formulated in terms of approximations: "a long way," "close," "a lot," "after supper," "many," "few," and the like. Through the years, as these and other questions arise, they call for more explicit answers. This development of quantitative thinking, communicating, and problem solving takes place through improvisation, imitation, and instruction.

Many experiences with sets may be identified in the life of the young child. He and his brother have matching sets of toy soldiers; his set of eating utensils has fewer members than his parents' set; he joins his set of blocks with his friend's set to build a big castle; he leaves a game, taking his set of marbles with him; his sets of fingers and toes match exactly; he loses a wheel off his toy car and finds fewer wheels in this set than in the set of wheels for another car; he counts the members of sets to find how many there are; in playing with his dump truck, tractor, and crane he finds this set of toys has three members regardless of the order in which he counts.

Even the very young child uses time in ordering his life. At first, the position of the hands on a clock determine important events in his life—lunchtime, time for television, or bedtime. His desire to know the number of days until Christmas or his birthday makes the calendar an important source of information.

Starting with such experiences as putting a penny in the gum machine, many situations that are important to the child demand knowledge of costs, values, and equivalent values of various coins. Part-taking experiences such as sharing candy bars, waffles, or sandwiches lead to the need for vocabulary and concepts of fractions.

The situations just described are but a sample of the many demands for understanding numbers that continually confront the small child as he attempts to make order of his surroundings and learns to understand, communicate, and solve his problems.

Pupils entering school have had widely varying experiences with numerical situations, and the degree of refinement of numerical understanding differs considerably among them. The teacher's task, therefore, is to identify each child's level of development and to provide experiences which will increase his competence, while taking into account his natural interests and curiosity.

On the following pages are effective experiences for helping pupils discover the mathematical ideas of the K-2 curriculum. To be effective in planning and guiding these activities the teacher needs to:

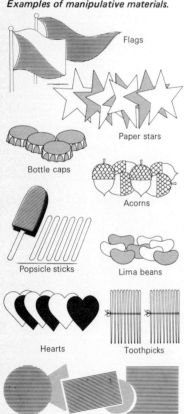

Figure 3-1
Examples of manipulative materials.

Flags

Paper stars

Bottle caps

Acorns

Popsicle sticks

Lima beans

Hearts

Toothpicks

Regions cut from paper

● Understand the mathematics now being learned in the K-2 program.
● Have access to a huge variety of learning experiences in order to plan for the great range of differences among beginning pupils.
● Fit the learning experiences into lessons in order to accomplish specific objectives for his class and for each individual pupil.
● Know the major topics of the K-2 mathematics program and the developmental steps through which pupils progress as they learn each.
● Have available experiences for pupils that may be used by an entire class, groups of pupils or by individuals.

TYPICAL NUMBER EXPERIENCES FOR PRIMARY GRADES

The particular learning experiences that are most effective for any topic vary with the teacher and class. The following are illustrations of useful types of important, though not necessarily independent, experiences which are used repeatedly in beginning mathematics instruction. How each of these may be utilized in conformity with the principles and practices of effective learning is described in the sample lessons which follow.

Experiments with Sets of Objects

A collection of manipulative materials (Fig. 3-1) is a necessity for every primary classroom. Pupils use them to solve numerical problems, to illustrate concretely a mathematical idea, and also to set up experiments, make observations, collect data, and draw conclusions.

If the pupil is to learn "What is five?" for example, he should have many experiences in manipulating sets. A few of these manipulations, using a set of five children, are:

● Arranging the members in different positions and finding that the set still has five members
● Matching exactly with other sets of five members
● Comparing with sets having more or fewer members
● Arranging in two or more disjoint subsets
● Joining a set of two members and a set of three members so that the result is a set of five members

Techniques for teaching pupils how to work with sets on the flannel board are seen in a summary of some lessons in Mr. Willard's first grade. The class had been studying sets with as many as nine members. Mr. Willard believed they were ready to learn the concept of place value. To start the lesson, he whispered to Doris, asking her to place a set of 13 pennies (play money) on the flannel board (Fig. 3-2). As Doris stepped away, Mr. Willard asked the class to tell him how many pennies were in sight. After a very short interval, he turned the flannel board so that it could not be seen and asked, "How many pennies?" No one had been able to count the number of pennies. Replies were: "The time was too short." "The pennies were scattered." and "There were too many pennies." Mr. Willard then replaced ten pennies with one dime (Fig. 3-3), and most of the children readily recognized the amount as 13 cents. This procedure was repeated with other numbers of pennies, and the children agreed that the replacement of ten pennies by one dime, where possible, simplified the counting.

Next the class took lima beans, plastic bags, and rubber bands from their arithmetic kits. Each pupil placed 11 beans on his desk and found groupings such as five and six, four and seven, and three and eight that totaled 11. They agreed that partitioning the sets of beans into subsets facilitated finding totals but disagreed on the best patterns. Jim suggested using 10 because it worked so well with pennies and dimes. The children then placed 10 beans in a plastic bag and had one left over. They showed twelve beans as one bag of 10 and two left over, and they continued this process for other numbers. They saw the convenience of having 10 beans in every bag so that these would be known as 1 ten rather than counting the 10 single beans. They repeated the process, using cards and toothpicks bundled in tens to illustrate the concept, and summarized their investigation by making statements such as:

Twelve pennies is the same as one dime and two pennies.
Twelve beans are one bag of 10 beans and two left over.
Twelve cards are one package of 10 cards and two more.

Figure 3-2
13 pennies on a flannel board.

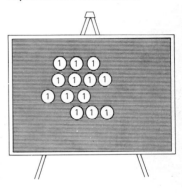

Figure 3-3
One dime and 3 pennies on a flannel board.

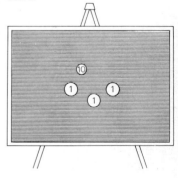

After a number of experiences with other materials and pictures, the children generalized without naming the materials, saying, "Twelve is 1 ten and 2 ones." and used the numeral 12 as a convenient way of recording it.

In the early stages of his mathematical learning, the young child manipulates real, socially significant materials to answer his quantitative questions. For example, "The small bus has five seats on each side and each seat will hold two children. How many children can ride on the bus?" He may answer this question by actually lining up five pairs of children and then five more pairs and counting the resulting total. Later he may answer the same question by letting sets of toothpicks represent children, arranging them to simulate the problem.

In the kindergarten and the beginning of grade one, problems are usually made concrete, and answers to them are secured by manipulating the materials mentioned in the problem. A problem about books is solved by manipulating books; a problem about milk cartons, chairs, pencils, or pennies is solved by combining or separating sets of materials.

In the later, more abstract stage, representative materials replace socially significant objects. Each child should have a mathematics box containing sets of different materials—acorns, popsicle sticks, bottle caps, tongue depressors, applicator sticks, play money, lima beans, and squares, triangles, and circles cut from colored paper. Joining sets, separating them into subsets, bundling into sets of 10 with rubber bands, placing counters on cards labeled with numerals, and paralleling computations by manipulating objects are but a few of the uses for these materials. As individual pupils represent number relations with their materials, cutouts backed with sandpaper or velours paper are used to demonstrate on the flannel board.

Figure 3-4
Identify different sets in the picture.

Drawing and Studying Pictures

Pictures that illustrate mathematical ideas afford another common type of experience in primary mathematics instruction. For example, the picture in Fig. 3-4, cut from a magazine and pasted on a poster, was used by Ms. Gilbert to review some of the elementary ideas of sets. She asked pupils to describe and point out any sets they saw. Some descriptions were: "The set of persons not taking a bite." "The set of persons wearing glasses." "The set of women."

Pupils solve problems by drawing pictures to represent the story. For example, Mary had eight tulips in her garden, and she picked five for the table. How many were left may be pictured by the children as they cross out five tulips from a picture of eight tulips. Other pupils may circle a set of five to show a set of three remaining.

When Ms. Mead's first grade class studied the triangle, square, and rectangle, she first had them cut models of these geometric figures from paper and construct wire models. Later they discussed examples of these figures as they appeared in their daily lives, e.g., the frame of a window, a tire, and the edges of a sheet of paper. One day Ms. Mead said, "Tell me in words what a square is." (The drawings she made are shown in Fig. 3-5).

Joe said, "A square has four sides."

"Then *a* is a picture of a square." said Ms. Mead as she drew it on the board.

Mary said, "A square has four corners."

"Then *b* is a picture of a square." said Ms. Mead.

Bob said, "All sides of a square are the same."

"Then *c* is a picture of a square." said Ms. Mead.

Ellen said, "A square is a figure that is the same across both ways."

"Then *d* is a picture of a square." said Ms. Mead.

The class agreed with Bill who said that it was "hard" to tell in words what a square was. It was further agreed that for the present they would use the wire model as an example of a square and would learn some more geometry before trying to describe a square in words.

Ms. Wilson thought her class had understood the idea of an empty set and the number of members in this set was expressed by the numeral 0. However, the text used in the class emphasized again and again that 0 was only a place holder, and many of the children seemed confused. She had pupils manipulate objects in a previous lesson and decided to use pictures as pupils restudied the use of 0 in naming certain numbers.

She first asked various pupils to draw pictures of sets that suggested two. Some of the results are shown in Fig. 3-6a, *b* and *c*. She asked whether each picture represented one set of two members or two sets of one member each. It was agreed that both interpretations could be made. She then asked if anyone could picture sets that still suggested two, yet were somewhat different from those already identified. After some trial and error, followed by discussion, the example in Fig. 3-6d was composed with two, here meaning *two sets*. The class agreed that when this picture was meant to represent two, it would have to be specified as *two sets*. Ms. Wilson then drew on the board the pattern shown in Fig. 3-7. The class decided this pictured two sets, or more specifically, two sets of 10 members each. They wrote the total

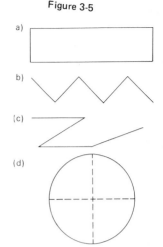

Figure 3-5

Figure 3-6

(a)

(b)

Sets of 2

(c)

(d)

Two sets

Figure 3-7

Two sets of ten.

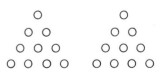

Figure 3-8
Two sets of ten and a set of one.

number of elements in both sets as the numeral 20. Then the question was raised, "What does the 0 mean?" The answer "No ones" was rejected because 20 can be thought as "20 ones." It was finally agreed, "If a set of 20 members were arranged in subsets of 10 each, there would be no ones left over. The 0 in the ones place shows this."

Next the pupils drew dot pictures illustrating 21, as shown in Fig. 3-8. They found one dot left over after two disjoint sets of 10 had been pictured. They agreed that the 0 and 1 in 20 and 21 respectively performed the same function; each represented the number of ones left after all sets of 10 had been collected. Pictures representing 30 and 40 were drawn, and the meaning of 0 was found to be the same as that described for 20.

Pictures cut from magazines or inexpensive picture books, found in textbooks or workbooks, drawn by teacher or pupils, or projected from filmstrips or films form a basis for studying numerical relations in a semisymbolic setting. Pupils move a step closer to understanding abstract manipulation of numerals as they parallel pictured operations with symbols, create problems from information given in pictures, answer number questions about pictures, and draw pictures to illustrate problems.

Number Experiences in Daily Affairs

In the transition from the unorganized use of number by the preschool child to its more systematic study in the schools, it is essential that the teacher capitalize on the mathematical experiences in the child's "community." Daily affairs in the classroom, parties, dramatizations and dramatic play, and selected stories and songs are examples of the regular, continuing primary classroom life that frequently can be utilized as "mathematics laboratory" experiences.

Classroom routine To give his pupils experiences in counting and to develop concepts of number and numeral, Mr. Robertson had his first-grade class check the daily attendance. One child counted and reported for each table; another placed the proper numerals on a chart on the chalkboard. (The teacher read and interpreted the words on this chart early in the year.) Another child counted the total number present and the number of empty chairs to find how many were absent (Fig. 3-9). These data were written on the chalkboard in a weekly attendance chart.

As their knowledge of number increased, the children compared the number present and absent on various days, and after a while they totaled the number absent for each week.

Later in the year, after the class had studied mathematical

Figure 3-9
Daily attendance.

Attendance		
	Present	Absent
Boys	_____	_____
Girls	_____	_____
Total	_____	_____

sentences, pupils wrote on the chalkboard each day a description of the attendance, which was compiled as shown in Fig. 3-10. For Monday they wrote $32 + 1 = 33$ and noted the same information could be expressed as $33 - 1 = 32$. One day Bill said he would like to write the mathematical sentence for tomorrow's attendance. The class wondered how he knew in advance how many would be present.

Bill wrote $33 - \triangle = \square$. The next day the pupils wrote in the frames the numerals that represented the number absent and present.

Much of the daily "business" of the classroom contains elements that can be utilized to increase pupils' facility in understanding and applying number. The effective teacher is sensitive to these opportunities. They arise, for example, in taking from the cupboard and passing out enough books, straws, or napkins for the pupils at a table; taking inventory of supplies; collecting and counting lunch money; placing the date on the chalkboard or crossing it off on the calendar; recording the classroom temperature; and finding pages in books.

Social activities In planning a picnic, Ms. Nixon's second-grade class needed to learn the units in which groceries are sold and the vocabulary required to make purchases at the grocery store. Arrangements were made for the class to visit a market. During the trip through the store, articles sold by the pound, quart, can, dozen, bag or package were pointed out; the need for scales was discussed; the pupils found various commodities by the numeral identifying certain shelves (bread being on 17, cereals on 19, etc.). The next day, pupils made various comments and raised further questions such as, "The two-pound carton of cheese is different in shape from two pounds of butter. Will the scales help us see if they weigh the same?" "Why aren't oranges sold by the dozen?" "Why do peas and corn come in different-sized cans?"

During the "sharing" period, Mary told the class that her parents knew a family who were in need of help for Christmas. The class decided to think about helping the family as they brought things for the Christmas drive.

After discussing what would be suitable for this family, the children started accumulating gifts. Each day they counted the number of toys and articles of clothing, took inventory of the canned food, and counted the money. They kept track of the number of days remaining to complete the project. Two days before school was to be dismissed for Christmas vacation, they counted the money and found that they had $2.58. They discussed what could be purchased for the two children with this money and appointed a

Figure 3-10
Weekly attendance.

	Mon	Tues	Wed	Thurs	Fri
Number present	32	33	30	33	31
Number absent	1	0	3	0	2

committee to accompany the teacher in shopping.

Dramatization and dramatic play Ms. Dalton's first graders held up both hands with all fingers extended, folding under two fingers at a time as they showed the action while Ms. Dalton read:

Ten little chickadees, staying up so late;
Two fly away, and then there are eight.
Eight little chickadees, sitting on some sticks;
Two hop away and then there are six.
Six little chickadees, running to their door;
Two fly away and then there are four.
Four little chickadees, friends oh so true;
Two run away and then there are two.
Two little chickadees, day's work all done;
Both go to sleep, and then there are none.

Figure 3-11
Learning the language of position by placing cutouts.

At other times, verbal descriptions by the teacher may be represented by pupils using materials on the flannel board. For example, a teacher provided cutouts of a mouse, stool, cat, canary, and moon; as she described the mouse under the stool, the cat on the stool, the canary over the cat, and the moon above them all, pupils placed the cutouts in the correct positions on the flannel board (Fig. 3-11).

Dramatic play with the class airport, train, store, post office, or house affords opportunity to weigh, make change, total prices, find the price of a number of like articles such as 10-cent stamps, or choose the correct money to pay for articles.

Simple problem situations are acted out through sociodrama, helping the pupil understand and identify with the problem. For example, "Ms. Shirer had 15 sweet peas, and she wanted to arrange them so as to give an equal number to Ms. Williams, Ms. Brown, and Ms. Baron. How many will each receive? Pretending that these pieces of chalk are the flowers and the children at the table are the ladies, can you do the problem?" Or, "Butter is 79 cents a pound. How much change will you get if you pay for the butter with a dollar? Mary, pretend that you are the storekeeper and your book is a pound of butter. John, take play money from the shelf to buy Mary's butter. Mary, you take the play money that you need to answer the question. William, will you count John's change and see if Mary gave him the right change?"

The imaginative child solves problems readily as he applies his natural ability to play-act and to identify himself with situations. Doing so, he learns to use numbers to cope with those situations.

Stories and songs Hearing stories followed by discussion, dramatization, and illustration helps small children develop their understanding of number. Later, as they learn to read, these concepts are broadened. Similarly, songs, although they are sung for purposes other than number development, frequently contribute indirectly to number understanding.

Ms. Johnson read the book *Chicken Little Count-to-ten*[1] to her kindergarten class, showing pictures of Chicken Little meeting one cow, two elephants, and so on. Later, as she reread the story, one child played the part of Chicken Little and the other children acted the roles of the various groups of animals.

One of the children's favorite songs was "Band of Angels."[2] Different pupils sat in front of the class with triangles, bells, castanets, and other instruments. The correct number stood and played as the group sang, "There was one, there were two, there were three little angels..."

Through careful planning pupils broaden their mathematical understanding as they observe, take trips, listen to other pupils or visitors tell about how number is used, and view films and filmstrips. They count the number of blocks from the firehouse to various pupils' homes, see the numeral on stamps and learn the prices, shop for a party, learn their own and friends' telephone numbers and street addresses, hear the fireman describe speed and number of gallons of water pumped by the fire engine, and hear the postman tell of the amount of mail he delivers and the distance he walks each day. Riding in the family car, they ask about road signs with numbers of miles, watch the gasoline pump register gallons and money, or talk about the distances and speeds registering on the speedometer. An expanded program of real or simulated experiences must be provided for pupils who lack such experiences of the typical middle-class environment.

Other Experiments and Experiences for Pupils

While mathematics books for every grade have numerous exercises, they do not always have sufficient variety to allow each child to work at the level best suited for him. It is necessary, then, for the teacher to provide additional activities. The following have been used effectively:

● Before pupils can read, there are many exercises that can be presented orally. Each pupil may have his box of materials from which he selects objects to complete the following experiments. Children at a table can check the correctness of each other's results.

(a) Match this set. (The teacher shows a set on the flannel board.)

[1]By M. Friskey and K. Evans, Children's Press, Chicago, 1946.
[2]From *Songs to Grow On,* arranged by B. Landeck, Edward B. Marks Music Company, William Sloane Associates, New York, 1950, p. 54.

Figure 3-12

(a)

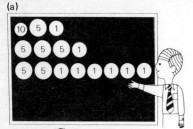

"There are two
other ways to do this."

(b)

"Here are two of the
six ways to match
these two sets."

Figure 3-13

(a)
$$2 + 1 = 1 + \underline{\quad}$$
$$3 + 4 = 4 + \underline{\quad}$$
$$1 + 5 = 5 + \underline{\quad}$$
$$3 + 2 = 2 + \underline{\quad}$$
$$8 + 197 = 197 + \underline{\quad}$$

(b)
$$0 + 7 = 7 + \square$$
$$0 + 1 = 1 + \triangle$$
$$0 + 5 = 5 + \triangle$$
$$0 + 9 = 9 + \triangle$$
$$0 + 276 = 276 + \square$$

(c)
$$8 + 1 = \underline{\quad} + 0$$
$$5 + 1 = \underline{\quad} + 0$$
$$9 + 1 = \underline{\quad} + 0$$
$$10 + 1 = \underline{\quad} + 0$$
$$87 + 1 = \underline{\quad} + 0$$

(b) Show a set with more members than this set.

(c) Show sets that suggest 2 + 1. (The pupil shows a set of 2 and a set of 1 and then rings his arms around them.)

(d) Put five circles in a line. Point to the first circle with one finger, the second circle with two fingers, and so on

● Have contests, using problems such as these:

(a) Write as many different names for 6 as you can in one minute.

(b) Find how many different ways there are to pay exactly for a 16-cent purchase (Fig. 3-12 a).

(c) Draw pictures of two sets of three members each. Find all ways to show these are matching sets (Fig. 3-12 b).

● The pupil completes a set of related exercises and then tries to discover a pattern, as illustrated by the examples in Fig. 3-13, where the blanks or frames are to be filled in so that the mathematical sentences are true. Either blanks, as in (a), or (c), or frames, as in (b), may be used. Neither form causes any special difficulty after a short introduction and discussion of the meaning of a true mathematical sentence.

● Number games serve to supplement and diversify practice. For example, when Ms. Winter's first-grade pupils entered the room early or stayed in at recess because of rain, they read numerals and kept score as they rolled a ping-pong ball through numbered arches on the game table (Fig. 3-14 a) and tossed bean bags onto a target drawn on oilcloth and spread on the floor (Fig. 3-14 b). The first pupil to score 10 points won the game.

The pupils particularly liked the "Red Riding Hood and the Wolf" game. On the flannel board, Ms. Winter mounted a house made of tag board, placing the additions and subtractions to be practiced in each window and door (Fig. 3-14 c). A cutout wolf was advanced one step toward the house each time an incorrect response was given as the leader pointed to a fact on a window or door. If the response was correct, the shutters were closed, the contest being to see if all windows and doors could be closed before the wolf advanced to the house. Numerous other appealing games are found in primary number books, syllabuses, and professional magazines.

AN ILLUSTRATIVE LESSON

Ms. Rodregues' first-grade class was reviewing, early in the school year, the concepts of triangles, squares, and rectangles. She decided to introduce the geoboard (pictured in Fig. 2-7) as a way of extending those ideas. Its construction is described in the Appendix on page 390.

Each set of three pupils was given a geoboard with elastics of different colors. Pupils were asked to show triangles, squares, and rectangles by putting elastics around the pegs.

Ms. Rodregues said, "Show me the smallest square you can.... Show me the largest square you can.... Show me other squares of different sizes." Through experimentation the pupils found four squares (Fig. 3-15).

Ms. Rodregues wanted pupils to make observations about a square. So she had pupils show a square on the geoboard, then said, "Tell me something about your square." Some answers were:

It has four sides.
The sides are straight.
It has four corners.
The corners are square.
All sides are the same length.

Bill said he could prove the corners were square. He showed how the corner of a page fitted each corner of the square.

In a similar way, properties of a triangle were introduced. Ms. Rodregues asked the pupils to show triangles with one square corner. There were many-sized examples. Then pupils were asked to show triangles with two square corners. Repeated attempts failed to produce such a triangle. The pupils discovered that it was impossible to have a triangle with two square corners.

Attention was next focused on special triangles such as those with two sides the same length. Though they tried, pupils were unable to show on the geoboard a triangle with three sides the same length.

Then pupils reviewed the ideas of inside, on, and outside a rectangle. They put their fingers on such points for a rectangle. Bob thought he'd be smart and arranged his geoboard with a triangle and a rectangle (Fig. 3-16). He showed a point inside both the rectangle and the triangle. Other pupils found points inside the triangle and outside the rectangle, and so on.

Pupils next completed pages in the textbook that required them to underline rectangles, draw circles around squares and name points inside triangles.

Pupils searched their environment for examples of the geometric figures. Illustrations of squares and rectangles were easy to find. Finding examples of triangles was more challenging, but the list grew. A few were found in stained-glass windows, in the steel structure of a bridge, and in the letter A.

Pupils brought in problems and suggestions for further study.

Sam's father told him the names of special triangles. The pupils "showed off" by using the words *scalene* (no sides congruent), *isosceles* (two congruent sides), and **equilateral** (three congruent sides) to identify triangles.

Figure 3-14
Examples of number games.

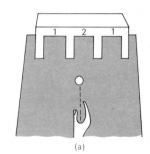

(a)

(b)

(c)

Figure 3-15
Four squares on a geoboard.

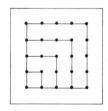

Figure 3-16
Rectangle and triangle on a geoboard.

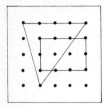

Figure 3-17
Marking a triangle to show congruent sides.

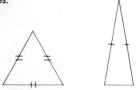

Figure 3-18
Another square on a geoboard.

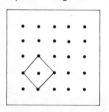

Figure 3-19
How many shapes in each figure?

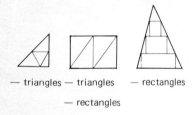

— triangles — triangles — rectangles

— rectangles

Figure 3-20
Bulletin board display of a triangle and a rectangle.

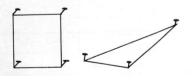

Jean's older sister showed her how to mark the sides of triangles to show which were of the same length (Fig. 3-17).

Van discovered a "different" square on the geoboard (Fig. 3-18). This started the class searching for other squares.

Ms. Rodregues drew some patterns on a ditto (Fig. 3-19), and pupils found the number of different shapes in each pattern.

Pupils used starched knitting wool and pins to show models of triangles, squares, and rectangles on the bulletin board (Fig. 3-20).

MATHEMATICS CONTENT AND SAMPLE EXPERIENCES

What are the principal topics included in the mathematics program for grades K-2? What are some of the developmental steps through which pupils progress in learning each of these? What are some experiences for promoting learning of these topics? Descriptions of experiences are catalogued here to answer these questions. Under 11 major topics covered in the primary mathematics program, suggested outcomes and appropriate experiences are arranged in one possible developmental order. The task of selecting, augmenting, and organizing is left to the teacher, to be adapted to his individual background and ingenuity, the needs of his particular class, and the textbook being used. The more detailed descriptions given under Typical Number Experiences for the Primary Grades and Experiences Combined in Lessons will serve as a guide in planning for use of these suggestions in the classroom.

As this list of experiences is studied, it should be recognized that:

● Because this is an overview of the program, it does not include all details.
● The topics are not independent categories. There is considerable overlap.
● The organization is more or less logical but does not represent a teaching order. However, the abilities within each category are in an order acceptable for their introduction.
● Individual pupils will be at different levels of development in the various categories.
● Individual pupils will not necessarily pass through all steps on the way to mastery of a topic.
● Some topics, such as geometry, fractions, problem solving, addition, and subtraction, are considered in more detail in later chapters.

Concepts of Shape and Position

Shape   The pupil:

1   Finds a difference in shapes of three-dimensional objects.
2   Identifies three-dimensional shapes by name and compares to familiar objects (Fig. 3-21).
3   Identifies plane shapes, such as circles, rectangles, and squares, and associates them with forms found in the environment.
4   Refines observations of properties of shapes; e.g., it has square corners, it has three sides.

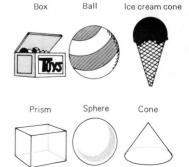

Figure 3-21
Identifying by name some three-dimensional shapes.

Box   Ball   Ice cream cone

Prism   Sphere   Cone

One pupil may observe or the teacher may call attention to the fact that the bottom of the light globe is like a ball. This can be the basis for discussion and identification, in which pupils point out or mention other objects, such as oranges and beads, that are shaped like a ball. At other times things shaped like a block or an ice-cream cone are identified. As familiarity with various shapes increases, the proper names for them may be learned; qualities such as the squareness of corners, the rolling of a ball, or the eight corners on blocks may then be recognized and discussed. Similarly, pupils find squares, circles, and triangles in picture frames, wheels, the music triangle, and other places in the classroom and community. Through handling, drawing, and discussing, they discover the number of sides and angles and other properties of the geometrical shapes around them.

Position   The pupil:

1   Progressively refines the concept listening, speaking, reading, and writing vocabulary for the following terms:

inside-outside	from-to	begin-end
left-right	into-out	east-west
near-far	off	middle
upper-lower	side	on
back-front	with	around
backward-forward	at	behind
before-after	beside	between
bottom-top	center	corner
ahead-behind	halfway	high-low
close-far	here-there	north-south
down-up	in-out	above-below
first-next-last	over-under	by

Figure 3-22

Joe   Ellen   Mac   Kay   Angelo

"Kay is second in line and Joe is fifth."

2   Refines concepts to include use of number for more accurate descriptions (2 meters behind, 3 feet above).
3   Uses numbers in the ordinal sense to designate *which one* (Fig. 3-22).

Like the development of all beginning vocabulary, this starts at an early age. Words and concepts take on meaning through descriptions of everyday occurrences: the book is *on* the top shelf; Jim is in the *first* seat; the girls will go *before* the boys; we will stay *inside* because it is raining. Games such as "Hide the thimble" afford vocabulary practice—it is *above, near, far,* 6 feet *away,* 20 centimeters *under.* Seatwork exercises include "Color the *longest* picture," "Circle the *shortest,*" "Draw a square around the one on the *left,*" or "Match the word with the picture". Later the words are introduced as part of the reading vocabulary and some in the spelling vocabulary. As they are discussed and dramatized, many of the stories and poems used in primary lessons enlarge concepts and vocabulary.

In addition to various experiences directly related to the child and his environment, experiments with tangrams can aid in accomplishing many objectives concerned with the ideas of size and shape which are continual parts of his life. The tangram is an old Chinese puzzle consisting of seven pieces that fit together to form a square (Fig. 3-23). Its construction from tag board is described on page 392. To make identification easier in this book the pieces have been labeled *A-G.*

Some experiments for pupils to complete with the tangram are the following:

1 Use pieces *C* and *G* to make a square region.
2 Use two pieces to make Fig. 3-24*a.*
3 Use pieces *D, E,* and *F* to make Fig. 3-24*b.*
4 Use tangram pieces as needed to cover the regions in Fig. 3-25.
5 Use tangram pieces to make as many different shapes as you can.

General objectives of the mathematics program that are furthered through experimentation with tangram pieces are:

- Development of motor skills by placing regions on figures of various shapes.
- Development of an intuitive idea of area as "covering a region."
- Development of the idea that different shapes may have the same area.

Rote Counting

Pupils recite the names for numbers in sequence. Learning the names in order holds a certain amount of fascination for children; many of them are able to perform rote counting to 20 or more when they enter school. Rhymes, songs, and games are an

Figure 3-23
Tangram pieces.

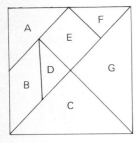

Figure 3-24
Cover with two tangram pieces.

(a)

(b)

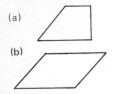

Figure 3-25
Cover with tangram pieces.

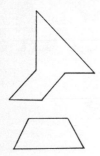

appealing and effective means for developing this ability. Pupils individually or in unison recite poems such as "One, two, buckle my shoe." Similarly, songs like "One little, two little, three little Indians" are sung with actions that point up the counting activity in the song. Rote counting is motivated by games such as "hide and seek," counting off for games, or having children count around the room, starting with 1 or some other number designated by the teacher or leader.

Number Concepts

Developing the meaning and vocabulary of sets   When they enter school, pupils have had considerable experience with sets of soldiers, dolls, cards, and so on. They may not have referred to these collections as sets, but nevertheless they have thought of them as entities and have associated numbers with some of them. In starting a systematic study of sets, the teacher may ask questions such as: "Will the members of the set of all boys come to the front of the room?" "Bill, will you bring me the set of red books?" "Will the members of the set consisting of Joe, Mary, and Bill stand up?" "Will the members of the set of all girls with long hair form a circle?" The emphasis is on thinking about a collection of materials, pictures, or symbols as a whole, with the word *member* used to designate any one object in the set.

Later, pupils identify sets in the classroom, at home, on the playground, or at the zoo. They describe various sets by naming the individual members, "The members of my set are Tony and Ellen." or by making a precise statement, "The members of my set are the children sitting at Becky's table." They list examples of sets of which they are members, such as "the set of children who have bicycles," or sets of which they are not members, such as "the set of children who live on Cedar Street."

The concept of a set is not difficult, but it takes time to develop the precise language used in describing sets. Pupils should have many opportunities to formulate and answer questions ("Is Joe a member of the set of boys wearing green sweaters?") as well as to name members of various sets and give word descriptions of them.

The idea of the empty set is one that is grasped readily by young children, especially if strange examples are used: "Show me the members of the set of girls in this room with orange hair," or "Will the members of the set of all boys with two noses stand up." If asked to give a name to such sets they may say "None" or "No such set." The term *empty set* is then supplied by the teacher. Because of their vivid imaginations, many children will be able to suggest interesting examples of the empty set.

Pairing members of matching sets Pairing members of sets may start with those having the same number of members. A set with Pam, Sue, and Fay as members may be lined up in the front of the room next to a set whose members are Jack, Greg, and Paul. Instructions are to march around the room in pairs. After the first pairing, which might be Pam with Jack, Sue with Greg, and Fay with Paul, pupils should suggest other pairings. The teacher then asks questions to bring out the idea of matching sets: "Does the set of girls match the set of boys?" "How can you tell?" "Does the set of boys match the set of girls?" Experiences like walking to the library or going to lunch provide further opportunity for pairing. From these, pupils should also grasp the idea that it is not always possible to pair members of two sets.

Counting the members of a set, associating the last number name with the number of members in the set The teacher may choose a set of four objects and ask a pupil to count the members of the set. At first he may be asked to touch each member of the set as he counts, "One, two, three, four." Later he may point to the members and, eventually, merely look at them as he counts.

Other pupils count the members in the set starting with different members. Then another set of four objects is selected and counted by the children, with emphasis on the idea that matching sets have the same number property. This may be phrased in a number of ways, e.g., "This set helps us think about what number?"

The importance to pupils of learning to associate a number with a given set cannot be stressed too strongly. They need many experiences over a period of time in counting sets with different numbers of members. Such experiences start before children have learned to write numerals to represent numbers, and the variety of activities is continually broadened after the symbols are introduced.

As pupils learn to associate a number with a set, they also arrange sets in order, according to the number of members in each. One teacher wrote letters on square pieces of felt and formed sets as shown in Fig. 3-26. The pupils arranged the sets in order, with the one having the fewest members on the left. Then they associated the numbers one, two, etc., with the sets. Various arrangements, such as the set with the fewest members placed on the left, right, bottom, or top (Fig. 3-27) were made.

Forming subsets of a given set The study of subsets may be introduced by the teacher asking members of the set of all girls in the room to stand up, then asking those who are wearing sweaters

Figure 3-26
Sets not arranged in order.

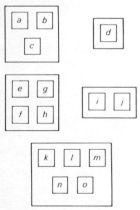

Figure 3-27
Sets arranged in order.

to move to the front of the room. Children may describe the sets as "The set of all girls," "The set of all girls wearing sweaters," and "The set of all girls not wearing sweaters." Members of the last two sets are identified by the teacher as "in" the set of all girls. Children often describe the last two sets as "part of" the original set. While this is satisfactory during early instruction, the word *subset* should be introduced as soon as the children are ready.

There are many possibilities for finding subsets. A set of books of various colors may be put on the desk. The children stack the set of red books and the set of blue books, then combine these subsets so that they once again form the original set. A set of classroom materials may be put on the desk, with the children arranging subsets composed of those items with which they write or those items on which they draw.

Finding various subsets in a set Pupils may select a set of six objects from their individual boxes of materials. They first show this set as two disjoint subsets, as pictured in Fig. 3-28. Then they display a set of six members arranged as three disjoint subsets. They should experiment to find the many possible arrangements and show each to the class on the flannel board. Then arrangements into other numbers of subsets are studied.

Pupils find a set of nine objects in a row difficult to distinguish from a set of eight or ten, but with experience, groupings such as those shown in Fig. 3-29 are identified with nine. An effective manipulative device for studying a set of nine, for example, is a wire with nine beads, as shown in Fig. 3-30. Pupils manipulate the beads into subsets and show their results to the class. The number of beads may be increased or decreased as other sets are studied.

Names for Numbers

The pupil:
1 Reads names for numbers 0, 1, 2, 3,..., 9 and uses each as the name for the number of objects in a certain set.
2 Writes names 0, 1, 2, 3,..., 9 and forms symbols, beginning the stroke as indicated in Fig. 3-31.
3 Reads and writes names: zero, one, two, three,..., nine.
4 Extends the above to 200 or more, in symbols and verbally.

The generally accepted sequence for learning about number is from the concrete to the abstract. Thus pupils first study sets of real objects, then sets of representative materials, and then pictures, with the emphasis in all cases on the number property of the set. Finally the numerals that name the number of objects in a set

Figure 3-28

A set of 6 as 2 sets of 3

A set of 4 and a set of 2

A set of 5 and a set of 1

Figure 3-29

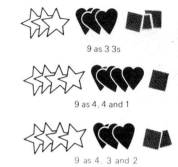
9 as 3 3s

9 as 4. 4 and 1

9 as 4. 3 and 2

Figure 3-30
Nine shown by beads on a wire.

Figure 3-31
Writing numerals.

0 1 2 3 4 5 6 7 8 9

are introduced.

The distinction between *number* (the idea) and *numeral* (the name for the idea) is made early in the primary program in most courses of study. While it is not expected that pupils will fully appreciate this distinction, the teacher can provide many examples to help pupils discriminate between an object or idea and its name. This study is begun as the teacher writes a pupil's name, Bill, on the board and the class discusses the difference between these marks on the board and their classmate Bill. Other distinctions are suggested by pupils, such as that between the written word *dog* and the animal itself or that between the written word *candy* and the actual delicacy. The concept is reinforced from time to time by other illustrations.

The teacher must recognize that Hindu-Arabic numerals are convenient symbols to represent the number of members in a set. He helps children understand this by displaying a set and asking about its number in different ways:

What numeral helps you think about the number in this set? (Teacher displays a set.)

What is the numeral for the number of objects in this set?

What numeral tells how many are in this set?

Pupils answer the question by writing the correct numeral on paper or on the chalkboard.

Some experiences for helping pupils use numerals to name the number of members of a set are:

Paste numerals cut from calendars on cards. As shown in Fig. 3-32*a*, pupils place on the cards the number of lima beans suggested by each numeral.

Display cards with numerals and patterned materials or pictures, as shown in Fig. 3-32*b*.

On a chalk tray or table match cards with numerals, as shown in Fig. 3-32*c*.

Make charts showing the numerals and the corresponding set, as pictured in Fig. 3-32*d*.

Make various types of moving devices. For example, the device pictured in Fig. 3-32*e* consists of two strips of tag board threaded through slits in a poster board. Pictures of sets on one strip are to be matched with the numeral on the other by sliding the strips.

Through imitation, pupils must learn to write numerals quickly and accurately. Some teachers favor having children trace over well-formed numerals or run their fingers along a wool-stitched numeral or around numerals notched in clay to develop some feel for the motion used in writing them. Others prefer to have them look at a numeral and attempt to imitate it, refining their work through repetition, self-criticism, and teacher appraisal.

Figure 3-32

Manipulative devices for studying numerals.

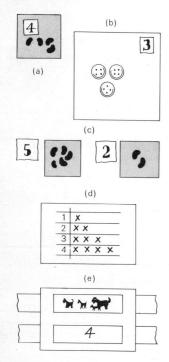

As pupils continue this study, wood rods may be introduced. These may be made from blocks of wood (see Appendix page 393 for suitable dimensions), popsicle sticks, or even strips of tag board. Coloring different-sized rods a different color is a common practice. These rods with the 1 through 5 rods pictured in Fig. 3-33 are constructed with marks to show the number associated with each and the numeral to identify it. There are many possible experiments with these rods, such as having pupils arrange them in order and make such observations as "The 4-rod is 1 more than the 3-rod". Other experiments are found on the following pages and on the Activity Cards near the end of the chapter.

Figure 3-33
Wood rods arranged in order.

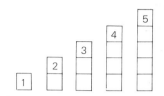

Associating numbers with points on a number line   The concept of *number* is first introduced by associating certain numbers with certain sets of concrete items. This procedure provides the young child with a tangible representation of number and one that he meets often in daily life. To avoid having the child think of numbers only as they are associated with specific sets, other representations such as the number line are introduced.

Figure 3-34
Pupils make a number line.

The teacher may mark a number of points equally spaced along a straight line on the floor in the front of the room. A child is designated to stand on each point. The child on the left is to be the number zero with other children in sequence as the following whole numbers, as shown in Fig. 3-34. To emphasize the arbitrary nature of the scale, the activity is repeated with other congruent spacings between points.

The teacher now draws on the board a number line (Fig. 3-35), using arrows to show that it continues in both directions. He places evenly spaced marks along the line. A pupil is asked to name each point (Fig. 3-36). Other experiences include completing the labeling of a number line (Fig. 3-37), and showing two steps or a jump of two starting from a point (Fig. 3-38).

Figure 3-35
Equally spaced points on a line.

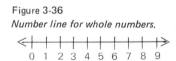

Ideas of *greater than* and *less than* may be studied using the number line. Questions such as the following are effective:

Tell me something about the points 7 and 5. (Point 7 is to the right of point 5. Point 5 is to the left of point 7.)

Tell me something about the numbers seven and five. (Seven is greater than five. Five is less than seven.)

What whole numbers are between six and nine? How is this shown on the number line?

Figure 3-36
Number line for whole numbers.

0 1 2 3 4 5 6 7 8 9

Figure 3-37
Pupils complete the numbering.

3 4   6

Place Value

The pupil:

1   Represents two-digit numerals with materials organized as tens and ones, and writes numerals corresponding to grouped

Figure 3-38
Jumps of two.

0 1 2 3 4 5 6 7 8 9 10 11 12 13 14

Figure 3-39
Fifteen in various groupings of beads.

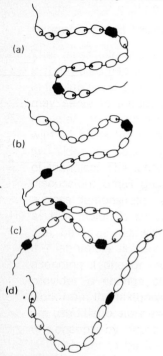

(a)

(b)

(c)

(d)

Figure 3-40
Showing fifteen with wood rods.

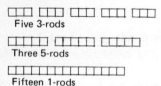

Five 3-rods

Three 5-rods

Fifteen 1-rods

Figure 3-41
Geoboard pegs grouped to show fifteen.

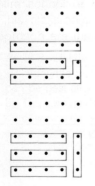

materials.

2 Understands that in recording numerals he is limited to using the symbols 0 through 9 in any place.

3 Understands the function of 0 in writing two-place numerals such as 20 or 80.

4 Generalizes that 10 ones = 1 ten and 10 tens = 1 hundred.

5 Understands that 23, for example, may be interpreted as 2 tens and 3 ones, 23 ones, or 1 ten and 13 ones.

6 Extends the above understanding to three-digit numerals and finally to millions by the end of grade three.

Emphasizing the idea of number   The teacher's desire to provide paper-and-pencil work often overrides the child's all-important need to have many concrete experiences with a number of things before he writes the numeral or code for that number using our subtle place-value system. Toward this end small groups of pupils experiment with concrete materials and report their findings to the class:

Using beads on a string.   Each group of pupils is given a supply of light and dark wooden beads and a string with instructions to show fifteen in as many ways as possible. The teacher may start by demonstrating one way with six, seven, and two beads (Fig. 3-39a). Pupils find other ways by experimenting and report: "My fifteen is nine and six" (Fig. 3-39b); "My fifteen is three and six and six" (Fig. 3-39c); "My fifteen is ten and five" (Fig. 3-39d).

Using wood rods.   The wood rods may be manipulated with a variety of instructions such as "Show fifteen using rods of only one size." In this case pupils discover that they can show fifteen in only three different ways (Fig. 3-40): as three 5-rods, as five 3-rods, or as fifteen 1-rods.

Using the geoboard.   With the geoboard pupils show fifteen pegs by using three elastics, then four elastics. One solution for each is in Fig. 3-41.

Effective teachers recognize that the place-value idea used in writing 15 as a standard name for fifteen objects is not a simple one, as evidenced by the hundreds of years it took to invent in its final form. Young children must explore fifteen objects in many different arrangements before writing its name.

Such experiences as the foregoing will make the arbitrary selection of base ten more meaningful. They will also help the pupil gain an intuitive understanding of the need for a standardized coding system. The more formal work with packaged materials, number strips, number blocks, and multibase blocks will then permit a more natural transition to the formal symbolic coding system.

Emphasizing the ideas of place value and base ten In developing the concept of place value, pupils stack and bag objects and arrange materials in sets of tens and ones and later in sets of hundreds, tens, and ones. Among the varied materials and experiences are the following:

Arranging materials as sets of tens and ones (Fig. 3-42).

Using the hundreds board. The hundreds board is a piece of plywood with 10 rows of 10 nails each. The 100 nails display, by means of disks hung upon them, the numerals from 1 to 100 (Fig. 3-43). Pupils see 16, for example, as one row of ten and six toward the next ten, or they investigate the difference in meaning of 26 and 62, two numbers with different meaning but expressed with the same symbols.

Using dimes and pennies to represent numbers. For example, 34 is objectified as three dimes and four pennies.

Representing numbers on the bead frame (10 wires with 10 beads on each wire). The partial frame illustrated in Fig. 3-44 shows the number 26.

Representing numbers with cards in a pocket holder. Six bundles of 10 cards each and 5 single cards illustrate 65, for example (Fig. 3-45). Conversely, groupings of cards in the pocket holder are examined, and the number so suggested is identified.

These or similar materials form the basis for understanding numbers expressed by numerals with two or more digits. As pupils name the numbers represented by various materials, the meaning of each digit of the numeral is clarified. Through writing numerals as they place cards in the pocket holder, they come to understand that the numerals 0 through 9 are the only symbols allowed in any given place. For example, they write 29 to indicate two packages of 10 cards and 9 single cards. When one more card is added, there are 10 in the ones pocket, and these are bundled as 1 ten and moved to the tens place, making a total of 3 tens; 3 tens with no ones left over is now written as 30.

Figure 3-42
Arranging materials in tens and ones.

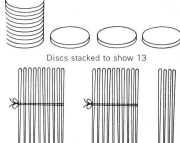

Discs stacked to show 13

Toothpicks bundled to show 24

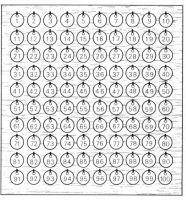

Lima beans packed in cellophane bags to show 35

Figure 3-43
Hundreds board.

Figure 3-44
Bead frame showing 26 as 2 tens and 6 ones.

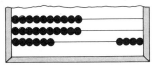

Figure 3-45
Place value chart showing 65.

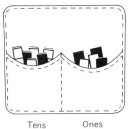

Tens   Ones

Figure 3-46
Abacus showing 70.

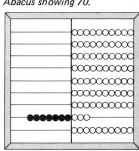

Pupils understand that the function of 0 in 30 is to show that there are no ones left after the 3 tens have been grouped. Similarly, representing 70 on an abacus (Fig. 3-46) indicates that after 7 tens are grouped there are no ones left. To show this they write 30 and 70 respectively.

An experiment that has proved effective in helping pupils understand the idea of place value is the following. When the code (numerals 1, 2, 3,...10, 11,...) is introduced, a supply of 2 cm-by-2 cm square regions each representing one, 2 cm-by-20 cm strips each representing ten, and 20 cm-by-20 cm square regions each representing one hundred may be made from tag board and given to each child. He also has a dittoed sheet with columns labeled hundreds, tens, and ones as shown in Fig. 3-47. The pupil shows the numbers one through nine with sets of small square regions. He is taught the exchange rule: Trade ten small square regions for one strip. When the first exchange is made at ten he writes 1 in the (new) tens column and 0 in the ones column (since he has no small square regions left). Similarly, at nineteen he adds one small square region making ten of them and exchanges them for one strip. Now he has two strips, so he writes 2 in the tens column and 0 in the ones. As this is continued, he discovers the next exchange rule: Trade ten strips, each representing ten, for one square region representing one hundred.

Extensive experiences with these and similar materials can aid a child in learning the coding system and what is meant by grouping by tens.

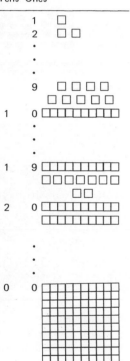

Figure 3-47
Squares and strips represent numbers.

Counting by Twos, Tens, Fives, and Threes
The pupil:

1 Groups objects in pairs and counts by ones.
2 Counts sets of two by ones, emphasizing the even numbers.
3 Counts objects by twos.
4 Identifies the tens in the right-hand column of the hundreds board. Says 1 ten, 2 tens, 3 tens, and so on.
5 Reads ten, twenty,..., one hundred from the hundreds board.
6 Observes that the numerals in the counting-by-tens series end in zero and that "ty" is used to indicate tens in twenty, thirty, etc.
7 Counts by fives, referring to the hundreds board and sets of five, and observes that the numerals end in 5 or 0.
8 Examines sets of materials in threes, counts by ones, and may count a few sets by threes.

Some experiences for learning to count by twos are the following:

Line up a set of two pupils and say "Two," point out another set of two and say, "Four," and so on.

Count pupils' shoes, fists, eyes, and ears by ones, emphasizing that there are pairs, or two, of each.

Count sets of two by ones and emphasize the even numbers: one, *two*, three, *four*, etc.

Count objects or pictures by ones, writing only the numerals for even numbers.

Read the numbers two, four, six, eight, etc., in sequence.

In a duplicated hundreds square, color in the numerals of the counting sequence for twos.

Say the twos, and, to check, turn over the corresponding tag on the hundreds board.

To learn to count by tens, pupils may color the tens on a hundreds square, count the ten objects in each of several plastic bags, count dimes, write the numerals 10 to 100 by tens, connect successive tens to complete a picture, such as that shown in Fig. 3-48. Experiences for learning to count by fives are similar, stressing the position that 5, 15, and so on, hold with respect to multiples of 10 on the hundreds chart.

Figure 3-48
Connecting numerals in order.

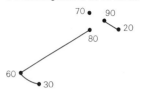

Addition and Subtraction

Before performing addition and subtraction using symbols exclusively, the pupil:
1   Observes sets of objects, recognizing disjoint subsets (sees in a set of seven objects disjoint subsets of six and one, four and three, three, three, and one, etc.).
2   Joins sets of materials to form a new set; by counting, finds how many there are altogether.
3   Relates addition of two numbers to the joining of two sets.
4   Removes a subset from a set and counts to find the number in the remaining subset.
5   Compares two sets of objects, matching the sets and counting the objects in the larger set.
6   Relates the subtracting of numbers to the removal from a set of one of its subsets.
7   Pictures addition and subtraction on a number line.
8   Uses mathematical sentences for recording addition and subtraction.

Initial experiences in determining "how many" in sets of materials and pictures are designed with the immediate aim of producing the ability to count and to develop concepts such as "What is five?" At the same time, these activities contain elements that, with minor changes and slightly different emphasis, form a familiar basis for introducing addition and subtraction.

The operation of *union* (joining) of two sets may be dramatized by placing a set of three girls on one side and a set of two boys on the other side of the classroom, then having them join to form a new set. The pupils first tell the number in each of the three sets, then they relate this set operation to the operation of adding of numbers, "Three and two are five." Later they use numerals to record the mathematical sentence $3 + 2 = 5$, which becomes a written record of the experiment.

In a similar manner, the child places a set of five members on his desk. He removes a subset of two members, and counts the members of the remaining set. Then he relates the removal of a subset to the operation of subtraction on numbers, recording the mathematical sentence $5 - 2 = 3$.

The importance of a program in which pupils discover results for addition and subtraction cannot be overemphasized. Examples of experiences for such a program are described below.

Discovery using materials   At first, sets of objects such as books, crayons, pennies, cards, or wooden dowels are joined, or a subset is removed from a given set. For example, to understand the mathematical sentence $3 + 4 = 7$, the pupil joins a set of three books and a set of four books and observes the same relationship as he joins other sets of three and four objects. He is not *proving* that $3 + 4 = 7$ as he manipulates materials, but he is making the result plausible. As the answer is verified each time, he begins to realize that $3 + 4 = 7$ is a true mathematical sentence, describing the number of elements in the sets formed by joining any set of four members to a set of three members. At this stage the learner has progressed a long way toward a meaningful generalization.

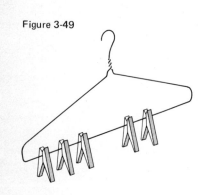

Figure 3-49

Using objects on a wire.   One ingenious teacher furnished each child with a wire clothes hanger with clothespins hung on the straight segment (Fig. 3-49). Since the number of pins could be varied by attaching or removing them, this device was used to objectify any facts being studied. Here are a few of the many concepts that may be explored by using this device:

The pupil removes a set of two (pins) from an original set of five (pins). He observes a set of three (pins) left. He relates this to the subtraction of numbers and records the mathematical sentence $5 - 2 = 3$.

He joins a set of two (pins) with a set of three (pins) to represent $3 + 2$. Then he joins a set of three with a set of two, representing $2 + 3$. He observes that $2 + 3 = 3 + 2$.

He solves $2 + n = 5$ by showing first a set of two members. When he thinks of joining this with an unknown set to form a set of five members, he discovers that he needs a set of three members.

Using scales. Pupils may use scales such as a ruler, the hundreds board, a calendar, or a clock face to discover answers to additions and subtractions and establish a basis for a somewhat different interpretation of these operations. Pointing off 7 centimeters on a ruler and then 4 more, for example, suggests the mathematical sentence $7 + 4 = 11$.

The number line, described earlier in this chapter, can be adapted for class use when drawn on the blackboard, or for individuals when drawn on a sheet of paper. The wood rods used in conjunction with the number line provide a more concrete representation of the addition facts. The pupil is given a number line drawn so that the unit is of the same length as the 1-rod. To find $3 + 5$ he places a 3-rod and a 5-rod on his number line and finds that they match the 8-rod (Fig. 3-50). After completing a number of similar experiences. He discards the rods and begins to draw number-line pictures. To show $3 + 5 = 8$ (Fig. 3-51), he draws an arc from 0 to 3, thinking of this as three steps or a jump of three. Now he sees that he must take five more steps or a jump of five. He finds that this is the same as eight steps or a jump of eight starting. 0.

Using the wood rods with the number line is recommended because pupils have been observed to count the arcs in the pictures and not recognize the number of units represented by the arc.

After pupils have shown addition on the number line as merely "counting on" and subtraction as "counting backwards," they can invent a picture to show subtraction. For $9 - 3 = \square$, they show nine as a jump from 0 to 9. Then they make a jump of three to the left from 9 and land on 6 (Fig. 3-52). Hence $9 - 3 = 6$.

A linear slide rule can be made from two pieces of tag board or from a manila folder. Cut two pieces the same length, but one wider than the other (Fig. 3-53). Subdivide each into segments of the same length and number from 1 to 10 or 18. Fold the larger card along the dotted line and insert the smaller. The rule (Fig. 3-54) is set to show any number through 7 added to 3, or subtraction facts with 3 as a difference. For example, to find $3 + 5$ we locate the sum 8 below the 5 on the inside scale. To take 6 from 9 we place 6 above 9 and read the difference below the left end of the inside scale.

Using a peg board. A peg board may be made from acoustical tile or a piece of wood with holes bored in it (see Appendix, page

Figure 3-50
Using wood rods on a number line to show 3 + 5.

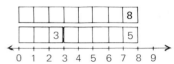

Figure 3-51
Number line picture of 3 + 5.

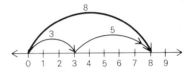

Figure 3-52
Showing 9-3 on a number line.

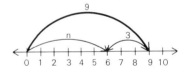

Figure 3-53
Homemade linear slide rule.

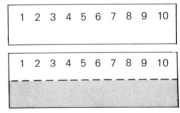

Figure 3-54
Slide rule for addition.

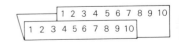

Figure 3-55
Facts, sum 6 on a peg board.

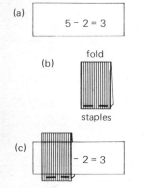

○○○○○○	0 + 6	6 − 6
●○○○○○	1 + 5	6 − 5
●●○○○○	2 + 4	6 − 4
●●●○○○	3 + 3	6 − 3
●●●●○○	4 + 2	6 − 2
●●●●●○	5 + 1	6 − 1
●●●●●●	6 + 0	6 − 0

391 for details on its construction). Different-colored golf tees or pegs are inserted in the holes to illustrate the idea being studied. Pupils may display facts with sum 6 as show in Fig. 3-55 They describe to other pupils at their table or to the class how $4 + 2 = 6$ and $5 + 1 = 6$ are related or how $5 + 1 = 6$ and $6 - 1 = 5$ are related. They also illustrate that the order of adding two numbers does not change the sum by comparing the result of $2 + 4$ and $4 + 2$.

Special difficulties Learning to solve equations such as $2 + \square = 7$, $\triangle - 2 = 4$, and $5 - \triangledown = 3$ is difficult when pupils do not have sufficient concrete experiences to relate to these sentences. A major portion of the difficulty associated with the study of these equations can be removed if pupils are guided through a number of experiments designed to help them visualize the meaning of each.

For $2 + \square = 7$ the pupil thinks, "I have two stars. I need some more so I will have seven stars." He manipulates his stars, joining a set of two to various sets, until he finds that a set of five will give him a set of seven.

For $\triangle - 2 = 6$ the pupil thinks, "I have some circles. If I take two away, I will have six left." He experiments, possibly starting with seven circles. When he takes two away he has only five left; so he must try again. Through intelligent trial and error, he finds if he starts with eight and takes two away he will have six left.

For $5 - \triangledown = 3$ the pupil thinks, "I start with 5. I take some away. Then I will have 3 left." Again, by experimenting with objects, he finds through trial and error that removing a set of two from a set of five leaves a set of three.

A device that has proved effective for practice after concrete activities is a card with mathematical sentences written on it and a slide that covers one of the numerals. For example, the sentence $5 - 2 = 3$ is written on a card (Fig. 3-56a). The slide is made by folding a piece of construction paper and stapling (Fig. 3-56b). The pupil covers one numeral in the sentence with the slide (Fig. 3-56c) and gives the answer for the numeral covered. He can check the correctness of his answer immediately by moving the slide.

Fractional Numbers

The pupil:

1 Separates one object into two parts of the same size. Names each one-half.
2 Distinguishes between one-half and either of two different-sized parts of one object.

Figure 3-56
Manipulative device for $\square - 2 = 3$.

(a) $5 - 2 = 3$

(b) fold

staples

(c) $- 2 = 3$

3   Finds, by sharing members of a set of objects equally with a friend, that each has one-half of the objects.
4   Performs these activities for one-fourth and one-third and possibly two-fourths and two-thirds.
5   Uses fractions in describing measures, such as one-quarter hour or one-half dollar.

While the topic of fractional numbers does not constitute a major portion of the primary program, there are at least two reasons for studying elementary concepts of fractions early: (1) pupils encounter the idea of fractional numbers in their environment; and (2) an early and continuing physical representation of difficult concepts is essential.

The program, as generally developed, helps children associate commonly used fractions, such as one-half, with a certain part of a physical object and a particular subset of a given set of objects.

The difficulty inherent in the concept of a fractional number is made apparent when one thinks about sandwiches. Generally, two slices of bread with an appropriate filler are referred to as "a sandwich." However, this may be cut in half, and either half may still be referred to as "a sandwich." The idea that one-half has a meaning only when the meaning of one has been identified is a very subtle one.

A child's first contact with the idea of one-half is the use of the word as he receives one of two parts of an orange, cookie, etc. This idea must be refined so that its meaning becomes one of two equal parts. The concept develops through halving many materials—pieces of string, sheets of paper, ribbons, stars—and saying and hearing "one-half." Through discussion and experiments with materials separated into two parts of different size, the generalization evolves that one-half of a whole is one of the two parts of the same size into which the whole has been divided. However, the meaning of *the whole* must always be kept clearly in mind.

Pupils may be given rectangular sheets of paper and asked to show a half by cutting. They should be urged to discover experimentally various ways of doing this, as shown in Fig. 3-57*a*. After cutting, they place the pieces one on top of the other. If they "fit," each may be named one-half of the original paper. Some pupils may be ready to explore other possibilities for cutting, as shown in Fig. 3-57*b*, and to test whether they actually have two pieces of the same size. Pictorial experiences include selecting pictures that illustrate halves; coloring halves of pieces of paper, hearts, and clowns; and marking to separate pictures in half.

The geoboard and dot paper help pupils understand the meaning of fractions after experiences such as the foregoing. Some useful

Figure 3-57
Halves of square regions.

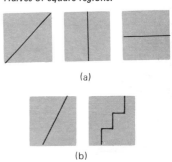

(a)

(b)

Figure 3-58

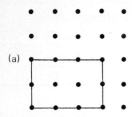

(a)

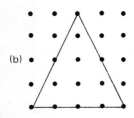

(b)

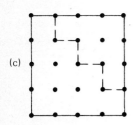

(c)

Figure 3-59

About 5 toothpicks long

About 3
pencils
long

projects are the following:

Form this figure (Fig. 3-58*a*) on your geoboard. Let this figure be 1. Use elastics to show one-half. How many ways can you do it?

Draw this figure (Fig. 3-58*b*) on your dot paper. Let this figure be 1. Draw a mark to show one-half. Cut out your figure. Tell the class how you know you have shown one-half.

Draw this figure (Fig. 3-58*c*) on your dot paper. Does the dotted mark cut the figure into two one-halves? Tell why.

Beginning experiences in finding half of a set come about through equal sharing. Four marshmallows or six jacks are shared equally by two pupils. As pupils perform these partitions, the idea is introduced that each receives one-half. Through continued sharing and partitioning of materials and pictured objects into two sets with the same number of members, the concept of one-half of the members of a set is built.

The experiences are continued with pictures as pupils enclose a subset which has a number of members half as many as a set of eight members.

The concept of one-fourth is introduced in a similar manner. One approach is for each pupil to fold a sheet of paper in half and then fold it in half again. As the paper is unfolded, four parts of the same size are observed. After establishing the sheet of paper as 1, the teacher may ask questions such as the following:

Show me one-fourth.
Show me one-half.
How many fourths make a half?
A fourth is what part of one-half?
How many halves are there in 1? How many fourths?

Because two-fourths and one-half are represented by the same piece of paper, this serves to introduce different names for the same fractional number. Although a thorough study of this idea is not made in the primary program, pupils may discover it experimentally, thus laying an early foundation for final understanding.

Measure

To learn linear measure, the pupil:

1 Compares the lengths of objects by observation.
2 Uses words such as *longer* or *shorter* in comparing objects.
3 Compares the lengths of objects by physically matching them.
4 Compares lengths of objects by matching models of them.
5 Uses pieces of chalk, pencils, or toothpicks to describe the lengths of objects (Fig. 3-59).

6　Makes a scale to determine the lengths of objects.

Other methods, such as measuring with a ruler, are treated in Chap. 9.

Early experiences with linear measure consist of describing, discussing, and comparing objects. Pupils make their first decisions on this basis of observation. They decide which segment appears longer (the first cases should be those where there can be no doubt). Initially, they may make decisions by comparing the top edge of a book and the edge of a sheet of paper, Jim's pencil and Mary's pencil, or a piece of chalk and a toothpick. The words used should be "The edge of the paper *seems* to be longer than the edge of the book."

The teacher may ask, "Who is taller, Bob or Greg?" If the answer is Bob, the teacher might ask, "Are you sure?" To a "yes" reply she might say, "Show me." The action of placing the boys back to back and observing the relative positions of the tops of the heads should make a definite decision possible. The advantages of this physical comparison over judgments by observation are then stated.

Next, pupils may compare the sides of two books by placing them edge to edge. Similarly, two pieces of chalk or a pencil and a piece of string held taut may be compared by laying them side by side.

The need for more refined methods is suggested when the problem "Compare the length of the book shelf and the length of a door" is raised. It is inconvenient, perhaps even impossible, to place the objects edge to edge. Now the teacher may choose two objects whose lengths cannot be compared physically such as the width of the door and the width of the teacher's desk. Pupils are asked to suggest ways of comparing these. Some answers are:

Use a tight piece of string to fit the width of the door, and compare it to the width of the teacher's desk.

Cut a piece of wood so it fits the width of the desk, and compare it to the door.

Figure 3-60

See how many pencils fit across the door and how many fit across the desk.

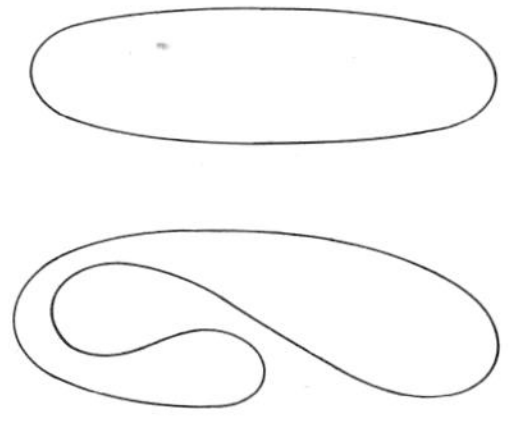

The occasion may be designed so that the pupils need to compare the lengths of closed figures such as those in Fig. 3-60. Here, pupils discover, the best method is to fit a piece of string to each curve as accurately as possible and then compare the lengths of the strings.

From these procedures pupils progress to using a new pencil,

Figure 3-61
Measuring with toothpicks.

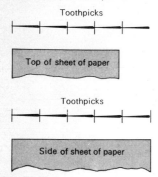

Figure 3-62

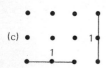

a piece of chalk, or a toothpick as an arbitrary unit of measure. They may place toothpicks along the top and side of a sheet of paper, as shown in Fig. 3-61. They conclude in this case that the side is longer than the top of the sheet. They should describe their measurements in such terms as "The top of the sheet is a *little less* than 4 toothpicks long" and "The side of the sheet is *about* 5 toothpicks long," so that they begin to grasp the idea that all measurements are approximate.

At a later time when units of measure are introduced, the geoboard becomes an effective device. Individual pupils or small groups may perform the following experiments on the geoboard and record their results on dot paper. For all experiments a length of 1 is established as shown in Fig. 3-62a.

Show a length of: (a) 2, (b) 3, (c) 4.
You must have "straight" segments.

Show a figure of length 2 that is not a segment.

Have a contest to find all figures that have a length of 3. One is shown in Fig. 3-62b.

Experimentation may be continued with the unit segment changed as shown in Fig. 3-62c.

Pupils study measurement of weight, liquid, area, and temperature through similar sequences of experiences. They may first describe their observations by saying, "The book is heavier than the tablet." "The can holds more water than the jar." or "The top of the teacher's desk is larger than the top of my desk."

The concept of weight and units for measuring weight evolves as pupils hold materials in both hands and decide which handful is heavier. They develop individual referents by comparing to a known weight: "It is about as heavy as my puppy"; "It is heavier than my arithmetic book." Later they place objects on scales and observe that the indicator points to numerals representing larger numbers as heavier objects are placed on the platform. They guess the weight of a book, shoe, or chalk box, and then weigh the object and compare the estimated and measured weight.

In a similar manner, pupils explore various means of measuring liquids by pouring them. They fill a container with water and determine whether this amount of water is more or less than enough to fill another container. They fill jars with cups of sand count the number required, and decide which jar holds the most. They discover, too, that two containers may hold the same amount of liquid while varying in size.

Since the metric system of weights and measures will be in extensive use very soon, it is important to start building the concept of metric units in the primary grades. The following activities may be used effectively:

Place signs around the classroom: "This door is about 1 meter wide"; "These 10 workbooks weigh about 1 kilogram"; "This jar holds about 3 liters."

Make lists of the approximate lengths of commonly used objects.

Make a collection of bottles that hold about 1 liter.

Make a collection of objects that weigh about 1, 2, or 3 kilograms.

Find places on the school ground that are about 10 meters or 20 meters from the classroom door.

Reading a thermometer follows the study of two-digit numerals. Children keep a record of daily temperatures on a calendar and set the ribbon thermometer to duplicate the actual termperature. This device is made from a piece of cardboard with a scale and a ribbon, part red and part white. The ribbon slides through the cardboard at 20 and 100 degrees. In Fig. 3-63 the juncture between the red and white ribbon is set at the 70-degree mark.

Starting on page 241 the sequence for learning to measure area, including the experiences for the primary grades, is considered in detail.

Figure 3-63
Ribbon thermometer.

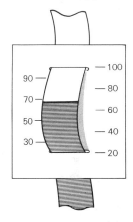

Money and Time

To learn about money, the pupil:
1. Learns about each coin (cent, nickel, dime, quarter, half-dollar, and dollar), recognizes the coin, knows its worth in cents, knows its worth in other coins.
2. Discusses items that can be bought with various amounts of money.
3. Selects the coins necessary to pay for articles.
4. Makes change, first in pennies, later in mixed coins.
5. Interprets 50 cents and 25 cents as half and quarter of a dollar.

In addition to the foregoing experiences, pupils set up equivalences in chart form; count money paid for milk, lunch, class pictures, and Red Cross; learn the abbreviations ¢ and $; and take turns acting as bookkeeper or clerk at the class store.

Figure 3-64
Manipulating the hands to show hours.

To learn time by the clock, the pupil:
1. Relates general statements of time to events, such as before lunch, noontime, morning.
2. Notes positions of hands of the clock (integral hours) for various activities (Fig. 3-64).
3. Reads hourly time.

4 Studies movement of the hands on the clock; noting the difference between the minute hand and the hour hand.

5 Reads and sets the clock to read various times.

6 Knows that there are 60 minutes in an hour and 30 minutes in a half hour.

7 Correctly writes the hour and half hour as, for example, 9 o'clock or 9:30 o'clock.

8 Writes the time to the quarter hour, 5 minutes, and nearest minute.

Figure 3-65
Clock jigsaw puzzle.

When the child enters school, he normally has some concept of the importance of time in ordering his life and some appreciation of approximate times in relation to events in his life. In school these concepts are refined, and the ability to use the clock is developed. While making clock faces on paper pie plates or fitting together a jigsaw puzzle of a clock face (Fig. 3-65) are effective learning activities, the seasoned teacher recognizes that most of the experiences in telling time grow out of the class schedule. Pupils read the clock at arithmetic time, lunch time, etc., daily reinforcing their concepts and skills.

To learn about the calendar, the pupil:

1 Senses different days of the week by activities or events: Sunday school on Sunday, beginning the school week on Monday, etc.

2 Builds a vocabulary of words such as *today*, *tomorrow*, and *yesterday*.

3 Senses a day in terms of time between events and begins to have some understanding of a week.

4 Identifies days with numerals on the calendar.

5 Learns names and sequence for days of the week.

Figure 3-66
Changeable classroom calendar.

"Today is Monday, September 15."

Understanding of the day, week, and calendar is enhanced through marking off days on the classroom calendar (Fig. 3-66); placing the date in the slot of the changeable calendar; writing the date on the board and announcing it to the class; counting the number of days until special events—Jimmie's birthday, or Christmas; keeping track of the number of days necessary for the germination of seeds; and keeping daily weather records.

Background of experience with money and the sense of time varies considerably among pupils. For this reason, teachers must provide different kinds of activities to be sure that these concepts are developed by *all* pupils.

Problem Solving

Much of the mathematics program in the first two grades consists of problem solving on a level appropriate for young children. Pupils are solving problems as they compare belongings, count possessions, or perform experiments such as those discussed earlier in the chapter. According to his stage of development, the pupil obtains answers by manipulating the sets of materials mentioned in the problem, representing the conditions of the problem using popsicle sticks or other materials, drawing stick figures, using tallies, or actually writing numerals and performing the appropriate operation. Whenever he uses the best means he knows to answer a numerical question for which he has not memorized a response, he may be said to have solved a problem. As we have already seen, the problem-solving program need not be delayed until children can read. Simple problems, first stated by the teacher and later by the class, are solved from the first day of school.

Some of the typical experiences through which primary children develop ability to solve problems follow. The pupils:

1 Describe problem situations during sharing period: "Uncle George gives me a nickel every time I spell a hard word for him. I spelled two words for him yesterday." With the help of teacher and pupils, the question, "How much did she get?" is formulated, and ways of solving the problem are discussed.
2 Formulate and state orally problems from data supplied by the teacher or other pupils. The teacher tells the class, "It is three blocks from school to June's house and two more blocks to Linda's house," and pupils make up problems from the data, drawing pictures to represent the problems as they solve them.
3 Read problems that are written on the board by the teacher, following oral statements by pupils. For example, during early study of addition, John said, "Two books and one book are how many books?" The teacher wrote on the board, "2 books and 1 book are ___." Pupils learning to read their own simply stated problems is a first step in solving written problems.
4 Act out, demonstrate with materials, or draw pictures to represent simply stated problems read by the teacher.
5 Read problems in workbooks or duplicated sheets and fill in blanks, drawing pictures to illustrate or showing computation according to level of development.

Helping pupils improvise solutions to new problems is of special importance because it encourages experimentation. For this purpose, those problems are appropriate which require a computation not yet studied, but which can be solved by adapting known procedures. After her pupils had learned the concept of subtraction and some subtraction facts, Ms. Peters gave them this problem:

Figure 3-67

$$n + 5 = 7$$

$$n = 2$$

The number thought of is 2

"Joan had 50 cents. She spent 4 cents. How much did she have left?" She urged pupils to suggest ways to do the problem. Here are some of the improvised solutions:

Write 1, 2, 3, and so on, to 45, 46, 47, 48, 49, and 50. Cross off 50, 49, 48, and 47. She had 46 cents left.

Obtain a set of 50 cards. Remove a set of 4. There is a set of 46 left.

If she spent 5 cents, she would have 45 cents left. She only spent 4 cents, so she has 46 cents left.

One procedure that has helped pupils improve their ability to solve word problems is the use of mathematical sentences. Here pupils first extract the numbers from the situation to write the mathematical sentence, perform any necessary computations to solve the sentence, and then make a word statement that answers the question in the problem. The procedure is illustrated in Fig. 3-67 for the problem: "I'm thinking of a number. If I add 5 to it the result is 7. What is the number?" With oral statements replacing written ones, this pattern can be used even before children are capable of organizing and writing such a solution.

Out of a planned program in problem solving, the primary pupil learns to use numbers to solve many of his daily problems, makes some progress toward learning to formulate problems, and learns to read and solve simply stated problems. Throughout the elementary school mathematics program, emphasis is placed on the expansion and development of these skills.

In summary, instruction in the primary grades lays a foundation for mathematics that follows. In an effective program, the child's interest in number is captured and intensified; sensitivity to number in his environment grows; a beginning is made in developing the concepts of whole numbers, fractions, and measures; and an important start is made toward facility in problem solving. Here, the emphasis is upon concrete, socially significant experiences; however, it is within this framework that the first steps toward mastery of symbolic arithmetic are taken.

During the primary years, the pupil is beginning to discover relations through investigative procedures—one of the most important results of all instruction. In brief, a start is made toward "learning to learn."

EXPERIMENTS FOR PUPILS

Instructions on each of the following Activity Cards guide pupils in performing an experiment through which they may discover a pattern, find a new way to do a mathematical problem, investigate a new use of mathematics, or extend their understanding of symbolism.

One objective directly related to the content of this chapter is given for each experiment. If the apparatus required for an experiment has not already been described, its construction is detailed in Appendix A.

In order to maximize the effectiveness of the Activity Cards, it should be remembered that:

They may be given to an individual pupil or a group of pupils.

Although one objective is listed on each Activity Card, for any experiment different objectives are attained by different pupils. For some pupils it may be an introduction to a concept, for others enrichment, or for still others review.

The amount of guidance needed in performing any experiment by a pupil or group of pupils will vary. Pupils with difficulties in reading, for example, may be included in a group activity. While some pupils may derive greater gain from discussing procedures and discoveries, other, faster ones work better alone.

The format of the card is fill-in, although space for answers has not in general been allowed here.

Each experiment can be simplified or expanded.

Activity Cards do not constitute a complete program. They are to be used at those times when they maximize learning.

ACTIVITY 1

Apparatus needed: wood rods   *Objective:* To show all ways to make 4, 5, or 6 with wood rods and write equations for them.

1   Use your rods to make the 3-family like this:
2   Make a 4-family. Write the equations.
3   Make a 5-family. Write the equations.
4   *Brainbuster.* Make a 6-family. Write the equations. Be sure you find all members of the 6-family.

3-family	Equations
3	
2 1	2 + 1 = 3
1 2	1 + 2 = 3
1 1 1	1 + 1 + 1 = 3

ACTIVITY 2

Apparatus needed: wood rods   *Objective:* To show 12 with wood rods.

1   Use two rods. Make 12 in as many ways as you can.
2   Use three rods. Make 12 in as many ways as you can.

ACTIVITY 3

Apparatus needed: circular geoboard

Objective: To show various times on a "geoboard clock."

Think of your geoboard as a clock face. Use a green elastic for the minute hand and a red elastic for the hour hand. Show these times on your geoboard clock:

1   3 o'clock.
2   Half past 7.

3   Quarter past 10.
4   Quarter to 1.

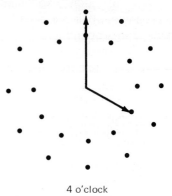

4 o'clock

ACTIVITY 4

Apparatus needed: circular geoboard

Objective: To invent pictures and show them on a geoboard.

Make this picture on your geoboard. Make up other pictures to share with your class.

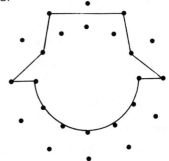

ACTIVITY 5

Apparatus needed: newspaper page

Objective: To locate numerals on a newspaper page.

1   Draw a ring around every numeral you see on your newspaper page.
2   Count the number of numerals you circled.
3   Which members of the class found the most numerals?

ACTIVITY 6

Apparatus needed: wood rods

Objective: To show the place-value meaning of numerals using wood rods.

1   You may use only 10-rods and 1-rods. Make each of these lengths. Use as many 10-rods as you can.

      14   21   27   35   49   63

2   Fill in this table:

	14	21	27	35	49	63
10-rods used	1	—	—	—	—	—
1-rods used	4	—	—	—	—	—

ACTIVITY 7

Objective: To find different names for the same number.

Cut out the six squares. Fit them together so that the edges that touch name the same number.

ACTIVITY 8

Objective: To recognize names for 8 and to write names for 7.

1   Draw a ring around all names for 8.

6 + 2   10 – 3   1 + 5   9 – 1   4 + 4   2 sets of 4

2   Have a contest with a friend. See who can write the most names for 7 in one minute.

ACTIVITY 9

Apparatus needed: wood rods   *Objective:* To measure a length using wood rods.

Use your rods to measure the length of the top of this card.
Write the length using each rod.
a   Length using 1-rods is about ___ 1-rods.
b   Length using 2-rods is about ___ 2-rods.
c   Length using 3-rods is about ___ 3-rods.

ACTIVITY 10

Apparatus needed: 3 dozen small stones   *Objective:* To use a pebble computer to illustrate the idea of place value.

1   On a sheet of paper make three marks and name them like this:
2   Use the pebbles as counters to show:

(a)   4 (b) 13 (c)   54
(d)   91 (e) 156 (f) 217

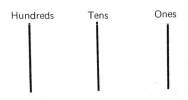

QUESTIONS AND EXERCISES

1 Make a list of 10 kinds of concrete materials or devices that may be used by primary children in performing experiments in mathematics. Under each item write the concepts that it helps to develop.

2 List six experiences with the empty set that aid primary children in understanding the idea.

3 A game that young children like to play is started by the teacher saying, as she looks toward a certain place in the room, "I'm thinking of a set that. . ." The pupil is expected to answer, "Is your set the set of. . .?" If the answer is correct, the pupil may describe a set. Describe six different sets that may be used.

4 Describe six examples of joining sets within the classroom environment. (For example, the joining of the set of art papers from Bill's table to the set of art papers from Sally's table.)

5 Describe some laboratory experiences for primary pupils in learning: (a) What is six? (b) What is a subset? (c) What is one-half?

6 The idea of place value is a very subtle one. What experiences with number should precede the introduction of this concept?

7 List the properties of triangles, squares, and circles that primary children may identify and discuss. For example, they may find that a rectangle has four sides and four square corners, and that all sides are not always the same length.

8 List experiences through which pupils may discover: (a) The amount various containers hold. (b) How 5 + 1 and 4 + 2 are related. (c) Different ways to match two sets of three members each.

9 (a) What mathematical ideas of the primary level can be illustrated by a number line? (b) How are color rods used with the number line to make illustrations of addition less abstract?

10 List ten experiences with the hundreds board that bring out the meaning of each number and the relations among numbers. (One example is, "Find the numbers for counting by ten.")

11 Supposing each child has a stiff wire with nine beads on it, list six things he could do to show the meaning of nine. (For example, he could show nine as one more than eight.)

12 What experiences should a young child have with measuring before he actually uses a ruler to determine the length of a segment?

13 What should a pupil learn about telling time by the clock in the primary grades?

14 Describe experiences in the primary grades that may be classified as *problem solving*. What criteria are used to determine if a certain experience may be called problem solving.

PROJECTS

1 Look through a series of recently published textbooks and teacher's manuals for grades K-3. Report to the class the following: (a) List experiences for pupils for learning a topic, such as counting by ones, measuring liquids, place value or fractions. (b) Outline the program in geometry (exclusive of measuring). Describe experiences with concrete materials and those with pictures. (c) List examples of seatwork activity that are on the thinking level (see Chapter 2 for illustrations). (d) Make a list of suggested manipulative materials and the important concepts they help develop. (e) Describe games that are suggested for building concepts or fixing skills. (f) List experiences through which pupils are guided in discovering concepts. (g) Suggest activities for the mathematics laboratory.

2 Describe some of the daily activities of the classroom that furnish experiences with number and geometry. Write an objective for each activity.

3 You are to take a walk with your kindergarten class in the vicinity of the school. (Assume it is late in the school year.) Plan some experiences with numbers that might arise. (Examples are: Counting the number of houses on each side of the street for one block, finding the number of front steps for each house, counting how many houses have fences in front, finding the largest tree, and so on.)

4 Demonstrate for the class the use of the following: (a) abacus in learning the concept of zero in writing numerals; (b) pocket holder for learning place value; (c) hundreds board for counting by fives; (d) cutouts of rabbits on a flannel board to show the meaning of ordinal numbers, such as first or second; (e) wire with beads on it to show addition facts with a sum of 8.

5 Write experiments for pupils for discovering each of the following concepts: (a) numbers used in the ordinal sense—first, second, and so on; (b) counting by 5; (c) 10 ones = 1 ten. (d) comparing lengths of objects by physically matching them.

6 Answer a mother who, when visiting your first-grade class which is experimenting with removing a subset from a set and writing the corresponding subtraction sentence, asks when her son will stop playing and start learning mathematics.

7 Use the evaluation scale for teaching aids in *The Arithmetic Teacher*, December 1971, pages 592-594 to evaluate commercially available materials for the primary grades.

Bibliography

1 Charbonneau, M.: *Learning to Think in a Math Lab*, National Association of Independent Schools, Boston, 1971. Contains many examples of activities for mathematical experiments.

2 Copeland, R. W.: *How Children Learn Mathematics*, Macmillan, New York, 1974. Helps the teacher see mathematics from the point of view of the child as he progresses through the various stages of development as defined by Piaget.

3 Immerzeel, G.: "Geometric Activities for Early Childhood Education," *The Arithmetic Teacher*, vol. 20, pp. 438-443, Oct. 1973. Geometric experiences that help bring a world filled with geometry into the classroom.

4 Inskeep, Jr., J. E.: "Primary-grade Instruction in Geometry," *The Arithmetic Teacher*, vol. 15, pp. 422-426, May, 1968. A plea for geometry in the primary grades and effective methods for teaching it.

5 Laycock, M., and G. Watson: *The Fabric of Mathematics*, Activity Resources Company, Hayward, Calif., 1972. Specifies objectives for primary grades and suggests various materials used to accomplish them.

6 Norman, L.: "Kindergarten in the Arithmetic Teacher: A Decade of Growth," *The Arithmetic Teacher*, vol. 18, pp. 253-256, April, 1971. Summarizes forty articles dealing with early childhood education in mathematics.

7 Rinker, E.: "Eight-ring Circus: A Variation in the Teaching of Counting and Place Value," *The Arithmetic Teacher*, vol. 19, pp. 209-216, March, 1972. A set of lessons for teaching place value using homemade materials.

8 Shulman, L.: "Psychology and Mathematics Education," in *Mathematics Education*, National Society for the Study of Education, Sixty-ninth Yearbook, NSSE, Chicago, Ill., 1970. Helps the teacher develop a philosophical point of view regarding the relationship between process and product.

9 Stern, C., and M. Stern: *Children Discover Arithmetic*, Harper and Row, New York, 1971. Of special interest to primary teachers will be chapter two, which deals with number games without number names or numerals.

4

ADDITION AND SUBTRACTION– whole numbers

The very young child is actually showing a model for addition as he joins sets of blocks to build a wall or sets of animals to form a zoo. He shows subtraction as he takes away a set of crayons from a box. Experiences in joining and separating sets are expanded in the kindergarten, with more formal work on addition and subtraction of whole numbers constituting a large portion of the curriculum in grades 1 and 2, and their study ordinarily completed in grade 4.

To be effective in planning and guiding experiences for learning addition and subtraction, the teacher needs to:

● Understand the properties of addition for the set of whole numbers.

● Know the relationship of subtraction to addition.

● Develop activities ranging from concrete to abstract through which pupils learn the important ideas and skills so they understand and perform addition and subtraction with ease and accuracy.

● Help pupils see the wide applicability of these two operations in solving relevant problems encountered in the routine of everyday life.

● Have a huge variety of experiments to aid in individualizing instruction.

DIRECTING LEARNING OF ADDITION AND SUBTRACTION

In directing learning of addition and subtraction, the teacher is concerned with answers to two questions:

What must the pupil learn? Here *up-to-date* textbooks and teacher's manuals may safely be followed in nearly all cases. Only slight variation in content occurs among the various series. In cases where the textbook and manual do not emphasize understanding the nature and the properties of operations on sets and their applications in algorithms, the teacher will need to supply additional content and appropriate experiences.

What experiences are appropriate for promoting learning? On the following pages this question is answered with special emphasis on three aspects: how pupils achieve mathematical understanding, insight, and maximum growth in the use of mathematical methods; how they acquire facility with the processes of addition and subtraction; and how they learn to identify applications of addition and subtraction in life situations.

The Facts

Mathematical sentences such as $8 + 5 = 13$ and $2 + 3 = 5$ are called *addition facts*. Addition facts have two addends that are numbers represented by one-place numerals. Because there are 10 of these $(0,1,2,3,\ldots,9)$, and because each may be added with any of these 10, there are 10×10 or 100 facts. In some curricula pupils memorize 100 subtraction facts. This is unnecessary because pupils can more easily learn addition facts and their relation to subtraction facts. Even the names for the terms in addition and subtraction are the same. In $6 + 5 = 11$, 5 and 6 are addends and 11 is the sum. In $11 - 6 = 5$, 5 and 6 again are addends and 11 again is the sum. All addition and subtraction facts are displayed in tabular form in Fig. 4-1. In this table the sum 9 is found by locating a cell in the row headed by one addend 5 and the column headed by the other addend 4. Likewise the result for $9 - 4$ is found by locating 9 in the column headed by the addend 4 and reading the unknown addend at the head of the row in which the 9 falls.

The kind of program through which pupils discover answers for the simpler addition and subtraction facts was discussed in Chapter 3. The importance of procedures whereby addition and subtraction are related to set operations and pictures on number lines cannot be emphasized too often. However, these are gradually replaced by experiences in which pupils reason their answers without reference to sets. Finally, tables are studied to focus attention on important ideas, with practice and application following. Methods for teaching various stages of this sequence follow.

Figure 4-1

Table of addition and subtraction facts.

+	0	1	2	3	4	5	6	7	8	9
0	0	1	2	3	4	5	6	7	8	9
1	1	2	3	4	5	6	7	8	9	10
2	2	3	4	5	6	7	8	9	10	11
3	3	4	5	6	7	8	9	10	11	12
4	4	5	6	7	8	9	10	11	12	13
5	5	6	7	8	9	10	11	12	13	14
6	6	7	8	9	10	11	12	13	14	15
7	7	8	9	10	11	12	13	14	15	16
8	8	9	10	11	12	13	14	15	16	17
9	9	10	11	12	13	14	15	16	17	18

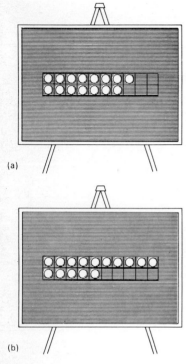

Figure 4-2
8 + 7 = 10 + 5

(a)

(b)

Techniques for promoting relational thinking   In the early stages it is perfectly natural for the child to obtain the result for 4 + 3 by counting three popsicle sticks beyond four, giving a total of seven. Later, however, when he begins to know some facts he is encouraged to use them to obtain unknown facts. For example, if he knows that 4 and 4 are 8, he may reason, "4 and 3 are 7, since the result must be 1 less than that from 4 and 4." Or if he knows 14 – 6 is 8, he may reason, "14 – 5 is 9, since subtracting 5 gives an answer 1 greater than subtracting 6."

As the pupil discovers one of these techniques, he describes it to the class, who are encouraged to check it for accuracy and to see how it is simpler than the approach through counters or other methods they have been using.

The mastery of additions and subtractions with sums 10 to 18 sometimes gives pupils difficulty. Before such facts are memorized, there are a number of specific ways in which relational thinking can help the pupil discover answers.

Discovery of answers for additions such as 8 + 6 and subtractions such as 14 – 6 is facilitated by thinking in terms of sets of 10. A helpful aid for emphasizing grouping to 10 is a paper frame for the flannel board or a wooden frame constructed to hold exactly two rows, with 10 disks in each row. To add 8 and 7, eight disks are placed in one row and seven in the other (Fig. 4-2*a*). Two disks from the row of seven transferred to the row of eight reveal the result as 1 ten and 5 ones, or 15 (Fig. 4-2*b*).

For 15 – 7, the 15 is represented by a full row of disks and five in the second row. Taking away 7 is accomplished by first removing the five disks and then removing two disks from the full row.

From a slightly different point of view, the pupil adds 9 by adding 10 and subtracting 1, or adds 8 by adding 10 and subtracting 2. The thinking for 6 + 8 becomes "6 plus 10 is 16, less 2 is 14." Subtraction of 9 may be thought of as subtracting 10 and adding 1. For example, 16 – 9 becomes (16 – 10) + 1.

At all stages of studying subtraction facts, the relationship to addition facts is stressed. The pupil who knows 6 + 8 = 14 may reason his answer to 14 – 6 by remembering that 8 is the number added to 6 to make 14. When relating to the easily learned "doubles," an exercise that helps reveal the relation is to have pupils

Figure 4-3
Relating facts to doubles.

8	8	8
+7	+8	+9

7	8	9
+8	+8	+8

1   Write groups of related facts on the chalkboard as in Fig. 4-3 (facts on either side of the double may be called *near doubles*).

2   Obtain answers by any means.

3 Describe how they can obtain sums for near doubles by reference to the doubles.

During lessons that stress facts through relational thinking, pupils should be asked to complete statements such as the following:

Because $8 + 10 = 18$, then $8 + 9 = ?$
Because $16 - 10 = 6$, then $16 - 9 = ?$
Because $13 - 8 = 5$, then $13 - 5 = ?$
If $6 + 7 = 6 + 7 = \square$, what is $6 + 8$?
If $5 + \square = 13$, what is $6 + \square$?
If $\square - 8 = 7$ what is $\square - 9$?

It must be emphasized that while using relational thinking to discover answers is desirable, this is but one step on the way from exploratory activities to automatic response. The teacher's responsibility is to see that pupils move to responses on a higher level before skill in any immature method is over-developed. A pupil should not continue indefinitely to relate to known facts, group to 10, refer to doubles, or change the order of addends. He must progress to responding automatically with the correct answer to a fact.

Techniques for fixing skills   Beyond the necessary seatwork practice found in textbooks, many teachers use mathematical games for short periods of time to add variety. Some of these may be found in Appendix B. A few examples of the many possibilities for keeping practice on the rational level follow. Others which aid in individualizing the skill-fixing program are exemplified by the Activity Cards near the end of this chapter.

Find n (n is a whole number) so that each mathematical sentence is true:

(a) $6 + n = n + 6$ (d) $n = n + 1$
(b) $n = n$ (e) $n + 2 = n + 3$
(c) $17 + n = n + 17$ (f) $10 - n = 11 - n$

For Exercises (a), (b), and (c) the answer is "Any whole number," and for Exercises (d), (e), and (f) "No whole number." These are not trick questions. Pupils should learn not only that mathematical problems often have one answer, but also that some, have many answers, and some have no answer.

Write numerals in each frame so that each mathematical sentence is true:

a. $\square + \triangle = \triangle + \square$ c. $\square + \triangle = \square$
b. $\square + \square = 12$ d. $12 + \triangle = 42 + 12$

Emphasizing basic ideas   The variety of methods for promoting understanding and skill with addition and subtraction is apt to obscure the fact that there are only a few basic ideas. The pupil is given many opportunities to study these when he completes an addition table. Some experiences used by creative teachers follow.

Studying the completed table (Fig. 4-4), the pupil finds that when the diagonal is drawn as shown, the two parts formed are related. He sees that sums *above* the diagonal repeat those *below* it. For example, 8 from $2 + 6$ is in the third row and seventh column, and 8 from $6 + 2$ is in the seventh row and third column. He identifies other examples of the commutativity of addition and argues, "Because $8 + 7 = 15$, then $7 + 8 = 15$."

To emphasize the role of zero as an addend, the teacher asks, "How do you know the sums in the first column or the first row?" Pupils gradually refine their statements and eventually say, "If zero is added to any whole number or any whole number is added to zero, the result is that whole number."

In a similar manner, the generalization to cover sums in the second row and second column is illustrated and finally formulated: "Any whole number plus 1 or 1 plus any whole number is the *next* whole number."

Pupils, by searching for examples, discover that properties for addition do not hold for subtraction. They try to find counting numbers for the frames to make true sentences for each of the following:

(a) $\square - \triangle = \triangle - \square$ (commutativity)
(b) $\square - (\triangle - \triangledown) = (\square - \triangle) - \triangledown$ (associativity)
(c) $\square - \triangle = \triangle - \square = \square$ (identity)

Since for each sentence they can find one example that is not a true sentence, they conclude the properties do not hold.

Studying mathematical sentences The pupil first uses mathematical sentences to record the results of his experiments with joining and partitioning sets. He writes $3 + 6 = 9$ after determining the number in the union of sets of three and six members; he records the separation of a set of two members from a set of eight members as $8 - 2 = 6$. Later he uses mathematical sentences to record a numerical situation with symbols. For example, he may represent the total cost of a 95-cent purchase on which there is a 4-cent sales tax as $95 + 4 = n$. Here n represents the total cost as a number of cents.

If open mathematical sentences such as $95 + 4 = n$ or $n - 7 = 16$ are to be of maximum use, pupils must have understandable procedures for solving them. As some experiences toward this end, pupils may:

Learn to identify n as an addend or the sum in sentences. One form for doing this is suggested in Fig. 4-5. Here the mathematical sentence is given, and pupils are required to determine the addends and sums.

Figure 4-4
Addition table.

+	0	1	2	3	4	5	6	7	8	9
0	0	1	2	3	4	5	6	7	8	9
1	1	2	3	4	5	6	7	8	9	10
2	2	3	4	5	6	7	8	9	10	11
3	3	4	5	6	7	8	9	10	11	12
4	4	5	6	7	8	9	10	11	12	13
5	5	6	7	8	9	10	11	12	13	14
6	6	7	8	9	10	11	12	13	14	15
7	7	8	9	10	11	12	13	14	15	16
8	8	9	10	11	12	13	14	15	16	17
9	9	10	11	12	13	14	15	16	17	18

Figure 4-5
Identifying addends and sums.

Mathematical sentence	Addends	Sum
$2 + 7 = n$	2, 7	n
$8 - 5 = n$	5, n	8

Generalize their observations: "For $2 + 7 = n$, I know two addends. The sum is unknown. I add to find the sum. For $8 - 5 = n$, I know the sum 8 and one addend 5. One addend is unknown. I subtract the known addend from the sum to find the unknown addend."

Rewrite sentences in a form for which the solution is easier to find. For $8 - n = 3$ they write $8 - 3 = n$. The thinking is "8 is the sum with 3 and n as addends." For $n - 4 = 6$, they think that n is the sum with 4 and 6 as addends as they write $n = 4 + 6$. Solutions of simple sentences such as these are intuitively obvious; however, a systematic procedure must be learned in order to determine n so that sentences such as $298 + n = 972$, $n - 572 = 104$, or $671 - n = 149$ are true.

Picture numerical situations described in words. They draw the number line in Fig. 4-6 for the problem: "Bob and his family drove 8 kilometers to the zoo and then drove some more to the park. In all they drove 11 kilometers. How far is it from the zoo to the park?" They then write the mathematical sentence $8 + n = 11$, or $11 - n = 8$, to represent the data in the problem.

Figure 4-6
Number line picture for $8 + n = 11$ or $11 - n = 8$.

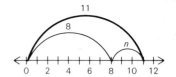

The Addition Algorithm

Computing the sum for two-place addends, such as $34 + 45$, is simpler than for $34 + 48$. The first, $34 + 45$, may be called the "noncarry" type, while $34 + 48$ is the "carry" type. The term *carry* is currently being replaced by terms such as *regroup* or *rename,* which describe more explicitly the nature of the procedure. Thus in computing $34 + 48$, the first addition, $4 + 8$, results in 12 ones, which is regrouped as 1 ten and 2 ones.

Procedures for understanding and learning computational techniques for additions requiring regrouping are described in the following paragraphs. These experiences may be readily adapted to teaching additions with no regrouping which are ordinarily taught first through the study of significant problems, use of manipulative materials, and discovery of a working pattern through study of expanded algorithms, such as in Fig. 4-7.

Figure 4-7
Expanded algorithm for addition.

$$
\begin{array}{rclcrcr}
34 & = & 30 & + & 4 \\
45 & = & 40 & + & 5 \\
\hline
& & 70 & + & 9 \\
& = & 79
\end{array}
$$

Exploration   Numerous demands for adding numbers represented by two-place numerals are present in the environment of the small child. Finding the total cost of two articles, such as 40 cents for the turtle and 12 cents for its food, the total number of pupils in two classes, the total weight of two children, and the total of numbers of various sorts of school supplies provides typical problems significant to pupils. As problems are presented, pupils are encouraged to find solutions through use of counting, grouping materials, or other improvisations.

For example, "Jim had 27 cents and earned 15 cents more running errands. How much did he have altogether?" Pupils first

Figure 4-8
Objectifying 27 + 15 with play money.

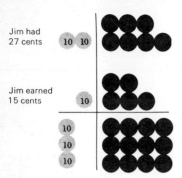

Jim had
27 cents

Jim earned
15 cents

Figure 4-9
Showing 13 + 19 with squares and strips.

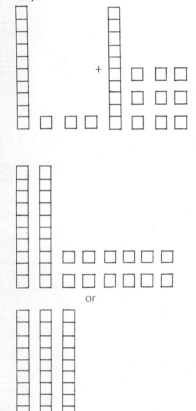

improvise the solution, using play money to represent dimes and pennies. The slowest pupil may pile up 27 pennies and count 15 more as 28, 29, 30, and so on, up to 42. More ingenious pupils may try methods that they have seen store clerks use: 27 and 10 (the dime of the 15 cents) are 37; then they count one penny at a time: 38, 39, 40, 41, 42. Or some may reverse the order, first combining 5 pennies and the 27 to make 32 and then adding the dime to make 42.

With a few hints, pupils may represent the solution with play money (Fig.4-8). At this stage they interpret the answer of 3 dimes and 12 pennies as 42 cents. The step of changing 12 pennies to 1 dime and 2 pennies is not necessary in the situation where money is involved. When numbers are added and the sum of the ones is more than 10, the renaming as a number of tens and ones must be done prior to adding the tens.

The square and strips described for exploring the idea of place value (page 60) are useful materials for the pupil to improvise an addition algorithm. With an understanding of place value and the idea that + means push together, count, and exchange as necessary, the pupil's manipulations in the early learning stages for 13 + 19 are shown in Fig. 4-9. Here he is not concerned with regrouping 12 ones as 1 ten and 2 ones prior to adding the tens. He merely wants to find 13 + 19 as 32. With the exchange rule well established, no distinction between the "carry" and "noncarry" types needs to be made in the early concrete stages.

Understanding the algorithm A pocket chart, with three rows of pockets for the two addends and sum, is useful for objectifying the addition algorithm (Fig. 4-10). Individual holders are made for each pupil by sewing butcher paper or tag board. This device has the advantage that the objectification can be performed in an order paralleling the solution with symbols.

Successive steps in solving the addition 37 + 26 are pictured in Fig. 4-11:

1 The addends 37 and 26 are represented in the top two pockets (Fig. 4-11*a*).
2 The ones are combined in the ones pocket of the last row, giving 13 ones (Fig. 4-11*b*).
3 The 13 ones are regrouped as 1 ten and 3 ones; the 1 ten is moved to the tens pocket (Fig. 4-11*c*). The tens are combined and placed in the last row. The result is seen as 6 tens and 3 ones (Fig. 4-11*d*). The sum is written as 63.

In this example, regrouping of 13 ones to 1 ten and 3 ones was performed *prior* to combining the tens. This order is important since it illustrates the order in performing the algorithm.

Expanded algorithms Expanded algorithms are very useful for helping pupils understand exactly what they are doing before they start to practice with an abbreviated form. The methods of recording shown in Fig. 4-12 help pupils visualize the actual additions, 8 + 7 and 50 + 20, that are performed. A comparision of the two forms reveals the commutative property for addition: the order of adding does not change the sum. Two other algorithms shown in Fig. 4-13 demonstrate that computing sums relies on the concept of place value and renaming a number of ones as a number of tens ones.

The final abbreviated thinking to be used by pupils in adding 67 + 25 is: 12 (from 7 + 5); write 2, remember 1 ten; 1, 7, 9; write 9. This short form is developed from the pattern used in the early stages of learning through objectification and verbalization of details of the operations. The aim is to achieve, finally, a simplified shortcut that can be rationalized as need arises. Even after the short form is mastered, teachers frequently have pupils verbalize the steps in their solution in order to show their understanding

When pupils have learned the rationale of renaming a number of ones as a number of tens and ones, they apply these same ideas to examples in which a number of tens are regrouped as a number of hundreds and tens. Sets of 100 counters or sticks are rather cumbersome, and so teachers generally prefer to use materials such as the modern computing abacus and possibly the pocket holder to objectify these additions. In general, less concrete experience is required at this stage. Meanings may be emphasized through having pupils verbalize the addition 267 + 359 in the form: 7 ones and 9 ones are 16 ones; 16 is 1 ten and 6 ones; record 6, remember 1 ten; 1 ten, 6 tens, and 5 tens are 12 tens; 10 tens are 1 hundred; record 2 tens and remember 1 hundred; 1 hundred, 2 hundred, and 3 hundred are 6 hundred. Objectification of a few examples, followed by verbalization, is a realistic program for most pupils, with additional concrete experiences provided for those who need that help.

Column Addition

After mastering addition facts, or simultaneously with the study of facts, pupils learn to add two addends such as 17 + 2, 28 + 5, or 77 + 8, ordinarily called *higher-decade addition;* they also learn to add three or more addends, usually written vertically and called *column addition.* These skills require understanding beyond that needed in learning the facts.

Addition in the higher decades Occasions for adding numbers

Figure 4-10
Pocket chart for addition.

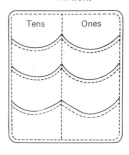

Figure 4-11
Objectifying 37 + 26 with a pocket chart.

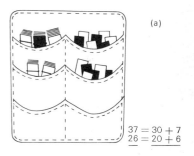

(a)

$$37 = 30 + 7$$
$$26 = 20 + 6$$

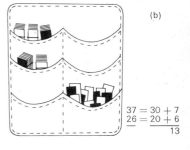

(b)

$$37 = 30 + 7$$
$$26 = 20 + 6$$
$$\overline{13}$$

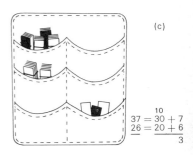

(c)

$$10$$
$$37 = 30 + 7$$
$$26 = 20 + 6$$
$$\overline{3}$$

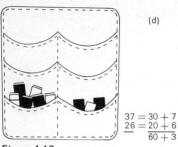

(d)

$$37 = 30 + 7$$
$$26 = 20 + 6$$
$$\overline{ 60 + 3}$$

Figure 4-12
Expanded algorithms for 58 + 27.

58	58
27	27

$$70 = 50 + 20 \qquad 15 = 8 + 7$$
$$15 = 8 + 7 \qquad 70 = 50 + 20$$
$$\overline{85} \qquad\qquad \overline{85}$$

Figure 4-13
Expanded algorithms for 58 + 27.

$$58 = 50 + 8 \qquad 58 = 5 \text{ tens} + 8 \text{ ones}$$
$$27 = 20 + 7 \qquad 27 = 2 \text{ tens} + 7 \text{ ones}$$
$$\overline{70 + 15} \qquad \overline{7 \text{ tens} + 15 \text{ ones}}$$
$$= 80 + 5 \qquad\quad = 8 \text{ tens} + 5 \text{ ones}$$

Figure 4-14
Related higher decade additions.

(a)
4	14	24		84	94
5	5	5	• • •	5	5

(b)
6	16	26		86	96
7	7	7	• • •	7	7

Figure 4-15
Number line pictures of related additions.

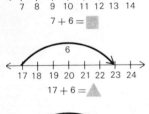

$$7 + 6 = \blacksquare$$

$$17 + 6 = \blacktriangle$$

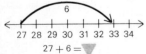

$$27 + 6 = \blacktriangledown$$

represented by two- and one-digit numerals, such as 27 + 5, arise from problem situations in life and also in multiplication and column addition. For example, in finding the product 9 × 36, after multiplying 9 × 6 as 54, the 4 is recorded and the 5 added to 9 × 3, with the final step being 27 + 5. Likewise, 27 + 5 occurs in the column addition 8 + 7 + 6 + 6 + 5 when the column is added from left to right. These higher-decade additions have a number between 10 and 99 as one addend and, as the other addend, a number 1 through 9.

Pupils may first improvise answers for higher-decade additions, such as 23 + 5, 46 + 8, or 68 + 3, by examining a hundreds board or number line. Next, they study a set of related higher-decade additions. They observe, for example, that all additions in Fig. 4-14a have 4 and 5 in the ones place and those in Fig. 4-14b have 6 and 7 in the ones place. Thus the right-hand digit of sums in Fig. 4-14a is 9, and in Fig. 4-14b it is 3. Groups of related additions such as these may be visualized with the hundreds board. For example, the answers to 4 + 5, 14 + 5, and 24 + 5 are seen to fall in the same column, revealing the important relationship that exists among these facts.

Other means for visualizing a series of related additions are number-line pictures, shown in Fig. 4-15. As more examples from 37 + 6 = □ up to 97 + 6 = □ are studied, pupils find a pattern: "7 and 6 are in the ones places of the addends and a 3 in the ones place of the sum."

Pupils must eventually learn to perform these additions automatically. They do not add ones and then tens, as they normally do when performing with paper and pencil. On the way to this level of mastery, some intermediate steps have proved useful. These are illustrated for the sequence of additions 6 + 7, 16 + 7, 26 + 7, etc.:

1 Think, "The sum of 6 and 7 is more than 10; therefore the sum of 16 and 7 is more than 20, and 26 + 7 is more than 30."

2 Think, "In each example the sum has a 3 in the ones place because the addends are 6 and 7."

3 For 36 + 7 think, "The sum of the ones is more than 9; therefore the number of tens in the sum is 1 more than 3."

4 Add 26 + 7 as "2 tens and 13 ones, which is 3 tens and 3 ones."

5 Add 46 + 7 by saying, "13, 53."

6 Finally, omit the 13 and say only, "53."

When practicing the higher-decade combinations written horizontally (26 + 7), pupils are less likely to add the ones and tens separately. Furthermore, they are practicing a form that more nearly resembles the pattern to be used later in multiplication and column addition. Exercises like "Count to 100 by sevens, starting with 9" or "Count to 100 by sixes, starting with 5" give practice with these additions.

Teaching column addition Additions with three or more addends are commonly referred to as *column* addition. Since addition is an operation on two numbers, the associative property for addition must be applied to obtain a sum. The form for recording the application of this property to finding the sum of 2, 3, 4, 5, and 6 is very complex: $\{[(2+3)+4]+5\}+6$. While pupils will not ordinarily write the addition in such a form, they should be aware that they add two numbers first, add a third number to this sum, and so on.

Column addition is usually introduced after the first few addition facts are learned, so that it may be used to vary practice with the basic facts. For example, the addition in Fig. 4-16a can be performed when children have a grasp of the concept of addition and know the facts $2+1$ and $3+4$. The only new skill here is adding an "unseen addend"; the 3 resulting from adding 2 and 1 must be retained mentally and added to 4. In Fig. 4-16b the first addition is performed on two "seen numbers," 4 and 5. All subsequent additions in this example require adding an "unseen addend." Adding the column down, the additions are $4+5$, $9+7$, $16+8$, $24+3$. The 9, 16, and 24 are unseen addends to be added to the seen addends 7, 8, and 3, respectively.

Column addition may be introduced readily in a social situation. Pupils encounter problems on costs of school supplies, such as "If pencils cost 3 cents, erasers 1 cent, and rulers 5 cents, find the total cost for one of each." Other significant problems requiring column addition are total team or individual scores in games, total number of children if the number at each table is known, and total number of books if the number in each pile is given. The actual objects mentioned in the problem or representative materials can be manipulated initially to find solutions or to verify answers.

Pictorial representation. Pictorial representation of numerical situations helps the pupil visualize the situation in the early stages of instruction. Such a representation is shown in Fig. 4-17 for the following problem: "Jim had four blocks, Mary had three, and David had two. How many did they have in all?" Here the pictures assist the child in his transition from the use of materials to the representation of the solution with symbols; they help him see that column addition is the process for finding the number in the union of three or more disjoint sets.

Figure 4-16
Examples of column addition.

(a)	(b)
2	4
1	5
4	7
	8
	3

Figure 4-17
Picturing column addition.

4

3

+ 2

Figure 4-18

Number line pictures of 4 + 3 + 2 = □.

(a)

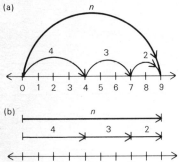

(b)

Pupils may draw a number-line picture as in Fig. 4-18*a* to visualize this problem: "Mary took four steps, then three steps, and then two more steps. How many steps did she take in all?" Later, after geometric ideas are introduced, they draw the picture, as in Fig. 4-18*b*, to represent *n* as a line segment that is the union of three line segments. In each case, they use the mathematical sentence $4 + 3 + 2 = n$ to represent the problem.

Unseen sums. Since "unseen sums" are a source of difficulty, special attention is given to their use. Some techniques for this purpose are:

Figure 4-19

Adding to "unseen numbers".

(a)	(b)		(c)	
4	4		4	
7	7	11	7	11	not $4 + 7 = 11$
8	8	19	8	19	not $11 + 8 = 19$
5	5	24	5	24	not $19 + 5 = 24$
6	6		6	30	not $24 + 6 = 30$
	30				

Record sums as they occur. To add in Fig. 4-19*a*, the sums 11, 19, and 24 may be written as indicated in Fig. 4-19*b* to provide a perceptual aid during beginning instruction. Pupils are encouraged to discard this aid when it is no longer needed. They should eventually perform by thinking *only* (not writing) the sum, as indicated in Fig. 4-19*c*. They should adopt a rhythm that can be maintained and speeded up as they master the more difficult higher-decade additions.

Figure 4-20

Race track game.

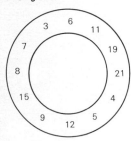

Use a *"race track."* Numerals are placed inside a circle (Fig. 4-20). The pupil is asked to think of a number, 8, for example, with instructions to add it to each of the numbers represented on the circular track. Circles of varying difficulty can be made: those that require only easy or difficult basic facts, only easy or difficult higher-decade additions, or a mixture of all types.

Questions on teaching column addition. Add up or down? A column such as that shown in Fig. 4-21 can be added, starting with the 4, obtaining 11, 19, 28, and 33; or, starting with the 5, obtaining 14, 22, 29, and 33. The sums are the same, but different additions are performed. There is no conclusive evidence to show that adding up is better than adding down, or vice versa. However, pupils should be encouraged to adopt one method and use it consistently, since there is some evidence that errors are avoided by following a consistent pattern. It is recommended that pupils add down since they are in a position to record the sum when completing the addition. In either case, it is useful to check the result by adding in the opposite direction.

Figure 4-21

4
7
8
9
5
—

Should addends be grouped? A common but dubious practice that some pupils adopt is to look in the column for addends that add to ten. For example, the addition in Fig. 4-22 could be completed by grouping 7 and 3, 8 and 2, 6 and 4, with 5 remaining, for a total of 35. In general, this practice is a substitute for learning all the facts. A column should be added by taking each addend as it occurs. Considering addends out of order, to secure additions which are either easy or which add to special totals, is likely to

Figure 4-22

7
2
8
6
3
5
4
—

introduce errors of omitting an addend or adding it more than once.

The Subtraction Algorithm

Subtractions with numbers expressed as two-place numerals are often classified into two types. No special renaming (borrowing) is required in solving the example 67 – 24 because basic facts may be applied directly. The thinking is "7 minus 4 is 3 and 6 minus 2 is 4" or "3 added to 4 is 7 and 4 added to 2 is 6." For 52–37, renaming or regrouping 52 (a change in form of 52 to 4 tens + 12 ones) is necessary because 2 minus 7 cannot be named as a whole number.

Subtractions with no regrouping are normally introduced very shortly after the subtraction facts necessary for their solution. Experiences for discovery using manipulative materials are similar to those for developing addition. The following procedures for examples requiring regrouping can be readily adapted for teaching examples where no regrouping is necessary.

Using money One of the simplest and most useful devices for introducing and developing an understanding of the procedure for subtracting with renaming is by analogy to money. For example, Jill owed May 8 cents. She counted her money and said, "I can't pay you today. I have two dimes but no pennies." Jill's mother said, "I'll give you 10 pennies for one of your dimes. Then you can pay May the 8 cents." The problem may be solved as follows: Jill shows two dimes on the flannel board (Fig. 4-23a). She sees that she cannot take eight pennies from two dimes. After converting one dime to 10 pennies, she takes away eight pennies, leaving one dime and two pennies as an answer (Fig. 4-23b).

Using a pocket holder The pocket holder is used to objectify a problem such as "Mary read 62 pages and Jane read 37. How many more pages did Mary read than Jane?" The teacher and pupils show 62 as six bundles of ten and 2 ones in the pocket holder (Fig. 4-24a). From this grouping of cards, 37 must be taken. Starting with ones as in previous subtractions, a result for 2 – 7 is not possible within the set of whole numbers; more ones, therefore, are needed in the sum. The only source is the tens pocket, so 1 ten is taken, the elastic removed, and the 10 ones placed in the ones pocket (Fig. 4-24b). The sum, 6 tens and 2 ones, is renamed as 5 tens and 12 ones. Now it is possible to take 7 ones from 12 ones (Fig. 4-24c), leaving 5 ones. Next, 3 tens are taken from 5 tens, leaving 2 tens (Fig. 4-24d). As a last step, these 2 tens and 5 ones are expressed as 25, the number of

Figure 4-23
Objectifying 20-8 with play money.
(a)

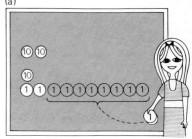

(b)

	2 dimes	0 pennies	
		8 pennies	
	1 dime	10 pennies	20
		8 pennies	−8
	1 dime +	2 pennies are 12 ¢	

Figure 4-24
Objectifying 62-37 with a pocket chart.

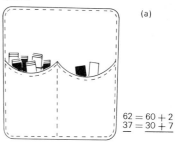
(a)

$$62 = 60 + 2$$
$$37 = 30 + 7$$

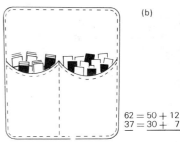
(b)

$$62 = 50 + 12$$
$$37 = 30 + 7$$

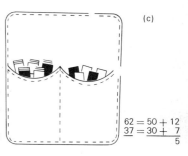
(c)

$$62 = 50 + 12$$
$$37 = 30 + 7$$
$$\overline{5}$$

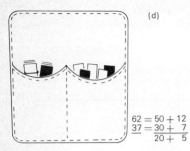

(d)

$$62 = 50 + 12$$
$$37 = 30 + 7$$
$$20 + 5$$

Figure 4-25
Expanded algorithm for 62-37.

    (a)   (b)

$$62 = 60 + 2 = 50 + 12$$
$$37 = 30 + 7 = 30 + 7$$

Figure 4-26
Using crutches in subtraction.

62	⁵6̷¹2
37	3 7

Figure 4-27
18-bead abacus to understand subtraction.

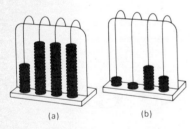

    (a)   (b)

Figure 4-28
Performing 103-75 with a pocket chart.

(a)

pages that Mary read beyond Jane.

Using an expanded algorithm As with addition, an expanded algorithm helps pupils understand the use of place value in performing subtraction. For example, to find 62 – 37, the pupil may first name 62 as 60 + 2 and 37 as 30 + 7, as shown in Fig. 4-25a. Since 7 > 2, 2 – 7 cannot be named as a whole number; therefore, 60 + 2 is renamed as 50 + 12 (see Fig. 4-25b). Now 12 – 7 and 50 – 30 can be performed.

Often, as developmental steps on the way to mastery, crutches are used to help pupils remember what they have done and to avoid mistakes. For example, as shown in Fig. 4-26, pupils should understand ⁵6̷¹2 means that 60 + 2 has been renamed as 50 + 12. In some cases crutches tend to give pupils confidence; in others they show how the computation was performed. Some pupils never need crutches; others will not be able to succeed without them. Any crutch is useful when it helps the pupil see the rationale of the operation, but all pupils should be encouraged to use them only as long as they are needed.

As a final outcome of instruction, each pupil is to complete such subtractions without recourse to materials. He must use a simple, short, direct pattern, thinking for 62 – 37, "7 from 12 is 5; 3 from 5 is 2; answer, 25." This working pattern characterizes mature solutions; it comes after experiences which develop an understanding of the "why" of the process. Practice is needed in varying amounts by different pupils with the skill further developed by applying the algorithm in solving practical problems.

Next, the subtraction algorithm is extended to exercises such as $\frac{467}{-285}$, where 1 hundred must be changed to tens, and $\frac{5,726}{-1,863}$, where 1 thousand and 1 hundred must be changed to hundreds and tens, respectively. Pupils rationalize such subtractions as logical extensions of the procedure developed for expressing 1 ten as 10 ones. Less use is made of objective materials. However, using an abacus (Fig. 4-27a) with 18 beads on each wire will aid in making this extension. In subtracting 3,285 – 1,673, for example, the sum, 3,285, is represented on the abacus (Fig. 4-27b). Beads representing 3 ones and 7 tens are taken away. Now one bead on the thousand wire is removed and replaced by 10 beads on the hundred wire so that the subtraction can be completed.

Subtractions with zeros in the sum Special attention must be given to learning the decomposition method when zeros occur in the sum. The use of the pocket holder for helping pupils understand the procedure is pictured for 103 – 75 in Fig. 4-28. The sum 103 is set up in the pocket holder (Fig. 4-28a). Subtraction cannot be started because there are not enough ones; further, there are no tens to change to ones. Hence, the hundred must be converted to 10 tens (Fig. 4-28*b*), and finally one of these tens must be shown as ten ones (Fig. 4-28*c*). Subtraction can now be performed. The use of crutches to record the operation is shown in Fig. 4-28*d*. The same method may be represented with money, as shown in Fig. 4-29.

Later, pupils may rationalize the same subtraction more simply if they recognize 103 as 10 tens and 3 ones. Then they rename one of these tens as 10 ones, so that 103 is thought of as 9 tens and 13 ones. This is shown with crutches in Fig. 4-30*a*. Likewise, for a subtraction such as 8,000 – 1,234, the pupil recognizes 8,000 as 800 tens and makes the decomposition as shown in Fig. 4-30*b* where 800 tens is renamed as 799 tens and 10 ones. Under this procedure, the sum must be interpreted to meet the conditions of the problem. For example, in 8,000 – 1,234, 8,000 is thought of as 800 tens and renamed 799 tens and 10 ones. For 8,000 – 6,720, 8,000 is more conveniently interpreted as 80 hundreds and is renamed as 79 hundreds and 10 tens.

Adding and Subtracting Mentally

The need for performing additions and subtractions without using pencil and paper is demonstrated daily in the activities of adults: checking on the total of purchases, planning the number of chairs needed for a party, budgeting, and the like.

Beyond its personal value, learning mental computation provides further opportunity for pupils to study carefully the application of the place-value scheme and various properties in explaining the "why" of certain procedures.

Probably no one technique for performing mental computations is better than another. However, pupils can benefit from studying approaches such as the following and adopting the ones which seem best for them:

The result for 32 + 45 may be obtained by thinking

$$32 + 45 = (32 + 40) + 5$$

Here the steps are 32 + 40 = 72 and 72 + 5 = 77.
Or the pupil may think, for 27 + 58, = (27 + 8) + 50.

It is more difficult to add 46 and 29 mentally than to add 45 and 30. The procedure for expressing 46 + 29 as 45 + 30 is based on the principle "The sum is unchanged if a number is added to one addend and the same number subtracted from the other addend." For the example in Fig. 4-31, 1 is subtracted and also added.

Two similar approaches for subtracting mentally are:
The difference 86 – 62 may be thought of as 86 – 62 = (86 – 60) – 2.

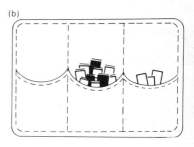

(b)

(c)

(d)

$$\begin{array}{r} \overset{9}{\overset{\,\,1}{\cancel{10}}}3 \\ -\ 75 \end{array}$$

Figure 4-29
Using money to perform 103-75.

Dollars	Dimes	Cents		Dimes	Cents		Dimes	Cents
1	0	3	=	10	3	=	9	13
	7	5	=	7	5	=	7	5

Figure 4-30
Simplifying subtraction by using place value.

(a) (b)

(a)
$$\begin{array}{r} \overset{9}{\cancel{1}}\overset{\,}{0}3 \\ -\ \ 75 \end{array}$$

(b)
$$\begin{array}{r} \overset{7}{\cancel{8}}\overset{9}{\cancel{0}}\overset{9}{\cancel{0}}\overset{1}{0} \\ -1\,234 \end{array}$$

Figure 4-31
Adding 46 and 29 mentally.

$$\begin{aligned} 46 + 29 &= (46 - 1) + (29 + 1) \\ &= 45 + 30 \end{aligned}$$

Figure 4-32
Subtracting 48 from 81 mentally.

$$81 - 48 = (81 + 2) - (48 + 2)$$
$$= 83 - 50$$

Here the steps are $86 - 60 = 26$ and $26 - 2 = 24$.

Or the pupil may think, for $73 - 48$, $73 - 48 = (73 - 8) - 40$. Here the steps are $73 - 8 = 65$ and $65 - 40 = 25$.

It is more difficult to subtract 48 from 81 than to subtract 50 from 83. The procedure for expressing $81 - 48$ as $83 - 50$ is based on the principle "If the same number is added to both the sum and known addend, the unknown addend is unchanged." For the example in Fig. 4-32, 2 is added to both 81 and 48.

Applying the relationship of addition to subtraction is another means of subtracting mentally. For $103 - 75$, the pupil thinks, "75 to 100 is 25 and 100 to 103 is 3. Therefore 75 to 103 is 28." Numer-line pictures, as in Fig. 4-33, help pupils visualize their reasoning for such examples.

Figure 4-33
Thinking of $103 - 75$ as "What added to 75 is 103?"

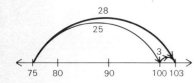

The Drill Program

A program of practice is essential. However, to be effective in fixing skills it must be of such nature that the pupil is motivated, and, further, that he thinks while he practices. Some examples of exercises that meet these criteria are the following:

- Write $<$, $=$, or $>$ in each blank so that each mathematical sentence is true:

  a. $57 + 49$ ___ $151 - 39$ b. $127 + 396$ ___ $271 + 264$
  Here pupils must perform two operations and then make a decision as to which result is greater.

- Pupils discover the rule that governs writing each of these sets of numbers and fill in the blanks.

  (a) 1, 1, 2, 3, 5, 8, 13, ___, ___, ___, ___. (This is the famous Fibonacci sequence. After the first two numbers, each number is the sum of the two numbers preceding it.)

  (b) 6, 7, 13, 20, 33, 53, 86, ___, ___, ___. [This sequence is derived by the same rule as in (a) above.]

  (c) 1, 2, 4, 7, 11, 16, ___, ___, ___.

  (d) 99, 97, 93, 87, 79, ___ ___, ___.

- In as many ways as possible express 36 as (a) the sum of two even numbers, (b) the sum of two odd numbers, (c) the sum of one odd and one even number. (c is impossible.)

- After studying the set of prime numbers, 2, 3, 5, 7, 11, 13, 17, 19, 23, 29, 31, 37, 41, 43, 47, 53, 59, 61,...,pupils may (a) write an even number such as 26 as the sum of two primes, the sum of three primes, and the sum of four primes; (b) find the even number less than 30 that can be expressed as the sum of two primes in the most different ways.

• Find all possible whole numbers for which the following mathematical sentences are true:

a. $\square - \triangle = \triangle - \square$ b. $38 - (2 + \square) = 21$

• Write all possible mathematical sentences that indicate a relationship among n, 58, and 97, if n is an addend; for example, $n + 58 = 97$. Answers are $n = 97 - 58$, $97 - n = 58$, and $58 + n = 97$. Pupils come to recognize $n = 97 - 58$ as the best form for obtaining the number represented by n. In order to write the relationship in all forms, pupils generalize that for any mathematical sentence in the form addend + addend = sum, another form is sum − addend = addend.

• Pupils insert parentheses in expressions with three addends in order to complete the computations in the easiest way. For example, by the associative property for addition $(36 + 25) + 75 = 36 + (25 + 75)$. The expression on the right of the equals sign is easier to deal with as $36 + 100$.

Learning to Solve Problems

Emphasis in this chapter has been placed upon understanding as well as skill—understanding of concepts, properties, relations, and operational techniques. Understanding such properties as closure, identify elements, and commutativity facilitates learning of other operations and is essential in contemporary algebra courses. The experience of discovering answers on one's own, provided in gaining this understanding, affords the pupil considerable experience in solving mathematical problems, recognized as an important ability in the mathematics curriculum.

Ability to describe in mathematical sentences problem situations which are solved by means of addition and subtraction also continues to be an essential part of the program. It is clear that this ability is not distinct from that of mathematical problem solving. Pupils who have discovered answers while studying addition and subtraction and who understand these operations appear superior in ability to determine and use the correct operation for solving applied problems.

The ability to solve applied problems is improved further through a planned program in which the nature of the processes is continually related to manipulations and to problem situations calling for their use, as described in Chapter 3. Some of these experiences in applying addition and subtraction in progressively more mature situations are:

Experiences in combining and separating sets, followed by writing and solving mathematical sentences to show the addition and subtraction of the numbers of elements.

Frequently introducing new steps, such as facts, multiplace addends, column addition, and subtraction with regrouping, through significant problems with amounts of money, numbers of pupils, and the like.

Providing specific sets of exercises that require pupils to use addition and subtraction to answer questions drawn from a wide variety of situations. Here special attention must be given to learning the terminology used in asking questions that are answered through addition and subtraction and to the formulation and solution of the appropriate mathematical sentences.

Mastery of addition and subtraction has been achieved only when pupils understand the operations and their properties, can compute with facility, and can use the algorithms to answer applied problems.

DIFFICULTIES WITH ADDITION AND SUBTRACTION

Young children use addition and subtraction often and with pleasure in their everyday life prior to entering school. They join sets of animals to make a circus; from a set of dolls they remove a subset. Yet in school they often encounter difficulty when these operations become more formalized. Teachers must, therefore, plan meaningful learning experiences.

IDENTIFYING DIFFICULTIES

There are opportunities throughout the school day and of course during the mathematics period to diagnose "trouble spots."

Observation during the mathematics laboratory. Here the teacher may observe some pupils having difficulty not with addition or subtraction but in following directions, or he may observe other pupils able to make discoveries but unable to record their findings with correct symbols. He will also locate pupils who are able to manipulate materials to find answers but have no desire to verbalize or record answers.

Observation during seatwork. While observing pupils during seatwork activities, talking to them, or correcting papers, the teacher may isolate inability to read or difficulty with regrouping in addition, column addition, or subtraction when zeros are in the sum.

Observation during a test and while correcting it. At what exercise in the test did Jimmy start making errors? Is there "something special" about these problems? Were Mae's difficulties due to lack of understanding of the symbolism? Does it seem that Alex has memorized certain facts or rules but does not understand what he is doing? Why does Jane do well in computation but not on questions concerning concepts?

Observation beyond the mathematics classroom. Bob says, "We won

by 4 points in volley ball, 21-17." However he has difficulty with
21 – 17 = n on a test. Why? Susie made an inventory of mathematics books in the library. She had to add a column of numbers. She did it correctly. On a test in column addition she had a poor score. Is there a reason for this?

One generalization is evident from the foregoing: The major difficulty encountered by pupils with addition and subtraction seems to be the symbolism.

REMEDIAL EXPERIENCES

Too often pupils' difficulties are diagnosed correctly but proper remedial experiences are not provided. In most cases, for example, a pupil having trouble with examples such as 62 – 37, where regrouping of the sum is required, needs more learning experiences rather than extensive drill on similar exercises.

The body of this chapter contains many different activities for discovering and learning important skills and concepts. The pupil will not ordinarily complete every one of these. Those not used may be completed in a remedial program in later grades when the topic is restudied. The abacus, for example, is not the best device for introducing the algorithms for addition and subtraction since pupils often do not see why one bead on the tens wire can replace ten beads on the ones wire. Since older pupils can handle this idea more readily, they may profit from a restudy of the algorithms with the abacus.

Some appropriate remedial experiences for two common difficulties with addition and subtraction are the following:

The meaning of + , – , and = . Pupils must learn that the symbols + and – , along with numerals and frames, are merely codes or labels for games they have played often. Only by concrete experiences can they identify addition with the action of joining two or more sets and subtraction with the removal of a subset from a set. (Other meanings of – such as comparing of the members in two sets are emphasized also.) In the mathematics laboratory the pupils' experiences should include first joining sets of 5 and 4 and verbalizing "Five and four are nine," or removing a set of 3 from a set of 8 and verbalizing "Eight take away 3 are five." Later he replaces the spoken word with the correct symbolism writing 5 + 4 = 9 and 8 – 3 = 5. Planning by the teacher must be done carefully so that pupils relate the physical manipulation of objects to the representation with symbols.

When, as often occurs, a pupil writes 5 + 4 = 11 + 2 after joining sets of 5, 4, and 2 and counting a set of 11, it becomes apparent that the statement, "The $=$ is placed between names for the same number", has little meaning for him. Learning the meaning of $=$ requires experiences beyond the verbal level. He must actually show himself that $3 + 4 = 7$ means that, starting with sets of 3 and 4, a set of seven is obtained and $3 + 4$ will *balance* 7.

Toward this end pupils may use a beam balance. They show experimentally, for example, that a 3 and a 4 on one side balances a 7 on the other side of the scale. When this happens, they write $3 + 4 = 7$. For experiments with the beam balance see page 97.

The algorithm for 62 – 37. Some pupils in the middle grades may not know how to find the result for $62 - 37$; others may write 25 with no confidence in their answer. For these pupils no amount of talk about place value and regrouping will help. And it is doubtful if expanded algorithms alone will be of aid. Further experiences in manipulating concrete materials are generally a necessity. One such experience follows, using square regions representing ones and strips representing tens.

First the pupil must think for $62 - 37$, "I can get 62 beans, remove 37 of them, and I have the result." He finds he can "speed up" his procedure with strips representing tens. He shows 62 as 6 strips and 2 squares (Fig. 4-34a). The symbolism $62 - 37$ says to the pupil, "Take a 37 from this." He finds he is asked to take away 3 strip and 7 squares. When 7 squares cannot be removed, the exchange rule of replacing 1 strip of 10 by 10 squares is used in order to obtain enough squares. The exchange with "crutches" in the algorithm is shown in Fig. 4-34b. The pupil removes 7 squares and writes his action (Fig. 4-32c). He now removes 3 strips to complete the experiment and records his result (Fig. 4-34d).

Some pupils may remove the strips first and then the squares. While they can invent a way to get the correct result in this manner, they must be encouraged to discover (rather than told) that it is simpler when the concrete materials are discarded and symbols used exclusively to perform the exchange rule first.

Teachers ask, "How can I work with some pupils needing remediation when I have twenty other pupils who do not need it?" One of the most valuable features of the mathematics laboratory is the possibility for many activities of varying degrees of difficulty from which all pupils can profit. While faster pupils are working independently or in small groups, the teacher can provide the needed guidance for remedial experiences, and vice versa. While such a program requires careful organization, it can be initiated and continually improved by every teacher.

Figure 4-34

Performing 62-37 with squares and strips.

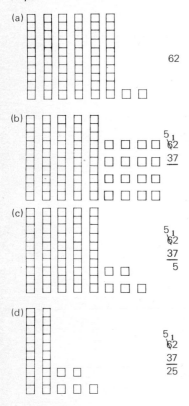

(a)

62

(b)

$\begin{array}{r} 51 \\ \cancel{6}2 \\ 37 \\ \hline \end{array}$

(c)

$\begin{array}{r} 51 \\ \cancel{6}2 \\ 37 \\ \hline 5 \end{array}$

(d)

$\begin{array}{r} 51 \\ \cancel{6}2 \\ 37 \\ \hline 25 \end{array}$

EXPERIMENTS FOR PUPILS

On the following pages are a number of Activities for pupils concerned with addition and subtraction of whole numbers. As we have seen, these may be written on cards and given to individual pupils or groups of pupils. (In order to understand the advantages and limitations of Activity Cards pages 72-73 should be reviewed.)

For each Activity there are many adaptions and extensions. In Activity 1, for example, one washer may be placed on the right arm and the pupil asked to achieve a balance with four washers on the left. (See page 389 for a picture of a beam balance.)

ACTIVITY 1

Apparatus needed: beam balance

Objective: To achieve a balance with a beam balance and write the equation which shows it.

1   Place one washer on 9 on the right arm. Place one washer on 1, one washer on 2, and one washer on 6 on the left arm. Does it balance? The equation is $1 + 2 + 6 = 9$.
2   Place the three washers at other places on the left arm so they balance the 9 on the right. Write the equation for your experiment.
3   Place the three washers at still other places on the left arm so they balance 9 on the right. Write the equation for your experiment.
4   Put one washer on 10 on the right arm. Balance it with three washers on the left. Do it in four different ways. Write an equation for each way.
5   Make up an experiment like this. Give it to your partner.

ACTIVITY 2

Apparatus needed: beam balance

Objective: To achieve with certain restrictions a balance with a beam balance and then write the corresponding equation.

1   Place one washer on 7 on the right arm. Place three washers on different numbers on the left arm so you get a "balance". Write the equation.

$$\underline{\quad} + \underline{\quad} + \underline{\quad} = 7$$

2   Repeat this experiment with one washer on 8 on the right; place one washer on each of three different numbers on the left. Be sure to get two answers. Write the equations.

$$\underline{\quad} + \underline{\quad} + \underline{\quad} = 8 \qquad \underline{\quad} + \underline{\quad} + \underline{\quad} = 8$$

3   *Brainbuster:* Repeat this experiment with one washer on 10 on the right and one washer each on three different numbers on the left. Write the equations.

4   Make up some equations and check them on your beam balance.

ACTIVITY 3

Apparatus needed: tiles numbered 1, 2, 3, 4, 5, 6, 7, 8, 9

Objective: To find experimentally how to arrange numbers to make sums of 12.

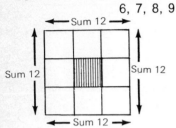

Place one tile on each unshaded square so the sum is 12 in four ways.

ACTIVITY 4

Objective: To discover how to arrange numbers so their sums are certain numbers.

Draw one straight mark on each circle. Look at Example 1.

Sum 11 and Sum 10

Sum 3 and Sum 7

Sum 7 and Sum 8

Sum 10 and Sum 11

ACTIVITY 5

Apparatus needed: 2 sheets of paper, 9 paper clips

Objective: To determine all ways of arranging items in two piles.

Number of clips on Sheet A	Sheet B	Equation
3	0	3 + 0 = 3

Sheet A		Sheet B		
2	+	0	=	2
___	+	___	=	2
___	+	___	=	2

1   Write A on one sheet of paper and B on the other.

2   In how many ways can you place 3 clips on Sheet A and Sheet B? One way is 3 clips on A and none on B. Write all ways in the table.

   You should have found 4 ways to do this.

3   Do the experiment again with 2 clips. One way is 2 clips on *A* and none on *B*. Write all ways.

4   Do the experiment again with 1 clip. You should find two ways to do this. The equations are ___ + ___ = 1 and ___ + ___ = 1.

5   Do the experiment again with 4 clips. Do the experiment again with 5 clips. Then do it again with 6 clips, 7 clips, and 8 clips. Record your results in the table.

6   *Brainbuster:* Guess how many ways you can put 9 clips on sheets A and B. Check your answer by placing the clips.

Number of clips	Number of ways to put on Sheet A and Sheet B
1	2
2	3
3	4
5	
6	
7	
8	

ACTIVITY 6

Objective: To write equations that are related to given equations.

1   Suppose you know that $6 + 5 = 11$. Then you also know that $5 + 6 = 11$ and that $6 + 4 = 10$ because $6 + 4$ is one less than $6 + 5$. You also know that $11 - 5 = 6$. These are related facts to $6 + 5 = 11$.
2   Suppose you know that $7 + 6 = 13$. Write as many related facts as you can.
3   Make up a problem like this for yourself. Then write the answers.

ACTIVITY 7

Apparatus needed: piece of string   *Objective:* To discover how to read the sum of two numbers from a nomograph. To invent a way to use the nomograph to subtract.

1   The three number lines show a nomograph. The string is placed to show $4 + 2 = 6$.
2   With your string show $2 + 2 = 4$. Now show $1 + 3 = 4$. Now show $3 + 3 = 6$.

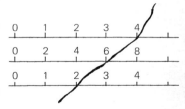

3   Write numerals for other points on each number line.
4   Use your string to find answers for $3 + 5$ and $5 + 1$.
5   Mark points for 1, 3, 5, 7, 9, 11, 13, and 15 on the middle number line. Now use your string to find $5 + 2$; $1 + 4$; $0 + 1$; $5 + 4$.
6   Invent a way to find answers to $5 - 2$; $4 - 1$; $3 - 2$; $5 - 3$.

ACTIVITY 8

Apparatus needed: 20-bead abacus   *Objective:* To find the sum of two numbers using a 20-bead abacus.

1   The 20-bead abacus shows $23 + 12$.
2   On your abacus show $54 + 32$. Remove the pins from the wires to find the result for $54 + 32$. Answer:____.
3   Use your abacus to find the results for each of the following:

        $46 + 23 =$ $61 + 34 =$

        $28 + 46 =$ $53 + 39 =$

ACTIVITY 9

Apparatus needed: 2 duplicated hundreds boards   *Objective:* To study higher-decade addition facts with a hundreds board.

Use a separate sheet showing a hundreds board for each of problems 1 and 2. On your hundreds board circle the answer for each addition in each problem.

1   On one hundreds board circle answers for 4 + 5, 14 + 5, 24 + 5, 34 + 5, 44 + 5, 54 + 5, 64 + 5, 74 + 5, 84 + 5, and 94 + 5. What can you say about each answer?

2   On the other hundreds board circle answers for 4 + 7, 14 + 7, 24 + 7,..., 94 + 7. What can you say about each answer?

3   Count by 6s starting with 7. ____, ____, ____, ____, ____, ____, ____

ACTIVITY 10

Objective: To follow directions, practice subtraction, and make an interesting discovery.

1   Choose a 4-digit numeral such as   3087
2   Write the largest number possible   8730
3   Write the smallest number possible   0378
4   Subtract   8352
5   Repeat steps 2, 3, and 4 until   8532
     you discover something interesting   2358
                                              6174

6   You choose a 4-digit numeral and do the experiment again. If you don't discover something after eight subtrations or less, you've made a mistake.

ACTIVITY 11

Objective: To practice computing while completing a puzzle.

Write + -, >, or < in the empty boxes. Make each sentence true reading left to right and top to bottom.

2		3		4
	■		■	
3		4		5
	■		■	
4		5		6

QUESTIONS AND EXERCISES

1 What basic ideas should a pupil discover and study in order to learn the addition facts?

2 On pages 81 - 82 , the basic ideas found in a table of addition facts were discussed. The same table, of course, can also be used for subtraction facts. Describe specific questions and ideas that might be discussed by groups of pupils for subtraction.

3 Why is it necessary that pupils have many experiences with the relationship between addition and subtraction and operations on sets of physical objects?

4 How may a pupil reason the result for 9 + 7 or 15 - 9 by thinking in terms of a set of 10 objects?

5 *True* or *false*? (Defend your answer.) (a) If a pupil can produce an answer of 7 to the question "What is 5 + 2?" we can assume he has mastered the fact. (b) The final outcome for learning addition facts is to apply such reasoning as "Because 8 + 8 = 16, 8 + 9 = 17" or "Because 14 - 7 = 7, then 15 - 7 = 8."

6 Make a list of topics for which the pupil should practice relational thinking. Record your answers in a form such as the following: *Facts with zero:* Pupil thinks, "Because 6 + 1 = 7, then 6 + 0 = 6."

7 What may happen when pupils bypass concrete representation and expanded algorithms and move quickly to use of abbreviated algorithms?

8 Describe in three ways how second- and third-grade pupils may improvise the solution for 37 + 45. For 72 - 47.

9 (a) Draw pictures of a pocket chart and decribe in words how 138 + 276 might be objectified. (b) Use pictures of an 18-bead abacus to illustrate how the addition is performed.

10 Draw pictures and describe how the 18-bead abacus is used to objectify: (a) 82 - 57; (b) 543 - 269.

11 In regrouping to perform the following subtractions what is the best name to use for the sum? (a) 6,010 - 1,234; (b) 7,000 - 1,234; (c) 8,100 - 1,234; (d) 8,110 - 1,234.

12 List concepts and procedures for computation associated with the program of addition and subtraction that may be: (a) discovered by pupils, and (b) best learned in the mathematics laboratory.

13 Summarize difficulties that some pupils have with column addition. What are some effective experiences for helping them overcome (or avoid) these difficulties?

14 Describe how you would help your middle-grade pupils learn to find n mentally for each of the following: (a) 53 + 38 = n; (b) 47 + 65 = n; (c) 78 - 49 = n; (d) 94 - 67 = n.

15 What emphases are made in teaching addition so that pupils will recognize situations calling for the operation.

PROJECTS

1 Study a recently published series of textbooks and answer the following for addition and subtractions of whole numbers: (a) List the major concepts and topics that are introduced in each of grades one, two, and three. (b) For each major topic in (a), list the concrete materials that are suggested for objectification. (c) Find examples of rational thinking. (One example is: "Because 6 + 1 = 7, 6 + 0 = 6.") (d) Find examples of expanded algorithms and crutches. (e) It was indicated on page 20 that practice should be kept on a rational level. Find exam-

ples that illustrate this kind of practice. (f) List experiences for learning the facts. (An example is emphasizing the relationship between addition and subtraction; that is, because 3 + 4 = 7, then 7 – 4 = 3.) (g) List experiences through which pupils may learn to recognize problems that are solved by addition and subtraction. (h) List activities that are recommended for the mathematics laboratory. (i) Describe experiences through which pupils may discover ideas.

2 Demonstrate to the class how to use toy money on a flannel board, an 18-bead abacus, or a pocket holder to objectify 23 + 34, 26 + 37, 34 – 21, and 36 – 19.

3 Plan a lesson for teaching the commutative property of addition, higher-decade addition, or adding zero and subtracting zero.

4 Write experiments for the mathematics laboratory through which pupils may (a) Study additions and subtractions with sums of 9 using a wire with 9 beads. (b) Learn to draw number-line pictures to illustrate addition and subtraction. (c) Use the 18-bead abacus to objectify subtractions such as 103 – 68 (a zero in tens place of the sum).

5 (a) Repeat the experiment in Activity 5, using 3 sheets of paper. (b) In Activity 7 invent a way to use the nomograph to subtract.

6 Some mathematics educators would replace at least some of the present emphasis in early instruction on the commutative and associative properties for addition by "the any-order idea for addition," which is known intuitively by pupils. Discuss with members of your class: (a) What is meant by this "any order idea for addition." (b) Does the above suggestion have any merit?

7 Use the squares and strips on page 84 to show how a pupil can improvise the answers to 209-146 in the early concrete stage of learning. Repeat this for 207 – 149.

Bibliography

1 Ashlock, R. B.: "Teaching the Basic Facts: Three Classes of Activities," *The Arithmetic Teacher*, vol. 18, pp. 359-364, Oct., 1971. Instructional activities are classified as understanding, relating, and mastering the facts.

2 Brownell, W. A., and H. E. Moser: *Meaningful vs. Mechanical Learning: A Study in Grade III Subtraction*, Duke University Press, Durham, N.C., 1949. Study of teaching subtraction, using decomposition in a meaningful way to some pupils and a mechanical way to others.

3 Fletcher, R. F.: "Elementary School Mathematics: A Word of Caution and a Question," *The Arithmetic Teacher*, vol. 19, pp. 645-647, Dec., 1972. Is the curriculum in addition and subtraction becoming too formal?

4 King, I.: "Giving Meaning to the Addition Algorithm," *The Arithmetic Teacher*, vol. 19, pp. 345-348, May, 1972. Illustrates the addition algorithm using blocks.

5 Marion, C.: "How to Get Subtraction into the Game." *The Arithmetic Teacher*, vol. 17, pp. 169-170, Feb., 1970. Experiences to motivate learning subtraction.

6 Pagni, D.: "The Computer Motivates Improvement in Computional Skills," *The Arithmetic Teacher*, vol. 18, pp. 109-112, Feb., 1971. Shows how to use the computer to motivate drill.

7 Quast, W. G.: "Method or Justification," *The Arithmetic Teacher*, vol. 19, pp. 617-623, Dec., 1972. The distinction, which should also be made by every teacher, between an algorithm and its justification is clearly discussed.

8 Smith, W.: "Subtraction Steps," *The Arithmetic Teacher*, vol. 15, pp. 458-460, May, 1968. Useful for helping teachers determine a sequence of steps in learning subtraction.

9 Stern, C., and M. B. Stern: *Children Discover Arithmetic*, Harper and Row, New York, 1971. Contains many concrete approaches to teaching addition and subtraction.

10 Weaver, J. F.: "Some Factors Associated with Pupils' Performance Levels on Simple Open Addition and Subtraction Sentences," *The Arithmetic Teacher*, vol. 18, pp. 513-519, Nov., 1971. Levels of difficulty for solving sentences of the form $a + b = c$ and $a - b = c$ with the place holder in various positions.

5

MULTIPLICATION AND DIVISION— whole numbers

Multiplication of whole numbers is ordinarily studied concurrently with its inverse, division. These two operations, generally introduced in grade 2 and culminating in the middle grades, complete, for the most part, the first phase of the program related to the set of whole numbers. In general, a higher level of mathematical maturity is required for successful study of multiplication and division than for addition and subtraction because some ideas are more subtle and the algorithms for computing are more complex. For effective teaching of these operations, the teacher needs to:

- Know the meaning of multiplication, its properties, and its relation to division.
- Have a huge variety of experiences through which pupils first discover the multiplication facts and then practice them.
- Understand the algorithms for multiplication and division and provide concrete activities for pupils that will lead to the abstract representation.
- Guide pupils to recognize numerical situations that call for multiplication and division and help them find uses for these in their environment.
- Prepare experiments for individual pupils or groups of pupils through which the program can be individualized.

DIRECTING LEARNING OF MULTIPLICATION AND DIVISION

The program of instruction in multiplication and division starts in the primary grades and extends through the elementary grades and beyond. The extent and diversity of the program are explained by the variety of required outcomes, including understanding of the properties of the operations and recognition of the situations calling for their applications, as well as mastery of the skills. Modern textbooks are designed to provide effective support for this program.

Additional instructional ideas and materials are supplied by the teacher.

The Facts

Mathematical sentences such as $6 \times 9 = 54$ consisting of two one-place *factors* , 6 and 9, and a *product,* 54, constitute the *multiplication facts.*

The number of facts There are 100 multiplication facts. These may be arranged as 10 sets of 10 facts each, with every number, 0 through 9, multiplied by each of the other ten numbers. Fig. 5-1 shows the multiplication facts, with products located at the intersection of the row to the right of one factor with the column headed by the other. Thus $5 \times 7 = 35$, as is indicated.

There are 10 facts like 0×0, 1×1, 2×2, 3×3, 9×9—a number times itself; the remaining 90 consist of 45 facts and the reverse of each.

While the expression "division facts" remains in use, it is not necessary. Even the modern vocabulary shows the relationship of 6×9 and 9×6 to $54 \div 9$ and $54 \div 6$. While in $54 \div 9 = 6$, *quotient* for 6, *divisor* for 9, and *dividend* for 54 are sometimes used, the names *product* for 54 and *factors* for 6 and 9 indicate the definition of division. So to find n if $54 \div 9 = n$, the thinking is "$54 \div 9 = n$ means $n \times 9 = 54$ (or $9 \times n = 54$)." Here 9 and n are definitely shown as factors with 54 as the product. Hence, divisions are displayed in the multiplication table. In Fig. 5-1 the product is found in the body of the table and the factors are located at the top of the given column and the front of the row.

Overview for learning the facts Generally a sequence of experiences, leading from manipulation of objects to the symbolic and generalization levels, is provided separately for several sets of related multiplication and division facts. Thus experiences with the twos are followed by a similar sequence for the threes. After manipulation of objects to illustrate the facts, relations between various facts are explored. A relation with the twos in multiplication is that each successive product is two greater than the preceding fact: 5×2 is two greater than 4×2. Another relationship is that multiplication is commutative, as illustrated by $2 \times 5 = 5 \times 2$.

The program leading to the fixing of skills includes many activities with objects, while studying the simpler facts and learning the basic ideas, with progressive guidance toward reliance on reasoning as the pupil matures. Thus, concrete experiences are gradually replaced by processes emphasizing *thinking* of answers and studying relations between known and unknown facts. At the same time, the methods for expressing multiplications and divisions be-

Figure 5-1
Multiplication-division table.

x	0	1	2	3	4	5	6	7	8	9
0	0	0	0	0	0	0	0	0	0	0
1	0	1	2	3	4	5	6	7	8	9
2	0	2	4	6	8	10	12	14	16	18
3	0	3	6	9	12	15	18	21	24	27
4	0	4	8	12	16	20	24	28	32	36
5	0	5	10	15	20	25	30	35	40	45
6	0	6	12	18	24	30	36	42	48	54
7	0	7	14	21	28	35	42	49	56	63
8	0	8	16	24	32	40	48	56	64	72
9	0	9	18	27	36	45	54	63	72	81

come more mature. At first, multiplications are expressed as "six 5s" or "four 3s," implying the idea of a number of equivalent sets. When the word *times* and symbol × are introduced, the original spoken form is continued, but its use is gradually dropped. Divisions are initially stated as "twos in eight." The more mature expressions "Eight divide by two" and "What number times two is eight?," along with the symbols ÷ and $\overline{)}$, are introduced as the occasions arise.

Throughout this program, the mathematical and applied emphases are interwoven. Pupils use the operations to solve problems from their environment, and then learn to apply them in less familiar situations described verbally or in writing. Skill in computation and mathematical understanding progress concurrently with the study of vocabulary and applications.

Experiences for discovery of facts Modern textbooks include or suggest many useful experiences for helping children discover the basic facts. The teacher's responsibility is to select and supplement these with other experiences appropriate to his class and to individual pupils.

Finding applications. Pairs of children in a line, stacks of three books, several nickels or dimes, sections in a milk carrier or a cupcake tin, packages of rolls, and sets of shoes, overshoes, fists, eyes, and ears illustrate a few of the situations readily available to furnish a significant basis for study of multiplication and division facts. Pupils are encouraged to improvise solutions in progressively more mature ways in order to find answers to such questions as the number of blocks in four stacks of three each. After observing the objects, pupils may count by ones; next, they may count by threes—three, six, nine, twelve; as they come to recognize three stacks of blocks as 9, they see four stacks as three more, or 12, or they recognize two piles as six and four piles as twice as many, or 12. They can organize the cost of different numbers of articles, such as 5-cent pencils, as follows:

Number of pencils	1	2	3...
Cost at 5 cents each	5	10	15...

Similarly, pupils manipulate materials to verify that twelve blocks contain four piles of three each or that a set of twelve blocks separated into four matching subsets gives three in each subset. Packing materials, e.g., placing 20 lollypops into cellophane bags of four each, and sharing materials equally among a given number of pupils provide a perceptual base for division.

As materials are combined or separated, the action is verbalized in a form that aids in visualizing a multiplication and division: four

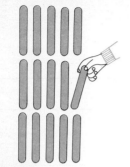

Figure 5-2
Three 5s or five 3s.

Figure 5-3
Bead frame showing 6 × 4.

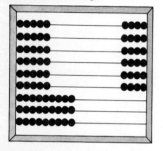

Figure 5-4
(a) Eight sets of 4. (b) Eight sets of 4 = three 10s and two 1s.

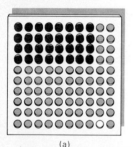

(a)

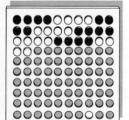

(b)

3s, four sets of three, threes in 12, and so on. Through objectification, verbalization and recording results of experimentation pupils recognize that a multiplication situation may be pictured as a number of sets, each with the same number of elements. Similarly, a situation requiring division is seen either as a set being separated into a given number of matching sets, or as a set being partitioned into disjoint sets with a given number of members in each.

Manipulation of materials. For purposes of improvising solutions or developing mathematical meanings, each pupil is supplied with materials, such as plastic disks, cardboard squares, and wooden dowels, that can be stacked, grouped, or packaged. Discovery experiences in which individual pupils group these materials are accompanied by demonstrations on the flannel board.

Each pupil lays on his desk such objects as three rows of tongue depressors (Fig. 5-2), meanwhile observing that he has depicted three 5s. He reexamines his display and discovers that it also reveals five 3s when considered as five columns of three each. These experiences afford a natural basis for later generalization of the commutative property for multiplication and a foundation for exploration of division.

A bead frame, composed of nine horizontal wires with nine beads on each wire, can be manipulated to represent any multiplication fact. In Fig. 5-3, a pupil has moved beads to show six 4s.

The pupil extends his concept of multiplication as he illustrates a fact such as 8 × 4 with colored pegs and a square of masonite with 10 holes in each of 10 rows. He first relates 8 × 4 to eight disjoint sets with four members in each, as shown in Fig. 5-4a. Then he displays the product, 8 × 4, by filling holes alternately with sets of four black pegs and four white pegs as illustrated in Fig. 5-4b. The answer, 32, is seen as three sets of ten and two more. Similarly, he observes 32 as eight sets of four each, showing that 32 ÷ 4 = 8.

Analyzing and drawing pictures. Pictures of such objects as triangles, circles, or squares may be cut from magazines or drawn on charts. These form a basis for experiences on a semiconcrete level, similar to those described for real materials. The pupil draws pictures to accompany his groupings of objects or to aid his visualization of a number of matching sets. He pictures four sets of two objects each to illustrate 4 × 2 (Fig. 5-5a). He sees from this the relation between 4 × 2 and 2 + 2 + 2 + 2. Or he finds how many twos can be subtracted from 8 by successively circling pairs of triangles from an original total of eight triangles to illustrate the relation of subtraction to division (Fig. 5-5b).

Reaching answers through relations. During the period when pupils are studying multiplication facts and before responses have become automatic, answers to unknown facts may be obtained by reference to known facts (for example, $7 \times 5 = 35$; therefore $8 \times 5 = 35 + 5 = 40$). While a certain amount of relational thinking may be done naturally, a planned program emphasizing relations begins with experiences using objects. For example: "There are twice as many windowpanes in 8 rows of 2 each as in 4 rows of 2 each"; "Our classroom has 7 rows of chairs with the same number in each. Because there are 30 chairs in 6 rows, there are 35 in 7 rows"; "There are half as many pupils at 3 tables of 5 each as at 6 tables of 5 each."

Pupils may systematically produce a multiplication or division table by means of relational thinking. As they build a table for 8, they may reason:

2×8 is $8 + 8$, or 8 more than 1×8, or 8×2.
3×8 is 8 more than two 8s.
4×8 is twice 2×8, or 2×16, or $16 + 16$.
5×8 is half of 10×8, or $5 \times 2 \times 4$, or 10×4.
6×8 is double 3×8, or triple 2×8, or 8 more than 40.
Eights in 40 are 5, so there is one less eight in the number $40 - 8$. There are six 8s in 48, so there are three 8s in a number half as great.

A number of related multiplications listed on the chalkboard, as in Fig. 5-6, affords opportunities for examining relationships. Studying the products reveals that 7×8 is one less eight than 8×8. Similarly, 9×8 is one more eight than 8×8.

Important concepts to be emphasized The teacher should remember that the many suggestions on the previous pages can be classified into a few broad categories. The following are some of the emphases that should pervade learning the multiplication facts and related divisions.

Relation between multiplication and division. This relationship is clarified for pupils when multiplications and divisions are represented in a rectangular arrangement. The pupil uses tiles as pictured in Fig. 5-7a to illustrate $4 \times 5 = 20$, $5 \times 4 = 20$, and the related divisions $20 \div 4 = 5$ and $20 \div 5 = 4$. At the same time he shows that if he starts with four sets of 5 tiles each, their union is a set of 20 members, and the mathematical sentence describing this is $4 \times 5 = 20$. If, however, he starts with 20, shown in Fig. 5-7b as 2 tens, and arranges the set into four subsets, each with the same number of members, the mathematical sentence describing this model is $20 \div 4 = 5$. To emphasize such relationships, pupils

Figure 5-5
(a) Four 2s. (b) 2s in 8.

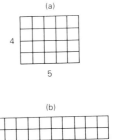

Figure 5-6
Relating multiplication facts.

8	8	8	7	7	7
$\times 7$	$\times 8$	$\times 9$	$\times 6$	$\times 7$	$\times 8$
	64			49	

Figure 5-7

Figure 5-8

"Here are 20. I put them into four sets of 5 to show 20 ÷ 4 = 5."

Figure 5-9

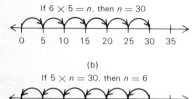

(a)

If 6 × 5 = n, then n = 30

(b)

If 5 × n = 30, then n = 6

Figure 5-10

Partial multiplication table.

×	1	2	3	4	5
1	1	2	3	4	5
2	2	4	6	8	10
3	3	6	9	12	15
4	4	8	12	16	20
5	5	10	15	20	25

Figure 5-11

5 × (3 + 1)

(5 × 3) + (5 × 1)

make statements such as, "Because 4 × 5 = 20, then 20 ÷ 4 = 5 and 20 ÷ 5 = 4."

When pupils are asked, "Show that 4 × 5 = 20," or, "Demonstrate that 20 ÷ 4 = 5" (Fig. 5-8) they display a rectangular arrangement. Thus as the pupil learns the multiplication facts and the relationship between multiplication and division, it becomes unnecessary for him to memorize divisions.

This idea is found in most texts presently available for use in the schools, but in some books is not emphasized to the extent necessary for understanding by pupils. It is the responsibility of every teacher to provide the experiences needed for a logical and pedagogically sound approach to computation with division and problem solving requiring division.

Further experiences through which pupils learn the meaning of division as well as its relation to multiplication are the following:

They draw similar number-line pictures for related multiplication and divisions. For 6 × 5 = n they think "Six 5s" and draw number-line pictures such as that in Fig. 5-9a. For 30 ÷ 5 = n they think "How many 5s in 30?" and draw as in Fig. 5-9b. They may or may not rewrite 30 ÷ 5 = n in the form n × 5 = 30 before drawing the picture.

They use a multiplication table to obtain results for divisions. They find n if 15 ÷ 3 = n from the partial multiplication table (Fig. 5-10) by locating the product, 15, in the body of the table opposite the factor 3 on the left. Then the unknown factor, 5, is located at the top of the column containing the 15.

They interpret a division as finding the unknown factor. As a result of concrete experiences, pupils learn to generalize the meaning of the factors in 3 × 5 = n as:

$$3 \qquad \times \qquad 5 \qquad = \qquad n$$
number of sets   number in each set

Then they discover similar interpretations for related situations that imply division. For the problem "Bill pasted 15 stamps in his book. He had 5 rows with the same number in each row. How many were in each row?" the pupil thinks, "How many sets of 5 in a set of 15?" He writes n × 5 = 15, with n as the number of sets and 5 as the number in each set.

For the problem "Joan had 15 pieces of candy. She gave the same number of pieces to each of three friends. How many pieces did she give to each?" The pupil thinks, "3 sets of how many form a set of 15?" He writes 3 × n = 15 where 3 is the number of sets and n is the number in each set.

The commutative property for multiplication. The commutative property for multiplication provides a means for decreasing the number of facts to be memorized. Here the pupil who knows $6 \times 8 = 48$ should, using this property, learn readily that 8×6 is also 48. He meets this idea when he is studying objects and pictures illustrating multiplications. He makes statements such as "I see four rows with eight items in each row and I also see eight columns with four items in each column. I see the same total in each case."

Later he learns commutativity of multiplication for whole numbers as seen in the multiplication table (Fig. 5-10). Here he observes that the diagonal acts as a mirror, with the 10 from 2×5 above the diagonal, for example, being the mirror image of the 10 from 5×2 below the diagonal. He notes that this was also the case for the addition table.

The pupil discovers that commutativity of multiplication, beyond its usefulness in learning the facts, is also applied in checking multiplication. He finds that performing 693×48 is one way of checking 48×693.

The distributive property. The many applications of the distributive property, some of which have already been demonstrated in this chapter, must be made explicit. Pupils who know $5 \times 3 = 15$, for example, learn to reason the result for 5×4.

Using poker chips to show $5 \times (3 + 1)$, they see that it is also equal to $(5 \times 3) + (5 \times 1)$ as in Fig. 5-11. After concrete and pictorial representations such as this, they reason "without pencil and paper" that 5×4 is one more 5 than 5×3 and get the answer almost automatically. Other illustrations of the distributive property, using a 5 by 4 arrangement of ⊗s, are pictured in Fig. 5-12.

In a similar manner, to divide, the pupil applies the property that division is right-hand distributive. He thinks, for example, "$18 \div 3$ is 6; 21 is 3 more than 18; therefore, $21 \div 3$ is 7." He first uses poker chips to show 3 as one set of three chips and 18 as six sets of three chips each (Fig. 5-13). Then he shows 21 (which is $18 + 3$) as seven sets of three chips each. Pupils should continue arranging their chips as shown in Fig. 5-14 to illustrate other distributions of 21 when dividing by 3.

Facts with zero as a factor. Many problems that seem to call for multiplication with zero may be solved without multiplying. This is seen in a situation where multiplication of zero may be performed—our team made zero points for each of four turns, so that our score is zero. Here the pupil knows without performing the multiplication 4×0 that there was no score.

A strictly mathematical approach of illustrating 5×0 as the number in five empty sets and 0×5 as an empty set of fives or even an array of 0 rows with 5 members in each row has not been completely convincing to pupils.

The only way to draw pictures of multiplication facts with zero factors is by drawing line segments. The picture in Fig. 5-15a shows 3 horizontal and 4 vertical segments. The 7 is the total number

Figure 5-12

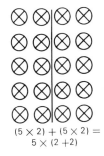

$(5 \times 2) + (5 \times 2) =$
$5 \times (2 + 2)$

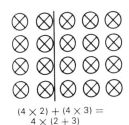

$(4 \times 2) + (4 \times 3) =$
$4 \times (2 + 3)$

Figure 5-13

$(18 + 3) \div 3$

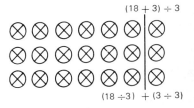

$(18 \div 3) + (3 \div 3)$

Figure 5-14
Pictures for $21 \div 3$.

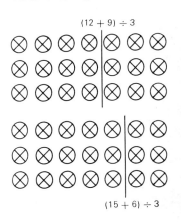

$(12 + 9) \div 3$

$(15 + 6) \div 3$

Figure 5-15
A picture showing multiplication with 0 is (c) or (d).

(a)

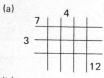

(b)

(c)

```
   4   0
4 _____
  _____
  _____
       0
```

(d)

Patterns showing results for 0 x 4 and 4 x 0.

(a)	(b)
4 x 4 = 16	4 x 4 = 16
3 x 4 = 12	4 x 3 = 12
2 x 4 = 8	4 x 2 = 8
1 x 4 = 4	4 x 1 = 4
0 x 4 = 0	4 x 0 = 0

of segments and the 12 is the number of intersections. This shows 3×4. Similarly, 5×2 is pictured in Fig. 5-15b. Now to show 4×0 the pupil draws 4 horizontal and 0 vertical segments and finds 0 intersections as in Fig. 5-15c. In a like manner 0×3 is illustrated with 0 horizontal and 3 vertical segments as in Fig. 5-15d.

Further, products such as 3×0 are discovered by using the idea of multiplication as a shortcut method of adding equal addends. The pupil interprets 3×0 as $0 + 0 + 0$ and finds that the answer is 0. Then the product for 0×3 is determined by applying the commutative property to 3×0.

Many pupils see the plausibility of products with 0 as a factor as they examine patterns. They write products for a set of multiplications such as shown in Fig. 5-16. Their thinking is that 3×4 is four less than 4×4, and so on, until 0×4 is seen as four less than 1×4. The reasoning is similar for the pattern in Fig. 5-16b. where 0 is the second factor.

The following is a description of how one teacher helped his class understand divisions with zero after a pupil had asked, "Why doesn't $0 \div 0 = 1$? I thought any whole number divided by itself was 1."

The teacher said, "First examine $0 \div 6$. Can you illustrate this problem?" The pupils supplied, "Members of the empty set separated into six equal parts," and, "How many sixes in zero?", suggesting intuitively an answer of zero. Next the class reviewed the relation of multiplication and division, seeing that another way for expressing $6 \div 2 = n$ is, "What number times two equals six?" (written $n \times 2 = 6$). The pupils then reasoned:

If $0 \div 6 = n$, then $0 = 6 \times n$.

If $0 = 6 \times n$, then n must be 0 because 0 is the only number that multiplies 6 so that the product is 0.

Now attention was directed to $6 \div 0$. Thinking of separating a set of six members into sets of zero members and attempts to subtract 0 repeatedly from 6 did not seem to bring any valid conclusions. The pupils suggested, "Let $6 \div 0 = n$, where n represents a number as yet unknown," and reasoned as follows:

If $6 \div 0 = n$, then $6 = 0 \times n$.

But if $6 = 0 \times n$, there is no number for n because there is no number which multiplies 0 so the product is 6.

Therefore, $6 \div 0$ is undefined.

Next, pupils tried to determine a result for $0 \div 0$. Their reasoning was recorded as follows:

If $0 \div 0 = n$, then $0 = 0 \times n$.

If $n = 1$, then $0 = 0 \times n$ is $0 = 0 \times 1$, a true sentence.

If $n = 23$, then $0 = 0 \times n$ is $0 = 0 \times 23$, a true sentence.

They found that any replacement for n in $0 = 0 \times n$ made the sentence true.

Therefore, $0 \div 0$ is meaningless.

After these experiments, the class generalized their findings:

> When zero is divided by any number except zero, the quotient is zero.

> Division of any whole number by zero is undefined.

Fixing skills After pupils have discovered facts and learned to reason results using the methods described above, they must master them for automatic response. Some of the variety of procedures for drill, aside from exercises in the textbook and workbook, are the following.

What am I thinking? The leader gives a product and asks the class, "Of what fact am I thinking?" Different members of the class give a pair of factors until they give the pair that the leader has in mind. For example, the leader might write 16 on the board. Successive children might suggest 4×4, 8×2, and then 2×8, the fact that was in mind.

Emphasizing factors. Because the idea of a factor is so important, pupils should use it in a variety of situations, of which the following are illustrative:

> For 12, list the set of all factors, the set of even factors, the set of odd factors, and the set of prime factors.

> For 36, list the set of one-place factors.

> List all facts with products between two numbers. One form for this list is shown in Fig. 5-17, with all answers listed in the 60-69 column.

> Make lists of all divisions with a certain number as a factor. For 6, they tabulate $6 \div 6 = 1$, $12 \div 6 = 2$, $18 \div 6 = 3$, and so on.

Experiences described in Chapter 4 for practicing the addition facts are readily adapted for use with multiplication and division. Numerous other practice materials, such as mathematical bingo (see page 35), electric boards, card games, and spinning games are also useful. A number of these may be found on the Activity Cards near the end of this chapter. Others are in Appendix B.

Figure 5-17
Organizing multiplication facts by products.

1 – 9	10 – 19	20 – 29	30 – 39	40 – 49	50 – 59	60 – 69	70 – 79	80 – 89
						8 × 8		
						7 × 9		
						9 × 7		

Figure 5-18
Array showing 6 × 15.

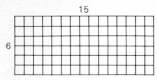

Figure 5-19
Picturing 6 × 15.

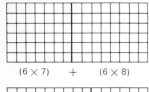

(6 × 7)   +   (6 × 8)

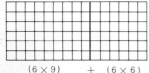

(6 × 9)   +   (6 × 6)

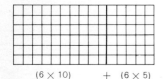

(6 × 10)   +   (6 × 5)

Figure 5-20
Ways of finding the result for 7 × 12.

(a)   (b)   (c)

```
12              12              12
12              ×7              ×7
12              14 = 7 × 2      84
12              70 = 7 × 10
12              84
12
12
14 = seven 2 s
70 = seven 10s
84
```

Figure 5-21

(a)

```
43
7
```

(b)

```
40            3
7
```

(c)   7 × 43 = 7 × (40 + 3)
            = (7 × 40) + (7 × 3)

Distinguishing the differences   While the emphasis in the foregoing has been on the relationship of multiplication and division, experiences are also needed that guide the pupil to discover differences between them. Two examples of investigations leading toward achieving this objective are the following:

Does the commutative property hold for division? Try to find different numbers for $\square$ and $\triangle$ so that $\square \div \triangle = \triangle \div \square$ is true.

Is division associative? Is this sentence true?
$$24 \div (6 \div 2) = (24 \div 6) \div 2.$$
Make up other sentences like this. How many are true?

The Multiplication Algorithm

In practice, related multiplications and divisions, such as 7 × 45 and 315 ÷ 7, are taught consecutively. Procedures for teaching the algorithms for multiplication and division are considered separately here in order to analyze their unique features. At appropriate places, however, their interrelationships are stressed.

Improvising solutions   When confronted with the problem "Find n, if $n = 6 \times 15$," pupils may draw an array, as shown in Fig. 5-18. With a background of application of distributive property gained while studying the multiplication facts, pupils may suggest possible solutions, such as those shown in Fig. 5-19.

The teacher can prepare a 6-by-15 rectangular region and may have pupils fold along different vertical segments to illustrate any of the solutions suggested. As a summary experience, pupils should state the advantage of (6 × 10) + (6 × 5) over other forms.

Using addition   For $n = 7 \times 12$ pupils can use addition in which the sums 14 and 70 have meanings, as indicated in Fig. 5-20a. Next, an expanded form of the multiplication algorithm is developed (Fig. 5-20b). Comparison with the results obtained from the addition reveals the reasonableness of the products 14 and 70. Later, pupils can develop the contracted algorithm with the 14 regrouped as 1 ten and 4 ones and the 1 ten added mentally to the result of 7 × 1 ten (Fig. 5-20c).

Studying the algorithm carefully   When attention is shifted to understanding a method for determining the product using only symbols, pupils study carefully how place value and the distributive property are applied. This is done by first picturing a multiplication, such as 7 × 43, in the usual rectangular form (Fig. 5-21a). This picture is next revised to show 43 as 40 + 3 (Fig. 5-21b). As pupils see 7 × 43 in this figure as the sum of two multiplications, 7 × 40 and 7 × 3, they make a written record of what they have pictured

(Fig. 5-21c). Next they use a vertical form as a convenient way of recording computations (any of those in Fig. 5-22 is useful).

Many teachers report that pupils give incorrect answers for examples such as 4 × 28, doing them as shown in Fig. 5-23. The product is computed as 4 × 8 = 32; record the 2 and "carry" the 3 tens. Then 3 tens + 2 tens (in 28) are 5 tens, and 4 × 5 tens are 20 tens, giving an answer of 202. This difficulty may arise when pupils are only shown *how* to multiply without sufficient experiences (such as those described above) to promote understanding.

An expanded form, such as for 6 × 34 in Fig. 5-24a, provides a rational transition to the final contracted algorithms. Examination of the multiplication recorded in this form reveals that 6 × 34 = (6 × 30) + (6 × 4); it also reveals the necessity for adding 2 tens after the multiplication 6 × 3 tens. The use of the crutch 2 (Fig. 5-24b) to indicate that 2 is to be added to the product of 6 and 3 is permissible if it promotes understanding of the process and aids those pupils who find it difficult to retain it mentally. As with other crutches, the teacher has the responsibility of discouraging its use by fast learners and guiding other pupils to discard it as soon as possible.

The extent to which pupils understand the process may be checked by asking such questions as the following, referring to the multiplication 4 × 28 = 112:

How is the 2 in the product obtained?
Why is the 2 placed where it is?
How is 11 obtained?
Why is the 11 placed to the left of the 2 instead of to the right?
How would you check the answer?

After pupils have generalized the algorithm and answered questions such as these, attention then should be turned to practice for fixing skills and varied experiences in application.

Multiplications with factors of 10 and 100

A complete understanding of products with factors of 10 and its multiples is a prerequisite to completing the study of the multiplication algorithm. The following techniques are useful for aiding pupils to explore and understand such multiplications.

A product, such as 6 × 10, is pictured by the usual rectangular arrangement. Pupils readily relate six dimes to 6 × 10. Correct results for a product such as 3 × 10 may also be discovered by thinking "3 × 10 = 10 + 10 + 10" or "3 × 1 ten = 3 tens = 30."

Results for multiplications such as 10 × 6 or 10 × 13 are verified by counting, adding, or applying the commutative property for multiplication, under which 10 × 6 = 6 × 10.

Figure 5-22
Expanded algorithms for 7 × 43.

$$
\begin{array}{cc}
40 + \;\; 3 & 40 + \;\; 3 \\
\times 7 \quad \times 7 & \times 7 \\
\hline
280 + \;\; 21 & 280 + \;\; 21
\end{array}
$$

$$
\begin{array}{c}
4 \text{ tens} + \quad 3 \text{ ones} \\
\times 7 \\
\hline
28 \text{ tens} + 21 \text{ ones}
\end{array}
$$

Figure 5-23
A common error in computing 4 × 28.

$$
\begin{array}{r}
28 \\
\times 4 \\
\hline
202
\end{array}
$$

Figure 5-24
Forms for finding the result of 6 × 34.

(a)

$$
\begin{array}{rl}
34 & \\
\times 6 & \\
\hline
24 & = 6 \times 4 \\
180 & = 6 \times 30 \\
\hline
204 & = 6 \times 34
\end{array}
$$

(b)

$$
\begin{array}{r}
{\scriptstyle 2} \\
34 \\
\times 6 \\
\hline
204
\end{array}
$$

Figure 5-25

Steps for showing that 20 × 7 = 10 × 14.

$$20 \times 7 = 10 \times 2 \times 7$$
$$= 10 \times 14$$
$$= 140$$

Figure 5-26

Expanded algorithm for 8 × 210.

$$
\begin{array}{r}
210 \\
\times\,8 \\
\hline
80 = 8 \times 10 \\
1600 = 8 \times 200 \\
\hline
1680
\end{array}
$$

Figure 5-27

Expanded algorithms.

$$8 \times 201 = 8(200 + 1)$$
$$= (8 \times 200) + (8 \times 1)$$

$$
\begin{array}{r}
201 \\
\times\,8 \\
\hline
8 \\
1600
\end{array}
$$

$$208 \times 372 = (200 + 8)(372)$$
$$= (200 \times 372) + (8 \times 372)$$

$$
\begin{array}{r}
372 \\
\times\,208 \\
\hline
2976 \\
74400
\end{array}
$$

Figure 5-28

Shortcut algorithm for 270 × 432.

$$
\begin{array}{r}
432 \\
\times\,270 \\
\hline
30240 \\
864 \\
\hline
116640
\end{array}
$$

Examining a number of separate cases where answers are obtained by these methods, the pupil sees zero in the ones place of the product in each instance (15 × 10 = 150; 10 × 23 = 230). He generalizes:

The product for a whole number times 10 (or 10 times a whole number) has a zero in the ones place.

Further examination leads to this conclusion:

Multiplication by 10 gives a product with each digit of the other factor moved one place to the left.

If one of the factors is a multiple of 10, such as 20, 30, etc., products may be discovered by extending the principle described above. For 20 × 7, the pupil first thinks of 20 as 10 × 2; then he thinks 10 × 2 × 7 as 10 × 14. Many teachers have their pupils record their reasoning for a few examples, as shown in Fig. 5-25 for 20 × 7.

Pupils learn to handle products with factors of 100 or its multiples, using the methods described for factors of 10. They may discover 4 × 100 by counting "100, 200, 300, 400," by adding, by thinking, "Four $1s are $4 or 400 cents, and therefore 4 × 100 is 400," or by reasoning, "4 × 100 = 4 × 1 hundred = 4 hundreds = 400."

Next, multiplication by numbers such as 200 or 300 is rationalized by expressing them as 2 × 100 and 3 × 100, using the same approach described for multiples of 10.

Multiplications with zeros in either factor such as 8 × 201, 7 × 210, 208 × 372, or 270 × 432 are sources of many errors. This difficulty is overcome if pupils use expanded algorithms such as shown for 8 × 210 in Fig. 5-26. Some pupils achieve greater understanding if they apply the distributive property and relate its use to the vertical algorithm. One way to show this is pictured in Fig. 5-27 for 8 × 201 and 208 × 372. Shortcut methods such as shown for 270 × 432 in Fig. 5-28 should be taught only after pupils know the reasons underlying the manipulations.

Factors of more than one digit Teachers find that many pupils can improvise a solution for multiplications such as 12 × 23. A few methods they may invent are:

Add 23 twelve times.

Add six 23s and six more 23s, or find 6 × 23 and double it.

Add eight 23s and four 23s, or five 23s and seven 23s.

Add ten 23s and two 23s.

Pupils are guided in recognizing the conventional pattern if the expression twelve 23s is stressed. They are asked, "About how much is the product?" Most pupils recognize it as slightly more than 230 (10 × 23). Then the teacher asks, "Exactly how many more than ten 23s?" An answer is, "Two 23s more," recorded as $12 \times 23 = (10 \times 23) + (2 \times 23)$. Comparing these improvised methods, the pupil sees the advantage of multiplying by 10 and 2. Since this is the form used in the algorithm, it remains only to find a suitable pattern for recording the work that has been performed.

Developing the algorithm Pupils see the reasonableness of the algorithm for multiplication such as 12×23 as they use an expanded algorithm such as the one illustrated with rectangles in Fig. 5-29. They observe that the four partial products are represented by the four regions in the array for this multiplication. Later, when they shorten the algorithm to the final form (Fig. 5-30), they add the 6 and 40 to obtain the first partial product, 46, then add 30 and 200 for the second partial product, 230.

The rectangular region in Fig. 5-29 helps reveal that the key to estimating lies in choosing the part that contributes most to the product. In this case, 10×20 represents the largest part; however, it is obviously less than the exact answer. In actual practice, the pupil is most likely to estimate by using 12 as 10 and 23 as 25, thus estimating 12×23 as 10×25.

The teacher should not be premature in pushing forward to shortcuts. At the same time, pupils who demonstrate readiness should be encouraged to adopt abridged algorithms. As pupils move toward the conventional algorithms, they may use a form such as shown in Fig. 5-31. While the 0 in 230 is often omitted in the final stages of learning, it is included here to show the meaning of 10×23.

Finally, when they use the conventional algorithm, pupils retain and record partial products more or less mechanically, without thinking specifically in terms of place value. However, they still are able to check their work or recall the algorithm at any stage through their understanding of basic properties.

Division with a Remainder

Pupils encounter remainders in division at an early age. If three children try to share seven toy trucks by giving one truck and then another to each child, they find that each of them receives two trucks, with one remaining. In spite of such frequent occurrences in their personal lives, it is necessary to provide pupils with considerable experience with divisions without remainders prior to systematic study of division with remainders.

Developing the idea of remainder As long as solutions remain on the concrete level, the concept of remainders is rather easy. Pupils encounter it many times during the normal school day: in

Figure 5-29
Array, expanded algorithm and use of the distributive property for 12×23.

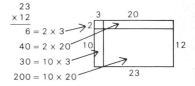

$$
\begin{array}{r}
23 \\
\times 12 \\
\hline
\end{array}
$$

$6 = 2 \times 3$
$40 = 2 \times 20$
$30 = 10 \times 3$
$200 = 10 \times 20$

Figure 5-30
Short cut algorithm for 12×23.

$$
\begin{array}{r}
23 \\
12 \\
\hline
46 \\
230 \\
\end{array}
$$

Figure 5-31
Expanded algorithm for 12×23.

$$
\begin{array}{r}
23 \\
\times 12 \\
\hline
46 = 2 \times 23 \\
230 = 10 \times 23 \\
\hline
276 = 12 \times 23 \\
\end{array}
$$

separating the class of 31 into two teams, in passing out 17 pieces of paper to five children, or in finding how many 4-cent pencils can be bought at the class store for 15 cents.

As pupils separate members of a collection of children, paper, or coins, their attention focuses on the number left over as the *remainder*. In finding how many 4-cent pencils can be bought for 15 cents, for example, the pupil illustrates three sets of four cents in a rectangular arrangement and has three cents left over as shown in Fig. 5-32.

Pupils may also improvise solutions to problems such as these through repeated subtraction. For the problem "Find the number of 6-cent tickets that can be bought for 25 cents and the amount of change," the thinking, using the subtractive approach, is: If one ticket is bought, we pay 6 cents, receiving change of 19 cents. We have 13 cents left after paying for two and 7 cents change from buying three, and, finally, 1 cent after paying for four tickets. This remainder is not enough to buy another ticket, and therefore the solution is complete." This is summarized and recorded as the series of subtractions shown in Fig. 5-33.

With a background of improvisation, the concept of remainder is established on the physical level, and the pupil is ready to shift to a consideration of the idea on the symbolic level.

Shifting to abstract representation When the pupil is learning to divide and interpret remainders in symbols, a dual presentation of algorithm and objects or picture is effective. An organization (Fig. 5-34) helps the pupil depict the situation, state it in language that shows what is meant, and perform the computation. It should be noted that $11 \div 2 = 5r1$ is not used because $5r1$ does not name a number. Rather, the pupil learns to perform the division and write the mathematical sentence $11 = (5 \times 2) + 1$, which describes the division.

The pupil's idea of division should be continuously related to the union of sets. For $6 \div 3$, six is related to the union of two sets of three members each; then for $7 \div 3$, seven is related to the union of two matching sets of three and a set with one member; and for $8 \div 3$, eight is related to the union of two matching sets of three and a set of two members. This pattern of thinking about related divisions helps to prevent the common mistake of solving $17 \div 3$, as shown in Fig. 5-35, where the remainder is greater than the divisor. When a pupil makes such errors, he should reexamine sets of objects and pictorial representations. Finally, he should realize that it is always possible to find a solution for which the remainder is less than the divisor.

Figure 5-32

$$15 = (3 \times 4) + 3$$

Figure 5-33
25 ÷ 6 related to subtraction.

$$
\begin{array}{r}
25 \\
-6 \\
\hline
19 \\
-6 \\
\hline
13 \\
-6 \\
\hline
7 \\
-6 \\
\hline
1
\end{array}
$$

Figure 5-34
Picture, statement and symbolization of division.

Picture	Statement	Symbol
▪▪ ▪ ▪▪ ▪ ▪▪ ▪	Five 2s in 11 and 1 left over	$\begin{array}{r} 2 \\ 5\overline{)11} \\ -10 \\ \hline 1 \end{array}$ $11 = (5 \times 2) + 1$
1 2 3 4 5 6 7 8 9 10 11 12 13 14	Four 3s in 14 with remainder of 2	$\begin{array}{r} 4 \\ 3\overline{)14} \\ 12 \\ \hline 2 \end{array}$ $14 = (4 \times 3) + 2$
●●●●● ●●●●● ●●●●● ●●●●● ●●●	Four 5s with 3 over in 23 or 4 nickles in 23 cents and 3 pennies left over	$\begin{array}{r} 4 \\ 5\overline{)23} \\ 20 \\ \hline 3 \end{array}$ $23 = (4 \times 5) + 3$

To emphasize this idea further, pupils may also be told the quotient and remainder and asked to find various divisors and dividends, write the mathematical sentence, and draw a picture for each. For example, with a quotient of 5 and a remainder of 3, a pupil may think, $23 \div 4$, and write, $23 = (4 \times 5) + 3$; however, for $23 \div 4$, it is wrong to write the mathematical sentence $23 = (4 \times 4) + 7$ to interpret the division because the remainder is greater than the divisor.

Added insight into the concept of remainders is acquired, along with an introduction to the long-division algorithm, by formalizing the repeated subtraction approach, described above. To find the number of sixes in 25, for example, the pupil subtracts 6 four times, with remainder 1, organizing his work as shown in Fig. 5-36*a*. As he recognizes a number of sixes in 25, he subtracts that multiple of 6 (12, 18, or 24), recording the number of sixes being subtracted as shown in Fig. 5-36*b* or *c*. These expanded forms have the advantage that they contract readily to the algorithm shown in Fig. 5-36*d*.

Through experience, the pupil's ability to deal with remainders progresses through various stages of maturity: picturing the number left over; the fractional notation $25 \div 6 = 4\ 1/6$; discarding the remainder where conditions of the problem may so require (the number of 6-inch ribbons that can be cut from 15 inches of ribbon); increasing the quotient by 1 ("If available tables seat eight people each, how many tables are required for a banquet of 27 people?").

Figure 5-35
A common error in division.

$$3\overline{)17} \atop \begin{array}{r} 4 \\ \underline{12} \\ 5 \end{array}$$

Figure 5-36
Algorithms for $25 \div 6$.

(a)
$$\begin{array}{r} 1+1+1+1 = 4 \\ 6\overline{)25} \\ \underline{6} \\ 19 \\ \underline{6} \\ 13 \\ \underline{6} \\ 7 \\ \underline{6} \\ 1 \end{array}$$

(b)
$$\begin{array}{r} 2+2 = 4 \\ 6\overline{)25} \\ \underline{12} \\ 13 \\ \underline{12} \\ 1 \end{array}$$

(c)
$$\begin{array}{r} 3+1 = 4 \\ 6\overline{)25} \\ \underline{18} \\ 7 \\ \underline{6} \\ 1 \end{array}$$

(d)
$$\begin{array}{r} 4 \\ 6\overline{)25} \\ \underline{24} \\ 1 \end{array}$$

The Division Algorithm

Some of the reasons why division is generally considered the most difficult of the processes with whole numbers are:

The algorithm is the most difficult to rationalize.

In some computations trial quotients are arrived at by estimation and often require corrections that demand insight beyond the ability of some pupils. In 46 322, for example, an estimated quotient of 8, obtained from $32 \div 4$, must be corrected. Likewise, 6 found from $32 \div 5$ is also in error.

Computations begin at the left, contrary to the pattern learned for the other processes.

Multiplication is performed with the factors in positions different from those previously used. In the division $23\overline{)976}$ with the 4 above, errors often arise in the multiplication 4×23 because these factors are not located as they are in the conventional algorithm $\begin{array}{r} 23 \\ \times 4 \end{array}$.

Figure 5-37
Algorithm for 72 ÷ 8.

$$\begin{array}{r} 9 \\ 8\overline{)72} \\ 72 \\ \hline 0 \end{array}$$

Figure 5-38

(a) ° OOOOOOOOOO
    OOOOOOOOOO
    OOOOOOOOOO
    OOOOOOOOOO
    OOOOO

45 = (4 x 10) + 5

(b) OOOOOOOOOO OOOOO
    OOOOOOOOOO OOOOO
    OOOOOOOOOO OOOOO

45 = 3 x (10 + 5)

Figure 5-39
The number of 3s in 45.

(a) OOO   OOO
    OOO   OOO
    OOO   OOO
    OOO   OOO
    OOO   OOO
    OOO   OOO
    OOO   OOO
    OOO   OOO

  8 threes   7 threes

(b)   8 + 7
        3$\overline{)24 + 21}$

(8 + 7) x 3 = (8 x 3) + (7 x 3)

To overcome these difficulties, the teacher must understand the algorithm as well as methods for teaching it effectively. The goal is for all pupils to perform and apply division with understanding; yet not all pupils can completely understand long division when the process is first introduced. Subsequent reexamination of the mathematical meanings, as well as reteaching the algorithm, is required. As the topic is retaught in later grades, the process is rationalized from various points of view. It is recognized that the principal emphasis on rationalizing the algorithm will be made with one-digit divisors; much of the computation with two-digit divisors will be performed, using the algorithm based on meanings developed previously.

No one approach for rationalizing the long-division algorithm has been demonstrated as most efficient. The most convenient is usually the one presented in the textbook series or syllabus. To supplement the approach of the textbook, it is useful for the teacher to have available a variety of effective methods for introducing long division and for helping children understand it. This does not necessarily mean that all of these will be used with the same class. Those not used initially may be introduced when the topic is restudied.

Introducing the division algorithm While facts are being studied, pupils learn to use the algorithm form (Fig. 5-37). Next they need experiences leading to the mastery of the algorithm for divisions such as $3\overline{)45}$, $8\overline{)2771}$, and $37\overline{)851}$. Here, as with the division facts, understanding of procedures depends upon seeing applications of the distributive property in the algorithm. These applications are first studied through concrete representation and then expressed using symbols.

One effective series of development steps illustrated for $3\overline{)45}$ is the following:

1   Pupils improvise solutions, thinking of $45 \div 3 = n$ as requiring arrangement of 4 tens and 5 ones (Fig. 5-38a) into three matching sets. They do this by placing one disk in each of three rows, until all 45 disks are distributed. The result, 10 + 5, is seen as the number in each row (Fig. 5-38b).

2   Next pupils view the division in terms of removing various numbers of sets of three and observe the application of the distributive property. For example, they remove eight sets of three and seven sets of three to exhaust 45 (Fig. 5-39a). Pupils may record this and show the use of the distributive property, as in Fig. 5-39b. The work shown in this figure is also recorded in the form: $(24 + 21) \div 3 = (24 \div 3) + (21 \div 3)$.

While attention is directed to understanding, pupils may remove *any* multiple of the divisor that they recognize, continuing this procedure until a remainder of zero is achieved. Their work is recorded in an expanded algorithm, as shown in Fig. 5-40 for 2)156.

Examples of possible solutions for 851 ÷ 37, using an expanded form, are shown in Fig. 5-41. As experience progresses, pupils are encouraged to reduce the steps, preferring the solution in Fig. 5-41*b* to that in Fig. 5-41*a*.

Cases in which the remainder is not zero are treated similarly, continuing to stress the idea that the remainder must be less than the divisor when the work is completed. Two solutions for 79 ÷ 6 are shown in Fig. 5-42. Here, through discussion, pupils may be led to see that the second solution is a simpler one and to observe that $79 = (13 \times 6) + 1$.

Studying various algorithms for division Many algorithms for division have been found helpful in promoting understanding by pupils. No one of them has been demonstrated to be superior to all others. Each is effective to the extent that pupils understand it. Actually they differ only in the position where the quotient is located. Any differences in their effectiveness exist probably in the thinking process employed by the pupil.

Besides the form suggested in Fig. 5-41, the one shown in Fig. 5-43 for 2,771 ÷ 8 is commonly used. Trying 100, 200, 300, and 400 times 8, the pupil finds the quotient lies between 300 and 400. He writes this as 300 and subtracts three hundred 8s (2,400) from 2,771, leaving a remainder of 371. There are over forty but less than fifty 8s contained in 371, so he subtracts forty 8s (320). Then he places 40 in the quotient in its proper relation to the 300 already there. The 51 yields six 8s with remainder of 3. This 3 contains no more 8s, so he writes $2,771 = (346 \times 8) + 3$.

Many pupils feel more secure by first subtracting 100×8 and then 100×8 again, as shown in Fig. 5-44. They continue subtracting a familiar multiple of 8 and thus are able to write the same mathematical sentence $2,771 = (8 \times 346) + 3$. The first solution for 2,771 ÷ 8 is far more sophisticated than the second; all pupils are encouraged to work toward this thoughtful procedure. At the same time, any number of multiples of 8 may be removed successively using this algorithm, and each pupil should work at a level commensurate with his ability.

Another advantage in this extended form is that the pupil is aware at all times of what the solution means. Furthermore, he can learn the meaning of each numeral he writes in the solution; he can see the reason for "bringing down numerals from the divi-

Figure 5-40
Expanded form for 156 ÷ 2.

(a)
```
        50 + 25 + 3
     2)156
        100   (50 × 2)
        ───
         56
         50   (25 × 2)
        ───
          6
          6   (3 × 2)
```

(b) $(50 + 25 + 3) \times 2 =$
$(50 \times 2) + (25 \times 2) + (3 \times 2)$

or

$(100 + 50 + 6) \div 2 =$
$100 \div 2 + (50 \div 2) + (6 \div 2)$

Figure 5-41
Expanded algorithms for 851 ÷ 37.

(a)
```
          10
     37)851
        370   =  10 × 37
        ───
        481
        370   =  10 × 37
        ───
        111
        111   =   3 × 37
        ───
```

(b)
```
          20 + 3
     37)851
        740   =  20 × 37
        ───
        111
        111   =   3 × 37
        ───
```

Figure 5-42
Two algorithms for 79 ÷ 6.

(a)
```
        7 + 5 + 1
    6)79
      42 = 7 × 6
      ──
      37
      30 = 5 × 6
      ──
       7
       6 = 1 × 6
      ──
       1
```

(b)
```
        10 + 3
    6)79
      60 = 10 × 6
      ──
      19
      18 = 3 × 6
      ──
       1
```

Figure 5-43
Expanded algorithm for 2,771 ÷ 8.

```
            6  ⎫
           40  ⎬ 346
          300  ⎭
       8)2,771
         2,400
         ─────
           371
           320
         ─────
            51
            48
         ─────
             3
```

Figure 5-44
*Another expanded algorithm for
2,771 ÷ 8.*

```
       100
       100
  8)2,771
       800
   ─────
     1,971
       800
   ─────
     1,171
```

Figure 5-45
Pocket charts showing 131 ÷ 3.

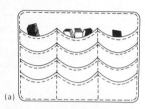

(a)

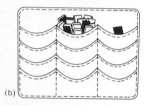

(b)

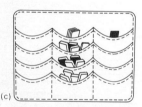

(c)

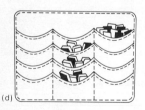

(d)

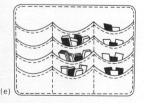

(e)

dend"; and the concept of remainder is emphasized at every step in the process. The same procedure is equally applicable to examples with two-digit divisors.

Using the pocket chart A means for rationalizing the division algorithm for 131 ÷ 3 is shown in Fig. 5-45.

1   Arrange the pocket holder to show 131, as in Fig. 5-45*a*. It is necessary that this number of cards be separated into three sets with the same number of members (if possible).

2   First, consider partitioning the one bundle of 100 cards (in the hundreds place) into three equivalent subsets. This cannot be accomplished with the one bundle of 100 left intact, and so the rubber band is removed, and the 100 is converted to 10 tens. Now the original 131 is pictured as 13 tens and 1 one, as shown in Fig. 5-45*b*.

3   Separate 13 tens into the three matching subsets. There will be 4 tens in each subset, with 1 ten that cannot be distributed (Fig. 5-45*c*). The quotient at this stage is 4 tens, as the cards indicate. Three times 4 tens (12 tens) are subtracted, and a remainder of 1 ten results. In the algorithm, progress has been made to the stage shown in Fig. 5-46*a*.

4   The 1 ten left over is converted to 10 ones and added to the 1 one for a total of 11 ones, as shown in the pocket chart in Fig. 5-45*d* and in the algorithm in Fig. 5-46*b*. Separating 11 into three parts of the same size yields three sets of 3 each with 2 left over (Fig. 5-45*e*). The completed algorithm is shown in Fig. 5-46*c*.

During early stages, pupils should be urged to tell exactly what has been done in each step. The representation with objects is then accompanied by the written record or algorithm.

Manipulation of materials to picture divisions in which divisors have two or more digits is difficult and cumbersome, and objectification is not ordinarily recommended.

Determining the number of places in the quotient After division has been introduced through such methods as the foregoing, the position of the numerals in the quotient can be determined through estimation. To find the number of sevens in 3,874, we first ask, "Are there as many as ten 7s?" Yes, because ten 7s are only 70. "Are there as many as one hundred 7s?" Yes, because one hundred 7s are 700, which is less than 3,874. "Are there as many as one thousand 7s, which is 7,000?" No, because the dividend is only 3,874. Since the quotient is greater than 100 but less than

1,000, it must contain three digits, or must fill the ones, tens, and hundreds places. So the first numeral in the quotient is located in the hundreds place, above the 8 in the dividend. Organizing the work, as shown in Fig. 5-47, simplifies comparison of the dividend to the results of the successive multiplications.

Pupils who can determine places for quotient digits mentally should not be required to make the written record. All pupils should try to achieve the mental solution.

Similarly, for a division such as 56)5,020, the divisor 56 is multiplied by successive powers of ten, starting with 1 as recorded in Fig. 5-48a. These multiples of 56, compared to the dividend 5,020, reveal that there are more than ten 56s (560) but less than one hundred 56s (5,600). The correct number of 56s, then, is between ten and one hundred, and therefore the quotient has two digits.

After the number of digits in the quotient has been determined, marks such as dashes can indicate the places to be filled in the quotient, as illustrated in Fig. 5-48b.

Operation at the level of the algorithm When the pupil has been introduced to the meanings of long division and has experimented with the intermediate steps described in previous pages, he is ready to develop facility with the long-division algorithm. As he works with the algorithm, he develops effective procedures for estimating quotient digits and perfects a systematic pattern of work, so that he can operate quickly and accurately. In performing the algorithm, practice is directed toward perfecting a technique that may be illustrated in the following computational steps for finding 32)1,675:

1 Estimate the quotient and determine the number of digits in the quotient. There are more than ten 32s (320) but less than one hundred 32s (3,200) contained in the dividend 1,675, and so the quotient has two digits (Fig. 5-49a).
2 Find the first trial quotient. Estimate the quotient by thinking "How many threes in 16?" (Fig. 5-49b).
3 Multiply 5 × 32. The product, 160, is placed below 167 (Fig. 5-49c).
4 Subtract 160 from 167 (Fig. 5-49d).
5 Compare the difference, 7, with the divisor, 32, to make sure the remainder is less than the divisor.
6 Bring down the next digit (Fig. 5-49e).
7 Find the next trial quotient: 2.

Following step 6, repeat the cycle; estimate the next quotient digit, multiply, subtract, compare, and bring down, until the division

Figure 5-46
Algorithm for 131 ÷ 3.

```
(a)    4      (b)    4      (c)   43
   3 )131      3 )131      3 )131
      12          12          12
       1          11          11
                               9
                               2
```

Figure 5-47
Estimating 3,874 ÷ 7.

```
   10 × 7 = 70
  100 × 7 = 700       7 )3,874
1,000 × 7 = 7,000
```

Figure 5-48
Places where digits occur in quotient for 5,020 ÷ 56.

```
(a)  1 × 56 = 56     (b)      --
    10 × 56 = 560         56 )5,020
   100 × 56 = 5,600
```

Figure 5-49
Algorithm for 1,675 ÷ 32.

```
(a)        --     (b)        5     (c)        5
    32 )1675          32 )1675         32 )1675
                                          160

(d)        5      (e)        5
    32 )1675          32 )1675
       160              160
         7              75
```

Figure 5-50

What do the 7,161, and 15 really mean?

$$23\overline{)1764}$$
$$7$$
$$161$$
$$\overline{15}$$

is completed.

Frequently pupils should be stopped during the process and asked to tell what they have done and to give the meaning of the numbers used. For example, in the incomplete division in Fig. 5-50, a pupil making the following statements shows insight into the operation: "So far I have found seventy (7 tens) 23s in 1,764. The 161 is actually 161 tens (7 tens × 23). The 15 is the number of tens left over after subtracting 161 tens. When the 4 is brought down, I will have a remainder of 154."

If pupils feel more secure with some elongated algorithm, they should be encouraged to use it. The teacher's objective is to help all pupils operate at a level appropriate to their ability.

TYPES OF PROBLEMS SOLVED BY DIVISION

Two kinds of problems solved by division require special attention because they commonly occur in social situations, and because divisions may be represented in a way identifiable as each kind. For example, to find n if $12 \div 3 = n$, these two models may be built:

- Think of representing $12 \div 3 = n$ or $3 \times n = 12$ by separating a set of 12 members into three matching sets. For a set of 12 ⊗s this may be done as follows with three sets named A, B, and C. One ⊗ is included in A, one ⊗ in B, and one ⊗ in C. This assigning of one ⊗ to each set in turn is continued until all 12 ⊗s have been distributed. That A, B, and C are matching sets is verified in Fig. 5-51. That $n = 4$ if $12 \div 3 = n$ is determined by counting the number of members in set A, B, or C.

Figure 5-51

4 members in each of
3 disjoint sets

In this example, we are given the number of members of a set and the number of matching subsets. We are to find the number of members in each subset; the operation for finding this number is called *division*. Some examples of this type of problem are:

(*a*) In dealing cards at bridge, the dealer gives one card to each of the four players, starting on his left, and continues until no cards remain to be distributed. The dealer has arranged it so that four people have matching sets of cards. $(52 \div 4 = n$ or $4 \times n = 52)$

(*b*) Four children are to share eight candy bars equally. How many candy bars will each have? $(8 \div 4 = n$ or $4 \times n = 8)$

(*c*) Twenty boys want to make four relay teams with the same number of runners but none in common. How many boys will be on each team? $(20 \div 4 = n$ or $4 \times n = 20)$

In each of these cases the process for finding the number of members in each of the disjoint matching sets is called *division*. In some texts these situations are called "partitive situations." The thinking is that a given set is to be *partitioned* into disjoint subsets with the same number of members.

Figure 5-52

• Think of representing $12 \div 3 = n$ or $n \times 3 = 12$ by arranging a set of 12 members into disjoint sets that have three members each. Starting with 12 (X)s, one set P of three members is formed; then a second set Q of three members, disjoint from the first, is formed. This is continued until all 12 (X)s have been placed in disjoint sets of three members. It is found that two more sets, R and S, can be formed. Figure 5-52 shows these disjoint sets. That $n = 4$ if $12 \div 3 = n$ or $n \times 3 = 12$ is verified by counting the number of subsets.

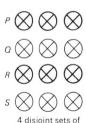

4 disjoint sets of
3 members each

In this example we are given the number of members in a set and the number in each of its disjoint matching subsets. We are to find the number of subsets that can be so formed; the operation for finding this number is division. Some examples of this type of problem are:

(*a*) A set of 52 cards is to be separated so that there are 13 cards in each pile. How many piles will there be? ($52 \div 13 = n$ or $n \times 13 = 52$)

(*b*) Eight candy bars are to be given out so that each person gets two bars. How many people can be so served? ($8 \div 2 = n$ or $n \times 2 = 8$)

(*c*) Thirty boys want to make relay teams of five members each who can run against each other at the same time. How many teams can be formed? ($30 \div 5 = n$ or $n \times 5 = 30$)

In each of these examples the process for finding the number of disjoint matching sets is called *division*. In some texts these situations are called "measurement situations." The thinking is that a given set is "measured" in terms of a set with a certain number of members.

While the names for these situations are not important, the concept that models for division situations can be illustrated in these two different ways is important. Furthermore, when division is first introduced, reference to these two situations is often made. For example, $8 \div 2$ may be thought of as "Eight objects separated into two parts of the same size." Technically this may be interpreted as "Finding the number in each of the two matching sets that can be formed from a set of eight members." The same example, $8 \div 2$, may be thought of as "twos in eight." Technically this means that from a set of eight members, the number of disjoint subsets of two members each is to be found.

The teacher should recognize that these two situations are illustrations of two major types of situations in which division is used. Language such as "twos in eight" helps pupils to visualize how a set is arranged into subsets, and this helps them to recognize division as the appropriate operation to solve certain problems that they encounter.

Figure 5-53
Array for 3 X 2.

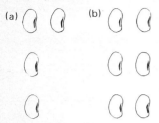

Figure 5-54
Squares and strips to show 4 X 3 = 12.

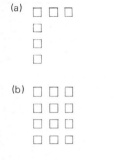

Figure 5-55
Showing 12 ÷ 3 = 4 and 3 X 4 = 12.

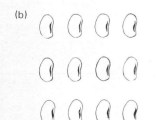

DIFFICULTIES WITH MULTIPLICATION AND DIVISION

The need for meaningful remedial experiences is greater among pupils for multiplication and division than for addition and subtraction. Because so many teachers lament, "If they only knew their facts they wouldn't have any trouble," the treatment of the teaching of the multiplication and division facts in this chapter was unusually extensive. Only a portion of the experiences suggested need be used when the facts are studied thoroughly. The others can be earmarked for pupils who need increased understanding or further practice.

While pupils' difficulties with multiplication and division are of great variety, many of them are associated with lack of understanding of the symbolism and insufficient manipulative experience. Too often pupils are simply handed a formal algorithm emphasizing a symbolic method, when they really need learning experiences illuminating the relationship between the concrete and the verbal, without which they cannot hope to understand the symbolic algorithm. Some special remedial experiences for this problem follow.

The Meaning of X and ÷

When pupils have difficulty with multiplication and division, the teacher should determine first if they can form physical models for the operations. Here are some suggested activities to guide pupils in building these models:

For 3 X 2. The pupil places 3 beans vertically and 2 horizontally (Fig. 5-53*a*); then he "fills in" with beans to make a rectangular array (Fig. 5-53*b*).

For 4 X 3. He places 4 squares vertically and 3 horizontally (Fig. 5-54*a*), then "fill in" with squares (square regions) to make a rectangular arrangement (Fig. 5-54*b*). As he progresses he replaces 10 of the squares with a strip (Fig. 5-54*c*) and finds that four 3s is the same as 1 ten and 2 ones.

For 5 X 3. He shows 5 horizontal lines and 3 vertical lines and counts the number of intersections to find the product. This is probably the quickest way to picture a multiplication and is very helpful. It is not as useful as the squares and strips, however, when the product is shown as numbers of tens and ones.

For 12 ÷ 3. He may build a model relating division and multiplication. Thinking, "Three times what is twelve?", he picks up 12 beans and places three of them vertically as in Fig. 5-55*a*. He then places one bean opposite each of the three beans and continues until the beans are exhausted as in Fig. 5-55b. He also thinks of 12 ÷ 3 as "How many threes in twelve?" As he places columns of three beans he also records what he has done in the algorithm form that he will use in more difficult examples (Fig. 5-56a,b,c,d,). In either case he sees the rectangular form previously identified with multiplication.

Only when the pupil knows the meaning of × and ÷ so that he can show models for each operation should he practice with exercises from the textbook. Drill prior to experiences that promote understanding of the symbolism is as useless for remediation as it is for initial instruction in a topic.

Restudying The Algorithm

When diagnosis indicates the pupil is having difficulties with the algorithm, remedial activities should also start at the concrete level.

For 4 × 12, for example, the pupil shows 4 squares vertically and 12 horizontally (Fig. 5-57a). As with other multiplications he must "fill in" his model to make a rectangular arrangement. As he experiments he may complete his array with single squares. Through discussion with classmates or teacher, he is encouraged to hunt for a quicker way to do this. With the exchange rule of replacing 10 squares with a strip of ten he can finish his array and is in a position to see how from his models he can identify the partial products in the algorithm (Fig. 5-57b).

He can even use this model for multiplications such as 12 × 13. He starts with 12 squares vertically and 13 horizontally. With the exchange rule in mind he finally completes the model in Fig. 5-58 and actually sees the four partial products in the algorithm.

The pupil finds the model for the division algorithm similar to the one he built for the "division facts." In fact he may soon realize that the only differences are dealing with larger numbers and making more exchanges. For 76 ÷ 5 he may begin by attempting to make a rectangular arrangement of 5s, or he may try to arrange 76 squares in 5 rows. Later he is encouraged to see 76 as 7 strips of ten and 6 ones and to try to arrange these in 5 rows. Different pupils will complete the experimentation in different ways. The "neatest" result is shown in Fig. 5-59a from which the pupil can observe "5 rows of fifteen and 1 left over are 76." He should try writing his results with (5 × 15) + 1 = 76 as one form. The relationship of his array to an algorithm must be observed also. If he writes 5 × 10 and 5 × 5 to represent his arrays in Fig 5-59a, he is aided to see how this is expressed in the algorithm in Fig. 5-59b.

Figure 5-56
Showing 12 ÷ 3 with squares and in an algorithm.

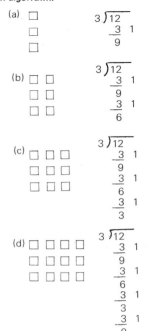

Figure 5-57
4 × 12 shown with materials and in an algorithm.

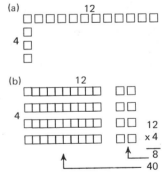

Figure 5-58
12 × 13 shown with materials and in an algorithm.

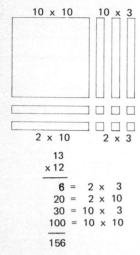

$$\begin{array}{r}
13 \\
\times 12 \\
\hline
6 = 2 \times 3 \\
20 = 2 \times 10 \\
30 = 10 \times 3 \\
100 = 10 \times 10 \\
\hline
156
\end{array}$$

Figure 5-59
76 ÷ 5 shown with materials and in an algorithm.

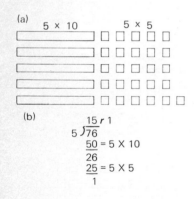

Of course, physical manipulation to depict multiplications and divisions becomes more complex with larger numbers. Hence computation with numerals only is a final outcome of instruction. To achieve this the pupil needs many learning experiences which lead him from the concrete to the symbolic with an emphasis also on verbal experiences to express the relationship between models and symbols. It is from such a sequence of activities that he becomes a symbolic learner with sufficient understanding and confidence to handle problems in the symbolic mode.

EXPERIMENTS FOR PUPILS

The following activities are concerned with multiplication and division of whole numbers. For each Activity there are a number of adaptions and extensions. In Activity 1, for example, the pupil may find the length of two of the 3-rods and two of the 4-rods and discover that this length equals two of the 7-rods. For this experiment he would be investigating the distributive property. In order to understand both the effective use and some of the limitations of Activity Cards, review pages 72-73.

ACTIVITY 1

Apparatus needed: wood rods

Objective: To use wood rods to show products.

1   Use your rods to find the length of:

    (*a*) 2 of the 3-rods.   answer: ____
    (*b*) 3 of the 4-rods.   answer: ____
    (*c*) 6 of the 4-rods.   answer: ____
    (*d*) 4 of the 5-rods.   answer: ____
    (*e*) 3 of the 2-rods.   answer: ____
    (*f*) 4 of the 3-rods.   answer: ____

2   Why are your answers the same for (*b*) and (*f*) and (*a*) and (*e*)?

3   Make up some more problems like these.

ACTIVITY 2

Apparatus needed: beam balance

Objective: To write multiplication and division sentences from experiments with a beam balance.

1   On the right arm place one washer on 10 and one washer
    on 2.
    (*a*)   How many washers on 4 balance it? ____
            You can write: $12 = \square \times 4$ or $12 \div 4 = \square$
    (*b*)   How many washers on 6 balance it? ____
            You can write: $12 = \square \times 6$ or $12 \div 6 = \square$

2   On the right arm place one washer on 10 and one washer
    on 8. Write two sentences for each of the following:
    (*a*)   How many washers on 3 balance it?
            ____   or   ____
    (*b*)   How many washers on 9 balance it?
            ____   or   ____

3   Make up some other problems like this.

ACTIVITY 3

Apparatus needed: peg board and straw   *Objective:* To illustrate the distributive property using
                                                a peg board.

1   Put pegs in your board like this. Write the multiplication equa-
    tion for this array.
2   Use your straw to show two parts for the array .
    Do you see that
    4×6 = (4×1) + (4×5) = $4 \times (1 + 5)$
    Original array   4 sets of 1   4 sets of 5   4 sets of $1 + 5$
3   Move the straw to show $(4 \times 2) + (4 \times 4) = 4 \times (2 + 4)$.
4   Move the straw to show $(4 \times 3) + (4 \times 3) = 4 \times (3 + 3)$.
5   Try some other arrays and write what you find.

ACTIVITY 4

Apparatus needed: beam balance   *Objective:* To discover a property of even numbers
                                        using a beam balance.

1   Place one washer on 1 on the right arm. Can you balance
    it with two washers on the same number on the left?
2   Place one washer on 2 on the right arm. Can you balance
    it with two washers on the same number on the left?
3   Try balancing with two washers on the same number on the
    left each of the following single washers on the right:
            (*a*)   3   (*b*)   4   (*c*)   5   (*d*)   6   (*e*)   7   (*f*)   8
4   What numbers can be balanced in this way?

ACTIVITY 5

Objective: To check division in a new way and to discover why it "works."

```
8 )1496
   800  |100
   ___
   696
   640  |80
   ___
    56
    56  |7
   ___
     0
```

1   A young boy checked the division by adding 800 + 640 + 56. His sum was 1,496, so he knew his division was correct. Study the division and discover what he did.

2   Use this method to check these divisions:

   (*a*)   3,375 ÷ 9   (*b*)   4,298 ÷ 7   (*c*)   35,692 ÷ 4

ACTIVITY 6

Objective: To discover a pattern by observing a number of cases.

1   Find: (2 × 2) – (1 × 3) =

   (3 × 3) – (2 × 4) =

   (4 × 4) – (3 × 5) =

   (5 × 5) – (4 × 6) =

   (6 × 6) – (5 × 7) =

   (7 × 7) – (6 × 8) =

   What is your guess for:

   (88 × 88) – (87 × 89) =

2   Find: (3 × 8 – (4 × 6) =

   (4 × 9) – (5 × 7) =

   (5 × 10) – (6 × 8) =

   (6 × 11) – (7 × 9) =

   What is your guess for:

   (7 × 12) – (8 × 10) =

   (10 × 15) – (11 × 13) =

ACTIVITY 7

Objective: To use a variety of symbols to write true sentences.

1   Use + , – , × or ÷ and = , > or < to make true statements: 7 __ 4 __ 3.   (Some answers are 7 = 4 + 3, 7 × 4 > 3 7 ÷ 4 < 3.

2   Follow the same directions for 9__ 2 __ 7. Get six different answers.

3   Follow the same directions for 6 __ 8 __ 12. Get eight answers.

ACTIVITY 8

Objective: To play a game about factors and to discover a winning strategy.

1   This game is for two players. Here are the rules:

   (*a*)   Choose a number.
   (*b*)   The first player can subtract any factor of that number except the number itself.
   (*c*)   The second player subtracts any factor of the result except the number itself.
   (*d*)   Players continue to take turns until one player is unable to subtract. He loses.

2   Al and Bob play.

The starting number is 12.	12
Bob can subtract 1, 2, 3, 4, or 6; he chooses 4.	− 4
	8
Al can subtract 1, 2, or 4; he chooses 2.	− 2
	6
Bob can subtract 1, 2, or 3; he chooses 2.	− 2
	4
Al can choose 1 or 2; he chooses 2.	− 2
	2
Bob can choose only 1; he chooses 1.	− 1
	1

   Al cannot play; he loses.

3   Choose a friend and play the game.
4   Try to find a way to always win this game.

Activity 9

Objective: To use mathematics to tell a person his birthday.

1   For this game use January as 1, February as 2, and so on with December as 12.
2   Ask a friend to do the arithmetic shown on the right. Suppose his birthday is May 21.
3   The result 521 shows May as 5 and the birthday as 21.
4   See if this works for your birthday.
5   Try this game with a friend.

Write birth month:	5
Multiply by 50	× 50
	250
Add 15:	+ 15
	265
Multiply by 2:	× 2
	530
Add birthday:	+ 21
	551
Subtract 30:	− 30
	521

ACTIVITY 10

Objective: To write names for numbers with restrictions on what numbers may be used.

In this experiment you can use addition, subtraction, multiplication, and division.

Here are some ways to make 8:

Use only 1s: $1 + 1 + 1 + 1 + 1 + 1 + 1 + 1 = 8$

Use only 2s: $2 \times 2 \times 2 = 8$

Use only 3s: $(3 \times 3) - (3 \div 3) = 8$

Now make 10:

Use only 1s:

Use only 2s:

Use only 3s:

ACTIVITY 11

Objective: To perform a "self-checking" division and to determine why the method "works."

1 Choose a 3-digit numeral such as 375.
2 Write the 6-digit numeral by repeating 375.
3 Divide 375,375 by 7. The quotient is:
4 Divide the quotient in Step 3 by 11.
5 Divide the quotient in Step 4 by 13.

If you've made no mistakes, you should have an interesting answer. What is your discovery?

6 Try other examples following Steps 1-5 above. Are your answers similar? Try to explain your results.
7 What is the smallest number with a factors of 7, 11, and 13?
8 What is $1,001 \times 375$?
9 Each of 289,289 or 684,684 or 926,926 has the same factor. What is it?
10 *Brainbuster:* Explain your discovery to a friend.

ACTIVITY 12

Objective: To follow directions, practice computation, and make a discovery.

A 2-digit numeral:	73
Same digits in reverse order:	37
Add:	110
Divide the sum by 11:	10
Is there a remainder?	No

1 Follow the steps at the left to complete the table in Ex. 2.
2 Choose some more 2-digit numerals and follow the steps in the table.

2-digit Numeral	Numeral with digits reversed	Sum	Factored form
62	26	88	11 X 8
18			11 X ___
98			
76			
13			

3   Tell a friend something about a factor of every sum.

QUESTIONS AND EXERCISES

1   Describe effective experiences through which pupils may discover multiplication and division facts.

2   Your objective is to help your pupils discover relationships among multiplication facts with 2 as one factor. Make a list of these relationships. (One is 5 X 2 is 2 greater than 4 X 2.)

3   One of your fourth-grade pupils is confusing the answers to 6 X 9 and 9 X 6 with the answers to 7 X 8 and 8 X 7. What experiences should be provided to help overcome this difficulty?

4   Describe relational thinking (as done in this chapter for facts with 8 as a factor) through which pupils may develop facts with 9 as a factor.

5   Why should pupils understand the relationship among multiplication and divisions facts? What are effective experiences for accomplishing this?

6   List five ways a pupil may improvise the result for 4 X 12.

7   Find the result for 6 X 123 by each of the extended algorithms described in this chapter.

8   What are experiences through which the generalization for multiplying a counting number by 10 is developed by pupils?

9   Perform the long division $37\overline{)1,040}$ using each expanded algorithm described in this chapter.

10   What are experiences for helping pupils understand multiplication by zero?

11   Draw pictures and describe the steps in words for showing $175 \div 4$ by means of the pocket chart.

12   One of your fifth-grade pupils asks, "For $3\overline{)135}$ why is there no numeral in the quotient above 1 in the dividend? After all, the 1 does represent 100 and $100 \div 3$ is more than 1." Answer him.

13   How may pupils in the second grade improvise an answer to the following: "How many apples at 8 cents each may be bought for 50 cents? How much change is received?"

14   Some of your fourth-grade pupils, when performing division, are leaving a remainder more than the divisor. What experiences would you provide for them?

15   Pupils use confidently the idea of remainder in division on the concrete level but have difficulties in dealing with this concept in the abstract. What experiences aid them in shifting to the abstract representation of remainders in division?

PROJECTS

1 Study a series of recently published textbooks and teachers' manuals and answer the following for multiplication and division of whole numbers. (a) List the major topics introduced for the first time in each of grades two through five. (b) Describe experiences for learning multiplication facts with 2 as a factor. Contrast the approach for facts with 2 with those having 8 as a factor. (c) Locate procedures for learning to compute mentally. (d) Find interesting drill exercises. (e) Illustrate all extended algorithms. (f) List suggested activities with materials and devices. (g) List suggestions for taking care of individual differences.

2 Some of your fourth-grade pupils are having difficulty with long divisions like $54 \div 2$, $72 \div 6$, and $84 \div 3$. Plan a one-day lesson for them. What activities will you use for the entire group and for individual pupils? Write an experiment for a group of three pupils. For pupils who do not need this review you will use an adaption of Activity 5. Rewrite it.

3 Write one mathematics-laboratory experiment for each of the following: (a) relating multiplication and division facts; (b) remainders in division; (c) picturing multiplication (1-digit times 2-digit) as a rectangular arrangement and writing the corresponding symbolism.

4 List ideas and procedures for computing that you think can be discovered by pupils. For each, describe one experience for pupils that would guide this discovery.

5 (a) Play the game in Activity 8. Discover the strategy. Write a variation of the game in which any factor of the number may be subtracted except 1 and the number itself. What is the strategy now? (b) Explain the check for division in Activity 5. (c) Do Activity 11.

Bibliography

1 Ando, M., and H. Ikeda: "Learning Multiplication Facts—More Than a Drill," *The Arithmetic Teacher*, vol. 18, pp. 366-369, Oct., 1971. Three stages for learning the multiplication facts are suggested: learning the concept, organizing into a table, and memorizing.

2 Ashlock, R.: "Teaching the Basic Facts: Three Classes of Activities," *The Arithmetic Teacher*, vol. 18, pp. 359-364, Oct., 1971. The author demonstrates the role of concrete material, verbal language, and symbolism in the acquisition of basic knowledge. The above issue of *The Arithmetic Teacher* has several excellent articles on multiplication and division.

3 Brownell, W. A.: "Rate, Accuracy and Process in Learning," *Journal of Educational Psychology*, vol. 35, pp. 321-337, Sept., 1944. An excellent analysis of what indexes can be applied to learning mathematics.

4 Cacha, F. B.: "Understanding Multiplication and Division of Multidigit Numbers," *The Arithmetic Teacher*, vol. 19, pp. 349-354, May, 1972. Using graph paper, multiplication and division are related to the idea of area. The method could easily be extended to the use of blocks.

5 Jerman, M.: "Some Strategies for Solving Simple Multiplication Combinations," *Journal for Research in Mathematics Education*, vol. 1, pp. 95-128, March, 1970. An interesting study using the computer to determine response times. May be useful in helping the teacher decide on a teaching strategy.

6 Kline, M.: "Logic versus Pedagogy," *The American Mathematics Monthly*, vol. 77, pp. 264-282, March, 1970. A clear statement of the need for a careful teaching approach to mathematics which avoids strict logical and axiomatic methods.

7 Quast, W.: "Method or Justification," *The Arithmetic Teacher*, vol. 19, pp. 617-622, Dec., 1972. The rationale for using a variety of methods to teach the four basic operations is clearly explicated.

8 Swart, W. L.: "Teaching the Division-subtraction Process," *The Arithmetic Teacher*, vol. 19, pp. 71-75, Jan., 1972. Levels of computation using the long-division algorithm should be known to all teachers.

9 Van Engen, H., and G. Gibb: *General Mental Functions Associated with Division*, State Teachers College, Cedar Falls, Iowa, 1956. An excellent piece of research comparing the achievement of two groups of pupils learning to divide, using two different methods.

10 Zweng, M.: "The Fourth Operation is Not Fundamental," *The Arithmetic Teacher*, vol. 19, pp. 623-627, Dec., 1972. A logical as well as a psychological approach to division is presented.

6
GEOMETRY

Introduction of geometry in the elementary school curriculum has the essential purposes of providing an opportunity for pupils to analyze further the physical world in which they live and providing an earlier foundation for the basic concepts and vocabulary that are necessary for continued study of mathematics. But at the same time, study of geometry may help pupils develop a genuine intellectual interest in mathematics. In addition, no other branch of mathematics affords so many opportunities for the learner to appreciate the aesthetic nature of the subject.

The study of geometry as a means of understanding and interpreting the environment begins during preschool years and develops with the pupil's interests. From an early age, experiences with concepts of line, angle, shape, curve, and other fundamental geometric ideas pervade his life. Playing with his toys, he finds blocks with square corners and builds fences to enclose his plastic animals. Later he finds the curve of the track for his train is too sharp, with the result that the engine jumps the track. As he matures he learns more about the one-, two-, and three-dimensional aspects of his environment; and he may, if he studies enough geometry, begin to speculate about the concept of a fourth dimension, which is shrouded in mystery and suspicion for the average citizen.

Geometry in the elementary school omits the formal aspects of the high school course, focusing instead on the physical environment of the pupil. The pupil is given a chance to explore, experiment, and discover and conjecture various ideas; yet he is encouraged to formulate precise statements, use logical thinking, and verify all conclusions.

In general the program is intuitive, with the emphasis on reasoning from objects and pictures. However, as the pupil gains confidence, the study is made somewhat more rigorous. For example, in the middle grades, the pupil may try to find the sum of the measures of the angles of a triangle by tearing off the corners of triangular regions and fitting them together, as shown in Fig. 6-1. Later, in the upper grades, he recognizes that this experimental approach makes the theorem plausible but does not prove it. He

Figure 6-1
The sum of the measures of the angles of a triangle.

then tries to discover a proof. Such a program, beginning with an exploration of the properties of geometric figures, discovering these properties through the study of models, and eventually, with a few topics, proving a generalized conclusion, characterizes much of the study of geometry in elementary school mathematics programs.

Geometry is often thought of as partitioned into two (not completely separate) categories—metric, or measurement geometry, and nonmetric geometry, in which measurement ideas are not applied. This distinction is disregarded in teaching, as ideas from the two "branches" are intermixed. The separation is useful here in order to emphasize in this chapter the nonmetric concepts, which constitute much of the new geometric content for the elementary grades, while leaving the measurement aspects to Chapter 9.

The effective teacher of geometry will need to:

● Prepare learning experiences which aid children to abstract the ideal geometry from the real world of physical objects.
● Understand the role of language and symbolism in expressing geometrical ideas.
● Be alert to the infinitude of geometric concepts embodied in every object of the universe.
● Guide pupils to conjectures about physical objects representing geometric ideas and assist them in the verification of such conjectures.
● Develop many learning experiences to meet individual needs and differences in learning geometry.
● Evaluate geometric understanding by observing pupil behavior, using class discussion as well as paper-and-pencil tests.

IDEAL VS. PHYSICAL GEOMETRY

The period at the end of this sentence is not a point but a model, illustration, or picture of a point. Similarly, the figures in Fig. 6-2 are not a rectangle and a triangle but models of them. In geometry points, lines, triangles, spheres, planes, and other figures are ideas. It is possible to produce a model, picture, or illustration of each. That the idea and the model for the idea differ is quite evident when the mathematician's concept of a point as having no length, width, or depth is contrasted to a dot on a paper, which does have dimensions. In the mathematician's *ideal geometry,* definitions are made and ideas developed by reasoning alone, without any necessary reference to objects in the environment.

The pupil comes to see the distinction between the idealized figures of geometry and the real objects that he is familiar with from numerous experiences. Thus, a line segment is illustrated by the intersection of the floor and a wall, the edge of a door or

Figure 6-2
Models of a rectangle and a triangle.

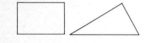

table, or a taut string. None of these examples exactly meets the idealized characteristics of a line segment, but all approximate them. By eliminating the irrelevant properties in each example, the pupil forms the idealized concept.

In the same way, the child sees the *rectangular prism* as the idealized common element among bricks, blocks of wood, breakfast-food cartons, and cigar boxes. Similarly, a sphere is illustrated by baseballs, oranges, basketballs, the moon, the sun, and the earth.

To avoid complicated language, drawings or concrete objects will often be referred to as if they were geometric objects. It should be remembered, however, that the drawing only represents a model for the idea. This distinction is made for children with expressions such as, "This pictures a square," as the teacher sketches the model of a square on the chalkboard. As the study continues the expression, "This is a square" may be used when the teacher is sure that incorrect concepts are not being developed.

The need for undefined terms, precise statements, and careful teaching of geometric concepts is indicated by the following example. In some books a straight line is defined as "the shortest distance between two points." If a line is a distance, then it can be measured, and a number indicating the number of units of length in the line may be associated with it. However, the same book may say, "A straight line can be extended indefinitely in either direction." Putting these statements together, one would reach the conclusion, "The shortest distance could be extended indefinitely." Obviously such definitions are not adequate. It is for this reason that great care must be taken to ensure that the learner understands a concept prior to any formal definition.

This chapter briefly summarizes much of the geometry content of the elementary school and suggests some effective experiences for pupils.

POINTS, PLANES, AND LINES

Words are defined in the dictionary by other words. These other words are defined by still others. Soon one of these words will be defined by the original word. This is known as a circular definition. Hence, in order to use a dictionary, the meaning of some words must be known.

To avoid circular definition in geometry some ideas are accepted as undefined. Then new ideas are defined in terms of these accepted ones. The undefined ideas may be different for different geometries or for different grade levels, depending on the nature of the course and the maturity of the pupil. For purposes of this chapter, *point, line, plane,* and *space* are undefined. At the same time these ideas can be described and illustrated, and their properties observed.

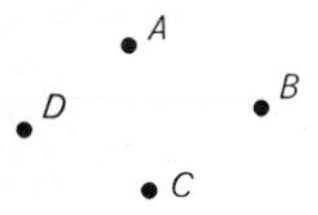

Point

The idea of a *point* is suggested by a dot, the tip of a pencil, or the corner of this page. These are illustrations of points only. Actually, geometric points are ideas; they are considered as something without size. The ordinary convention for labeling pictures of points is by capital letters, as is shown in Fig. 6-3. A point may be thought of as a specific location, and space may be thought of as the set of all points.

Plane

A *plane* is a special set of points suggested by a chalkboard, desktop, or door. These are somewhat misleading as representations because the ideal plane has no boundaries. Ordinarily, planes are pictured as shown in Fig. 6-4. Planes may be named by any three points not on the same straight line. The pictured plane is named *plane ABC.*

Line

A *line* is a certain subset of the set of points called a *plane.* There is no good model of a line in the physical world because the line extends without limit in both directions. Models of lines would be the extension of the edges of a ruler or a taut string. Pictures of lines include arrows to indicate that lines are endless. Two points on a line are used to name the line. The names of the lines in Fig. 6-5 are $\overleftrightarrow{AB}$ or $\overleftrightarrow{BA}$ and $\overleftrightarrow{CD}$ or $\overleftrightarrow{DC}$.

The vivid imagination of pupils is helpful in introducing the idea of a point in the early grades. Starting with (models of) points such as dots and progressing to points at the tip of a pencil or the corner of a desk, the teacher says, "These suggest points." Pupils then describe other physical referents such as "two centimeters above the corner of the book" or "six meters west of the drinking fountain on the playground." They may play a game by describing how to find the point where the treasure is buried. One pupil may say, for example, "The point locating the treasure is ten steps from the door toward the bookcase and then three meters up." Another pupil may find the point.

The concepts of planes, points, and lines are developed as pupils describe examples from their own environment. They may say, for example, "If a ruler is extended in both directions it is an example of a line," or they may make an extensive list of illustrations of planes. Examples in the classroom are the chalkboard, the floor,

Figure 6-3

{A,B,C,D}

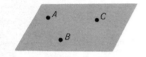

Figure 6-4
Plane ABC.

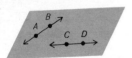

Figure 6-5
Lines $\overleftrightarrow{AB}$ or $\overleftrightarrow{BA}$ and $\overleftrightarrow{CD}$ or $\overleftrightarrow{DC}$.

or the cover of a book. The idea of a line as a set of points is built as two pupils hold a piece of string taut and various pupils touch the string and say, "This is one point on the line." As time goes on pupils realize that there are points on the line beyond those at which the string is being held.

When they start learning how to name lines, groups of pupils may have contests to see which can find all names for a line. They find the line in Fig. 6-6 has six names. (Can you discover how the names are organized so all are listed? Invent another way to organize the names.)

Figure 6-6
Names for a line.

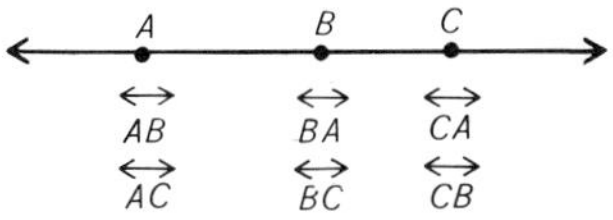

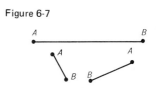

LINE SEGMENTS, RAYS, AND ANGLES

While *between* is difficult to define, it is agreed that this property implies, "If a point is between two points, then all three are on one line." Pupils should contrast this use of *between* with its less precise use in everyday life. Chicago is between San Francisco and New York for all practical purposes, but this does not agree with the strict mathematical interpretation of the term.

Line Segment

A *line segment* is a set of points that can be represented by a taut string or the edge of a book. Specifically, it is a set of points consisting of two points and all other points between them. In Fig. 6-7 the points A and B are *end points* of each line segment AB. The line segment is named $\overline{AB}$ or $\overline{BA}$.

Figure 6-7

To develop the pupil's concept of a line segment he should be asked to find many examples of line segments in the classroom—a pencil, a piece of chalk, a stretched string, the edge of a piece of paper. A variety of experiences is important so that he can acquire the intuitive notions of a line segment as being straight, having length, and being composed of points.

Once this is established, he can proceed to the next generalization, one which is beyond his experience—the unlimited extension from the line segment to the line. Actually, this is no strain on the pupil's imagination as he sees that any line segment he represents can readily be extended in both directions. The ends of the segment, then, become points on the line.

Figure 6-8

Ray

A beam of light from a source such as a lamp in a lighthouse is an excellent example of a ray. A *ray* is a set of points that is a subset of the set of points called a *line*. The rays pictured in Fig. 6-8 are each named $\overrightarrow{AB}$, with end point A and B any other point on the ray.

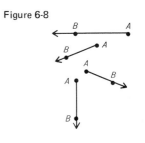

Figure 6-9
Angles ABC or CBA, ∠ABC or
∠CBA.

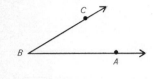

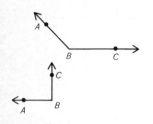

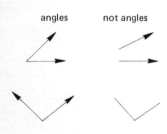

Figure 6-10

These are

angles   not angles

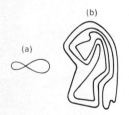

Figure 6-11
The simple closed curve is (b).

Angle

A set of points, consisting of two distinct rays that are not on the same line, with the same end point, is called an *angle.* The common end point is called the *vertex,* and the rays are often called *sides* of the angle. Angles are named, using letters for three points—the vertex and one point on each ray. The angles shown in Fig. 6-9 are each named angle *ABC,* angle *CBA* or, more simply, ∠*ABC* or ∠*CBA,* with the letter naming the vertex in the middle.

It is possible for pupils to discover the definition of an angle. Each group of pupils may be given a card with Fig. 6-10 on it and instructions "From these pictures tell me what an angle is." If the entire class is working together the figures may be drawn on the chalkboard. By observing the pictures carefully and refining their statements by discussion, pupils can find the unique properties of an angle. Another experiment with angles is in Activity 5 at the end of the chapter.

CURVES AND SIMPLE CLOSED CURVES

If only one of the curves in Fig. 6-11 could be described, using the word *simple,* most persons would probably choose (a). Strange as it may seem, (b) is an example of a simple closed curve, and (a) is not. This is another illustration of the difference between the technical meaning of a word and its everyday meaning.

Simple Closed Curves

Intuitively, a path may be thought of as a set of points in space that is traversed in going from one point to another. In geometry such paths are called *curves.* In this section only curves with all of their points in one plane (called *plane curves*) are considered. A plane curve may be thought of intuitively as a set of points that may be drawn without lifting a pencil off the paper. A curve is shown in Fig. 6-12*a, b, c,* and *d,* but not in Fig. 6-12*e* and *f.* From this figure it is seen that curves may or may not have straight portions.

If a curve is drawn in such a way that a return is made to the starting point—i.e., the first and last points coincide—the path is called a *closed curve.* All curves in Fig. 6-13 are examples of closed curves. If no point except the first is passed over more than once, meaning the curve "does not intersect itself," the path is called a *simple closed curve.* Fig. 6-13*g, h,* and *i* picture simple closed curves, while Fig 6-13*j, k,* and *l* do not because each "intersects itself."

Pupils may discover and formulate definitions, such as that for simple closed curves. The teacher draws a number of curves on the board, such as in Figs. 6-11, 6-12, 6-13. He asks first that the pupils make intelligent guesses as to which are simple closed curves. Some of these answers are written on the board. Then, using colored chalk, he traces the simple closed curves (Figs. 6-11*b*, 6-12*b* and *c*, and 6-13*g*, *h*, and *i*). From the tracing, pupils state the common properties. They readily see the following:

Each is drawn by starting at a point and returning to it.

There are no intersections, except at the "begining point."

The teacher may now say, "I can draw this figure (pointing to Fig. 6-12*f* on the board) by applying these conditions." Some pupils will discover the path in Fig. 6-14 starting at *A* going to *B*, removing the chalk from the board, and then tracing *C* to *D* and then *E* back to *A*. Pupils may then state the third property—that the chalk may not be removed from the board—and the definition is complete. The parts of the definition may be phrased first in the language of the pupils; more precise statements may be made, depending on the ability of the class.

Properties of simple closed curves From examination of examples, the fact that any simple closed curve separates a plane into three sets of points seems intuitively evident. These three sets are:

The curve itself.

The interior (the part of the plane enclosed by the curve).

The exterior (points neither on the curve nor in the interior).

Special simple closed curves Much of geometry is made up of a study of polygons. These are simple closed curves, consisting of the union of three or more line segments. Line segments that form polygons are often called *sides,* and the intersections of the segments are called *vertices.* Polygons are named by the letters that name the vertices. Thus, in Fig. 6-15 the polygons are named *triangle ABC* or△*ABC, quadrilateral DEFG, pentagon HIJKL,* and *hexagon MNOPQR.*

Geometric figures commonly found in the child's environment provide the natural setting for an introduction to geometry. Models of figures, such as the rectangle, triangle, and circle, can be identified in a variety of concrete objects. Pupils may suggest their individual properties and those common to two or more figures.

As a beginning, the teacher may show a wire model of a rectangle and ask pupils to trace the rectangle with a finger. Then he may ask, "Show me other examples of rectangles." A pupil may volunteer the answer that a sheet of paper is a rectangle. The teacher should

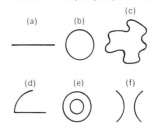

Figure 6-12
The curves are (a), (b), (c), and (d).

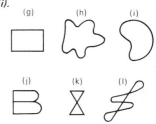

Figure 6-13
Simple closed curves are (g), (h), and (i).

Figure 6-14

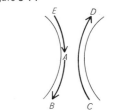

Figure 6-15
Polygons.

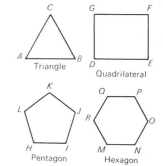

Figure 6-16
Rectangles.

(a)

(b)

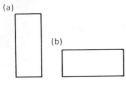

(c)

(d)

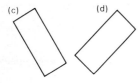

Figure 6-17
Quadrilaterals.

Figure 6-18

(a)

(b)

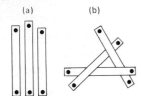

say, "Trace with your finger the part that suggests a rectangle." The pupil recognizes that he shows a rectangle as he moves his finger along the edges of the sheet. This is repeated with other examples, such as the edges of a door or a book cover. Continuing, the teacher draws a picture of a rectangle on the board, and the pupil traces the rectangle with his finger or another piece of chalk. Then pupils imagine a rectangle and trace it in the air with their fingers.

In studying rectangles, models and pictures should be held and drawn in various positions, and the pupils should be asked to select those that suggest rectangles. Too often, pupils see rectangles only in positions (a) or (b) in Fig. 6-16 and fail to see the same properties in (c) and (d).

Pupils may also draw closed figures, such as those pictured in Fig. 6-17, that are not rectangles but do have four sides. While technical names, such as *quadrilateral* and *parallelogram,* are not important in early instruction, many pupils enjoy using them and in some cases even spelling them.

The circle, square, and triangle are introduced in a similar manner. After some experiences with the triangle, pupils are furnished with strips of paper and asked to show a triangle. As the lengths of the three strips are varied, the pupils find triangles with three sides of the same length, two sides of the same length, or no two sides of the same length. The common element of three sides for all triangles is emphasized. Eventually the prefix *tri* should be identified as meaning three through examples such as *tri*cycle, *tri*o, *tri*ple, and *tri*pod.

The teacher may ask if three strips, such as shown in Fig. 6-18*a,* can be used to show a triangle. Then he should put the strips together, as shown in Fig. 6-18*b.* He should then ask, "Are the strips sides of the triangle?" The student should answer "no" and try to defend his answer in words; even if he cannot explain, he should place the strips in such a position so as to show them as sides of the triangle.

There is something magic about the way children enjoy making various designs and shapes on geoboards. They are strongly motivated to find answers for such questions as:

How many triangles can you make with two sides the same length?
Who can make a shape with more than six sides?
How many triangles can you make that have a square corner (right angle)?
Can you make a triangle with three sides the same length? Invent a new kind of geoboard so you can make such a triangle.

The idea of an interior and exterior of simple closed curves is intuitively evident to preschool children. This concept is emphasized and expanded as pupils:

Draw a triangle with red crayon.

Color the interior of the triangle blue.

Color the exterior of the triangle green.

Locate point A inside the triangle.

Locate point B in the exterior in the triangle, then draw line segment AB and count the number of intersections of segment AB and the triangle.

These latter activities help the pupil develop the notion of a *plane region*, an idea that makes the study of area more meaningful.

EXAMPLES OF CREATIVE TEACHING

The creative teacher can make mathematics exciting. Sometimes he accomplishes this by the way he introduces a problem. At other times it is the problem itself or the process of devising a method for solving it that fascinates pupils. Each of the following two lessons, although they deal here with an entire class, can be adapted for experimentation by groups of pupils in a mathematics laboratory.

A How Many Problem

Ms. Au often challenged the class with "I'll bet you can't tell me how many...," and found them extremely motivated by these questions. One day, after the idea of a simple closed curve had been introduced, she asked, "How many simple closed curves can you trace with your finger?", drawing Fig. 6-19a on the board. As with other problems Ms. Au had presented, her pupils were as intrigued with planning a way to solve the problem as with the answer. This concurred with the objectives she had outlined.

One group of pupils made a start by labeling the drawing as in Fig. 6-19b; then they proceeded to list systematically all of the simple closed curves.

1   First they found all of the simple closed curves that include point A. (Two of these were ABF and $ACDF$.)

2   Next they listed all of those that include point B but not point A. (Two of these were BCD and $BDEF$.)

3   Then they determined those with point C but not A or B. None was found.

4   They continued and found those with point D but not with points A, B, or C. (The only one was DFE.)

5   Starting with points E and F, they found no simple closed curves that had not been listed previously.

Figure 6-19

How many simple closed curves?

(a)

(b)

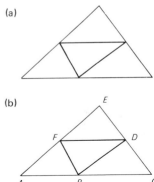

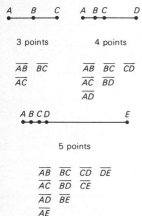

Figure 6-20

Figure	Number of simple closed curves
1—triangle	4
2—triangle	3
3—triangle	3
4—triangle	1
Total	11

Figure 6-21
How many segments?

Figure 6-22
Naming the segments.

A   B   C   A B C   D

3 points   4 points

$\overline{AB}$ $\overline{BC}$ $\overline{AB}$ $\overline{BC}$ $\overline{CD}$
$\overline{AC}$ $\overline{AC}$ $\overline{BD}$
             $\overline{AD}$

A B C D   E

5 points

$\overline{AB}$ $\overline{BC}$ $\overline{CD}$ $\overline{DE}$
$\overline{AC}$ $\overline{BD}$ $\overline{CE}$
$\overline{AD}$ $\overline{BE}$
$\overline{AE}$

Another group of students organized their experimentation by first defining a one-triangle figure as *ABC* or *BDC*, a two-triangle figure as *ABDF* or *CDFB,* continuing with three- and four-triangle figures. They argued that these are the only four *kinds* of simple closed curves in the drawing. These pupils finally determined 11 simple closed curves, as shown in Fig. 6-20. The teacher was especially impressed by some of the pupils' arguments in answer to the question, "Are you sure you have found all of the simple closed curves?":

A two-triangle figure must include triangle *BDF*. Figure *ABCDBFA,* for example, is not a simple closed curve. Thus, $\triangle BFD$ can be used with each of $\triangle ABF,$ $\triangle BCD,$ and $\triangle DEF$. The total is three.

A three-triangle figure cannot include all of $\triangle ABF, \triangle BCD,$ and $\triangle DEF$. Each must include two of these, along with $\triangle BDF$.

As with so many problems in mathematics, the answer was less important than the other outcomes. The pupils discovered procedures that not only led to a solution for this problem, but also could be applied to solving others. Also, they practiced organizing their work in such a way that they were sure their answers were correct. These are two of many outcomes sought from the study of mathematics which, although important, have not received enough attention.

Problems About Segments and Rays

Mr. Brent found his average class somewhat disinterested with the lessons that required learning new symbolism. Since he knew the importance of symbolism and the necessity for learning it, in order to create interest he introduced it combined with experiments and experiences with concrete materials. One of these procedures required pupils to examine a number of cases and then to suggest a general pattern. This method is called *inductive reasoning.*

Models of line segments, such as pencils, pieces of chalk, a taut string, and so on, were discussed and shown by members of the class. The idea of exactly two end points was discovered, and Mr. Brent asked how a line segment with end points *A* and *B* might be named. Suggestions from the class were the following:

Segment with end points *A* and *B*.   Line segment *AB.*

Segment *AB.*   *AB.*

The advantages of each were analyzed. The last, *AB,* was thought best, but the class agreed that a name which distinguished a line containing points *A* and *B* from a segment with end points *A* and *B* was necessary. The names $\overleftrightarrow{AB}$ or $\overleftrightarrow{BA}$ were found to be the symbolism most frequently used for this line segment.

Next Mr. Brent asked, "How many line segments can be named in Fig. 6-21?" Some pupils drew the figure on a piece of paper, but there was not complete agreement on the number of segments.

At this point, Mr. Brent had the class arrange itself into groups. The groups were told to find the number of segments, to organize their work, and then to report to the class. After some oral reports, the class decided that the method proposed by Jim's group was the best because they had discovered a way (Fig. 6-22) to list all segments and be certain none was omitted. They did this by naming all segments with end point A. Next they named all segments with end point B, but not containing A, then all with end point C, but not containing A or B, and so on.

Some pupils were interested in the pattern 1, 3, 6, 10 for the number of segments (Fig. 6-23). They located 6 points on a line and found 15 segments; they continued with 7 points to determine 21 segments. They studied these results and finally discovered the relationships shown in Fig. 6-24. A tentative generalization was formulated that $n(n-1)/2$ was the number of segments formed by n points on a line.

As a final problem for those who had a special interest Mr. Brent asked, "How many segments, each of a different length, can you find on the geoboard?" Some young mathematicians discovered the correct answer and a way to prove they were correct. Can the reader do this?

When rays were introduced, Mr. Brent again organized the lesson so that pupils might explore the idea and learn the necessary symbolism. He drew a line on the chalkboard and labeled it as in Fig. 6-25. He asked the class, "How many rays can you name?" Remembering the value of organizing their thinking, the pupils wrote these names for the rays:

$$\overrightarrow{RV} \qquad \overrightarrow{SV} \qquad \overrightarrow{TV} \qquad \overrightarrow{UV}$$

$$\overleftarrow{VR} \qquad \overleftarrow{UR} \qquad \overleftarrow{TR} \qquad \overleftarrow{SR}$$

Next, the pupils wanted to know if a pattern existed such as they had discovered for line segments. They drew pictures and completed the accompanying table for Fig. 6-26. Most pupils guessed 10 rays for 6 points and 12 rays for 7 points. These were verified with pictures. Some average pupils even guessed $2n-2$ rays for n points, and others said, "Double the number of points and subtract 2 for the number of rays."

Mr. Brent made sure that his pupils recognized that the conclusions discovered in the manner described above had not been proved, but the plausibility of these conclusions was suggested.

Figure 6-23

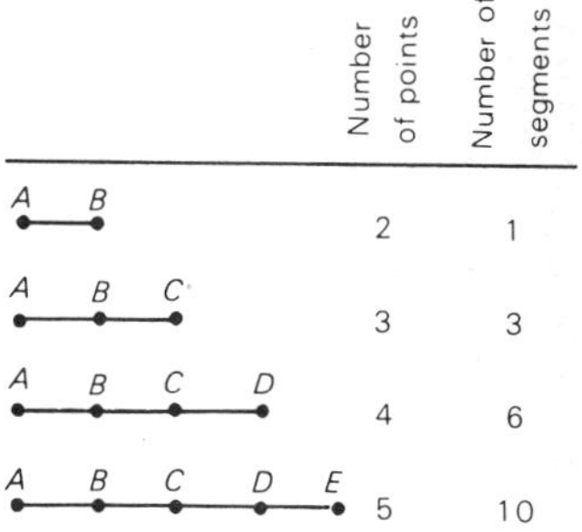

	Number of points	Number of segments
A B	2	1
A B C	3	3
A B C D	4	6
A B C D E	5	10

Figure 6-24

points	Number of segments
1	$\frac{2 \times 1}{2} = 1$
2	$\frac{3 \times 2}{2} = 3$
3	$\frac{4 \times 3}{2} = 6$
4	$\frac{5 \times 4}{2} = 10$

Figure 6-25
How many rays?

R S T U V

Figure 6-26

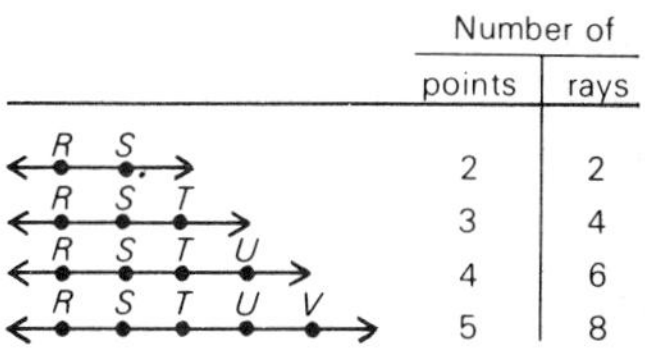

	Number of points	rays
R S	2	2
R S T	3	4
R S T U	4	6
R S T U V	5	8

Proof for an example such as this is learned considerably later in mathematics.

Two things are especially worth noting in this example of effective teaching. First, the primary interest of the class was directed to the study of line segments and rays, which was the purpose of the lesson. Second, the lesson as it developed gave pupils real experiences in discovering patterns, organizing data, and drawing tentative conclusions.

The same kinds of lessons can be developed from many of the Activities described at the end of this chapter. Some are appropriate for large groups and some for small groups, while some can be used for independent exploration.

COMPARING AND CONGRUENCE

Even young children make crude comparisons of magnitudes, using words such as *larger, smaller, taller, bigger,* and *less than.* Adults, too, often make comparisons relying on sight, feeling, or even intuition. Sometimes a physical comparison is made by placing an object on another. For example, to find whether region *A* or *B* is larger, *B* might be placed on *A,* shown in Fig. 6-27. In comparisons of this kind there are only three possible outcomes: the first is smaller than the second, the first is larger than the second, or they are the same size.

Congruence of Line Segments

Sometimes it is easy to determine which of these three possibilities is true. For $\overline{AC}$ and $\overline{AB}$ in Fig 6-28, with point *A* as a common end point, point *C* is between *A* and *B,* and therefore $\overline{AB}$ is longer. This procedure is commonly used when two children stand back to back. The one with the top of his head above that of the other is the taller.

Often the procedure is complicated because it is not convenient to transport and compare examples of segments by superimposing one on the other. For example, a person might want to know if a log is too long for a fireplace. He could get a stick the length of the log and move it to the fireplace. Likewise, to compare $\overline{XY}$ and $\overline{KJ}$, as shown in Fig. 6-29*a*, a model of $\overline{XY}$ is obtained with end points *S* and *T*. Point *S* is placed on point *K*. Now point *T* falls between *K* and *J,* as shown in Fig. 6-29*b,* and $\overline{XY}$ is said to be shorter than $\overline{KJ}$.

Now suppose two line segments *AB* and *GH* fit exactly. The segments are then said to be *congruent;* this is written $\overline{AB} \cong \overline{GH}$. It may seem that the segments should be called *equal* and the relation symbolized $\overline{AB} = \overline{GH}$. This is incorrect because the equals sign = is used between different names for the same number

Figure 6-27
Comparing regions A and B.

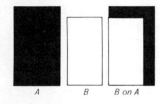

Figure 6-28

Figure 6-29
Comparing lengths by matching a model.

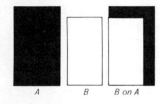

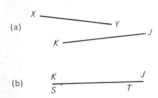

or set. Now $\overline{AB}$ and $\overline{GH}$ are not names for the same set of points; therefore, the equals sign cannot be used. The word *congruent*, then, is used to describe figures that have the same size and shape.

The variety of geoboard experiments concerned with congruent line segments is enormous. Pupils may, for example, show six segments congruent to a given segment, or find the segment on the geoboard that has (*a*) the greatest number of segments congruent to it, (*b*) exactly three other segments congruent to it, or (*c*) one other segment congruent to it.

Congruence of Triangles

Two triangles are said to be congruent if one fits the other exactly. This is an idealized notion and is not subject to physical verification; and, although the concept is developed by making physical comparisons, the difference between the idealized situation and the physical model must be remembered. If the physical models of two figures appear to fit exactly, they should be described as "seeming to be congruent."

While congruence exists in definition only, the precision of the language used may be relaxed in later instruction, and the words *"seem to be"* may be replaced by *"are."* If $\triangle XYZ$ and $\triangle STR$ (as shown in Fig. 6-30) are congruent, then the correspondence must be such that point S falls on point X, point T falls on point Y, and point R falls on point Z. Such correspondence is necessary for $\triangle XYZ$ to be congruent to $\triangle STR$. The fact of congruence is indicated as $\triangle XYZ \cong \triangle STR$. The formal idea of one-to-one correspondence of a set of points for congruence is avoided in early instruction. Rather, the idea of congruence is introduced through experiments with the geoboard, dot paper, and other materials. Some experiences are:

Figure 6-30
$\triangle XYZ \cong \triangle STR.$

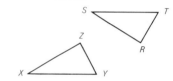

On the geoboard pupils form polygons that are congruent to given polygons.

One pupil forms three triangles on his geoboard, only two of which are congruent. His partner determines which two are congruent.

Pupils form on the geoboard "strange" figures (Fig 6-31) congruent to those they see on dot paper.

Figure 6-31

Pupils use tracing paper to obtain figures congruent to given figures.

Pupils use tracing paper to compare $\overline{AB}$ with $\overline{CD}$ and $\overline{MN}$ with $\overline{ST}$ (Fig. 6-32). These are common optical illusions. Some pupils may do library research and find other examples for the bulletin board.

When pupils use tracing paper or other devices to compare geometric figures, they develop an intuitive notion of relative size. These intuitive experiences are an important step in developing

Figure 6-32
Optical illusions.

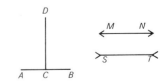

Figure 6-33
Drawing parallel lines.

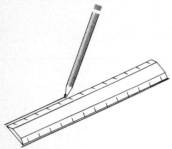

Figure 6-34
Forming parallel lines by folding paper.

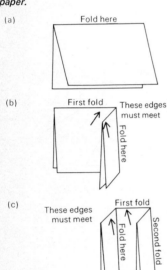

Figure 6-35
Finding the midpoint.

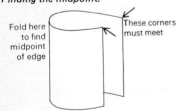

concepts. During such instruction, however, possible sources of error should be emphasized as pupils are encouraged to be as accurate as possible in making comparisons.

EXPLORING FOLDING OF PAPER

A number of geometric concepts may be discovered by pupils as they fold pieces of paper which they have prepared in various shapes. Such activity is especially useful in helping pupils visualize ideas. The pupil who folds paper to find the midpoint of a line segment or to find the bisector of an angle, for example, will learn faster, learn more, and be more interested than the pupil who relies exclusively on verbal descriptions.

Drawing Parallel Lines

Pupils first find in the classroom a number of examples of parallel lines, such as sides of window frames, the door, or the chalkboard. Then they are given rulers and pencils and asked to draw parallel lines. Most discover that one accurate way is by drawing along two edges of a ruler, as shown in Fig. 6-33.

Next they experiment to find how to fold the paper to show parallel lines. One possible way to do this is shown in Fig 6-34a, b, and c. After pupils observe the parallel lines in Fig. 6-34c, they may recognize that each of the parallel lines is perpendicular to the first fold. This is like the edges of two sides of a piece of paper—they are parallel, and each edge is perpendicular to the top edge.

Finding the Midpoint

Many pupils know and others can invent a way to find the midpoint of the edge of a sheet of paper. One way to do this is shown in Fig. 6-35. Using this procedure, they may find the midpoints of two sides $\overline{AC}$ and $\overline{BC}$, of triangle ABC (Fig. 6-36) and draw segment $\overline{DE}$ joining the midpoints. Then small groups of pupils may discuss and try to guess two relationships between $\overline{DE}$ and $\overline{AB}$. Most will see $\overline{DE}$ is parallel to $\overline{AB}$, and those who have studied angles formed when two parallel lines are intersected by a third line can prove it. If pupils do not guess the other relationship they may be told, "Use your ruler." (Can the reader guess this relationship?) The relationships are verified by joining with segments the midpoints of pairs of sides of other triangles.

A similar experiment is performed by locating the midpoints of sides of quadrilateral $MNOP$. (Fig. 6-37). If they join the midpoints as shown, pupils may guess that the figure is a_____.

A challenging experiment for pupils is to make triangles and quadrilaterals on their geoboards and verify the conclusions of the two experiments above.

Bisecting an Angle

Even before the definition of the bisector of an angle has been made, pupils have an intuitive feeling for its meaning. If given a triangle and asked to fold the paper so that the fold bisects one angle, many pupils discover the procedure shown in Fig. 6-38. (The teacher may wish to discuss the word *bisect*, and pupils may use expressive [although not precise] descriptions, such as "*Bisect means cut in half or cut into two equal parts.*") If pupils make three folds to show the three angle bisectors (Fig. 6-39), they will discover the interesting fact that the angle bisectors of a triangle intersect in one point.

A Circle through Three Points

Pupils may try to draw with a compass a circle through three points, such as *A*, *B*, and *C* (Fig. 6-40). They will find it a difficult job. Even continued experiments will produce, in most cases, only approximate answers. With this limited success, the teacher may suggest trying to solve a simpler problem: "Draw a circle through two points."

As pupils think about this problem, they may decide that a point for the center of the circle must be the same distance from each of the two points. Some pupils may locate point *E* equidistant from both *C* and *D* (Fig. 6-41) as the center of a circle that passes through points *C* and *D*. Many pupils may recognize that point *E* is not the only point for the center of a circle through *C* and *D* (Fig. 6-42). They may discover also that all centers seem to form a line. This line is found by putting the compass through the sheet of paper containing the two points *R* and *S* and folding, as shown in Fig. 6-43a and b. Any point on the fold (Fig. 6-43c) may be the center of a circle through *R* and *S*.

Now the problem of a circle through three points *R*, *S*, and *T* may be explored. Using the compass through points *R* and *S* (Fig. 6-44a) pupils see that the center must be on the fold so

Figure 6-36
What is the relationship of $\overline{DE}$ to $\overline{AB}$?

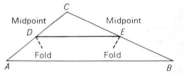

Figure 6-37
Name figure MNOP.

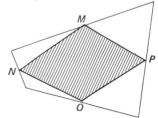

Figure 6-38
Bisecting an angle.

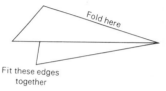

Figure 6-39
Angle bisectors meet in a point.

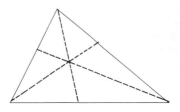

Figure 6-40
Try to draw a circle through A, B, and C.

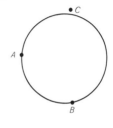

Figure 6-41
Points on a circle are equidistant from its center.

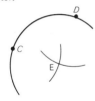

Figure 6-42
Circles through two points, C and D.

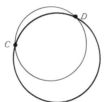

Figure 6-43
Circles through R and S will have centers on fold.

(a)

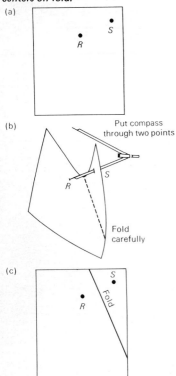

(b)

Put compass through two points

(c)

Fold carefully

Figure 6-44
Circle through R, S, and T has its center at M.

(a)

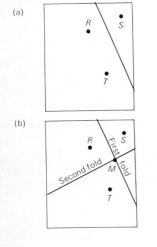

(b)

the circle passes through *R* and *S*. This procedure is repeated for points *R* and *T* (*T* and *S* would serve equally well), and the second fold (Fig. 6-44*b*) is determined. For the circle to pass through *R* and *T*, its center must be on this fold. Combining the two discoveries, the center must be on both folds, or point *M*, for a circle to pass through points *R*, *S*, and *T*.

USING A COMPASS AND STRAIGHT EDGE

Like the geoboard, the compass fascinates children. They soon learn how to construct many designs without instruction. One especially interesting activity is to draw arcs inside a circle and color the resulting regions. This illustrates the good advice, "Exploratory play should precede formal instruction."

The compass and straight edge (a straight edge differs from a ruler in that it does not have markings which permit measuring) play an important role in many geometric constructions.

In Fig. 6-45, with a center at *O*, a set of points with end points *A* and *B* is drawn with the compass. This set of points is named *arc AB* or *arc BA*. Pupils intuitively grasp the idea that, for every point such as *A*, or *B* on the arc, $\overline{OA} \cong \overline{OB}$. This is commonly stated, "All points on the arc are the same distance from the center."

Copying a Line Segment

Suppose $\overline{AB}$ is to be copied on line *g* in Fig. 6-46. The points of the compass are placed on *A* and *B*. Any point *P* on *g* is chosen, and the metal point is placed on it. Arcs are described on *g* at *Q* and *R*. Now $\overline{AB} \cong \overline{PQ}$ and $\overline{AB} \cong \overline{PR}$.

Copying a Triangle

$\triangle XYZ$ (Fig. 6-47*a*) may be copied because the problem is merely to copy three line segments and arrange them in a certain way, as in Fig. 6-47*b*:

1　Draw a line; name it *h*.
2　Copy $\overline{XY}$ on *h*; name it $\overline{KG}$.
3　Draw arc *m*, using *K* as the center and a radius congruent to $\overline{XZ}$.
4　Draw arc *p*, using *G* as the center and a radius congruent to $\overline{YZ}$.

Figure 6-45
Points A and B are equidistant from O.

(a) 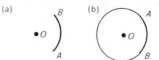 (b)

Figure 6-46
Copying segment AB.

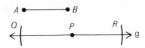

5   Arcs m and p intersect at H. Now, $\triangle XYZ \cong \triangle KGH$ because $\overline{XY} \cong \overline{KG}$, $\overline{XZ} \cong \overline{KH}$, and $\overline{YZ} \cong \overline{GH}$.

Copying an Angle

Suppose a copy of $\angle B$ (Fig. 6-48a) is required. This is not a new or different problem. In fact, its solution was described in the instructions for copying a triangle. If any point A is chosen on one ray of $\angle B$ and any point C on the other ray, $\triangle ABC$ may be formed by drawing $\overline{AC}$ as in Fig. 6-48b. Now a copy of $\triangle ABC$ will contain an angle congruent to $\angle B$.

Bisecting an Angle

Angle KXN (Fig. 6-49a) can be separated into two congruent angles that can be made corresponding angles of congruent triangles. This idea is shown in Fig. 6-49b with $\triangle XYZ \cong \triangle XWZ$. To make the triangles congruent, the corresponding sides are constructed congruent in the following manner:

1   Draw arcs of the same but arbitrary length, with center at X.
2   These arcs intersect $\overrightarrow{XK}$ at Y and $\overrightarrow{XN}$ at W, as in Fig. 6-49c. Now, $\overline{XY} \cong \overline{XW}$.
3   Draw an arc with center Y and an arc with center W, having the same radius. These arcs intersect at Z, as in Fig. 6-49d. Now $\overline{WZ} \cong \overline{YZ}$.
4   Draw $\overline{XZ}$, as in Fig. 6-49e.

Now $\triangle XYZ \cong \triangle XWZ$ because three sides of one are congruent, respectively, to three sides of the other. Hence, $\angle YXZ \cong \angle WXZ$ because they are corresponding angles of congruent triangles.

Many other constructions are possible with compass and straight edge. They include drawing a line perpendicular to a given line or parallel to a given line and separating a segment into two, three or four congruent segments. Even pupils in the lower elementary grades understand, enjoy, and can discover many of these constructions, suggestions for some of which are found in the Bibliography at the end of this chapter.[1]

SPACE FIGURES

Space figures, such as the sphere, cylinder, pyramid, and prism, are introduced in the primary grades in the form of models. Pictures and models may be used in the upper grades.

[1]It is interesting to note that certain constructions which appear simple cannot be made by compass and straight edge. For example, while every angle can be separated into two or four congruent angles by these instruments, it cannot be separated into three congruent angles.

Figure 6-47
Copying triangle XYZ.

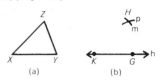
(a)   (b)

Figure 6-48
Copying angle B.

(a)

(b)

Figure 6-49
Bisecting angle X.

(a)

(b)

(c)

(d)

(e)

Space figures are sets of points not all in the same plane. Care must be exercised in selecting models to stress that the figure is the set of points on the surface (shell of the object). For example, the model of a sphere is a basketball rather than a solid baseball and the model of a rectangular prism is an empty box rather than a child's wooden block.

Sphere

Although children in the primary grades may first use the word *ball* to describe a sphere, many teachers recommend applying the correct name from the start.

Among first experiences, pupils are asked to tell as many things about the sphere as they are able. They may make such observations as "It is round." "It has no square corners." or "It is something like a circle." They will identify balls and marbles, certain kinds of light fixtures, breakfast foods, and knobs on doors as objects that are shaped like spheres.

The teacher will probably have to ask questions such as the following to help pupils see other properties:

Can you draw *straight* segments on a sphere? Can you draw *curves?* (Let children experiment and decide the answers.)

If you cut the sphere into two parts with a straight cut, what shape do you always get? (Let children try to get curves other than circles.)

Tell me how to cut the sphere to obtain the greatest circle.

Prism

A figure shaped like a cereal box is an example of what is technically known as a *rectangular prism*. In order to study and describe this figure, certain words must be introduced:

Faces: the flat sides of the prism.
Edges: line segments which are the intersection of faces.
Vertex, plural *vertices*: points where the edges intersect.

Then groups of pupils may discuss and report special properties of a rectangular prism. They discover that:

It has six faces, twelve edges, and eight vertices.
The faces are rectangular regions.
Every vertex is the intersection of three edges.
There are three sets of four congruent edges.

The teacher may guide pupils to discover other properties with such questions as:

What figure is formed when two faces meet?
How many regions meet at a vertex?

Figure 6-50
Rectangular prism.

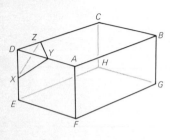

How many edges meet at a vertex?

Do exactly two edges meet anywhere on the prism?

What kind of a figure would we have if all of the faces were square regions?

In later grades, pupils refine their understanding of the rectangular prism (Fig. 6-50) by experimenting to answer:

Show the longest segment that may be drawn on face *ABCD*; on *ADEF*; on *EFGH*. (The teacher may point to the face.)

Name some opposite faces. What seems to be true about opposite faces?

What shapes do you see if a cut is made along the boundary *ACHF*? (The teacher demonstrates what is meant by using a model. Actually, the cut separates the rectangular prism into two congruent triangular prisms. The cut itself is rectangular in shape.)

How is the prism cut so that a triangle is formed? (See cut *XYZ* in Fig. 6-50).

Similar experiences may be used in study of the cube, which is a rectangular prism with congruent faces (Fig. 6-51a). Other prisms, such as those pictured in Fig. 6-51, may also be introduced.

Pupils may build models of various space figures. A pattern for constructing a model of a prism is shown on page 153, and one of a triangular pyramid is shown in Fig. 6-52.

Properties of other space figures are investigated by procedures such as described above. As part of their exploration, pupils may make a table, listing the number of edges, vertices, and faces for certain space figures, thus contrasting some of their properties.

Cylinder

A circular prism is a prism with circular bases. It is most often called a *cylinder*. A tin can is one example of a cylinder. Two circular cylinders are shown in Fig. 6-53.

First, pupils may suggest examples of cylinders, such as broom handles, circular steel rods, and telephone poles. They may then experiment to find answers to questions such as:

How can you form a cylinder (without bases) from a sheet of paper?

Draw on the cylinder a line segment and a curved path. (Do not use either base for this.)

If you were to cut along *ABCDA* in the cylinder in Fig. 6-54, what geometric shape would be cut? Answer for a cut along *LMNPL*. Tell how to cut so that the result is a circle.

Figure 6-51

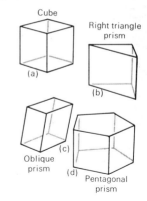

Cube
Right triangle prism
(a)
(b)
Oblique prism
(c)
(d)
Pentagonal prism

Figure 6-52
Model for a triangular pyramid.

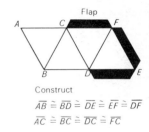

Construct
$\overline{AB} \cong \overline{BD} \cong \overline{DE} \cong \overline{EF} \cong \overline{DF}$
$\overline{AC} \cong \overline{BC} \cong \overline{DC} \cong \overline{FC}$

Figure 6-53
Circular cylinders.

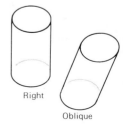

Right
Oblique

Figure 6-54
What figure is traced by ABCDA?

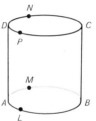

AN ILLUSTRATIVE LESSON

The following geometry lesson is organized according to the flow chart in Chapter 2 (Table 2-1). While the content of the lesson may not be one of the most essential parts of the present curriculum, it does illustrate how pupils discover answers, organize their findings, explore problems, and, in general, enjoy mathematics for the sake of mathematics. It should be recognized that this content may be adapted for effective use at many different grade levels.

The objectives of Ms. Porter (the teacher) for these lessons were to help pupils:

Construct models of geometric figures in space.

Discover properties concerning edges, vertices, and faces for cubes, pyramids, cones and prisms.

Identify examples of various space figures.

Preparation

Ms. Porter made a careful analysis of the background skills and concepts needed for success in learning about space figures. She found that there was considerable variation in what pupils knew about these figures, and decided that a review was necessary.

She showed the class pairs of plane figures and space figures, such as a coin and a ball, a piece of paper and a book, a flat piece of metal and a can of peaches.[1] The pupils made lists of how members of each pair were alike and how they were different. The lists were criticized, and mathematical items were retained, such as being *round* for the coin and the ball. Of course, the real difference in which Ms. Porter was interested was that one object of each pair was two-dimensional and the other three-dimensional. The pupils tried describing this difference in words:

The coin is flat, and the ball is not.
The book has thickness, and the piece of paper does not.
The can of peaches takes up more room.

Although the language of the pupils lacked the preciseness of maturity, it did indicate a feeling for the idea. Ms. Porter continued by showing models of prisms, cylinders, and spheres. She told the class they were called *space figures*. She also showed them a circular disk and a piece of cardboard and named them *plane figures*. The pupils then named items in the room that were space figures, for example, a chalk box, a volleyball, and a light globe.

[1] The coin, paper, and metal must be thought of as having no thickness.

Exploration

Near the end of the period Ms. Porter gave each pupil a mimeographed sheet on which was the figure shown in Fig. 6-55. Each pupil cut it out and folded and pasted it to make a cube. Ms. Porter asked the class to make up some problems about cubes after they had answered the following questions about the cube in Fig. 6-56.

1   For your cube, count the number of (*a*) faces; (*b*) vertices; (*c*) edges.
2   What is the fewest number of edges you can move your finger along to go from *A* to *B* ?
3   What is the greatest number of edges you can move along to get from *A* to *B* if you cannot go along the same edge twice?
4   Can you get from *A* to *B* by going along 5 different edges? Along 4 different edges?

Abstraction and Organization

On the next day, pupils first discussed answers to the problems given to them. Joe was sure that "Three was the fewest edges to move to get from *A* to *B*." When pressed for a reason he said, "Starting from *A*, if I move along any one edge"—which he showed with his finger—"I'm still two edges from *B*." The class agreed. Ms. Porter then asked someone to show how to get from *A* to *B* by moving along four edges. No one could do this. After trying, Debby suggested again, "It can't be done." Ms. Porter asked, "Why not?" Debby tried unsuccessfully to answer this a number of times. Finally Lois showed that after moving along three edges, her finger was either at *B* or two edges from it. So it was possible to get to *B* by moving along three or five edges but not four. The other problems were solved similarly as pupils actually moved their fingers along the edges, giving reasons for their answers.

    Ms. Porter's purpose in this step was to develop the pupils' confidence that they could discover solutions by critically examining models and then reasoning logically.

    Laura brought in a problem (given by her father) which she presented to the class. "Twenty-seven cubes are stacked in three layers of nine cubes in each (Fig. 6-57). If you can pick up the set of cubes and see all sides, how many cubes would you not see at all?"

    Many of the children could not understand or visualize the problem. Carl suggested putting 27 cubes together. This was done with scotch tape. Then, to understand the problem, Ms. Porter asked Mac to point to a cube that had one face showing. He did so,

Figure 6-55
Model for a cube.

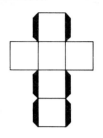

Figure 6-56

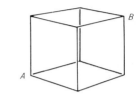

Figure 6-57
A set of 27 cubes.

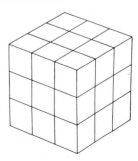

Figure 6-58

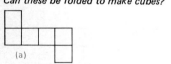

Number of faces showing	Number of cubes
0	1
1	6
2	12
3	8
4	0
5	0
6	0

Figure 6-59
Can these be folded to make cubes?

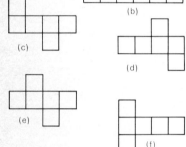

(a)

(b)

(c)

(d)

(e)

(f)

(g)

(h)

Figure 6-60
Matching models with labels.

and then the teacher went to other pupils, having each point to one or more of these. Marge suggested coloring the face red. This was done, and six cubes with one face showing were found. Faye said that a table should be made of what was found. She was asked to complete the chart (Fig. 6-58) on the chalkboard as the answers were found. The procedure was continued. Twelve cubes with two faces showing and eight with three faces showing were found. The pupils gave reasons why no cubes were found with four, five, or six faces showing. With $6 + 12 + 8 = 26$, and 27 cubes in the stack, Ginny argued there should be one with no faces showing. When some pupils doubted this, the stack was opened and the conclusion was verified.

Here again, the answer to the problem was not the most important outcome from the lesson. Its value lay in the way the pupils attacked the problem by building a model, examining it, and coloring the cubes with one face showing to avoid errors in counting them, and the fact that they wanted to make a table in order to see the data they were collecting.

The pupils wanted to study more about cubes, and so Ms. Porter mimeographed a sheet of pictures (Fig. 6-59). Pupils were instructed to cut out each arrangement of squares and decide if the pattern could be folded to make a cube.

Various kinds of pyramids with triangular and square bases and prisms with bases of the same shape were studied in a similar manner; models of each were made by individual pupils.

Maintaining and Extending Skills and Concepts

Since the purposes for these lessons did not include any skills, no drill was provided in the usual sense. Ms. Porter did, however, furnish games designed to fix abilities to recognize and name various three-dimensional shapes and discern some of their characteristics.

In one game, circles were drawn with chalk on the floor and labeled, as shown in Fig. 6-60. The children stood in a ring around the circles. A number of models of space figures were placed on a desk. A pupil was asked to take one model and place it in the correct circle. If he was successful, he could choose the next player, and the game continued.

Many variations of this game were played, with circles labeled according to the number of faces of prisms (Fig. 6-61) or the number of vertices. It was suggested that the game be made more difficult by using a label such as "space figures with six faces and eight vertices." Some pupils played this game during lunch hour and on rainy days.

Application

The real application of this lesson was in pupils' invention of methods for solving problems. They used models to discover answers and then applied logical reasoning to show that their answers were correct. At the same time, they became more aware of the great number of geometric shapes in their environment. They made a collection of examples, such as a cereal box, an ice cream cone, a cylindrical medicine bottle, a tennis ball.

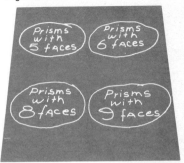

Figure 6-61

Some pupils found books on geometry in the library and read a number of them during free reading time. Other pupils with special interests made models of space figures at home. They described their models in words, and other pupils tried to reproduce the figures. Two examples of these were:

> Make a space figure with five sides; two sides are triangular and three are square.

> Start with a cube. Cut off a piece so that the figure has seven sides, fifteen edges, and eight vertices.

In planning the geometry activities for an elementary class the teacher keeps two basic ideas in mind. First, because pupils generally find these activities interesting, they help to enliven the entire program throughout the year. Second, the experiences are designed to make the pupils' later study of geometry more successful. Through well-chosen, interesting experiences, pupils explore the geometry of their environment, learn to recognize geometric figures and their properties, develop precise vocabulary and refine concepts, learn to use instruments, and learn to apply mathematical thinking in the geometric setting. In this study they extend their understanding of such familiar concepts as set and number, acquire new concepts, such as curve and congruence, and uncover procedures for exploration and discovery of new relationships.

EXPERIMENTS FOR PUPILS

From among the almost unlimited number of experiments that teachers use to help pupils learn about geometry, a few selected Activities are given here. They may be varied and adapted for introducing concepts, aiding discovery, providing practice, developing relationships, or, in general, enhancing mathematical process skills (mathematical thinking). A variation for Activity 1, for example, would be to have pupils look at buildings, bridges, and fences and find examples of parallel and perpendicular segments, of congruent figures, of angles, and so on.

ACTIVITY 1

Apparatus needed: magazines, scissors

Objective: To help pupils become more aware of geometry in their environment.

1. Look at a car. Make a list of all geometric figures such as segments, circles, and rectangles that you see. Find more examples on a truck or a house.
2. Cut pictures of geometric figures from magazines. Place the pictures under titles such as quadrilaterals, triangles, circles, and so on. Make a display on the bulletin board.

ACTIVITY 2

Apparatus needed: crayons

Objective: To practice making a conjecture about regions.

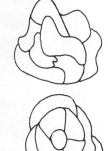

1. These are maps showing a number of countries. You are to color the countries. Here are the rules for coloring:

   (*a*) Use the fewest colors.

   (*b*) No two countries with a common boundary have the same color.

2. Draw some maps. Color, using the rules given above.
3. You and your partner draw some maps. Exchange and color them.
4. What is the fewest number of colors needed for all maps?
5. *Brainbuster:* Look up the famous "four color" problem in the library.

ACTIVITY 3

Objective: To refine concepts of closed curve and simple closed curve.

1. Which capital letters of the alphabet and which of the ten numerals are closed curves? Which are simple closed curves? Write your answers below. The letters *A* and *B* are done for you.

	Closed curve	Simple closed curve	Neither
Capital letters	B		A
Numerals			

2. Check your answers with those of a friend. If your answers

are not the same, decide who is correct.

3   The capital letters of the alphabet are separated into two sets. Discover the rule. Finish writing the letters.

First set	*A*	*EF*	*H*
Second set	*BCD*		*G*

B •

A •

ACTIVITY 4

Objective: To formulate hypotheses and generalizations.

1   How many lines through 2 points, *A* and *B*?
2   How many lines through 3 points, *C, D,* and *E*? Draw the lines.
3   Draw pictures to find how many lines through 4 points; through 5 points; through 6 points. Be sure no three points are on the same line. Write your answers on the table. Look for a pattern.
4   *Brainbuster:* Don't draw a picture. How many lines for 7 points? for 10 points?

D •

C •

E •

number of points	lines
2	1
3	
4	
5	
6	

ACTIVITY 5

Objective: To practice formulating hypotheses and generalizations.

1   Study the chart. Count the rays and angles. Fill in the blanks.
2   Draw the next picture using 6 rays. Fill in the chart.
3   Guess the number of angles for (*a*) 7 rays; (*b*) 8 rays. Check your answer by drawing a picture.
4   *Brainbuster:* Look for a pattern in your chart. How many angles for 10 rays? Don't draw a picture.
5   *Superbrainbuster:* How many angles for *n* rays?

Number of		
	rays	angles
	2	1
	3	3
	4	6
	5	10

ACTIVITY 6

Apparatus needed: ruler   *Objective:* To draw curves and appreciate their beauty.

1   Draw line segments *AA, BB, CC,* and so on. What do you see?
2   Draw another picture. Use more letters. What do you see?
3   Draw another picture with a different angle. How has your curve changed?
4   *Brainbuster:* Talk with your friend. Try to discover a way to do something similar with a circle.

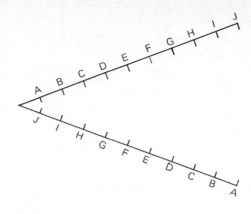

ACTIVITY 7

Apparatus needed: circular geoboard

Objective: To form geometric figures on a circular geoboard.

1 Make these figures on your circular geoboard: (*a*) a triangle with 2 congruent sides; (*b*) a triangle with no two sides congruent; (*c*) a rectangle; (*d*) a rhombus; (*e*) a trapezoid.

2 If possible, make the following polygons with all sides congruent: (*a*) 3 sides; (*b*) 4 sides; (*c*) 5 sides; (*d*) 6 sides; (*e*) the largest possible number of sides.

3 Which polygons (how many sides) with all sides congruent is it impossible to make?

ACTIVITY 8

Apparatus needed: wax paper

Objective: To fold wax paper triangular regions to form new figures.

1 Cut six triangular regions from your wax paper.

2 The picture shows two folds (dotted segments) to form four new triangles. Fold your triangular regions to make the figures: (*a*) one fold, two new triangles; (*b*) one fold for one new triangle and one quadrilateral; (*c*) two folds for two triangles and one quadrilateral.

3 Make up similiar wax-paper-folding problems. Give them to your friend to solve.

ACTIVITY 9

Apparatus needed: paper

Objective: To find examples of symmetry and congruence.

1 Make an airplane by folding paper.
2 Show your friend examples of symmetry and congruence in your airplane.
3 With your friend make a list of things you can see or think of that: (a) have symmetry; (b) are congruent.

ACTIVITY 10

Apparatus needed: drinking straws, scissors   *Objective:* To discover which three segments can and which three cannot form triangles.

1 Cut three straws for each length: 6 cm, 8 cm, 10 cm, 12 cm, 14 cm, 16 cm.
2 Choose 3 straws. Make some triangles. The picture shows a triangle 6 cm by 6 cm by 8 cm. List your triangles in the table. Try to find three straws from which you can't make a triangle.

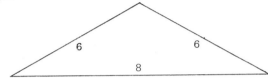

3 Tell your friend why you can't make some triangles.

ACTIVITY 11

Apparatus needed: pin, pencil, paper clip, straight edge   *Objective:* To invent a way to perform geometric constructions using only a pin, a paper clip, a pencil, and a straight edge.

1 Use only the apparatus given you, invent a way to: (a) draw a circle; (b) bisect an angle; (c) draw a triangle with all sides congruent.

QUESTIONS AND EXERCISES

1 What is meant by "The geometry program in the early grades is intuitive"?

2 Describe how the idea of a point may be introduced to pupils.

3 Discuss as you would with your fourth-grade class why the distinction between *line* and *line segment* should be made.

4 A boy in your fourth-grade class tells you that his father said that point Z is between points X and Y in the accompanying figure. Explain the meaning of *between,* illustrating with points that are and are not between X and Y.

$$x \bullet\!\!-\!\!\!\!-\!\!\!\!-\!\!\bullet y \quad {}^{\bullet z}$$

5 A teacher drew a picture of an angle on the

floor of the classroom. Pupils positioned themselves so they were on the angle bisector. What was the purpose of this?

6 A parent tells you when he went to school it was correct to speak of two equal segments. He wants to know why *congruence* has replaced *equal* in describing certain segments. What would you tell him?

7 Your class has studied parallel lines. What materials would you provide for each pupil in order to help make a definition of parallel line segments? Describe how you would have pupils use these materials.

8 A pupil asks you to explain the question "Why are two lines in the same plane if they intersect?" Prepare an answer, using concrete materials or pictures as needed.

9 One way to develop the ideas of geometric paths is to have the pupils play a game where the leader says, "I'm thinking of a geometric path in the classroom that is a straight path from the door to Jimmy's desk." A pupil then shows the path. Give some examples of statements like the one above for segments and nonstraight paths.

10 What purposes are served by having pupils perform experiments and organize their data in tables?

11 There are certain things that pupils cannot discover, such as the name $\overleftrightarrow{AB}$ for line AB. Name six other items associated with geometry that they cannot discover.

12 List properties of a triangular pyramid as was done for a prism. Summarize how you would conduct a lesson on the pyramid so that pupils might discover its properties.

13 How could you have pupils use tracing paper to determine intuitively the relative size of two angles?

14 *True* or *false*? Defend your answer. In the primary grades, pupils may be allowed to use words such as ball instead of sphere and box instead of rectangular prism.

15 *Brainbuster*: Draw a rectangular prism, a triangular prism, a triangular pyramid, and a rectangular pyramid. Each figure has a number of vertices v, edges e, and faces f. Make a table to show the number of each of these properties for each figure. Try to discover a formula that connects v, e, and f.

PROJECTS

1 Study a recent series of textbooks and teachers' manuals and answer the following about the geometry program: (a) What important topics and concepts are introduced at each grade level from one to six? (b) Describe some experiments that pupils perform with geometric figures. (c) Try to find statements that are vague or incorrect. (One example is: "A triangle is the union of three segments.") (d) To what extent is a distinction made between line and line segment? Between circle and circular region? If a distinction is made and then discontinued, what reasons are given for the change? (e) List examples of practice exercises. How do these differ from exercises about numbers? (f) What physical models are recommended for use by pupils?

2 Make a list of illustrations from the environ-

ment of circles, polygons, angles, and space figures, such as prisms, cones, and cylinders.

3 Demonstrate to the class the use of various materials in teaching geometric concepts. (Examples are wire loop and circular region of cardboard, basketball and baseball, triangle and parallelogram of wood strips with a single nail at each vertex, etc.)

4 You know how to copy a triangle with a compass and straight edge. Draw a quadrilateral. Invent two different ways to copy it using only these two instruments.

5 On pages 140, 150, and 151 are a number of questions and experiments. Complete each of these. Choose one of them and write it as an Activity Card to be given to a pupil to complete.

6 Write an experiment, the objective of which is to discover all possible intersections of two angles. What materials could be used? (You may wish to refer to the example of the intersection of two triangles in Chapter 2.)

7 The topic of symmetry was not mentioned in this chapter. Examine an elementary school mathematics series. Outline: (a) important ideas concerning symmetry for each grade, and (b) materials useful in the study.

8 On pages 160, 167, and 171 are questions of the reader. Investigate each and answer it. Describe to a friend your procedure for answering each.

Bibliography

1 Black, J.: "Geometry Alive in Primary Classrooms," *The Arithmetic Teacher*, vol. 14, pp. 90-93, Feb., 1967. Emphasizes teaching geometry in learning centers. Devoted to geometry.

2 Egsgard, J.:"Geometry All Around Us," *The Arithmetic Teacher*, vol. 16, pp. 437-445, Oct., 1969. Illustrates the geometrical nature of the environment.

3 Henderson, G. L. and C. P. Collier: "Geometric Activities for Later Childhood Education," *The Arithmetic Teacher*, vol. 20, pp. 444-453, Oct., 1973. Many illustrations of geometric activities that help pupils develop problem-solving abilities.

4 Ibe, M.: "Better Perception of Geometric Figures Through Folding and Cutting." *The Arithmetic Teacher*, vol. 17, pp. 583-586, Nov., 1970. Good example of the importance of physical experimentation.

5 Johnson, D. A., and W. H. Glenn: *Curves in Space*, McGraw-Hill, N.Y., 1963. Discussion of where curves are found in our environment.

6 Lulli, H.: "Polyhedra Constructions," *The Arithmetic Teacher*, vol. 19, 127-130, Feb., 1972. Explicit instructions for building several geometric models.

7 Ravielli, A.: *An Adventure in Geometry*, Viking Press, New York, 1957. Ideas from geometry made clear by pictures.

8 Skypek, D. H.: "Geometric Concepts in Grades 4-6," *The Arithmetic Teacher*, vol. 12, pp. 443-449, Oct. 1965. Discussion of concept development in geometry, based on Piaget's research and theory.

9 Walter, M.: "Some Mathematical Ideas Involved in the Mirror Cards," *The Arithmetic Teacher*, vol. 14, pp. 115-125, Feb., 1967. Fascinating discussion of experiences for children as they discover the idea of symmetry.

10 Williford, H.: "What Does Research Say About Geometry in the Elementary School," *The Arithmetic Teacher*, vol. 19, pp. 97-103, Feb., 1972. Affirms that many geometric ideas can be understood by young children.

7
FRACTIONAL NUMBERS

There are many everyday problems that are impossible to solve if only whole numbers are used. If three boys wish to share two apples equally, the result cannot be expressed as a whole number. Even a young child can solve the problem readily with a knife, but to express the answer mathematically demands using numbers other than whole numbers.

While adults normally know the set of numbers needed to solve the problem and know the answer, 2/3, frequently their logic is circular: "What do you get when you divide 2 by 3? The answer is 2/3. What is meant by 2/3? It means what you get when you divide 2 by 3." This reasoning is accepted on an immature level because practical experience gives a person confidence that such numbers exist, and operations with them conform to certain properties. Traditionally these numbers have been referred to as *fractions.* Presently in the elementary school, they are more commonly called *fractional numbers,* which are named by fractions such as 1/2, 4/5, 7/7, 18/5, 3/1, or 12/14.

Fractions have traditionally been a source of difficulty for both children and adults. Compared with the counting numbers, the historical development of a convenient notation was slow, and algorithms for computing with fractions were unwieldy. The fact that fractional numbers are recorded by naming a pair of whole numbers is only one of several sources of difficulty. There are many others: Each fractional number may be expressed in an infinite number of ways (2/3 = 4/6 = 6/9 = 8/12...); it is difficult to conceive of operating on a pair of numbers as though the pair were a single number. To be added and subtracted, fractional numbers must be expressed in the same denominator. The multiplication and division algorithms are difficult to rationalize. Furthermore, in application the same fractional number may be expressing a measure, a division, or a comparison situation.

None of these difficulties is insurmountable. To overcome them this chapter aids the teacher in:

● Maturing his knowledge of the concepts of fractional numbers and of the mathematical properties governing operations with them.

- Learning techniques for guiding pupils to discover concepts, understand algorithms, and maintain skills of operations with fractional numbers.
- Studying experiments through which the program with fractions can be individualized.

DIRECTING LEARNING OF FRACTIONAL NUMBERS

Some experiences for introducing fractions in the primary grades were described in Chapter 3. It was pointed out that motivation and mathematical understanding are most readily developed if pupils actually use fractional numbers in familiar situations. This emphasis should be continued in the middle grades, but there is increased attention to the mathematical properties of these numbers as the operations of addition and multiplication are introduced.

Extending Concepts

Pupils extend their concept of a fractional number as they manipulate materials, draw pictures, use number lines, and explore applications. A variety of experiences, each paralleled by appropriate symbolization, is necessary to accomplish this purpose. Following are two experiments through which pupils may discover the meaning of a fraction.

ACTIVITY I

Apparatus needed: graph paper, scissors   *Objective:* To form and compare regions representing 1/2, 1/3, 1/4, and 1/6.

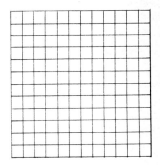

1   Cut out four square regions like this from your graph paper. Each region is a 1-region.
2   Cut a 1-region into two parts of the same size. Tell your partner how you know they are the same size. Write 1/2 on each part. The 1/2 means you have cut 1 into ___ parts of the same size and you are thinking of ___ of them.
3   Cut a 1-region into three parts of the same size. Write 1/3 on each part. Tell your partner what the 1 and the 3 in 1/3 mean.
4   Cut a 1-region into four parts of the same size. Write 1/4 on each. Tell your partner what the 1 and the 4 in 1/4 mean.
5   Cut a 1-region into six parts of the same size. What do you write on each? Tell your partner why your answer is correct.
6   *Brainbuster:* Which is larger—1/2, 1/3, 1/4, or 1/6? Tell your partner how you are sure you are right.

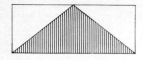

7 *Superbrainbuster:* Is the shaded part of this region half of the rectangle? Tell your partner how you can check your answer.

ACTIVITY II

Apparatus needed: 25-pin geoboard

Objective: To separate a given region representing 1 into parts of the same size.

1 Form each of these shapes on your geoboard. Think of each shape as 1. Use elastics so each shape is cut into four parts of the same size. Tell your partner why each part is 1/4.

2 Make a shape on your geoboard. Ask your partner to cut it into four parts of the same size.

3 *Brainbuster:* Put an elastic around the biggest square in your geoboard.

(*a*) Cut it into eight parts of the same size. The fraction for each is _____ .

(*b*) Cut it into sixteen parts of the same size. The fraction for each is _____ .

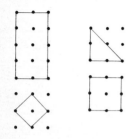

Figure 7-1
Shading regions to show ½.

Figure 7-2
Shading regions to picture fractions.

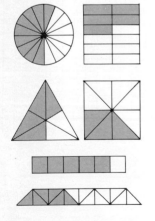

Following are some examples of other experiences for extending the concept of a fraction. Each is listed without detail. All can be adapted for group or individual instruction and can be used at different grade levels and for different purposes by shifting the emphasis. The pupil:

Cuts circular, rectangular, and square regions (each representing 1) in halves in various ways, as in Fig. 7-1. He labels each part 1/2. He decides in how many ways he might cut a given rectangular region in half.

Examines 1/2 inch and 1 inch and compares them by saying, "The inch is twice as long as the half-inch." He compares 1 centimeter to 2 centimeters, 1 kilogram to 2 kilograms, 1 meter to 2 meters and eventually sees that in each case the fraction 1/2 indicates a comparison in which one measure is twice the other. Similarly, he compares four rolls eaten to the twelve rolls in the package as 4/12 or 1/3; a 3-inch pencil to a 4-inch pencil as 3/4; the six blocks he has walked to the total distance of nine blocks as 6/9; ten books on one shelf to twenty on another as 10/20; five chairs at Jim's table to six at Bill's as 5/6.

Divides by 2 and finds one-half of a number, comparing answers to see that both processes yield the same result.

Draws pictures of regions separated into congruent parts. He shades a certain number of parts of each, as in Fig. 7-2. Thinking of the whole region as 1, he uses fractions to name the part shaded. He answers questions such as the following for each region: "Into how many congruent parts is it separated?" "How many parts are shaded?" "What fractional part of it is shaded?" "What fraction names the part unshaded?"

Discriminates between 2/3 as meaning two of three *congruent* parts of a whole and two of three parts of a whole. If each region in Fig. 7-3 measures 1, only in *b* is the measure of the shaded portion 2/3.

Illustrates the meaning of denominator as symbolizing the number of parts of the same size into which a whole is separated, and numerator as the number of those parts being considered.

Draws line segments with dots equally spaced. After some dots are labeled, as in Fig. 7-4*a*, *b*, and *c*, he labels others correctly. Describes how to find dots for 1/2, 3/2, 1/4, 2/4, or 3/4 on a number line.

Uses a number line to count: (*a*) by 1/4s, starting at 0; (*b*) by 3/4s, starting at 1/4; (*c*) backward by 2/4s, starting at 9/4.

Uses fractions to describe measures. He reasons from Fig. 7-5*a*, "If 1 is represented by the shaded region, then 5/2 is represented by the entire region." He reasons from Fig. 7-5*b*, "If 1 is represented by the shaded region, then 1/2 is represented by the unshaded region."

This list of concrete and pictorial experiences can be increased manyfold. As with other topics, the teacher should keep in mind his responsibility to guide pupils toward operation with symbols. During this development, materials and pictures are referred to often to develop or refresh concepts.

A mature understanding of the concepts expressed by fractions is a major outcome from the study of fractional numbers during the middle and upper grades. Their most common use in daily living is in communicating ideas. For example, from the newspaper, we find recovery is complete in three-fourths of cases of an illness that is diagnosed early; two-thirds of automobile accidents occur between sunset and sunrise; Pete Rose had one-half the hits his team secured off the opposing pitcher. Pupils must have experience in interpreting expressions from more mature social situations such as these. To this end they may search newspapers, magazines, reference books, texts from other subjects, and their daily experiences for applications. Bulletin board displays may be prepared, the class may discuss ideas suggested by fractions, and problems may be formulated and solved. Out of these experiences, the pupil learns to interpret situations described by fractions that he hears or reads and to express his own ideas and experiences with fractions.

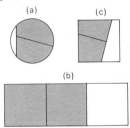

Figure 7-3
Only (b) shows 2/3.

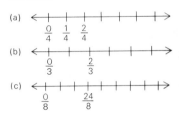

Figure 7-4
Labeling a number line to show fractions.

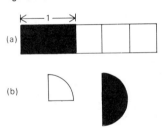

Figure 7-5

Figure 7-6
Common errors with fractions.

$$\frac{\cancel{6} + 8}{3 + \cancel{6}}$$

$$\frac{\cancel{10}^5 + \cancel{8}^3}{\cancel{3} + \cancel{2}}$$

$$\frac{\cancel{45}^2}{\cancel{27}}$$

Figure 7-7
Circular regions for showing relation-
ships.

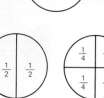

Different Names for the Same Number

Some strange errors made by pupils (Fig. 7-6) suggest the need for careful teaching of the idea of and skill in determining different names for the same fractional number. There is a need also to clarify the terms used at this stage of instruction since there is evidence that some nonmathematical terms hinder understanding and create situations which cause pupils to make errors.

A suitable vocabulary There is a good case for deleting some of the traditional language, such as *changing fractions, reduce,* and *cancel,* and substituting terms that are more accurately descriptive of the operations applied.

Changing fractions. Rather than *change,* it is more accurate to say *rename* or *express,* indicating that the change is merely to another name for the same number. Thus, "1/2 and 4/8 are different names for the same number," "1/2 is renamed 4/8," or "1/2 is expressed as 4/8" are preferred to "Change 1/2 to 4/8."

Reduce. This may imply a change in size. While possibly not quite so misleading as *changing,* it is preferable to use language that suggests the procedure to be used. In many texts we find, "6/12 is reduced to 1/2" and "15/10 is reduced to 3/2." Here, too, the procedure is one of renaming. If it is desired to express 6/12 as 1/2, the directions may be "Name 6/12 in *simplest form*" or, less often, "Name 6/12 in *lowest terms.*" There is a definite need for the idea of expressing in simplest form. To most people, for example, 2/3 is more comprehensible than 72/108, even though each names the same number.

Cancel. This word is not only unnecessary but also causes confusion. It should be avoided completely and replaced by *divide.*

Discovering different names for the same number After reviewing the meanings, vocabulary, and notation for fractional numbers and discussing some applications, Ms. Allison's class discovered the many names for the same fractional number through the following experiences.

1   First mimeographed sheets of circular regions were distributed to each pupil, who labeled the regions as shown in Fig. 7-7. The pupils cut out the regions and the individual parts of each. By placing the proper regions on top of others, they wrote numerals in each frame so that each mathematical sentence was true:

$$\frac{1}{2} = \frac{\square}{8} \qquad \frac{3}{4} = \frac{\triangle}{8} \qquad \frac{1}{3} = \frac{\square}{12} \qquad \frac{2}{3} = \frac{\square}{6} \qquad \frac{1}{2} = \frac{\triangledown}{12}$$

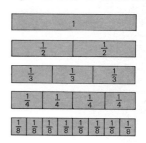

Figure 7-8
Rectangular cutouts for flannel board.

2   In a similar manner, the pupils experimented with rectangular cutouts (Fig. 7-8) on the flannel board.

3   The pupils then drew, labeled, and studied a number line and completed the empty columns in the chart started in Fig. 7-9. After the chart was completed, they examined their results to see if they could discover a pattern. Some of their remarks were: "1/2 must equal 2/4 because in 2/4 there are twice as many parts, but each part is only half as large;" "If we multiply numerator and denominator of 2/3 by the same factor, we get another name for 2/3. If the factor is 2, we get 4/6; if the factor is 4, we get 8/12." Through discussion, the class concluded that any fractional number could be renamed by multiplying the numerator and denominator by the same counting number. This was tested by expressing 1/4 as twelfths and 1/3 as sixths, using the rule and verifying the result with materials. Since the statement was correct in all cases tried, it was accepted.

Figure 7-9

Mathematical sentence	$\frac{1}{2} = \frac{\square}{4}$	$\frac{3}{2} = \frac{6}{\triangle}$
True mathematical sentence from using:		
Circular regions	$\frac{1}{2} = \frac{2}{4}$	
Rectangular regions		$\frac{3}{2} = \frac{6}{4}$
Number line		

4   Next pupils verified their rule by using a circular geoboard. The geoboard in Fig. 7-10 is arranged to show that 1/2 = 2/4 when the square represents 1.

Figure 7-10
Geoboard showing ½ = ²⁄₄.

5   Attention was then directed to the process of naming in *simplest form*. Using materials, pupils verified 4/8, 6/9, and 10/12 could be named, respectively, as 1/2, 2/3, and 5/6. The need for simplest form was discussed, and one pupil said, "It is easier to think about 2/3 than to think about 8/12 or 16/24 or 20/30."

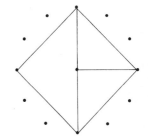

6   The question "What is simplest form?" was resolved as the pupils wrote sets of numerals. In set *A* each member represents 1/2, and in set *B* each member represents 3/4

$$A = \{1/2, \ 2/4, \ 3/6, \ 4/8, \ 5/10, \ldots \}$$
$$B = \{3/4, \ 6/8, \ 9/12, \ 12/16, \ldots \}$$

They agreed that 1/2 and 3/4 were the simplest names for members of sets *A* and *B*, respectively. Then they wrote other true mathematical sentences, such as the following:
    1/3 = 2/6 = 3/9 = 4/12 and 4/5 = 8/10 = 12/15 = 16/20.
They finally agreed that in simplest form the numerator and denominator of a fraction had only 1 as a common factor.

7   After reviewing the meaning of greatest common factor (g.c.f.), Ms. Allison had the pupils complete a chart like Fig. 7-11

Figure 7-11

Finding the simplest form of a fraction.

Fraction	$\frac{4}{10}$	$\frac{16}{24}$
Factors of numerator	1,2,4	1,2,4,8, 16
denominator	1,2,5,10	1,2,3,4,6 8,12,24
Factored expression using g.c.f.	$\frac{2 \times 2}{2 \times 5}$	$\frac{8 \times 2}{8 \times 3}$
Fraction in simplest form	$\frac{2}{5}$	$\frac{2}{3}$

for various fractions.

After pupils discovered the process for renaming fractions, they recognized that practice was necessary in order to increase facility. Textbook, workbook, and duplicated exercises provided material for practice until they could perform the process quickly and accurately. They returned to manipulating materials whenever difficulty was encountered in use of the algorithm.

Rufus invented an exercise which proved so interesting that other pupils wrote variations of it. His original exercise was:

Find a subset of three members from each set so each member names the same number

$$A = \{12/16, \ 16/24, \ 40/60, \ 72/108\}$$
$$B = \{ \ 9/16, \ 27/64, \ 3/8, \ 33/88, \ 21/56\}$$

The pupils next applied their new skill in solving word problems. They searched their environment for new uses of equal fractions and discovered applications such as:

In music, a quarter note is the same as two eighth notes; six eighth notes is the same as three quarter notes.

To secure 1/2 pound of candy, two 1/4 pound packages can be bought.

On the high school track, one half-mile and two quarter-miles are the same length.

Why was Ms. Allison's approach effective in producing understanding?

Through exploration, the pupils discovered the plausibility of properties and rules. Their discoveries did not *prove* a rule, but obtaining the same results using different materials gave them considerable confidence in it.

The pupils made many discoveries themselves. Ms. Allison planned the experiences and guided their efforts to solve problems, but the pupils had a purpose in manipulating regions, studying number lines, and drawing conclusions.

The pupils met the new situation at a low level of abstraction (using concrete materials) and progressed to a higher level of abstraction (using symbolic representation and generalizing their findings).

The pupils practiced because they understood the value of the skill.

The pupils learned to recognize situations where the process could be used.

Ms. Allison was able to ask appropriate questions that aided her in diagnosing and prescribing learning experiences.

Addition and Subtraction of Fractional Numbers

Addition and subtraction of fractional numbers require more sophisticated thinking than that used with whole numbers because pupils deal with pairs of numbers, renaming them so that the denominators are the same and "adding only numerators." Careful teaching is required to avoid errors, such as adding both numerators and denominators, as in the form

$$\frac{1}{2} + \frac{1}{3} = \frac{1+1}{2+3} = \frac{2}{5}$$

Difficulties may be avoided by effective selection of experiences whereby pupils name sums by the use of materials and adding fractional numbers is related to adding whole numbers, with pupils discovering the procedure.

Experimenting with addition and subtraction   The study of addition and subtraction is normally started with fractional numbers expressed with the same denominators. Here, the pupil learns to add or subtract numerators and place that sum or difference over the common denominator. A sequence of experiences that has proved effective in developing understanding and facility in adding fractional numbers is:

First, pupils manipulate materials to discover answers. For example, Joan's mother gave her 1/4 apple and later gave her 2/4 of the same apple. How much of the apple did she receive? The pupil uses parts of a circular region to represent the problem and writes the mathematical sentence as shown in Fig. 7-12.

Pupils draw number-line pictures. Joe's father said, "If you walk straight to school it is 3/8 mile. When you come home by way of Bob's place you walk 4/8 mile." How far does Joe walk if he goes directly to school and returns by way of Bob's house? Many pupils, remembering addition with whole numbers, suggest the number-line picture in Fig. 7-13a, and see 3/8 + 4/8 = 7/8 from the number line. An alternate picture for representing the addition is shown by line segments in Fig. 7-13b.

Next, pupils write the mathematical sentence for the shaded parts of rectangular regions in Fig. 7-14. The whole of each region represents 1.

Pupils may also count to find sums. For 3/4 + 2/4 they count by fourths from 3/4, "3 fourths, 4 fourths, 5 fourths." For 6/7 + 4/7 they count, "6 sevenths, 7 sevenths, 8 sevenths, 9 sevenths, 10 sevenths." This counting is comparable to the operation of adding two whole numbers, 3 + 2 in the first example and 6 + 4 in the second.

As a summary activity, pupils verify that the following are true mathematical sentences by the use of materials or pictures, or by counting.

Figure 7-12
Circular regions to show ¼ + 2/4.

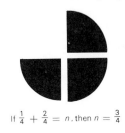

If $\frac{1}{4} + \frac{2}{4} = n$, then $n = \frac{3}{4}$

Figure 7-13
Number line pictures of 3/8 + 4/8 = n.

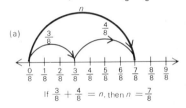

If $\frac{3}{8} + \frac{4}{8} = n$, then $n = \frac{7}{8}$

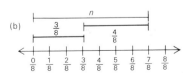

Figure 7-14
Using rectangular regions to objectify addition.

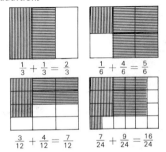

$$\frac{1}{3} + \frac{1}{3} = \frac{2}{3} \qquad \frac{1}{6} + \frac{4}{6} = \frac{5}{6}$$

$$\frac{3}{12} + \frac{4}{12} = \frac{7}{12} \qquad \frac{7}{24} + \frac{9}{24} = \frac{16}{24}$$

Figure 7-15

Intuitive justification for addition.

$\frac{3}{6}$	3 sixths	$\frac{7}{8}$	7 eighths
$+\frac{2}{6}$	2 sixths	$+\frac{6}{8}$	6 eighths
$\frac{5}{6}$	5 sixths	$\frac{13}{8}$	13 eighths

Figure 7-16

5 cm	2 liters
4 cm	7 liters
9 cm	9 liters

Figure 7-17

Forms for recording addition.

(a) $\frac{5}{8} + \frac{2}{8} = \frac{5 + 2}{8}$ (b) $\frac{5}{8}$

$\qquad = \frac{7}{8}$ $\frac{2}{8}$

$\qquad\qquad\qquad \frac{7}{8}$

Figure 7-18

Justifying steps for showing ¾ + ²⁄₄.

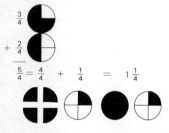

$\frac{3}{4}$

$+ \frac{2}{4}$

$\frac{5}{4} = \frac{4}{4} + \frac{1}{4} = 1\frac{1}{4}$

Figure 7-19

Names for terms in addition and subtraction.

Addition		Subtraction	
$\frac{3}{4} + \frac{7}{4} = \frac{10}{4}$		$\frac{10}{4} - \frac{7}{4} = \frac{3}{4}$	
$\frac{3}{4}$	addend	$\frac{10}{4}$	sum
$+ \frac{7}{4}$	addend	$- \frac{7}{4}$	addend
$\frac{10}{4}$	sum	$\frac{3}{4}$	addend

$$\frac{2}{6} + \frac{3}{6} = \frac{2 + 3}{6} \qquad \frac{4}{8} + \frac{2}{8} = \frac{4 + 2}{8} \qquad \frac{4}{3} + \frac{6}{3} = \frac{4 + 6}{3}$$

Estimation of answers is emphasized throughout the manipulation and discovery stage. Pupils answer questions such as the following for 1/3 + 1/3: "Why is the sum more than 1/2?" "Why is the sum less than 1?"

Pupils continually emphasize that numerators tell *how many*. For 3/6 + 2/6, they see they have three, each of size 1/6, and two more, each of size 1/6. For early instruction, then, many teachers instruct pupils to write additions in the form shown in Fig. 7-15. This helps them sense that numerators are added, and that denominators name "what is added." Although this is not a strict mathematical interpretation of addition, it does help avoid adding both numerators and denominators; it is analogous to adding a *number* of centimeters to a *number* of centimeters or a *number* of liters to a *number* of liters (Fig. 7-16).

After pupils have improvised methods for securing answers to a number of specific additions, they examine their results and conclude that in each the numerators are added to obtain the numerator of the sum, and the *common* denominator is the denominator of that sum. They apply this generalization to other examples and check the results where necessary by manipulating materials and drawing pictures. They learn to record their solutions in both the horizontal and vertical forms, as shown in Fig. 7-17. They continue to use the intermediate step, (5 + 2)/8 (Fig. 7-17a), until they have confidence in the procedure.

For additions with sums 1 or greater, the renaming in mixed form may or may not be emphasized at this time. For 3/4 + 2/4, an answer of 5/4 is considered correct, unless the pupil is given specific instructions to record the answer in mixed form. He may rename 5/4 as 1 1/4 using pictures to rationalize the procedure, as shown in Fig. 7-18. The renaming of 5/4 is not performed by dividing 5 by 4 at this stage. That shortcut is discovered later.

Subtraction of fractional numbers named by fractions with the same denominator is taught through a series of experiences similar to those for addition. Particular attention is given to the relation between addition and subtraction in the following ways as pupils:

Use the same words, *addend and sum,* for terms in an addition or subtraction, as shown in Fig. 7-19.

Illustrate 2/3 + 5/3 = 7/3 with a picture like 7-20. They see it also represents 7/3 – 5/3 = 2/3.

Think of 7/4 – 3/4 = *n* as finding the unknown addend *n* and write the same relationship as 7/4 = 3/4 + *n*.

Verify the commutative property for addition of fractional numbers by showing, for example, that 3/5 + 6/5 = 9/5 and 6/5 + 3/5 = 9/5. In a similar manner, they prove that the property does not hold for subtraction by a counterexample, such as 9/5 – 3/5 ≠ 3/5 – 9/5.

Write a mathematical sentence, such as 5/8 + 6/8 = n, in three other forms: 6/8 + 5/8 = n; n − 5/8 = 6/8; and n − 6/8 = 5/8.

More difficult additions and subtractions Pupils encounter difficulties as they attempt to improvise a solution to a familiar situation, such as: "Jim's mother made a pie and served one-half for lunch and one-third for midafternoon snacks. How much of the pie was served?" In attempting to improvise a solution, pupils find that methods previously used (Fig. 7-21) are not successful. In attempting to represent 1/2 + 1/3 with parts of circular regions or on a number line, they find they cannot name the answer immediately. Having represented 1/2 + 1/3, using rectangular and circular cutouts as shown in Fig. 7-22a and b, pupils are guided to search for a fractional part in terms of which the sum can be named. They discover that both 1/2 and 1/3 can be named as sixths, as shown in Fig. 7-22c and d, and that the sum is 5/6.

Developing a suitable algorithm   After several problems are solved experimentally, the results are recorded in the forms of Fig. 7-23, where 2/6, 3/6, and 5/6 are obtained by reference to the cutouts. Then results are examined for a symbolic approach without reference to materials. As pupils develop a method of solution by use of common denominators, they gain confidence through checking their steps by reference to manipulative materials or drawing pictures.

Finally, pupils are guided to discover that they can obtain a least common denominator (l.c.d.) by the following procedure: (1) Test the largest denominator to see if the other denominator is a factor of it. If so, it is the least common denominator. (2) If not, try successive multiples of the largest denominator until one is found that is divisible by the other denominator. For example, for 1/4 + 1/8, 8 is the l.c.d. because 4 divides 8. For 3/8 + 1/6, they try 8, 2 × 8 = 16, and 3 × 8 = 24, finding 24 to be the l.c.d. because it is the first multiple of 8 which is divisible by 6.

As they are learning the idea of l.c.d., pupils record all steps of their thinking, as shown in Fig. 7-24a. Shortcuts, including the vertical form (Fig. 7-24b), can be developed after pupils comprehend the basic ideas.

Subtraction, where the sum addend are expressed by fractions with different denominators, is learned through methods similar to those described for addition. At the algorithm level, subtraction differs from addition only in that numerators are subtracted rather than added.

Any addition or subtraction of fractional numbers can be performed by renaming both fractions with a denominator that is the

Figure 7-20
Picturing 2/3 + 5/3 = 7/3 or 7/3 − 5/3 = 2/3.

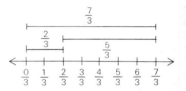

Figure 7-21
How can 1/2 + 1/3 be named as a fraction?

$$\tfrac{1}{2} + \tfrac{1}{3} = ?$$

$\tfrac{1}{2}$	1 half
$\tfrac{1}{3}$	1 third
$\tfrac{1}{?}$	?

Figure 7-22
Objectifying 1/2 + 1/3.

(a)

(b)
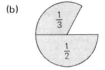

(c)
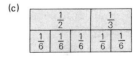

(d)

Figure 7-23
Ways of recording 1/2 + 1/3.

$$\frac{1}{2} + \frac{1}{3} = \frac{3}{6} + \frac{2}{6} = \frac{5}{6}$$

$$\frac{1}{2} = \frac{3}{6}$$
$$\frac{1}{3} = \frac{2}{6}$$
$$\phantom{\frac{1}{3}} \frac{5}{6}$$

Figure 7-24
Algorithms for ⅜ + ⅙.

(a)
$$\frac{3}{8} + \frac{1}{6} = \frac{3 \times 3}{8 \times 3} + \frac{1 \times 4}{6 \times 4}$$

$$= \frac{9}{24} + \frac{4}{24}$$

$$= \frac{13}{24}$$

(b)
$$\frac{3}{8} = \frac{9}{24}$$

$$\frac{1}{6} = \frac{4}{24}$$

$$\frac{13}{24}$$

(c)
$$\frac{3}{8} = \frac{3 \times 6}{8 \times 6} = \frac{18}{48}$$

$$\frac{1}{6} = \frac{1 \times 8}{6 \times 8} = \frac{8}{48}$$

$$\frac{26}{48}$$

Figure 7-25

Algorithm for adding numbers expressed in mixed form.

	Reason
$1\frac{1}{2} + 2\frac{3}{4} = \frac{3}{2} + \frac{11}{4}$	$1\frac{1}{2}$ and $2\frac{3}{4}$ renamed
$= \frac{6}{4} + \frac{11}{4}$	$\frac{3}{2} = \frac{6}{4}$
$= \frac{6 + 11}{4}$	$\frac{6}{4}$ and $\frac{11}{4}$ added
$= \frac{17}{4} = 4\frac{1}{4}$	$\frac{17}{4}$ expressed in mixed form

Figure 7-26

Objectifying 1½ + 2¾.

(a)

(b)

(c)

product of the two denominators. This denominator may not be the *least* common denominator, but it will always serve. Using this method, pupils may add 3/8 and 1/6 as shown in Fig. 7-24c. Many pupils may discover this approach, and slower pupils may continue to use it as a suitable level of achievement. There was a time when any denominator other than the l.c.d. was considered wrong. The l.c.d. does in general provide numbers with which computation it easier, but is may be questioned whether the additional time needed to find the l.c.d. is saved in the computation.

Systematic methods for finding the l.c.d. The intuitive procedure for finding the least common denominator is replaced by one or more of the following methods as pupils are able to comprehend and use them with confidence:

Rename each addend in many forms. In computing 3/8 + 1/6, the pupil may write the sets *A* and *B*, respectively, of names for 3/8 and 1/6.

$$A = \{3/8, \ 6/16, \ 9/24, \ 12/32, \ 15/40, \ 18/48, \ \ldots\}$$
$$B = \{1/6, \ 2/12, \ 3/18, \ 4/24, \ 5/30 \ 6/36, \ 7/42, \ 8/48, \ldots\}$$

Since any member of set *A* can replace 3/8 and any member of set *B* can replace 1/6, pupils may write

$$3/8 + 1/6 = 9/24 + 4/24 \ \text{or} \ 3/8 + 1/6 = 18/48 + 8/48$$

They try other multiples of 24, such as 72 and 96, and may write the set of common denominators {24,48,72,96,120,...} that can be used in adding 3/8 and 1/6. They further agree, through discussion, that the use fo 24, the l.c.d., requires simpler computation.

Apply common mutliple and least common multiple (l.c.m.). The concept of common multiple is often introduced when whole numbers are studied. This may be done in the following manner, illustrated for 6 and 8. *R* and *S* are the set of multiples of 6 and 8, respectively. Then

$$R = \{6,12,18,24,30,36,48,\ldots\}$$
$$S = \{8,16,24,32,40,48,\ldots\}$$

The members common to both sets are 24, 48, 72, 96, etc. This is symbolized as $R \cap S = \{24,48,72,96,\ldots\}$. The least number in $R \cap S$ is the l.c.m. of 6 and 8, and, therefore, it is the l.c.d. of fractions with denominations of 6 and 8.

Adding fractional numbers expressed in mixed form That fractional numbers named in mixed form can be added or subtracted without the necessity for new procedures is shown in Fig. 7-25 for 1 1/2 + 2 3/4. Sometimes it is convenient to perform the addition with the addends expressed in mixed form. For 1 1/2 + 2 3/4, pupils first use circular regions to represent both addends, as shown in Fig. 7-26a. The parts of circular regions are each pictured as fourths in Fig. 7-26b and combined in Fig. 7-26c. Now this representation is paralleled with symbols (Fig. 7-27). In early instruction, the 5/4 may be renamed as 4/4 + 1/4 as an intermediate step.

For 3 1/4 – 1 1/2, pupils represent the sum and known addend, as in Fig. 7-28a. In Fig. 7-28b, 1 1/2 is shown as 1 2/4, and so the computation is 3 1/4 – 1 2/4. In Fig. 7-28c, 3 1/4 is pictured as 2 5/4; the region representing 1 2/4 is removed, and the unknown addend is represented in Fig. 7-28d. Now these steps are paralleled with symbols (Fig. 7-29).

Multiplication of Fractional Numbers

In many texts, multiplication with factors expressed as fractions has been developed through consideration of many different cases: a whole number times a fractional number (3 × 4/5), a fractional number times a whole number (4/5 × 3), both factors fractional numbers (3/7 × 8/5), and many others. A less involved approach is to interrelate all these "types," stressing one operation (multiplication) and one algorithm for computation. Here also, emphasis is placed on relating the operation of multiplication of fractional numbers to operations on whole numbers. Attention is given to the fact that the set of fractional numbers under multiplication has every property observed for the set of whole numbers under multiplication. When this is done, results obtained mathematically agree with our intuitive expectations and with everyday experiences requiring multiplication of fractional numbers.

Multiplication of whole numbers was related to the union of a number of disjoint sets with the same number of members (three sets of four members each as a model for 3 × 4). That this relationship breaks down when the number system is extended to include fractional numbers is obvious because such numbers as 1/5, 3/2, or 7 2/11 cannot be associated with a number of members in a set. However, the idea of regarding multiplication as repeated addition—3 × 4 = 4 + 4 + 4, for example—may be used to help name some products when factors are fractional numbers.

Relating multiplication to addition Thinking of 4 × 1/2 as four 1/2s or 4 × 1 2/3 as four 1 2/3s seems to imply addition:

$$4 \times 1/2 = 1/2 + 1/2 + 1/2 + 1/2$$
$$4 \times 1|2/3 = 1\ 2/3 + 1\ 2/3 + 1\ 2/3 + 1\ 2/3$$

The pupil may read 4 × 1/2 as "four one-halves" or 4 × 1 2/3 as "four one and two-thirds" during early instruction.

Using significant situations Pupils relate a situation such as 3 one-quarter dollars to 3 × 1/4, or 4 one-half-hour time periods to 4 × 1/2, or five 2 5/8-inch lengths to 5 × 2 5/8. Answers to these

Figure 7-27
Algorithm for 1½ + 2¾.

$$1\tfrac{1}{2} = 1\tfrac{2}{4}$$
$$2\tfrac{3}{4} = 2\tfrac{3}{4}$$
$$3\tfrac{5}{4} = 3 + \left(\tfrac{4}{4} + \tfrac{1}{4}\right) = 4\tfrac{1}{4}$$

Figure 7-28
Objectifying 3¼ – 1½.

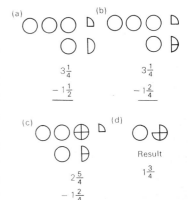

(a)

$$3\tfrac{1}{4}$$
$$-1\tfrac{1}{2}$$

(b)

$$3\tfrac{1}{4}$$
$$-1\tfrac{2}{4}$$

(c)

$$2\tfrac{5}{4}$$
$$-1\tfrac{2}{4}$$

(d)

Result

$$1\tfrac{3}{4}$$

Figure 7-29
Algorithm for 3¼ – 1½.

$$3\tfrac{1}{4} = 3\tfrac{1}{4} = 2\tfrac{5}{4}$$
$$1\tfrac{1}{2} = 1\tfrac{2}{4} = 1\tfrac{2}{4}$$
$$1\tfrac{3}{4}$$

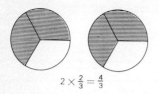

Figure 7-30

$$2 \times \frac{2}{3} = \frac{4}{3}$$

Figure 7-31

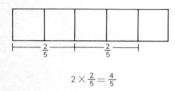

$$2 \times \frac{2}{5} = \frac{4}{5}$$

Figure 7-32

$$5 \times \frac{2}{3} = \frac{10}{3}$$

Figure 7-33
Pictures for multiplication with fractions.

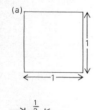

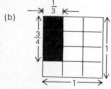

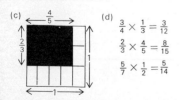

$$\frac{3}{4} \times \frac{1}{3} = \frac{3}{12}$$
$$\frac{2}{3} \times \frac{4}{5} = \frac{8}{15}$$
$$\frac{5}{7} \times \frac{1}{2} = \frac{5}{14}$$

problems are secured by using materials and interpreting the answer as a number of dollars, hours, and inches.

Using materials and pictures One pupil may represent 2 × 2/3 = 4/3 with circular regions (Fig. 7-30) on the flannel board, while other pupils represent it at their seats with their individual fractional cutouts. In a similar manner, 2 × 2/5 = 4/5 may be shown by means of rectangular regions (Fig. 7-31).

A number line is convenient for picturing a multiplication such as 5 × 2/3. Here the pupil marks off five segments, each measuring 2/3, and reads the product on the number line as 10/3 (Fig. 7-32). The foot ruler is a convenient device for discovering answers for products, such as 6 × 2/8, 5 × 2 1/4, or 3 × 7/2.

When the first factor is expressed as a fraction in multiplication, such as 1/2 × 5 or 2/3 × 6, the concept of repeated addition seems to be of no help. It can be explained, however, that we want the commutative property for multiplication to hold for fractional numbers just as it did for whole numbers. Then the pupil thinks of 1/2 × 5 as 5 × 1/2, and 2/3 × 6 as 6 × 2/3.

Developing an algorithm for multiplication Before undertaking the study of the product of two fractional numbers, the pupils review the idea of measure of area of a rectangular region.

For a rectangular region 4 cm long and 2 cm wide, for example, they determine the area as 8 square cm. The measure of the area is 8 (from 4 × 2) in square cm. After a number of similar experiences they generalize that the measure of the area of a rectangular region is the product of the measures of lengths of the adjacent sides.

Pupils now discover the rule for the product of two fractional numbers by the following procedures:

Drawing a rectangular region 1 by 1 (Fig. 7-33a). This is a unit square region whose measure of area is 1 (from 1 × 1).

Finding 3/4 × 1/3, for example, they draw and shade a rectangular region 3/4 by 1/3 (Fig. 7-33b), noting that its measure of area is 3/4 × 1/3. They reason that the shaded portion has 3 small rectangular regions and each has an area of 1/12 because the unit region has been separated into 12 parts of the same size. Therefore, the shaded portion is three-twelfths of the unit region and, therefore, its measure of area is 3/12. They see that the shaded region shows 3/4 × 1/3 = 3/12.

Finding 2/3 × 4/5 by similar procedures. As shown in Fig. 7-33c, the unit region is separated into 15 congruent regions; therefore each represents 1/15. Since there are eight of these shaded in the region 2/3 × 4/5, they write 2/3 × 4/5 = 8/15.

Examining the results, searching for a pattern. After studying a number of cases, as in Fig. 7-33d, they "guess": *The numerator of the product is the product of the numerators of the factors, and the denominator of the product is the product of the denominators of the factors.* They try this rule in other cases and find that it is correct.

Testing the rule for cases where the factors are greater than 1. They determine $3/2 \times 8/5$ by first drawing a unit rectangular region; from this picture they show $3/2 \times 8/5$, as in Fig. 7-34. They observe that the unit region is separated into 10 congruent regions, and, therefore, that the measure of each is 1/10. There are 24 of these in $8/5 \times 3/2$, so that $8/5 \times 3/2 = 24/10$. They check this by their rule:

$$\frac{8}{5} \times \frac{3}{2} = \frac{8 \times 3}{5 \times 2} = \frac{24}{10}$$

They find the product obtained by drawing a picture and the product obtained using their rule are the same.

Trying to generalize: *If a/b and c/d represent two fractional numbers,*

$$\frac{a}{b} \cdot \frac{c}{d} = \frac{a \cdot c}{b \cdot d}$$

They should recognize that this statement is a much simpler one than the word statement in the fourth item above.

Shortcut procedures The shortcut procedure, often called *canceling* or *reducing*, has been the cause of many unnecessary mistakes. These two terms are replaced by *divide*, and, when taught, shortcuts are justified not as tricks but through the mathematical ideas involved.

A procedure that has proved effective is the following. At first, pupils multiply and then express in simplest form, as in Fig. 7-35a. Next, they divide numerator and denominator by the common factor 2 at the step prior to performing the multiplication, as in Fig. 7-35b. At a later stage (Fig. 7-35c), they see the common factor 2 in the original expression and divide numerator and denominator by it as a shortcut for the procedure in Fig. 7-35a or b.

Working individually with pupils, the teacher can see that each child performs at his best level. Some pupils will continue to multiply and then rename in simplest form; others will be able to rename the factors before multiplying.

Using "of" (e.g., 1/2 of 8) The expressions "one-half of eight boys" and "two-thirds of a dozen" are commonly used and understood by adults and pupils alike. As early as grade three, the pupil has objectified 1/2 of 8 by separating eight boys into *two* sets with the same number in each and considering the number of boys in *one* of the sets. The pupil may also picture a situation such as 3/4 of 20 on a number line. He locates 0 and 20 and

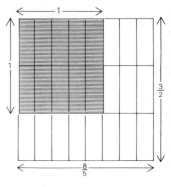

Figure 7-34
Picturing $\frac{3}{2} \times \frac{8}{5} = \frac{24}{10}$.

Figure 7-35
Three ways to find $\frac{3}{2} \times \frac{6}{5}$.

(a) $\dfrac{3}{2} \times \dfrac{6}{5} = \dfrac{3 \cdot 6}{2 \cdot 5} = \dfrac{18}{10} = \dfrac{9 \cdot 2}{5 \cdot 2} = \dfrac{9}{5}$

(b) $\dfrac{3}{2} \times \dfrac{6}{5} = \dfrac{3 \cdot \overset{3}{\cancel{6}}}{\cancel{2} \cdot 5} = \dfrac{9}{5}$

(c) $\dfrac{3}{\cancel{2}} \cdot \dfrac{\overset{3}{\cancel{6}}}{5} = \dfrac{9}{5}$

Figure 7-36
Finding ¾ of 20.

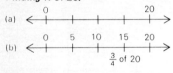

Figure 7-37
Finding ⅔ of 10.

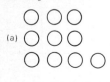

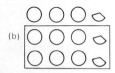

separates the segment into *four* congruent segments, as in Fig. 7-36*a*. Then he counts *three* of these, as in Fig. 7-36*b*, and finds 3/4 of 20 is 15.

Such intuitive ideas are extended as pupils improvise a solution for 2/3 of 10. They distribute ten circular regions into three piles of three each, with one left over, as pictured in Fig. 7-37*a*. The one "left over" is replaced by three thirds, and these thirds are distributed, giving the arrangements pictured in Fig. 7-37*b*. Now 2/3 of 10 is illustrated by two of these piles, or 6 2/3.

While the pupil is improvising solutions to statements such as 2/3 of 12, the generalization *"of* means *times"* should be avoided. It is ambiguous and, in fact, may be misunderstood since "3 of 4" is likely to be interpreted as a fraction rather than as 3 × 4. Attention should be directed to the whole question rather than merely to its wording.

At the same time, it is true that 3/4 of 20 and 3/4 of 20 have the same results. Pupils may verify this by determining 3/4 × 20 using models as described above, computing 3/4 × 20, and comparing answers. After examining a number of cases, the pupil may sense that a *fraction of a number*, such as 2/3 of 14, and a *fraction times a number,* such as 2/3 × 14, have the same result.

Reciprocals The concept of *reciprocal* can be introduced by having pupils find, by intelligent trial and error, the fractional numbers represented by *a/b, c/d,* and *e/f,* so that each of the following mathematical sentences is true:

$$\left(\frac{2}{1} \cdot \frac{a}{b}\right) = 1 \left(\frac{3}{4} \cdot \frac{c}{d}\right) = 1 \left(\frac{13}{7} \cdot \frac{e}{f}\right) = 1$$

Pupils quite readily find that (2/1)(1/2), (3/4)(4/3), and (13/7)(7/13) are all equal to 1. Here 1/2 is called the *reciprocal of* 2/1, or 2/1 may be called the reciprocal of 1/2. The product of any number and its reciprocal is 1.

Division of Fractional Numbers

Most everyday problems requiring division of fractional numbers can be performed without recourse to an algorithm for the operation. Problems where the computation could be completed by the use of fractions can usually be calculated with decimals or by changing units; for example, 3/5 ÷ 1/2 is computed as .5⟌.60; also, to find the number of 1/4-pound amounts in 4 pounds, 64 ÷ 4 is performed, after changing the weights from a number of pounds to a number of ounces.

Experience indicates that division with fractions can be a meaningful process, and that a minimum level of competence can be attained by most pupils. Every pupil can learn to secure answers for some of these divisions by means of number lines or other devices; all, or nearly all, can study with profit some intuitive procedures, while solutions using the idea of reciprocals is an appropriate level of attainment for others.

Studying division intuitively Divisions such as 1/4 ÷ 2 may be thought of as "one-fourth separated into two parts of the same size." This may be improvised by pupils as they replace a region whose measure is 1/4 by two regions, each with a measure 1/8 (Fig. 7-38a). Similarly, through experimentation 2/3 ÷ 4 is represented in Fig. 7-38b by replacing 2/3 with four parts of one-sixth each. On the flannel board, a similar procedure is used, as pictured for 1/3 ÷ 2 in Fig. 7-38c.

As the pupil examines the answers secured by the use of materials, he draws conclusions such as:

I picture dividing by two as finding one of two congruent parts. I also picture multiplying by 1/2 as finding one of two congruent parts. It seems that 1/4 ÷ 2 = 1/4 × 1/2.

I picture dividing by three as finding one of three congruent parts. I also picture multiplication by 1/3 as finding one of three congruent parts. It seems that 5/7 ÷ 3 = 5/7 × 1/3.

At this stage, some pupils may guess that dividing a number by 2 gives the same result as multiplying that number by the reciprocal of 2; that is, 3/5 ÷ 2 = 3/5 × 1/2. Similiar statements can be made about dividing by other counting numbers.

Answers to particular divisions may be obtained and the reasonableness of "multiplying by the reciprocal" established through manipulating materials. The result for 4 ÷ 2/3 can be obtained by repeatedly removing 2/3 cups from a measuring pitcher containing four cups of sand. The pupil can discover the answer to 2 ÷ 1/4 by counting the number of regions of area measure 1/4 that are needed to cover exactly a region of area measure 2 or by examining a foot ruler to determine the number of 1/4 inches in 2 inches.

Rationalizing a procedure whereby a solution can be obtained using symbols is initiated first with divisors that are unit fractions. For example, pupils use circular regions to find answers for 1 ÷ 1/2, 1 ÷ 1/3, and 1 ÷ 1/4 and record them as shown in Fig. 7-39. Next, they observe that the quotient in each case is 1 times the reciprocal of the divisor. Finally, they rationalize divisions, such as 6 ÷ 1/3, as follows: "1 ÷ 1/3 = 3/1; therefore, 6 ÷ 1/3 is 6 times as great or 6 × 3/1."

The same procedure can be followed for nonunit fractions, but the argument is somewhat more complex. Pupils examine strips

Figure 7-38
Picturing division by a counting number.

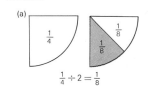

(a)

$$\tfrac{1}{4} \div 2 = \tfrac{1}{8}$$

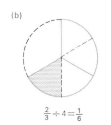

(b)

$$\tfrac{2}{3} \div 4 = \tfrac{1}{6}$$

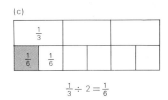

(c)

$$\tfrac{1}{3} \div 2 = \tfrac{1}{6}$$

Figure 7-39
1 divided by a unit fraction.

$$1 \div \tfrac{1}{2} = 2 = 1 \times \tfrac{2}{1}$$

$$1 \div \tfrac{1}{3} = 3 = 1 \times \tfrac{3}{1}$$

$$1 \div \tfrac{1}{4} = 4 = 1 \times \tfrac{4}{1}$$

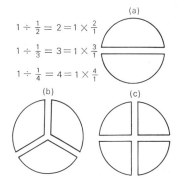

(a)

(b)   (c)

Figure 7-40

1 divided by a nonunit fraction.

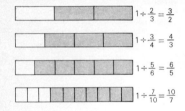

$1 \div \frac{2}{3} = \frac{3}{2}$

$1 \div \frac{3}{4} = \frac{4}{3}$

$1 \div \frac{5}{6} = \frac{6}{5}$

$1 \div \frac{7}{10} = \frac{10}{7}$

Figure 7-41

Details for showing that
$\frac{3}{7} \div \frac{2}{5} = \frac{3}{7} \times \frac{5}{2}.$

Computation

$\frac{3}{7} \div \frac{2}{5} = \left(\frac{3}{7} \times \frac{5}{2}\right) \div \left(\frac{2}{5} \times \frac{5}{2}\right)$

$= \left(\frac{3}{7} \times \frac{5}{2}\right) \div 1$

$= \frac{3}{7} \times \frac{5}{2}$

Figure 7-42

Expressing $\frac{3}{7} \div \frac{2}{5}$ as a division with whole numbers.

$\frac{3}{7} \div \frac{2}{5} = \left(\frac{3}{7} \times 35\right) \div \left(\frac{2}{5} \times 35\right)$

$= \left(3 \times 5\right) \div \left(2 \times 7\right)$

$= 15 \div 14$

$= \frac{15}{14}$

of paper, each representing 1 and marked as shown in Fig. 7-40. They see from the picture that in 1 there is one 2/3 and one-half of another 2/3. Now pupils have concluded that $1 \div 2/3 = 1\,1/2$ so that $1 \div 2/3 = 3/2$. Similarly, from the picture it seems that for $1 \div 7/10$, there is one 7/10 and 3/7 of another 7/10. Hence $1 \div 7/10 = 1\,3/7 = 10/7$. Pupils note that in each case the quotient is 1 times the reciprocal of the divisor. The pupils rationalize $4 \div 2/3$ as:

There are four times as many 2/3s in 4 as 2/3 in 1.

Since $1 \div 2/3 = 1 \times 3/2$, then $4 \div 2/3 = 4 \times 3/2$.

Pupils complete a number of such examples, then explain their methods to each other and to the class. They conclude their explanations with, "To divide by a fractional number, I multiply by its reciprocal."

An algorithm for dividing by a fractional number   Understanding the usual mathematical demonstration that $3/7 \div 2/5 = 3/7 \times 5/2$ depends on the idea, "if product and known factor are each multiplied by the same number (except 0), the unknown factor is unchanged." To review this idea, pupils should examine a number of mathematical sentences such as

$$12 \div 2 = (12 \times 3) \div (2 \times 3)$$

$$18 \div 3 = (18 \times 4) \div (3 \times 4)$$

$$24 \div 8 = (24 \times 5) \div (8 \times 5)$$

and show that they are true. For the first they may think, $12 \div 2 = 6$. In $(12 \times 3) \div (2 \times 3)$, the product 12 and known factor 2 are each multiplied by 3. Now $36 \div 6$ is also 6. Hence

$$12 \div 2 = (12 \times 3) \div (2 \times 3)$$

A demonstration that $3/7 \div 2/5 = 3/7 \times 5/2$ is shown in Fig. 7-41. One of the important ideas to be stressed is the reason 5/2 was chosen to multiply both 3/7 and 2/5. The reason is "So that the known factor will be 1." Capable pupils should be encouraged to use this procedure to show that $a/b \div c/d = (a/b)(d/c)$. An alternate way to divide with fractions is demonstrated in Fig. 7-42. Here, a common multiple of 7 and 5 is chosen to multiply both 3/7 and 2/5. This procedure avoids the *multiply-by-the-reciprocal* idea, and division with fractions is converted to one involving whole numbers in such a way that both divisions have the same quotient.

Other Experiments and Experiences for Pupils

Generalizations about products   Since their previous experience has been with whole numbers in which the product was generally greater than either factor, pupils frequently have difficulty understanding that multiplication with fractions can yield products less than either factor. To clarify this and develop added insight, a useful type of exercise is to have pupils complete a series of multiplications arranged as shown in Fig. 7-43. Through discussion, conclusions such as the following are formulated:

- If each factor is greater than 1, the product is greater than either.
- If one factor is unchanged and the other decreased, the product decreases.
- If one of two factors is less than 1, the product is less than the other factor.

Generalizations about quotients Because of their experience with division of whole numbers, pupils may wonder why the quotient may be greater than the dividend in some divisions with fractions. Through observation of the sequence of divisions shown in Fig. 7-44, pupils reason that halving the divisor with the dividend unchanged doubles the quotient. Thus, 24 and 48 from $12 \div 1/2$ and $12 \div 1/4$ are plausible. Generalizations such as those for multiplication in the preceding paragraph can be formulated through discussion of the relations observed in Fig. 7-44.

For more capable pupils, this pattern may be extended to solve exercises such as $12 \div 3/4$, and to check the algorithm. Since $12 \div 1/4 = 48$, the answer to $12 \div 3/4$ must be $48 \div 3$. This follows since the divisor is three times as great; therefore the quotient must be one-third as great. Now the *invert-and-multiply* procedure is justified, since

$$12 \div \frac{3}{4} = 48 \div 3 = \frac{48}{3} = \frac{12 \times 4}{3} = 12 \times \frac{4}{3}$$

Estimating answers When multiplying fractional numbers, special emphasis is given to approximation of products prior to computation. For example, consider Joe who was continually making mistakes, such as $3 \times 4/5 = 12/15$. He obviously multiplied both the numerator and the denominator of 4/5 by 3. This type of incorrect answer can be avoided through estimation. A few techniques for estimating are the following.

1/3 × 4. Some pupils may think, "1/4 of 4 is 1; therefore, the answer will be slightly more than 1 since 1/3 of 4 is greater than 1/4 of 4." Others may be able to establish bounds between which correct answers will fall. For example, since 1/2 of 4 = 2 and 1/4 of 4 = 1, the correct product will be between 1 and 2 but closer to 1. Still others may approximate, "1/3 of 3 is 1; therefore, 1/3 of 4 is slightly more than 1." There are numerous other possibilities, but a workable principle in estimating is to estimate the factors

Figure 7-43
When is the product less than the first factor?

$4 \times 8 =$	$6 \times 27 =$
$4 \times 4 =$	$6 \times 9 =$
$4 \times 2 =$	$6 \times 3 =$
$4 \times 1 =$	$6 \times 1 =$
$4 \times \frac{1}{2} =$	$6 \times \frac{1}{3} =$
$4 \times \frac{1}{4} =$	$6 \times \frac{1}{9} =$

Figure 7-44
When is the quotient greater than the dividend?

$$12 \div 4 = 3$$
$$12 \div 2 = 6$$
$$12 \div 1 = 12$$
$$12 \div \frac{1}{2} = 24$$
$$12 \div \frac{1}{4} = 48$$

Figure 7-45

Applying the distributive property.

$$\frac{2}{7} + \frac{4}{7} = \left(2 \times \frac{1}{7}\right) + \left(4 \times \frac{1}{7}\right) \text{ One meaning of a fraction}$$

$$= \frac{1}{7}(2 + 4) \text{ Distributive property applied}$$

$$= \frac{6}{7}$$

Figure 7-46

Algorithm and picture for $2\frac{1}{3} \times 3\frac{1}{4}$.

$$3\frac{1}{4}$$
$$\times\ 2\frac{1}{3}$$

$$\frac{1}{12} = \frac{1}{4} \times \frac{1}{3} \quad A$$
$$1 = \frac{1}{3} \times 3 \quad B$$
$$\frac{1}{2} = 2 \times \frac{1}{4} \quad C$$
$$6 = 2 \times 3 \quad D$$
$$7\frac{7}{12} = 2\frac{1}{3} \times 3\frac{1}{4}$$

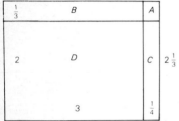

Figure 7-47

Applying the distributive property twice.

$$2\frac{1}{3} \times 3\frac{1}{4} = \left(2 + \frac{1}{3}\right)\left(3 + \frac{1}{4}\right) \quad \text{Distributive property applied}$$
$$= 2\left(3 + \frac{1}{4}\right) + \frac{1}{3}\left(3 + \frac{1}{4}\right)$$
$$= \left(2 \times 3\right) + \left(2 \times \frac{1}{4}\right) + \left(\frac{1}{3} \times 3\right) + \left(\frac{1}{3} \times \frac{1}{4}\right)$$

as numbers suitable for mental computation. It should be remembered that even rough approximations help to avoid mistakes such as that made by Joe in the example above.

2 1/3 × 3 1/4. Think, "2 × 3 = 6; the answer is slightly greater than 6, possibly 7, because in the estimating each factor has been decreased." From another point of view, an estimation may be 7 1/2, from 2 1/2 × 3. Here the 2 1/3 is increased slightly to 2 1/2, and the 3 1/4 decreased slightly to 3 to yield 7 1/2 as the estimate. Approximations will not prevent small errors, such as omitting the multiplication of 1/3 × 1/4 when 2 1/3 × 3 1/4 is performed in the vertical form, but they will help to avoid the bizarre results that are so frequently accepted without question.

Studying properties The properties of the fractional numbers under the various operations have not been discussed here as completely as was done for whole numbers. They are, however, equally important. The variety of experiences suggested in the chapters on whole numbers can be adapted for use with the fractional numbers. Some specific applications of the properties are worth noting.

For early instruction in adding fractional numbers, arguments were primarily made from pictures. The use of the distributive property and the meaning of a fraction are used, as shown in Fig. 7-45, to demonstrate adding fractional numbers without any reference to physical models. This may be thought of as an abstract justification of the rule for adding fractional numbers.

Sometimes it may be desirable to use a vertical algorithm for multiplication of fractional numbers expressed in mixed form. Frequently, this algorithm is omitted or reserved for use with fast learners. The algorithm for 2/3 × 3 1/4, together with the graphic representation, is shown in Fig. 7-46.

As pupils study the multiplication recorded in the horizontal form shown in Fig. 7-47, they find that the distributive property must be applied twice.

Pupils may study a series of steps, such as in Fig. 7-48, showing 2/3 + 4/5 = 4/5 + 2/3. They supply the reason for each step.

Studying patterns As pupils study a set of related expressions, as in Fig. 7-49, they have opportunities to discover patterns and draw conclusions. In Fig. 7-49c, for example, many pupils will recognize that "1 divided by a unit fraction is the denominator of that fraction."

The best order and level for introducing different properties and operations with fractions still depends in large measure upon the individual class and teacher. Each teacher should try various approaches, such as those suggested, in this chapter. Only through this kind of classroom experimentation can the most effective procedures be found.

RETEACHING THE SYMBOLISM OF FRACTIONS

Middle and upper grade and even high school pupils often make bizarre mistakes with fractions. In a standardized test given recently to eighth-grade pupils, one exercise was $1/2 + 1/4 = ?$ with a choice of four answers, one of which was correct. Only about 20% of the pupils gave the correct answer. While no generalization that this is truly typical is possible from this one example, most teachers can testify to less than adequate learning of concepts and skills with fractions by a significant number of pupils.

Teachers faced with this problem must isolate specific difficulties for each pupil and plan an organized sequential series of learning experiences. In many cases, difficulties will be diagnosed as lack of understanding of the symbolism of fractions. When such a diagnosis is made, experiences in the mathematics laboratory should be prescribed so the pupil can relate a physical model of a fraction to the symbol for that model. We have already seen several experiments that further attainment of this important objective. Six more are given here. The imaginative teacher will choose those experiments that are needed by specific pupils or groups of pupils and provide as many variations of each activity as are necessary. It should be remembered that this is a sample set of activities only.

Figure 7-48
Justifying commutativity for addition with fractions.

$$\frac{2}{3} + \frac{4}{5} = \frac{10}{15} + \frac{12}{15}$$
$$= \frac{10 + 12}{15}$$
$$= \frac{12 + 10}{15}$$
$$= \frac{12}{15} + \frac{10}{15}$$
$$= \frac{4}{5} + \frac{2}{3}$$

Figure 7-49
Sets of related expressions.

(a) $2 \div \frac{1}{3} =$ (b) $\blacktriangle \div \frac{1}{5} =$ (c) $1 \div \frac{1}{3} =$

$3 \div \frac{1}{3} =$ $\blacktriangle \div \frac{1}{6} =$ $1 \div \frac{1}{4} =$

$4 \div \frac{1}{3} =$ $\blacktriangle \div \frac{1}{17} =$ $1 \div \frac{1}{5} =$

$\blacktriangle \div \frac{1}{3} =$ $\blacktriangle \div \frac{1}{\blacktriangle} =$ $1 \div \frac{1}{\blacktriangle} =$

ACTIVITY III

Apparatus needed: scissors, 4 strips of paper each about 20 cm long

Objective: To show concretely the meaning of numerator and denominator of a fraction.

1   Each strip of paper is 1 unit.

(*a*)   Fold one strip into two parts of the same size. Write 1/2 on each part. Tell your partner what the 1 and the 2 in 1/2 mean.

(*b*)   Fold another strip into four parts of the same size. Write 1/4 on each part. Tell your partner what the 1 and 4 in 1/4 mean.

(*c*)   Fold another strip into eight parts of the same size. Write 1/8 on each part. Tell your partner what the 1 and 8 in 1/8 mean.

(d) Cut each strip on its folds.

2 Arrange your strips to show which is larger:
(a) 1/2 or 1/4   (b) 1/8 or 1/4

3 Put your strips together to show:
(a) 2/4 (2 pieces each 1/4)   (b) 3/8   (c) 3/4

4 *Brainbuster:* Put your strips together to show a strip.
(a) 1 1/2 times as long as the 1-unit strip.
(b) 6/8 as long as the 1-unit strip.
(c) 1 1/4 times as long as the 1-unit strip.

ACTIVITY IV

Objective: To show that 1/2 can be used to name regions of different size.

1 How many squares?
2 How many squares?
3 Are there the same number of squares in the first picture as in the second? In which were the squares larger?
4 This circle is cut in 2 parts of the same size. On each part write its fraction.
5 This circle is cut into 2 parts of the same size. On each part write its fraction.
6 Tell your partner why you wrote 1/2 on each part in both circles.
7 The part named 1/2 in Ex. 4 is larger than the part named 1/2 in Ex. 5. Tell your partner how two parts of different size can have the same name of 1/2.

ACTIVITY V

Objective: To show equal fractions with regions.

1 This square region is 1 unit. Cut it out. Each triangular region is the same size. Write the fraction for each triangular region on it. Cut out each triangular region.
2 Use your cutouts to explain to your partner that:
(a) 1/2 of the square region is the same as 4/8 of it.
(b) 1/4 of the square region is the same as 2/8 of it.
(c) The whole square is the same as 4/4 of it.

ACTIVITY VI

Apparatus needed: scissors

Objective: To compare fractions using concrete models for them.

1 Make copies of these strips.

2 To compare 1/4 and 1/3 you could do this:

1 unit

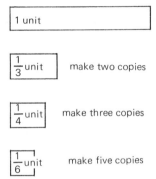 make two copies

make three copies

make five copies

You see that 1/3 is greater than 1/4. Use your strips to com-. pare: (*a*) 1/3 and 1/6; (*b*) 1/4 and 1/6.

3 To compare 2/3 and 3/4 you could do this:

You see that 3/4 is larger than 2/3. Use your strips to compare:
(*a*) 2/3 and 5/6; (*b*) 3/4 and 5/6; (*c*) 3/4 and 4/6.

ACTIVITY VII

Apparatus needed: strips from Activity IV

Objective: To picture additions on a number line.

1 You can place your strips on this number line to show that 1/3 + 1/4 = 7/12. Place your strips on the number line to find the sums.
(*a*) 1/6 + 1/4 =   (*b*) 1/3 + 1/6 =   (*c*) 2/3 + 2/4 =   (*d*) 1/3 + 1/2 + 1/4 =

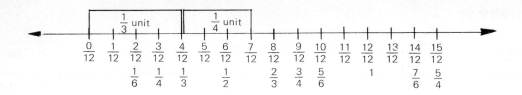

ACTIVITY VIII

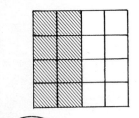

Objective: To picture and write the corresponding symbols for multiplication with fractions.

Study the pictures and fill in the blanks:

1   One half of 16 squares is _____ squares.

    $1/2 \times 16 =$ $16 \times 1/2 =$

2   One half of \$2 is _____ dollars.

    $1/2 \times 2 =$ $2 \times 1/2 =$

3   One half of 60 minutes is _____ minutes.

    $1/2 \times 60 =$ $60 \times 1/2 =$

4   One half of 12 eggs is _____ eggs.

    $1/2 \times 12 =$ $12 \times 1/2 =$

5   One half of a half hour is _____ hour.

    $1/2 \times 1/2 =$

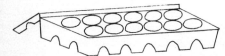

EXPERIMENTS FOR PUPILS

Here and on the following pages are more experiments designed to promote learning of concepts and skills with fractions.

For each Activity there are many adaptations and extensions. In Activity 1, for example, if half an egg carton is used, fractions with a denominator of 6 may be studied, or if two egg cartons are joined, fractions with a denominator of 24 may be shown.

ACTIVITY 1

Apparatus needed: egg carton and marbles

Objective: To illustrate fractions using an egg carton and marbles.

There is one rule for this game: Only one marble can be placed in each space.

1   Put in one marble. What fraction of the carton is filled?

2   Put in two marbles. What fraction of the carton is filled?

3   Keep going until all spaces are filled. Write your fractions here:

4   How many fractions with a denominator of 12 do you have?

5   Write all fractions in simplest form.

ACTIVITY 2

Apparatus needed: egg carton and marbles

Objective: To find the sum of two fractions using an egg carton and marbles.

There is one rule for this game: Only one marble can be placed in each space.

1   Fill one-half the spaces with marbles. Then fill one-fourth of the spaces. What fraction of all the spaces is filled? So $1/2 + 1/4 =$

2   Use the egg carton and marbles to find the answers.

    (a) $1/4 + 1/3 =$ (c) $2/3 + 1/4 =$ (e) $1/4 + 5/12 =$
    (b) $1/2 + 1/3 =$ (d) $1/12 + 3/4 =$ (f) $1/2 + 1/12 =$

ACTIVITY 3

Apparatus needed: 6 straws and scissors

Objective: To use straw and parts of straws to illustrate fractions equal to 1.

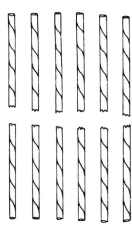

1   Cut each straw in half. Lay them out as shown. We can say that:

      1 straw equals 2 halves or $1 = 2/2$

      2 straws equals 4 halves or $2 = 4/2$

2   Show the following with your straws. Then fill in the blanks.

    3 straws equals ____ halves or $3 = \dfrac{}{2}$

    4 straws equals ____ halves or $4 = \dfrac{}{2}$

    5 straws equals ____ halves or $5 =$

    6 straws equals ____ halves or $6 =$

3 Cut each half straw in half again. Half of a half equals one-fourth. Show each of the following with your straws. Fill in the blanks.

1 straw equals 4 fourths or 1 = 4/4

2 straws equals ____ fourths or $2 = \dfrac{}{4}$

3 straws equals ____ fourths or $3 = \dfrac{}{4}$

4 straws equals ____ fourths or 4 =

5 straws equals ____ fourths or 5 =

6 straws equals ____ fourths or 6 =

4 Write four more equations like this:
   1 = 3/3   2 = 6/3

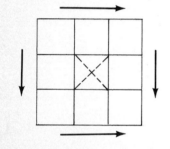

ACTIVITY 4

Objective: To find experimentally 1 as the sum of three fractions in four ways.

1 Cut out the 8 regions with fractions on them.

2 Put one fraction on each square on this figure so the sum is 1 in each of four ways.

ACTIVITY 5

Objective: To find experimentally a number expressed as the sum of three fractions in four ways.

1 Cut out the 8 regions with fractions on them.

2 Put one fraction on each square in this figure so the sum is the same in four ways.

ACTIVITY 6

Objective: To practice adding fractions.

1 Below is a ruler to find the number for your name. Write the fraction for each letter, *B, C, E, F,* and so on.

2   The number for MARY is

        M   A   R   Y

        3 +   0 + 4 1/4 + 6 = 13 1/4

3   What is the number for your name?

4   What is the number for each of these names?

    (*a*) PAUL   (*c*) ROBERT

    (*b*) ELLEN   (*d*) MARIA

ACTIVITY 7

Apparatus needed: geoboard   *Objective:* To show that, given a certain region as 1, one-half can be represented by regions of many different shapes.

1   Form this square on your geoboard. Let this region be called 1. Use an elastic to separate it into two parts each 1/2. Do it in two different ways.

2   Form this rectangle. Call this region 1. The shaded and unshaded regions can each be called 1/2. Find 3 other ways to separate it into two parts each 1/2.

3   Find many ways to separate each of these shapes into two parts each 1/2.

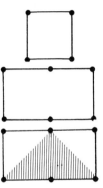

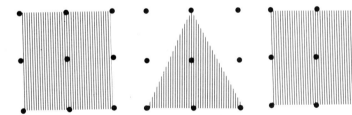

ACTIVITY 8

Apparatus needed: tangram pieces   *Objective:* To determine the number describing the size of a region given the size of another region.

    Place your tangram pieces on one another to find answers. (See page 52 for identification of tangram pieces as A,B,C,D,E,F,G.)

1   Suppose piece *D* is 1. What is the number for

    (*a*) piece *F?*   (*b*) piece *G?*

(a)

A	B	C	D	E	F	G
					2	
					3	
					5	

(b)

A	B	C	D	E	F	G
					1/2	
					1/3	
					1/4	

(c) piece *C?*　　　　　(d) piece *A?*

2　Suppose piece *A* is 1. What is the number for

(a) piece *G?*　　　　　(c) piece *D?*

(b) piece *C?*　　　　　(d) piece *F?*

3.　In each row of the charts the number for piece *F* is given. What is the number for each other piece in the row?

ACTIVITY 9

Objective: To write fractions as the sum of unit fractions.

1　The ancient Egyptians used fractions with numerators of 1. These are called unit fractions. 3/4 is expressed as 1/2 + 1/4 and 5/12 as 1/3 + 1/12.

2　Write as the sum of two unit fractions.

(a) 2/3 = ____ + ____　　　　(b) 7/12 = ____ + ____

3　Write as the sum of three unit fractions.

(a) 5/12 = ____ + ____ + ____　(b) 7/8 = ____ + ____ + ____

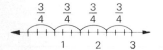

ACTIVITY 10

Objective: To find equivalent fractions.

Cut out the squares. Fit them together so that the edges that touch name the same number.

ACTIVITY 11

Objective: To read divisions with fractions meaningfully and to draw number line pictures of them.

1　Divisions are easier if you read them like this: 3 ÷ 3/4 is "How many 3/4s in 3." Then you can mark off on a number line as shown to get the answer of 4.

2　Fill in the blanks. Use the number line to get the answer if you need it.

(a) 2 ÷ 1/4 means how many ____ in ____. 2 ÷ 1/4 =

(b) 5 ÷ 5/4 means how many ____ in ____. 5 ÷ 5/4 =

(c) 4 ÷ 2/4 means how many ____ in ____. 4 ÷ 2/4 =

ACTIVITY 12

Objective: To discover a procedure for showing that two fractions are equal.

1 Find the products of the numbers:

(a) $\dfrac{2}{4}$ $\dfrac{3}{6}$ $2 \times 6 =$ $4 \times 3 =$ Is $\dfrac{2}{4} = \dfrac{3}{6}$?

(b) $\dfrac{1}{2}$ $\dfrac{5}{10}$ $1 \times 10 =$ $2 \times 5 =$ Is $\dfrac{1}{2} = \dfrac{5}{10}$?

(c) $\dfrac{4}{8}$ $\dfrac{2}{4}$ $4 \times 4 =$ $8 \times 2 =$ Is $\dfrac{4}{8} = \dfrac{2}{4}$?

(d) $\dfrac{2}{3}$ $\dfrac{6}{9}$ $2 \times 9 =$ $3 \times 6 =$ Is $\dfrac{2}{3} = \dfrac{6}{9}$?

2 (a) Is $\dfrac{3}{4} = \dfrac{6}{8}$? $3 \times 8 =$ $4 \times 6 =$ Is $3 \times 8 = 4 \times 6$?

(b) Is $\dfrac{2}{5} = \dfrac{6}{15}$? $2 \times 15 =$ $5 \times 6 =$ Is $2 \times 15 = 5 \times 6$?

(c) Is $\dfrac{3}{4} = \dfrac{9}{12}$? $3 \times 12 =$ $4 \times 9 =$ Is $3 \times 12 = 4 \times 9$?

3 Fill in the blanks.

(a) Because $\dfrac{1}{2} = \dfrac{4}{8}$ $1 \times \underline{\quad} = 2 \times \underline{\quad}$

(b) Because $\dfrac{2}{3} = \dfrac{4}{6}$ $\underline{\quad} \times 6 = \underline{\quad} \times 4$

(c) Because $\dfrac{2}{4} = \dfrac{8}{16}$ $\underline{\quad} \times \underline{\quad} = \underline{\quad} \times \underline{\quad}$

QUESTIONS AND EXERCISES

1 What are some sources of difficulty that pupils experience in learning fractional numbers?

2 Illustrate how to represent 3/4 by a rectangular region; by a point on a number line; by a comparison of the numbers of members of two sets; by the measure of length of a line segment.

3 Your class has studied unit fractions, such as 1/2, 1/3, 1/4, and so on. You will now introduce fractions with numerators of 2 or greater, such as 2/3 and 3/4. List some experiences you would prepare for your pupils.

4 A pupil shows you a rectangular region about the size of a postage stamp: He asks what fraction it represents. Answer him.

5 What are experiences with concrete materials through which pupils learn different names for the same fractional number?

6 "Is one-fourth or one-half closer to one-third?" If one of your pupils in a fifth-grade class asked you this question, what are several ways that you could help him discover the answer?

7 A pupil has circular regions representing 2/3 and 1/4 and others representing unit fractions. How may he name 2/3 + 1/4 by experi-

menting with the regions.

8 Explain what you would like your pupils to know about how to find a least common denominator by naming sets of multiples of the denominators of the two fractional numbers.

9 Some of your pupils consistently are adding denominators as well as numerators. That is, they are obtaining

$$\frac{3+2}{4+4}$$

for 3/4 + 2/4. What experiences would you provide for them?

10 Describe experiences you would provide for your pupils when studying multiplications with fractions prior to introducing the rule for multiplying?

11 In what ways may a pupil improvise the solution for 4 X 2/3?

12 Show how to picture the product by means of rectangular regions for the following: (a) 2/3 X 3/4; (b) 3/2 X 5/4.

13 A boy in your class missed the following exercises in a test: 3 X 4/5 = ?; 4 X 1/3 = ?; 5 X 2/3 = ?. His answers were 12/15, 4/12, and 10/15. Would you expect him to make the same mistakes if he were given similar exercises the next day? Describe experiences to help him recognize and correct his mistakes.

14 List intuitive procedures for studying 1/2 ÷ 3.

15 Describe how to show the following: (a) 1½ ÷ 3 using a clock face; (b) 6 ÷ 2/3 on a number line; (c) 3/4 ÷ 2 with rectangular regions.

16 *Brainbuster*: A quick general procedure to "reduce" 16/64 and 26/65 to 1/4 and 2/5, respectively, is 1̸6̸/6̸4 = 1/4 and 2̸6̸/6̸5 = 2/5. There are only two other examples like this, with two-place numerals for both numerator and denominator. What are they? (*Hint*: Try numerals with 9.)

PROJECTS

1 Look through a recent series of textbooks and teacher's manuals and answer the following concerning fractions: (a) List the major topics introduced at each grade one to six. (b) Describe the concrete aids that are suggested. (c) List activities that are suggested for the mathematics laboratory. (d) What concepts or algorithms are presented in a way to aid discovery by the pupil.

2 Demonstrate how each of the following is objectified: (a) The common denominator for 1/4 + 1/8 and 1/2 + 1/3, using cutouts of rectangular regions on a flannel board. (b) The subtraction 3/4 – 1/2, using circular regions. (c) The equality 2/8 = 1/4, using a linear scale or ruler. (d) The addition 2 3/4 + 1 5/8 and the subtraction 3 1/4 – 1 1/2 using circular regions. (e) The multiplication 4 X 2/3, using a number line. (f) The division 6 ÷ 3/4, using a number line.

3 Study the Ms. Allison example on pages 166-168. Write experiments for pupils for which the mathematics laboratory is the best method of accomplishing the objective.

4 Often it is stated that topics, when retaught at a higher grade level, are presented in a more mature and abstract manner. Choose a topic, such as addition, multiplication, or division of fractional numbers. Outline the experiences for pupils at the grade level where it is introduced. Compare this to the experiences provided in later grades. Is the topic merely reviewed in later grades or is it presented in a more mature way?

5 Below are some common errors found in papers of fifth and sixth graders. Determine the mistakes and give remedial experiments: (a) 3/4 + 1/2 = 4/6; (b) 7/8 + 5/8 = 12; (c) 1/2 + 3/4 = 3/8; (d) 6/8 ÷ 2/8 = 3/8; (e) 6 ÷ 1/2 = 3.

6 The multiplication property of 1 has sometimes been neglected in teaching. Look through the chapter carefully and find all uses for it in learning about fractions and computations with them. Look through a recent textbook series and locate all uses of the multiplication identity in the study of fractional numbers.

7 (a) Do Activities 4, 5, 9, and 12; (b) Make a 3-by-3 square like the 2-by-3 in Activity 10; (c) Write more exercises for Activity 9; (d) Do Activity 8. Write an experiment for fast pupils which is more difficult.

Bibliography

1 Anderson, R. C.: "Suggestions from Research-Fractions," *The Arithmetic Teacher*, vol. 16, pp. 131-135, Feb., 1969. Summary of research findings relative to teaching fractions and a listing of selected references.

2 Baumgartner, M.: "What Can You Do With an Egg Carton?," *The Arithmetic Teacher*, vol. 15, pp. 456-458, May, 1968. Activities children need to understand fraction concepts.

3 Bohan, H.: "Paper Folding and Equivalent Fractions-Bridging a Gap," *The Arithmetic Teacher*, vol. 18, pp. 245-249, April, 1971. Excellent article on fractions for two reasons: first, useful models are developed; and second, the dialogue that should be used with children is presented.

4 Duquette, R.: "Some Thoughts on Piaget's Findings and the Teaching of Fractions," *The Arithmetic Teacher*, vol. 19, pp. 273-275, April, 1972. Relates why laboratories with geoboard experiments are useful for learning fraction concepts.

5 Heddens, J. W., and M. Hynes: "Division of Fractional Numbers," *The Arithmetic Teacher*, vol. 16, pp. 99-103, Feb., 1969. Division with fractions done in a manner similar to division of whole numbers.

6 Jacobs, I.: "If the Hands Can Do It the Head Will Follow," *The Arithmetic Teacher*, vol. 19, pp. 571-577, Nov., 1972. Interesting method using egg cartons to show multiplication with fractions.

7 Kidd, K., S. Myers, and D. Cilley: *The Laboratory Approach to Mathematics*, Science Research Associates, Chicago, 1970. Illustrates the importance of the laboratory approach in teaching mathematics and provides models for fractions.

8 Nelson, D., and M. N. Nelson: "Pegboard Multiplication of a Fraction by a Fraction," *The Arithmetic Teacher*, vol. 16, pp. 142-144, Feb., 1969. A concrete model that could also be used with a geoboard for multiplication with fractions.

9 Shuster, A. H., and F. L. Pigge: "Retention Efficiency of Meaningful Teaching," *The Arithmetic Teacher*, vol. 12, pp. 24-31, Jan., 1965. Research study of the relative effectiveness of three methods of teaching addition and subtraction with fractions.

10 Stern, C., and M. Stern: *Children Discover Arithmetic*, Harper and Row, New York, 1971. Models, symbols, and rules for dealing with fractions in a rational framework discussed on pages 304-334.

8
DECIMALS AND PERCENT

The weatherman reports the rainfall from the storm as 0.58 inch in 1974 and as 1.47 centimeters in a few years. The commuter's timetable records the distance from the Loop to 63rd Street as 6.3 miles in 1974 and as 10.1 kilometers in a few years. The variety of situations in which decimals are found in everyday life will increase tremendously with the imminent use of the metric system. Then, units, tenths, and hundredths of the basic units for length, weight, volume, and so on will replace the awkward English units, subunits, and common fractional parts of them.

This chapter guides the teacher in:

- Understanding the concept of a decimal and of percent.
- Learning methods of developing experiences for pupils as they discover concepts and algorithms of decimals and become skillful in their use.
- Helping pupils explore and solve problems with decimals and percents.
- Developing experiments in order to individualize instruction.

As in previous chapters, the emphasis is on class experiences which in many cases may be readily written for use in the mathematics laboratory. The last section of the chapter provides specific examples of such experiments.

DIRECTING LEARNING OF DECIMALS

While the logic of the decimal notation is simple to the adult, its intelligent application demands understanding of the concept and ability to compute, both of which develop only through carefully guided experiences.

Developing Concepts And Notation

This chapter offers alternatives to the familiar use of money as an introduction to decimals. While this method is useful, since most children have had many experiences with money, it is not sufficient to learn the subtle ideas of our decimal system. The teacher, therefore, needs other strategies.

Tenths   The pupil first learns to use decimals as an alternate way of expressing certain fractions with which he is already familiar. The teacher may first write examples of decimals on the board, discuss them briefly, and ask pupils to search for those situations in their environment where decimals in tenths occur. The next day they report the examples they have found: automobile odometers in miles and tenths of miles, pedometers calibrated to miles and tenths of miles, stop watches calibrated to seconds and tenths of seconds, and rulers calibrated to tenths of centimeters. (Some of these units will change as the metric system is introduced.)

While studying the situations, the pupil acquires the concepts and the meaning of the notation through manipulative and pictorial experiences. The teacher refers to a rectangular region (Fig. 8-1) and asks the class to indicate what part of it is shaded. They respond with "three-tenths" and record this as 3/10. Now the teacher explains 0.3 as another way of writing the result. After repeating this experience for a number of different expressions with tenths, the pupils are helped to fix the meanings and notation of tenths as decimals by activities such as the following:

Color different parts of unit rectangular and circular regions and name the part colored as both a decimal and a fraction (Fig. 8-2).

Construct and study number lines. Here, the important ideas are that the decimal form is merely an alternate name for a fractional number and, hence, can be used to name points on a number line. Pupils construct number lines with a variety of labeling, such as those shown in Fig. 8-3, which illustrate counting by 0.1, by 0.05, and by 1.2.

Such activities are continued until the pupil understands that decimals such as 0.3 or 0.7 are names for fractional numbers, and he has a mental picture of these as "three" and "seven" of the 10 congruent parts of 1. He then is ready for interpreting tenths in terms of place value, understanding that tenths written in the decimal form are an extension of the place-value property that he has been using to name whole numbers.

A valuable set of experiences toward this end make use of the pocket holder. A cardboard pocket chart is labeled, as illustrated in Fig. 8-4. Cards representing ones are cut into 10 congruent strips to represent tenths.

Pupils write decimals represented by various combinations of cards in the holder and demonstrate the meaning of 3.8, 28.5, etc., in the holder.

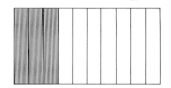

Figure 8-1
Rectangular region showing $\frac{3}{10}$ or 0.3.

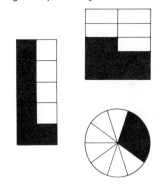

Figure 8-2
Regions representing decimals.

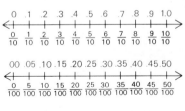

Figure 8-3
Decimals located on number lines.

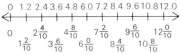

Figure 8-4
Pocket chart for representing decimals.

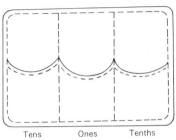

Tens   Ones   Tenths

Pupils place successively 1, 2, 3,..., 9 strips in the tenths pocket and record as .1, .2, .3..., .9.

When 10 strips are placed in the tenth pocket, pupils observe that the number of strips permitted in any one pocket has been exceeded, and, following the pattern used with whole numbers, the 10 tenths are replaced by one card in the ones place.

Hundredths Extension of the concept of decimals to hundredths follows understanding of tenths. Pupils find and bring to class examples of common situations in which decimals are expressed in hundredths. One example, 11.36 inches (28.85 cm) as the total rainfall is written by pupils both in the decimal form 11.36 and as $11\frac{36}{100}$, building the idea that these are two ways of expressing the same number. Similarly, other decimals from real situations are named as fractions. Actual materials serve as the basis for real problems: the decimal-equivalent chart seen in machine shops; the surveyor's chain, with each unit ruled to hundredths of a unit; and calipers and barometers that are graduated in hundredths.

Next, experiences in coloring and interpreting, similar to those described for tenths, are used with square regions partitioned into 100 congruent parts.

Pupils may also make 15 cm cardboard square regions and label them 1. Some are cut into 10 strips of the same size with dimensions 1.5 cm by 15 cm and labeled 0.1. Some of the strips are cut into 10 square regions, each 1.5 cm by 1.5 cm, and labeled 0.01 (Fig. 8-5). Sandpaper pasted on the back of the cardboard facilitates use on the flannel board. Pupils use these materials to represent fractional numbers, such as 5.36 or 2.34 (Fig. 8-6), and write as decimals the various numbers represented on the flannel board. They also show 10 one-hundredths equal to 1 tenth and 10 tenths equal to 1.

Finally, they study tables, such as in Fig. 8-7, and recognize the symmetry in the names and place values for decimals. They see tens and tenths, hundreds and hundredths, thousands and thousandths symmetrically located with respect to the ones place. Likewise symmetrically located are the places with values 10^1 and $(1/10)^1$, 10^2 and $(1/10)^2$, and 10^3 and $(1/10)^3$. Pupils find there is *not* symmetry with respect to the decimal point and begin to realize that it merely indicates that the place to its left has a place value of 1.

Extension beyond hundredths Pupils extend their concept of decimals to thousandths as they find magnitudes expressed as thousandths in newspapers, modify an abacus to display

Figure 8-5
Cardboard regions for representing decimals.

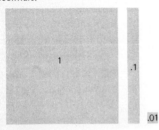

Figure 8-6

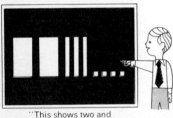

"This shows two and thirty-four hundredths."

Figure 8-7
Symmetry in names for decimals.

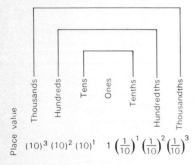

thousandths, and reason logically that 10 one-thousandths are equal to 1 one-hundredth (10/1,000 = 1/100; therefore, .010 = .01). It is impractical and unnecessary to use rectangular regions or other objects subdivided into as many as 1,000 congruent parts. By this time, pupils should be ready to rely on logic and symbolic notation. (See Activity 2 for the use of the abacus to show hundredths and thousandths.)

Expanded form Samples of the types of exercises which help pupils understand the notation for decimals so they can apply it automatically are the following:

- Fill in these blanks so that each mathematical sentence is true:

  .376 = ____ tenths and ____ thousandths

  = ____ hundredths and ____ thousandths

  = ____ thousandths

- Arrange the members of each set in order to express numbers from greatest to least:

  (a) {.28,.289,.298}   (b) {1.70,1.706,1.670}

- Complete each of the following sequences:

  (a) .15, .17, .19, ____ , ____ , ____

  (b) 1.43, 1.49, 1.55, ____ , ____ , ____

  (c) .95, .90, .85, ____ , ____ , ____

  (d) 3.71, 3.63, 3.55, ____ , ____ , ____

Addition and Subtraction

Procedures for teaching addition and subtraction of whole numbers are readily extended to fractional numbers expressed as decimals. Since these additions and subtractions present few new difficulties, the study of this topic offers opportunity to reemphasize important properties and maintain the skills in these processes with whole numbers. Some procedures for accomplishing this purpose are as follows:

1 The pupils are confronted with a problem such as: "According to John's pedometer, the Boy Scouts traveled 3.4 kilometers on Monday and 2.3 kilometers on Tuesday. What was the total distance they travelled?" Pupils first draw a picture (Fig. 8-8a) for the problem, using a number line. The same type of picture is used whether the addition is recorded by fractions, decimals, or numerals for whole numbers.

Figure 8-8
Picturing and computing 3.4 + 2.3.

(a)

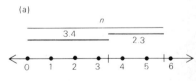

(b)

$$n = 3.4 + 2.3$$
$$= 3\tfrac{4}{10} + 2\tfrac{3}{10}$$
$$= \tfrac{34}{10} + \tfrac{23}{10}$$
$$= \tfrac{57}{10} = 5.7$$

Figure 8-9
Representing 3.4 + 2.3 with a pocket chart.

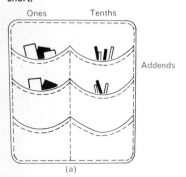

Ones   Tenths

Addends

(a)

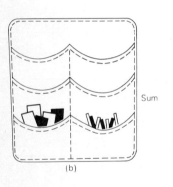

Sum

(b)

3.4
2.3
———
5.7   (c)

Figure 8-10
Picturing 0.6 × 0.7.

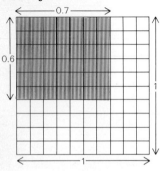

2   Next, pupils improvise solutions using the fraction form, as shown in Fig. 8-8*b*.

3   Pupils improvise solutions by using cards in the pocket chart, as in Fig. 8-9*a* and *b*.

4   Solutions using the pocket chart are paralleled by writing the addends one above the other, placing each digit as indicated by the improvised solutions, adding, and comparing results, as in Fig. 8-9*c*.

5   Written records of the solutions are carefully examined, and pupils conclude that places having the same place value are written in a vertical column as in the algorithm first encountered in the addition of whole numbers.

6   This algorithm is practiced, returning to the use of fractions or the pocket chart as required.

While this sequence of experiences was described for addition, similar steps serve to promote understanding of subtraction with decimals. Other experiences can be adapted from those suggested for addition and subtraction of whole numbers described in Chapter 4. When both addition and subtraction have been studied, one operation may be used to check the other.

Multiplication

As in the study of other topics, multiplication with decimals proceeds through appropriate readiness experiences, problems for motivation, careful attention to activities that promote understanding, and finally to practice and application. Special experiences for promoting mathematical understanding designed to help pupils verify or justify the rule for placing the decimal point in the product include the following.

Picturing multiplication with decimals   The product of two numbers expressed as decimals is verified by pupils with pictures of rectangular regions similar to those used for fractions. They are given a unit region 1 by 1, partitioned into 100 congruent parts as shown in Fig. 8-10. They observe that each of these parts is 0.01 of the region. They shade 42 of these parts to represent 0.42 and note that the shaded rectangular region has sides of 0.7 and 0.6 so its measure is 0.7 by 0.6. They conclude that $0.7 \times 0.6 = 0.42$.

Adding   Pupils obtain answers to a multiplication such as 3×4.2 by thinking, "three 4.2s" and adding $4.2 + 4.2 + 4.2$. At the same time, they sense the difficulties of this approach in solving 0.6 × 3.1, since the idea of 3.1 being added six-tenths times is meaningless.

Expressing decimals as fractions Pupils discover the rule for placing the decimal point in the product of two decimal factors if the factors are first expressed as fractions:

$$3 \times 0.2 = 3 \times \frac{2}{10} = \frac{3 \times 2}{10} = \frac{6}{10} = 0.6$$

$$0.3 \times 5.2 = \frac{3}{10} \times 5\frac{2}{10} = \frac{3}{10} \times \frac{52}{10} = \frac{156}{100} = 1.56$$

Pupils summarize the results of these and other calculations in a chart, as shown in Fig. 8-11. They study the data, discuss possible patterns, and suggest a tentative conclusion: the number in column 2 plus the number in column 3 equals the number in column 5. They check this generalization with other multiplications. Finally, through constructive criticism and refining of language, they reach the reasonable conclusion: the number of decimal places to the right of the decimal point in the product equals the sum of the numbers of decimal places in the first factor and the second factor. The teacher should understand that no rule has been *proved* by this inductive, or experimental, method. However, this approach makes the generalization plausible to pupils. See Activity 4 at the end of this chapter for an alternate method of placing the decimal point in products.

Emphasizing the distributive property As with multiplication of whole numbers, understanding the algorithm for multiplication with fractional numbers expressed as decimals is based on the place-value idea and the distributive property. Some experiences for the pupils that emphasize these ideas are:

Draw pictures to illustrate the distributive property, as shown in Fig. 8-12a for 2 × 4.8.

Apply the distributive property without completing the computation, as shown for 7 × 3.82 in Fig. 8-12b.

Figure 8-11 *The number of decimal places in a product.*

	Column				
1	2	3	4	5
	Decimal places in		Product	Number of decimal
Multiplication	First factor	Second factor	(using fractions)	places in product
3 × .2	0	1	$\frac{6}{10}$ = .6	1
3.1 × 4.71	1	2	$\frac{14601}{1000}$ = 14.601	3
.3 × 5.2	1	1	$\frac{156}{100}$ = 1.56	2

Figure 8-12
Applying the distributive property.

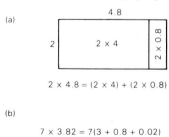

(a)

$$2 \times 4.8 = (2 \times 4) + (2 \times 0.8)$$

(b)

$$7 \times 3.82 = 7(3 + 0.8 + 0.02)$$
$$= (7 \times 3) + (7 \times 0.8) + (7 \times 0.02)$$

Figure 8-13
Expanded algorithm for 7 × 3.94.

$$
\begin{array}{r}
3.94 \\
7 \\
\hline
.28 = 7 \times 0.04 \\
6.3\ \ = 7 \times 0.9 \\
21\ \ \ \ \ = 7 \times 3 \\
\hline
27.58 = 7 \times 3.94
\end{array}
$$

Pupils show the factors used to determine each product, as illustrated for 7 × 3.94 in Fig. 8-13.

A reasonable answer through estimation Many multiplications with decimals can be estimated by elementary methods, while estimates that incorporate more mature concepts of place value or division by powers of ten are appropriate at later stages of instruction. To be useful, estimations should be performed mentally; hence, simplified procedures within the ability of most pupils are necessary.

Mental approximation by rounding. Beginning pupils learn to select the product of 5 × 3.8 from among 190, 19.0, and 1.90. Their estimation, 5 × 4 = 20, indicates the plausibility of 19.0. Similarly, their answer, 31.68, is plausible for 4.8 × 6.6, since 5 × 7 = 35.

Through experience, pupils recognize that, for purposes of estimating, the parts of both factors that contribute least to the product can be discarded in arriving at factors that are easy to handle. Even relatively large adjustments to simplify both factors provide useful approximations. Thus, in the multiplication 0.05 × 42.7, one estimation is 0.1 × 40 = 1/10 of 40 = 4. Here, they see that even doubling .05 yields a suitable estimation since possible exact answers might be 0.2135, 2.135, 21.35, or 213.5, and the one of these nearest to 4 is 2.135.

Pupils need many experiences to conclude that approximations may be less precise than is commonly realized and still be useful. For most multiplications, any of a wide choice of factors is adequate for locating the decimal point by estimation. Given 8.23 × 78.7, the factors may be rounded to 10 and 100. Although not providing the most accurate approximation, these numbers provide the simplest computation, and the estimated product (1,000) makes it possible to determine the correct answer from among a number of possibilities: 6.47701, 64.7701, 647.701, or 6,477.01.

Establishing bounds for products. Frequently it is possible to make two approximations: "less than" and "greater than." These are upper and lower bounds for the product. For example, given 3.6 × 4.82, the pupil who figures "3 × 4 = 12" recognizes his estimate as too small and knows the product is more than 12. If he uses "4 × 5 = 20," he realizes his estimate is too great and reasons that the product is less than 20. As a result, he has established 12 and 20 as numbers between which the exact product falls. With experience, he observes that the factors seem closer to 4 and 5 than to 3 and 4, indicating that the product is closer to 20 than 12.

One or more of these methods for estimating is within the capacity of most elementary school pupils. They are useful not only to develop confidence in computational procedures, but also to add variety in checking answers.

To find out whether these various procedures for rationalizing the process are producing the desired results, the teacher may seek answers to such questions as the following:

Are pupils increasingly sensitive to the reasonableness of answers?

Do they understand the reason for the rule they may use in placing decimal points in products?

Is the amount of repetitive practice necessary to complete learning reduced?

Are skill and understanding transferable to new situations having similar and related elements?

When pupils have forgotten the procedures normally used, do they substitute methods that secure the correct result or help them recall the usual approach?

Division

Division with whole numbers is taught before many pupils are ready to understand the details of the algorithm. As a result, they may come to division with decimals with some ability to perform long division, but with only a hazy grasp of the "why" of the procedure. Study of division with decimals offers an opportunity to refresh or extend understanding of the rationale for the process of division and to clarify basic ideas.

Instruction in division with decimals, accordingly, should be directed to broad objectives, including the following:

Appreciating the need for division with decimals and ability to apply the process.

Relearning and extending understanding of why: (*a*) numerals in quotients are placed where they are; (*b*) partial products are subtracted and what partial products mean; and (*c*) numerals are "brought down."

Refreshing comprehension of relation of division to subtraction and multiplication.

Learning why and how to treat decimal points in division.

Learning to estimate and check.

Achieving skill in computation: (*a*) reinforcing skill with the long-division algorithm; and (*b*) developing skill in division with decimals.

All of these, except the 4th and 5th items, are achieved with adaptation of methods described previously. Teaching pupils where the basic properties are applied and how to estimate and check answers requires special attention.

Divisor expressed as a counting number The pupil who has mastered the process of dividing a number named by a decimal by a counting number places the decimal point in the quotient directly above the decimal point in the dividend. Before operating on this level, the pupil has many exploratory experiences through which he discovers or verifies the rationale for the procedure:

● He objectifies the operation with the pocket chart.

Figure 8-14
Pocket chart for performing 8.6 ÷ 2.

Figure 8-14
Pocket chart for performing 8.6 ÷ 2.

Ones   Tenths

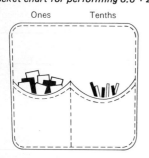

(a) He sets up the division $2)\overline{8.6}$ in the pocket holder, as shown in Fig. 8-14. He thinks of the example as 8.6 separated into two equal parts. He finds the answer by separating eight cards representing ones into two sets of four each, and six cards representing tenths into two sets of three each. The quotient 4.3 is written in the proper position:

$$\begin{array}{r} 4.3 \\ 2)\overline{8.6} \end{array}$$

Figure 8-15
Pocket chart for performing 8.4 ÷ 3.

Ones   Tenths

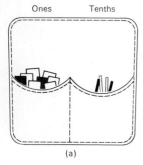

(a)

(b) The division $3)\overline{8.4}$ is set in the pocket chart, as pictured in Fig. 8-15a. First, the eight cards representing ones are separated into three sets of two each, with two left over. Since the two cards representing ones cannot be separated into three parts without breaking them up, they are renamed 20 tenths. The resulting 24 cards representing tenths are separated into three sets of eight each, as in Fig. 8-15b. Thus, the quotient is seen to be 2 ones and 8 tenths, and the division is writtten as

$$\begin{array}{r} 2.8 \\ 3)\overline{8.4} \end{array}$$

Many teachers have guided pupils to relate pocket chart experiments to the use of the distributive property in the algorithm. In the above example pupils may show the manipulation of the cards with numerals in this way

$$\begin{aligned} 8.4 \div 3 &= (6 + 2.4) \div 3 \\ &= (6 \div 3) + (2.4 \div 3) \\ &= 2 + 0.8 = 2.8 \end{aligned}$$

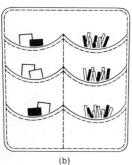

(b)

● The pupil secures answers by means of fractions, then locates the decimal point. Steps in this approach for $2)\overline{8.4}$ are as follows:

(a) He performs the division, disregarding the decimal point:

$$\begin{array}{r} 4\ 2 \\ 2)\overline{8.4} \end{array}$$

(b) He performs the division using fractions; the answer is renamed as a decimal:

$$\begin{aligned} 8\ 4/10 \div 2 &= 8\ 4/10 \div 2/1 \\ &= 8\ 4/10 \times 1/2 = 42/10 = 42/10 \\ &= 4.2 \end{aligned}$$

(c) He locates the decimal point in the correct position in the original division.

$$\begin{array}{r} 4.2 \\ 2\overline{)8.4.} \end{array}$$

- The pupil selects a reasonable answer by estimating. For $2\overline{)26.8}$ the pupil divides, disregarding the decimal point, obtaining 134. He sees the correct quotient is to be selected from among .134, 1.34 and 13.4. He sees the correct quotient is near 13 (from $2\overline{)26}$) or some other approximation, such as 15 (from $2\overline{)30}$) or 10 (from $2\overline{)20}$). Any of these suggests 13.4 as plausible.

From a number of divisions solved by these methods, the pupil sees the generalization that the decimal point in the quotient is placed directly above that in the dividend.

Annexing zeros A difficulty often encountered in division occurs where zeros must be annexed to the dividend. For example, in $2\overline{)3}$ or $4\overline{)8.6}$, the dividends must be named as 3.0 and 8.60, respectively.

After reviewing different names for the same number, such as .3 = .30 = .300, 2.7 = 2.70 = 2.7000, 5 = 5.0 = 5.00, the following sequence of experiences is one feasible approach:

1 Pupils find $2\overline{)5}$ (5 separated into two equal parts) intuitively and write the completed solution as 2 1/2.

2 They write 2 1/2 in the decimal form 2.5.

3 They find this same result is obtained by placing the decimal point, annexing a zero to the dividend, and dividing as previously learned (Fig. 8-16).

4 They conclude that an acceptable procedure for such divisions is placing a decimal point and annexing zeros as needed.

Figure 8-16
Annexing zeros in the dividend.

$$\begin{array}{r} 2.5 \\ 2\overline{)5.0} \\ 4 \\ \hline 10 \\ 10 \\ \hline 0 \end{array}$$

Divisor expressed as a decimal The same general sequence that has been suggested for numerous other topics is followed in learning division when the divisor is expressed decimally. The pupil first improvises solutions and then draws generalizations for placing the decimal point in the quotient.

Improvising solutions. Simple methods through which pupils improvise solutions are the following:

Locate the decimal point in quotients to conform with the result from division with fractions, applying the same procedure as described above.

Obtain answers through reference to a number line. The answer to $.3\overline{)1.8}$ is secured by counting the number of 3 tenths in 1 and 8

Figure 8-17
6 is the number of 0.3s in 1.8.

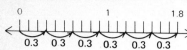

0   1   1.8

0.3   0 3   0.3   0.3   0.3   0.3

tenths, as shown in Fig. 8-17.

Estimate answers to some divisions with quotients 1 or greater by rounding off.

Division   **Thinking**

2.3)‾18.76 Twos in 18.

.3)‾7.44   Number of 3 tenths in 1 is about 3, so that the number of 3 tenths in 7.44 is about 7 × 3, or 21. Thus 24.8 is the most plausible answer from among .248, 24.8, and 248.

Later, when an algorithm is developed, pupils obtain answers through these rational methods and compare them to answers secured through the algorithm.

Mathematical justification. The most common technique for placing the decimal point in quotients is often referred to as the *caret method*. While it is possible for pupils to learn to use this method mechanically, they may, with proper experiences, understand as well as perform the process. Understanding is developed as pupils see the relation of division with a decimal to division by a counting number.

Before this new topic is undertaken, exercises should be provided to establish readiness. First, pupils perform related divisions, such as 2)‾32 and 20)‾320, 6)‾48 and 600)‾4,800 Then they find by examining these divisions that multiplying a divisor and dividend by the same nonzero number does not change the quotient; further, they see this generalization as one previously studied in renaming fractions

$$\frac{1}{2} = \frac{1 \times 3}{2 \times 3} = \frac{3}{6}$$

Now this same procedure can be applied so that division with decimals is performed with the divisor a counting number. The work may be summarized as in Fig. 8-18.

As pupils compile data from these and similar divisions, they can discover the following generalizations. Through a class discussion the statements are refined to a level of preciseness commensurate with their language ability. The conclusions may be posted on the bulletin board for future reference.

- By suitable choice of a factor, the division may be expressed with the divisor a counting number.
- The same factor that was used in column 2 must be used in column 3. (See Fig. 8-18.)
- If divisor and dividend are multiplied by the same factor, the quotient is unchanged (columns 3 and 4).
- Divisions need not be performed with the divisor expressed as a decimal. They may be rewritten as shown in columns 4 and 5. Some

1	2	3	4	5	
Division	So that the divisor is a counting number, multiply it by:	So that quotient will be unchanged, also multiply dividend by:	Division rewritten as:	Solution	
$.2\overline{)8}$	10	10	$2\overline{)80.}$	$2\overline{)80.}$ (40.)	
$2.4\overline{)3.12}$	10	10	$24\overline{)31.2}$	$24\overline{)31.2}$ (1.3)	
$.25\overline{)8}$	100	100	$25\overline{)800.}$	$25\overline{)800.}$ (32.)	
$.625\overline{)3.725}$	1,000	1,000	$625\overline{)3725.}$	$625\overline{)3725.00}$ (5.96)	

Figure 8-18
Placing decimal points in quotients.

pupils may see that the number of places the decimal point is moved in any division is the same as the number of zeros in the factor displayed in column 3.

As a result of the experiences required to complete the chart (Fig. 8-18), pupils may discuss and formulate a generalized rule stated in a form such as: "Multiply both dividend and divisor by ten or a power of ten, so that the divisor is a counting number. Then proceed as if dividing by a counting number."

In achieving a suitable level of understanding, pupils should recognize this procedure as another application of the multiplication property of 1. This is shown for $5.432 \div 0.56$ in Fig. 8-19, with 1 named 100/100.

Using an algorithm. For many pupils, the final working pattern may consist of using the following procedure, illustrated for $0.56\overline{)5.432}$:

1   Estimate the answer: $1 \div 0.56$ is about 2, so that $5.432 \div 0.56$ is about 2×5.

2   Multiply 0.56 by 100 so that the divisor is a counting number; multiply 5.432 by 100 also. This gives $56\overline{)543.2}$.

3   Perform the division using these numbers, and compare quotient with the estimate from step 1.

Many pupils are taught that computations are never performed with the divisor named as a decimal. As a first step they express the division with the divisor as a counting number. Many other pupils are capable of locating the decimal point in the quotient mentally. This mental operation is to be encouraged if pupils are thoroughly familiar with the justification for the procedure and if

Figure 8-19
Making the divisor as a counting number.

$$\frac{5.432}{0.56} = \frac{5.432}{0.56} \times \frac{100}{100}$$

$$= \frac{5.432 \times 100}{0.56 \times 100}$$

$$= \frac{543.2}{56}$$

Figure 8-20

Expanded algorithm for 8.64 ÷ 0.24.

$$
\begin{array}{r}
36 \\
0.24 \overline{)8.64} \\
7.20 = 30 \times 0.24 \\
\overline{1.44} \\
1.44 = 6 \times 0.24 \\
\overline{0}
\end{array}
$$

Figure 8-21

Set *A*

Set *B*

Figure 8-22

Set *A*   Set *B*

they obtain correct answers.

Most pupils will profit from using some form of an expanded algorithm. One is shown in Fig. 8-20. Pairs of pupils will profit from asking each other questions concerning the placement of numerals and the factors used to obtain partial products in such an algorithm.

For other experiences with division with decimals see Activities 1 and 5 at the end of this chapter.

DIRECTING LEARNING OF RATIOS

The idea of a ratio is applied so automatically in everyday life without the use of the word itself that the formal study of it in the classroom seems unduly complicated. Children interested in football understand and say, "Bob Griese completed 15 out of 25 passes"; but, if asked the ratio that expresses the number of pass completions to the number of passes, attempted, they are speechless. The wide daily use of ratios is indicated by a few examples: 23 hits in 79 times at bat (ratio 23 to 79 or 23:79 or 23/79); 63 kilometers on 16 liters of gasoline (ratio 63 to 16 or 63:16 or 63/16); 37 cents for 3 cans of dog food (ratio 37 to 3 or 37:3 or 37/3).

The mathematician prefers to write a ratio in the form 3:4 rather than as 3/4 to avoid confusing ratios and fractions. While there are legitimate reasons for this distinction, the fraction form expressing ratios will be used. If a circular region is separated into 3 congruent parts and 2 are being considered, then 2 is being compared to 3 as a ratio. The same model may be thought of as 2/3 of the entire region under consideration. Both interpretations are important; their differences are subtle, and using the same numeral to indicate each does not cause confusion. However, since both forms are in common use, both should be learned by pupils.

Experiences For Expressing Data

It is useful at first to have students make comparisons using both ratio and subtraction. Toward this end, they may complete the following experiments:

- How many more marbles in set *A* than set *B* (Fig. 8-21)? Fill in the blanks: ____ - ____ = ____ . You have compared set *A* and set *B* by subtraction.

  Complete this statement:

$$
\frac{\text{Number of marbles in set } A}{\text{Number of marbles in set } B} = \underline{\quad}
$$

The fraction you wrote compares the number in *A* to the number in *B* as a ratio.

- How many more pennies are in set *B* than in set *A* (Fig. 8-22)?

  Use ratio to compare the number of pennies in set B with the number of pennies in set A.

- Use ratio to compare the number of objects in set *A* with the number in set *B* for each pair of items in Fig. 8-23.

Figure 8-23

A	B
7 pencils	5 books
5 dogs	8 boys
4 balls	9 bats
7 hats	2 cans
3 shovels	8 hoes
7 plates	8 cups
11 spoons	5 forks

Simple word problems are useful in establishing the idea that ratios apply to situations both inside and outside the classroom. These may be examined as soon as it is evident that the pupils can express a comparison by means of ratio. The pupils, as well as the teacher, can suggest situations for comparison:

- There are 13 girls and 11 boys in Ms. Hansen's class.

  a. Use subtraction to compare the number of girls with the number of boys.

  b. Use ratio to make the same comparison.

- Jim earned $10 and spent $7. Use ratio to compare what he saved with what he earned.

Figure 8-24

(a)
(b)
(c)

The concept of ratios is extended as pupils complete activities such as the following:

Look at Fig. 8-24. The ratio of the number of triangles to the number of circles is: in Fig. 8-24*a*____ ; in Fig. 8-24*b*____ ; in Fig. 8-24*c*____.

The ratio 1/2 means 1 triangle for every ____ squares.

The ratio 2/4 means ____ triangles for every ____ squares.

The ratio 3/6 means ____ triangles for every ____ squares.

It is effective also to use ratio in developing a table in order to establish the idea of a constant factor in comparison by ratio:

- Use ratio to compare the number of leaves with the number of apples (Fig. 8-25).

  Using the same ratio, complete the following table:

  Number of leaves: 3 ? 12 ? ?
  Number of apples: 1 2   ? 5 6

Figure 8-25

- Use ratio to compare the number of dogs with the number of boys (Fig. 8-26).

  Using the same ratio, complete the following table:

  Number of dogs: 3 ? 9 ? 15 18 ?
  Number of boys: 2 4 ? 8 ? ? 14

An important outcome, then, in studying ratio is that in 2/3,

Figure 8-26

for example, 2 of something is being compared to 3 of something. If the ratio had been 3/2, then 3 would have been compared to 2. In this study many language forms should be used. As the pupil shows sets of 3 and 4 objects, he should compare them using a ratio by making statements such as:

3 compared to 4.
3 out of 4.
3 for each 4.
The ratio of 3 to 4.

There are many other familiar situations available for helping pupils to learn to use ratio: counting and comparing the number of steps two pupils take to walk from the classroom door to the basketball court, measuring and comparing different pupils' heights and weights or various items in the classroom, and so on. Other specific experiments concerned with ratio are found in Activities 10 and 11 at the end of the chapter.

DIRECTING LEARNING OF PERCENT

For many years, percent has been introduced in grade six, and its applications have been a central concern in grades seven and eight. Although the curriculum in these grades has been revised, percent is still a matter of concern, with mixed results. If the difficulty in learning percent is to be avoided, careful attention must be directed to helping pupils establish a clear concept of it. Carefully selected experiences are needed to focus attention on meaning rather than on manipulation.

The mastery of percent requires no new mathematical understandings or skills beyond those needed in using fractional numbers. The difficulties that the pupil encounters lie in the special vocabulary and conventions that accompany its various applications. For this reason, it is useful to examine the important situations in which percent is used, as well as to refresh pupils' skills in the operations that will be required, during the early stages of the learning steps in presenting the topic.

Percent In Use

The pupil needs only to examine the daily newspaper to discover that percent is one of the most widely used mathematical concepts in our environment. On a typical day, we find that the cost of living has risen 5 1/2 percent during the first six months of the year, but that wholesale prices have risen 7 percent. There is encouraging news that unemployment is now only 5 percent, but, on the other hand, automobile accidents decreased by 15 percent over the corresponding period last year.

The financial page is packed with information expressed in terms of percent, and the editorial page is often filled with percentage data that must be carefully interpreted by the reader.

Evidence that we need to reexamine the teaching of percent is found in the incidence of incorrect usage among the adult population. In most areas of communication, errors in usage are relatively harmless; however, the language of percent deals with an area where precision in thought and communication is essential. Errors in usage may cost money. The person who borrows on a 9 percent plan that turns out to be a 16 percent plan is paying a real penalty for his ignorance. Congress has undertaken to protect those who borrow or buy on installment loans by requiring a full statement of all pertinent terms in the transaction, but the best protection for the ignorant will always be education.

Incorrect usages of percent are startlingly easy to find. We often read that prices are reduced 100 percent or attendance has declined 300 percent. It is apparent that a large segment of our population is incapable of thinking or communicating effectively in an area in which precise thinking is essential. Seen in this light, the question "How can the teaching of percent be improved so that its meaning is understood and its applications are handled efficiently?" becomes extremely important.

Developing the Meaning of Percent

A variety of experiences with percent, progressing from concrete to semiconcrete and on to the symbolic stage, may be completed while the pupil is developing the ability to handle the ideas of percent. Many of the exercises used to develop the idea of ratio with common and decimal fractions are applicable for this purpose as well.

The hundreds board, with disks colored red on one side and blue on the other, is helpful to display visually the meaning of percent as *number per hundred*. For example, the pupil arranging 12 red and 88 blue disks can show 12 out of 100, or 12%, and 88 out of 100, or 88%. Here he sees that the total is 100%.

Graphic representation is widely used. Mimeographed 10-by-10 squares form the basis for pictorial activities showing percent as hundredths. Pupils consider the entire square as *one* and each small square as *one one-hundredth*. They color various sections—15, for example—as in Fig. 8-27, and say and record the result as .15, 15/100, 15 hundredths, and 15%. They shade squares in response to directions: "Color 17 percent, 35 percent, 65 percent, 78 percent."

Figure 8-27
Name shaded region in four ways.

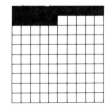

Figure 8-28
Rectangular regions for showing percent.

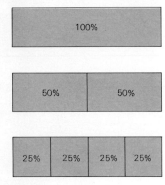

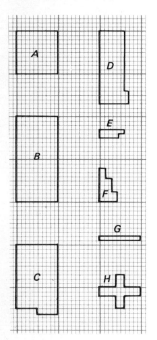

Rectangular regions similar to those described for decimals may be constructed for percent (Fig. 8-28). These are used by groups or individual pupils to discover relationships among percents. They find, for example, that it takes two regions labeled 50% to cover one region labeled 100%.

Using squared paper, the meaning of percent *can be* brought out with questions such as: "If square region *A* represents 100 percent (Fig. 8-29), what percent is represented by regions *B-H?*" or "In Fig. 8-30 the rectangle represents 100 percent. What percent is represented by each of the lettered parts? Why should the sum of the percents add to 100?" The purpose of these experiments is to bring pupils to an understanding of 18 percent as "18 out of 100," as "18 per 100," as "18 compared to 100" and as "the ratio of 18 to 100."

As a reinforcement experience, pupils find examples of the use of percent and report to the class. A newspaper article stating "10 percent of the land will be used for a park" can be restated in class: "If there are 100 acres of land, 10 acres will be for a park." If a survey of the school revealed that 75 percent of the pupils preferred a trip to Disneyland and 25 percent preferred a picnic at the beach, the pupil explaining may say, "This means 75 out of 100 wanted to go to Disneyland." It would be hoped that other pupils might ask, "Suppose there were 200 pupils and not 100. How would you explain 75 percent of that number?" An even more thoughtful question would be, "Does that mean 75 out of *every* 100 pupils?" Either question can institute a fine discussion of the meaning of percent.

As the study of percent progresses, the pupil can find more and more applications of the concept in everyday life. In order to make him aware of its manifold uses, the bulletin board may be the focus of activity. Individual pupils or committees may compile and select clippings from newspapers and periodicals and prepare displays of applications of percent. As new applications are found, they should be discussed. The bulletin board may be arranged so that a section is reserved for items about business, another for sports, another for consumer buying, and so on.

Of special value in this connection is a list of errors encountered in the usage of percent. In discussing these, pupils should tell what is wrong with each statement and try to determine the source of the error. While many classifications of errors are possible, pupils will find examples in the following categories:

● Comparison to something impossible to measure or very unlikely to have been measured: 40 percent milder; gets clothes 50 percent whiter; rides 30 percent smoother; 45 percent better shaves.

- Interpretation impossible because no comparison is possible:

  (a) If a quarterback completed 50 percent of his passes, did he have a good day? It is impossible to tell because we do not know how many passes he threw. If he completed 15 of 30 or 1 of 2, his record is expressed as 50 percent.

  (b) Is it very serious if 100 percent of the new students need dental attention? If there are 25 new students, the answer is probably yes, but it may be different if there is only one new student. In many cases, when a sample is small, the language of percent is used deliberately to create an impression of a larger sample.

- Comparison where the numbers compared to are different:

  (a) It is possible for prices to rise 200 percent but not to be cut 200 percent, or for attendance to increase 150 percent but not to decrease 150 percent.

  (b) A raise in pay of 10 percent followed by a cut in pay of 10 percent does not have the effect of *no* change in pay. Expressions such as "The number of students doubled or increased 200 percent" are very common.

Developing Computational Skills

Three skills, two of which the pupil has practiced, should be checked out prior to solving problems with percent because they will be used continually.

Expressing percent as a decimal To express a percent as a decimal the pupil argues, "5 percent may be thought of as 5 hundredths and therefore written as 0.05. Similarly, 29 percent is 29 hundredths and can be written 0.29." Pupils may note the similarity between 100 and %. When told this recently, a boy said, "Let's write 29% then as $\frac{29}{\%}$."

There is no need for the pupil to remember whether to move the decimal point two places to the right or left even with percents greater than 100. For example, he expresses 250% as 2.50, reasoning that 250 percent equals 250 hundredths. He obtains 2.5 by dividing 250 by 100, or he may reason

$$250\% = 100\% + 100\% + 50\%$$

$$= 1 + 1 + 0.5 = 2.5$$

Percents less than 1 percent (such as 1/2 or 0.7 percent), and percents greater than 100 percent present less difficulty if they are consistently associated from the beginning with fractions and decimals expressing the same ratios. In practice, pupils show different meanings such as the following:

Figure 8-30
What percent of the rectangular region is each lettered region?

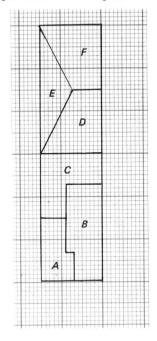

$$1/2\% = \frac{1}{2} \text{ of } 1\% = 0.5\% = 0.005$$

$$0.7\% = 0.7 \text{ of } 1\% = 0.7 \times 0.01 = 0.007$$

$$125\% = \frac{125}{100} = 1.25$$

Solving equations involving multiplication Pupils have solved equations such as $1/2 \times 6 = \square$, $\square \times 12 = 20$, and $5/6 \times \square = 35$. A necessary review in preparation for solving problems with percent by the factor-product method is illustrated by the following questions:

What are the factors and the product in $1/2 \times 4/5 = \square$?

In $\square \times 18 = 27$? In $0.16 \times \square = 67$?

How do you find a number for $\square$ if $3/7 \times 11/5 = \square$? If you know two factors, how do you find the product?

How do you find a number for $\square$ if $\square \times 1.35 = 5.535$? If $7/4 \times \square = 224$? If you know the product and one factor, how do you find the unknown factor?

Solving a proportion The computational skill required in the proportion method of attacking problems in percent is to solve equations in the form $\dfrac{n}{100} = \dfrac{8}{40}$ or $n:100 = 8:40$. Both of these equations show that two ratios are equal and are called proportions.

Equations in fraction form were used extensively when the pupil studied equal fractions. He learned, for example, that $1/2 = 3/6$, $7/5 = 28/20$, and so on. He discovered:

Because $1/2 = 3/6$, then $1 \times 6 = 2 \times 3$.
Because $7/5 = 28/20$, then $7 \times 20 = 5 \times 28$.

The important idea for the pupil to know is:

If $n/100 = 8/40$, then $40 \times n = 100 \times 8$.

Figure 8-31
Showing "If a/b = c/d then ad = bc".

$$\frac{a}{b} = \frac{c}{d}$$

$$\frac{a}{b} \times \frac{d}{d} = \frac{c}{d} \times \frac{b}{b}$$

$$\frac{ad}{bd} = \frac{bc}{db}$$

$$ad = bc$$

He now has the proportion written in the factor-product form and is able to solve for n. Some pupils may be able to prove this, often called "cross multiplication." One way to do this is shown in Fig. 8-31.

How pupils may discover this special property of equal ratios is illustrated by the following Activity. It should be recognized that this experiment does not constitute an effective teaching procedure because it develops the idea too quickly. Each of the steps requires more examples, discussion among pupils, and pupil participation in making up and solving similar examples.

ACTIVITY I

Objective: To check a property of equal ratios.

1   In the proposition 3:4 = 9:12 the 4 and 9 are called *means* and 3 and 12 are called *extremes*.

2   Fill in this table.

Proportion	Means	Product of means	Extremes	Product of extremes
5:10 = 8:16	10,8	10 × 8 = 80	5,16	5 × 16 = 80
8:100 = 20:250				
15:100 = 3:20				
125:100 = 75:60				

How do the products compare in each case?

3   Write each proportion as an equation with factors.

   (*a*)   4:5 = 20:25   5 × 20 =

   (*b*)   3:2 = 18:12

   (*c*)   150:100 = 12:8

   In any proportion the product of the _____ equals the product of the _____

4   Solve for ☐ or *n*.

   (*a*)   *n*:100 = 20:80
   (*b*)   140:100 = ☐:250
   (*c*)   75:100 = 60:☐

SOLVING PROBLEMS USING PERCENT

When the concept of percent has been mastered and the prerequisite skills reviewed, the only difficulty with problems using percent is the analysis of the situation expressed in the problem. Two different approaches to solving these problems are currently taught: the *factor-product* form and the use of *proportion*. There is little to choose between them since they differ only in the kind of mathematical sentence to which the analysis leads.

   Any systematic procedure for problem solving is most effective when it calls for a mathematical sentence. By this method the number relationships are separated from their social or physical setting, and irrelevant distractions are removed. For example, take this problem: "A salesman receives a commission at the rate of 15 percent. If he sells $60 worth of goods, what is his commission?" The mathematical sentence might be:

$$.15 \times 60 = p \qquad \text{(factor-factor-product form)}$$

or

$$\frac{15}{100} = \frac{n}{60} \qquad \text{(proportion form)}$$

The Factor-Product Approach

The goal in solving problems by this method is to express the problem as a simple percent statement in the form "Percent of a number equals a number" and then translate that percent statement to a mathematical sentence in the form "Factor times factor equals product."

In learning to analyze problems with this approach those stated in simple form are studied first:

Find 90 percent of 50. The pupil thinks, "I want to find 90 percent of a number. The factor-product expression is $0.90 \times 50 = n$."

What percent of 50 is 45? The pupil thinks, "I want to find what percent of 50 is 45. The factor-product expression is $n \times 50 = 45$."

90 percent of what number is 45? The pupil thinks, "90 percent of what number is 45? The factor-product expression is $0.90 \times n = 45$."

In solving problems, pupils try to isolate the relationships from the social situation. This is learned as pupils organize their solutions. One way of doing this is illustrated by the following:

- Eric earned $60 a week last summer. He saved 23 percent of it. How much did he save?

$$23\% \quad \text{of} \quad 60 \quad \text{is} \quad n$$
$$.23 \times 60 = n$$
$$13.80 = n$$

Eric saved $13.80.

- The Bears have won 75 percent of the games they have played. They have won 57 games. How many games have they played?

percent times number of games played equals number of games won

$$0.75 \times n = 57$$
$$n = \frac{57}{0.75} = 76$$

The Bears have won 76 games.

- Kay had $12.50. She spent $2.50. What percent of her money did she spend?

percent of her money equals money spent

$$n \times 12.50 = 2.50$$
$$n = \frac{2.50}{12.50} = 0.20 \quad \text{or} \quad 20\%$$

Kay spent 20% of her money.

The approach of teaching each of these problems as one of three cases and identifying the numbers in the factor-product equation by names of rate, base, and percentage has not in general been successful. The emphasis should be on having pupils make a word statement in the form of factor × factor = product, from which they write the equation.

A special type of application that requires careful teaching deals with rate of increase and decrease. Such problems are most effectively analyzed in the following way:

> The number in the junior history club last year was 60. This year it has increased 15%. How many are in the club this year?

As groups of pupils discuss this problem among themselves they make pertinent statements, such as:

> The number in the history club last year is 100% of the membership.
>
> This year we have 15% more than last year.
>
> This year's membership is 100% + 15% or 115% of last year's membership.
>
> The percent statement is 115% of last year's membership is this year's membership.
>
> The percent statement is, 115% of 60 is n.
>
> The equation is $1.15 \times 60 = n$. So $n = 69$.

Other pupils may analyze the problem by determining the increase in membership.

> This year's membership is last year's membership plus the increase in membership.
>
> We know last year's membership. The increase is 15% of last year's membership. This is 15% of 60.

If 15% of 60 is n, then, $.15 \times 60 = n$, and $n = 9$.

$$\text{Last year's membership} = 60$$

$$\text{New members this year} = 9$$

$$\text{Total membership this year} = 69$$

The Proportion Approach

This method is also based on understanding the meaning of percent. The convenience of using proportion is evident from a few illustrations:

> Jim sold 36 papers. He started with 120 papers. What percent of his papers did he sell?

A pupil's analysis could be: "He sold 36 out of 120 papers. This is 36/120. I want to express this ratio as a fraction with a denominator of 100. He sold n papers out of 100. This is $n/100$. The two ratios are equal. So $36/120 = n/100$."

Joan colored 14 squares of her chart. She said she had colored 40% of them. How many squares were on the chart?

A pupil's analysis could be: "If she had 100 squares on her chart she would have colored 40 of them. This is 40/100 of them. We want to express this as a ratio when she has colored 14 of them. This is $14/n$. The two ratios are equal. Then $40/100 = 14/n$."

Analysis of problems Ability to set up the proportion that expresses the relationships in a problem situation calls for insights that can be provided by carefully selected experiences. These insights should go beyond the idea of proportion as the equating of two fractions. It should be understood as two ways of stating the same ratio, each of which can be derived from the information in the problem. The following exercises suggest the kinds of analyses for developing abilities to sort out the numbers being compared, to disregard the irrelevant data in the problem situation, and to state the relationships between the numbers in the problem.

Each of the following examples can be written on a card and given to pupils for individual or group problem solving activities.

● In a mathematics test of 25 problems, Jack had 18 problems correct. What percent did he have correct?

(a) Express the ratio of number correct to total number of problems. (18/25)

(b) If there were 100 problems and Jack had the same ratio of correct problems to total number of problems, how would you express the ratio? ($n/100$)

(c) Since the two ratios are equal, then $n/100 = 18/25$. How do you know that $25n = 1,800$?

(d) What number can replace n to make the proportion true?

● Jane earned $80 last summer and saved 35 percent of her money. How much did she save?

(a) How many dollars would Jane have saved if she earned $100 and saved the same fraction of it?

(b) Express the ratio of her savings to earnings if n is the number of dollars she saved.

(c) Write the percent saved as a fraction with 100 as denominator.

(d) State the proportion.

(e) What number can replace n to make the proportion true?

● Twelve pupils had perfect test scores last Friday. This is 30 percent of the class. How many are in the class?

(a) If there had been 100 pupils in the class and the achievement had been the same, how many would have perfect papers?

(b) Express this fact as a ratio.

(c) You know that 12 pupils had perfect scores, and you have to find the total number of pupils. Express the ratio of perfect scores to total number of pupils, using b to express the total number of pupils.

(d) Explain the proportion 30/100 = 12/b. Where does each fraction come from? How do you know the fractions are equal?

(e) Find the number that makes the proportion true.

- Henry earned $84 last summer. This was 20 percent more than he earned the year before. How much had he earned the previous year?

  (a) Think: 84 is 20 percent more than b. Then: 84 is 120 percent of b.

  (b) If Henry had earned $100 the previous year and the ratio of last year's earnings to those of the previous year was the same, how much would he have earned last summer?

  (c) Which element of the statement is unknown?

  (d) Set up the proportion.

  (e) What number will make the proportion true?

For the sake of simplicity, the foregoing illustrations were selected from problems offering no computational difficulties and, with the exception of the last, no hidden questions. As the study progresses, problems should be introduced with more difficult computations and with irrelevant data that are to be ignored in determining the relationships among the numbers.

At some later date these same basic methods—factor-factor-product or proportion—are extended to other problems using percent in an almost endless variety of situations as identified through clippings for the bulletin board. Here the new vocabulary and conventions associated with special applications, such as profit, loss, markup, discount, sale price, and commission, must be discussed, dramatized, and illustrated. Some examples of a few of these problems and their analyses are given in Table 8-1.

Activities 3,7,8, and 9 at the end of this chapter describe further experiences for pupils with percent.

A MATHEMATICS AND SCIENCE LESSON

The study of mathematics and science jointly in the same lesson has been encouraged in many experimental projects, and materials for such lessons have been published. Examples are the Minnesota School Mathematics and Science Teaching Project, Elementary Science Study, Science: A Process Approach and Unified Science and Mathematics for Elementary Schools.

One such experimental lesson concerns the study of leaves. The objective of the experiment is purposely not given to the reader

TABLE 8-1 APPLICATIONS OR PERCENT

Profit and loss	A car sold for $1,800. If the profit was 25 percent of this price, how much was the profit?	A car sold for $1,800. If the profit was $450, what percent of the selling price was the profit?	If the profit on a car is $450 and this is 25 percent of the selling price, what is the selling price?
	$b = 1,800$, $r = 0.25$, p unknown $0.25 \times 1,800 = p$ or $$\frac{25}{100} = \frac{p}{1,800}$$	$b = 1,800$, $p = 450$, r unknown $r \times 1,800 = 450$ or $$\frac{r}{100} = \frac{450}{1,800}$$	$p = 450$, $r = 0.25$, b unknown $0.25 \times b = 450$ or $$\frac{25}{100} = \frac{450}{b}$$
Commission	A real estate salesman is paid 5 percent commission. Find his commission on a sale of $15,450.	A real estate salesman is paid $772.50 for selling a house for $15,450. What rate of commission is he paid?	A real estate salesman is paid 5 percent on his sales. If his commission is $772.50, what is the amount of his sale?
	$b = 15,450$, $r = 0.05$, p unknown $0.05 \times 15,450 = p$ or $$\frac{5}{100} = \frac{p}{15,450}$$	$b = 15,450$, r unknown, $p = 772.50$ $r \times 15,450 = 772.50$ or $$\frac{r}{100} = \frac{772.50}{15,450}$$	b unknown, $r = 0.05$, $p = 772.50$ $0.05 \times b = 772.50$ or $$\frac{5}{100} = \frac{772.50}{b}$$
Discount	A coat marked at $40 is marked down 20 percent. What is the discount?	A coat marked at $40 is reduced by $8. What is the rate of discount?	A coat is reduced 20 percent. If the reduction is $8, what is the original price?
	$b = 40$, $r = 0.20$, p unknown $0.20 \times 40 = p$ or $$\frac{20}{100} = \frac{p}{40}$$	$b = 40$, r unknown, $p = 8$ $r \times 40 = 8$ or $$\frac{r}{100} = \frac{8}{40}$$	b unknown, $r = 0.20$, $p = 8$ $0.20 \times b = 8$ or $$\frac{20}{100} = \frac{8}{b}$$

(nor should it be stated to the class). In this way the experimenter can act like many scientists—investigating a phenomenon and not knowing what the results will be.

The teacher may organize his class in groups of four pupils, with each group at a separate table. Then each group is given a ruler, marked in centimeters and tenths of centimeters, and about ten leaves from a shrub or tree. On examining their leaves, each group finds:

Their leaves are of varying sizes.
All leaves seem to come from the same tree.
Each group has leaves from a different tree.
Some leaves from a tree are bright green, others are turning yellow.

Next, the teacher asks the question, "For your leaves, what should we measure?" Various answers may include "The stem," "The length," and "The width." Because there is probably a difference of opinion concerning the meaning of these terms, the teacher may give instructions for measuring:

The length is measured along the blade of the leaf and does not include the petiole (stem). (See Fig. 8-32.)

Figure 8-32
Length of a leaf.

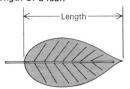

The width is measured across the leaf at the midpoint of the length (Fig. 8-33).

Next the pupils study their rulers, observing that each centimeter is subdivided into ten congruent parts. They agree to measure to the nearest tenth of a centimeter. Then they discuss how to determine the midpoint of the length and discover that the leaf can be folded (Fig. 8-34). The length of the fold can then be measured as the width. Next, they discuss the need for accuracy in measurement and in folding the leaf and the need for organizing their data in order that information can be used by other pupils.

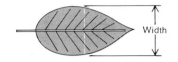

Next each group of pupils completes its measurements for the ten leaves. These are recorded as in columns 1, 2, and 3 (Fig. 8-35). Pupils are then asked, "What can we do with the data?" Observations are made and questions are raised:

Would length plus width mean anything?

Let's try to find the average of length and width.

Could we divide length by width?

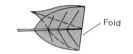

It is decided to try a number of suggestions.

First length plus width is determined and the results written in column 4 (Fig. 8-35). Pupils conclude that it seems the longest leaf also "has" the longest length plus width. Next, they determine length minus width (Fig. 8-35 column 5) and observe no startling results. Similarly, length times width (Fig. 8-35 column 6) and the average of length and width (Fig. 8-35 column 7) provide no new conclusions. They do, however, make one fundamental agreement concerning their data. Since their measurements have two or three places of accuracy (widths such as 3.6, 6.4, and 2.3 and lengths such as 4.1, 10.7, and 11.4), then numbers for length times width or the average of length and width should contain at most three digits.

Figure 8-35

1	2	3	4	5	6	7	8
	to nearest 1/10 cent.		Length + Width	Length − Width	Length × Width	Average Length and Width	Length Width
	Width	Length					
A	3.6	6.1	9.7	2.5	22.	4.9	1.69
B	2.3	4.1	6.4	1.8	9.4	3.2	1.78
C	3.6	6.4	10.0	2.8	23.	5.0	1.77
D	4.1	7.9	12.0	3.8	32.	6.0	1.92
E	6.1	10.7	16.8	4.6	65.	8.4	1.75
F	6.4	11.4	17.8	5.0	73.	8.9	1.78
G	3.9	6.6	10.5	2.7	26.	5.3	1.69
H	4.1	7.1	11.2	3.0	29.	5.6	1.73
I	2.3	4.1	6.4	1.8	9.4	3.2	1.78
J	4.8	8.9	13.7	4.1	43.	6.9	1.85

Average $\dfrac{\text{length}}{\text{width}} = 1.77$

When the ratio of length to width (length divided by width) is computed to three places (Fig. 8-35 column 8), some interesting observations are made by the pupils:

The numbers (ratios) are *close together*.

The ratio for the longest leaf is not the greatest.

The ratio for the shortest leaf is not the least.

Leaves from the same tree have about the same ratios of length to width.

Leaves from different trees often have quite different ratios.

Next pupils find the average of the ten ratios for leaves from each tree, and this number is assigned as a possible identifying number for the leaves of that tree. These data are organized and written on the board (Fig. 8-36). All leaves are then discarded, and each group of pupils is given a leaf from one of the trees. The problem is to try to determine the tree from which it was removed. The pupils measure length and width of the unknown leaves, compute length divided by width and compare it to the previously determined ratios. For example, the ratio of an unknown leaf is 1.65. This suggests it is from tree III. The conclusions reached are generally correct, except for one unknown leaf whose ratio is 1.54. While this is closer to the ratio for the leaf from tree VII (Fig. 8-36), the pupils decide it might also be from tree III.

Several interesting investigations may grow out of lessons such as this:

If the ratio of a leaf were 0.65, what would it look like? Answer for a ratio of 3.

Does this procedure work for leaves such as maples (Fig. 8-37) or other leaves where there are many indentations?

Several features of the organization and treatment of lessons such as this are worth considering:

Pupils see the usefulness of mathematics in studying other subjects.

Pupils have an opportunity to apply many mathematical concepts, such as precision in measuring (See Chapter 9.), average, and ratio. Many skills, such as adding, dividing, and finding averages, are practiced in a new setting.

Pupils plan their own procedures.

Pupils make many discoveries of both mathematical and scientific phenomena.

Such a study, in most cases, leads to continued investigation.

Some studies that could be initiated from this lesson are a more detailed study of leaves, graphing of results, and answers to ques-

Figure 8-36

Average ratio of length to width of leaves for seven trees.

Tree	Average of length ÷ width
I	1.77
II	.82
III	1.62
IV	1.01
V	2.11
VI	1.78
VII	1.49

Figure 8-37

tions such as: "Why was the ratio of length to width chosen?" "What would be found if the ratio of width to length had been determined?"

EXPERIMENTS FOR PUPILS

The following Activities are concerned with decimals, ratio or percent. For each there are many adaptions and extensions. In Activity 1, for example, divisions such as 1.5 ÷ 3 may be objectified with the rods by thinking "1 and 5 tenths into 3 parts of the same size." Cards may also be produced with the rods used to picture addition and subtraction with decimals.

ACTIVITY 1

Apparatus needed: wood rods

Objective: To use wood rods to obtain answers to divisions with decimals.

1 Change the names of your wood rods as follows: Name the 1-rod as 0.1, the 2-rod as 0.2, the 3-rod as 0.3, and so on. You name the 10-rod as ____.

2 Use your rods to find answers for divisions. For 1.5 ÷ 0.3 you think, "How many 0.3s in 1.5?" You set up the rods like this.

There are ____ 0.3s in 1.5.

3 Use wood rods to find answers for these divisions. Fill in the blanks.
   (*a*) 1.2 ÷ 0.4 =   How many ____ in ____?
   (*b*) 1.8 ÷ 0.6 =   How many ____ in ____?

ACTIVITY 2

Apparatus needed: abacus

Objective: To show the meaning of decimals on an abacus.

1 This abacus shows 28.09.

2 Move the beads on your abacus to show each of the following:
   (*a*) 3.14   (*b*) 10.73   (*c*) 36.90   (*d*) 0.54

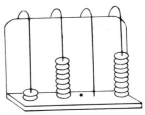

3 Place the decimal point on your abacus so you can show each of the following:
   (*a*) 1.623   (*b*) 7.504   (*c*) 3.007   (*d*) 0.0103

4 Show some decimal numerals on your abacus. Ask your partner to name the numerals.

ACTIVITY 3

Objective: To determine percents of a number.

1   Study these true statements:

10% of 80 = 8	80% of 80 = 64	150% of 80 = 120
30% of 80 = 24	20% of 80 = 16	300% of 80 = 240

Write true or false:

(*a*)   30% of 80 is 3 times 10% of 80.

(*b*)   20% of 80 is 1/4 of 80% of 80.

(*c*)   300% of 80 is 2 times 150% of 80.

(*d*)   10% of 80 + 20% of 80 = 30% of 80.

2   Study these statements. Then fill in the blanks.

(*a*)   If 10% of n = 8, then 20% of n = 2 × 8.

(*b*)   If 40% of n = 20, then 10% of n = 1/4 × 20.

(*c*)   If 50% of n = 12, then 100% of n = _____ × 12.

(*d*)   If 30% of n = 18, then 10% of n = _____ × _____ .

ACTIVITY 4

Objective: Discover generalizations concerning multiplication of decimals.

Fill in blanks in the chart below.

Multiplication	Statement	Product using fractions	Decimal part of product expressed by	Statement of how product was obtained
0.21 X 3	Hundredths times ones	$\frac{63}{100}$	Hundredths	Hundredths times ones are hundredths
0.6 X 0.8	Tenths times _____	_____	_____	Tenths times _____ ,are _____.
0.3 X 0.47	_____ times hundredths	_____	_____	_____ times _____ are _____ .

ACTIVITY 5

Objective: To find quotients after making the divisor a counting number.

1   Here are four ways to make the divisor a counting number for 3.2 ÷ 0.8.

$.8\overline{)3.2}$ becomes $.8 × 5\overline{)3.2 × 5}$ becomes $4\overline{)16}$

$.8\overline{)3.2}$ becomes $.8 \times 10\overline{)3.2 \times 10}$ becomes $8\overline{)32}$
$.8\overline{)3.2}$ becomes $.8 \times 2.5\overline{)3.2 \times 2.5}$ becomes $2\overline{)8}$
$.8\overline{)3.2}$ becomes $.8 \times 100\overline{)3.2 \times 100}$ becomes $80\overline{)320}$

Do the four divisions above. If your answers are not all the same, check your work.

2 Follow the pattern on Ex. 1 to do $1.2 \div 0.4$ in four ways. Be sure the divisor becomes a counting number.

ACTIVITY 6

Objective: To practice one way of estimating quotients.

1 Estimate □ if $0.65 \div 0.05 = □$

This equation means $□ \times 0.05 = 0.65$. Now try 1, 10, 100, 1000 and so on for □.

If □ = 1, $1 \times 0.05 = 0.05$. This is too small.

If □ = 10, $10 \times 0.05 = 0.5$. This is too small.

If □ = 100, $100 \times .05 = 5$. This is too large.

So □ is between 10 and 100.

2 Use this thinking to estimate:
   (a) $965.1 \div 8.2$ (b) $2.73 \div 0.41$

ACTIVITY 7

Apparatus needed: tangram pieces   *Objective:* To determine the relation of tangram pieces to each other using percent. See page 52 for identification of tangram pieces by letter.

1 Fit your tangram pieces to answer these questions.

   Suppose the D-piece is 10% of a number. Then the:
   (a) F-piece is ____ % of that number.
   (b) G-piece is ____ % of that number.
   (c) A-piece is ____ % of that number.

2 Suppose the B-piece is 200% of a number. Then the:
   (a) D-piece is ____ % of that number.
   (b) F-piece is ____ % of that number.
   (c) C-piece is ____ % of that number.

3 *Brainbuster:* Suppose the G-piece and the D-piece together are 60% of a number. Then the:
   (a) B-piece is ____ % of that number.

(*b*) A-piece and the F-piece together are _____ % of that number.

4 Make up some problems like this. Give them to your partner to solve.

ACTIVITY 8

Apparatus needed: wood rods

Objective: To name the wood rods as a percent of a number.

1 Suppose your 1-rod is 10% of a number. Write the percent of that number for each of these rods.

(*a*) 2-rod _____   (*b*) 3-rod _____   (*c*) 8-rod _____

2 Suppose the 5-rod is 150% of a number. Write the percent of that number for each of these rods.

(*a*) 10-rod _____   (*b*) 7-rod _____   (*c*) 2-rod _____

ACTIVITY 9

Objective: To write a story for a given computation.

1 If you were told to write a story about 75% × ☐ = 30, you might write:

(*a*) Joan had 75% of the problems correct on a test. She had 30 problems correct. How many problems were on the test?

(*b*) At a sale, all prices were 75% of the marked price. On sale, a coat cost $30.00. What was the marked price?

2 Write a story for each of these:

(*a*) 50 × 60 = ☐

(*b*) ☐ × 80 = 40

ACTIVITY 10

Objective: To write the ratios of the lengths of line segments.

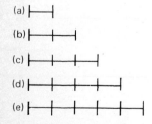

1 The length of line segment *a* is 1 unit. The ratio of the length of segment *a* to the length of segment *d* is 1 to 4 or to 1/4. Write the ratios of the lengths of these segments:

(*a*) *b* to *c* _____   (*c*) *e* to *a* _____

(*b*) *d* to *c* _____   (*d*) *c* to *e* _____

2 Draw line segments *f*, *g*, *h*, and *i*. The ratios of these lengths are given.

(*a*) *f* to *g* is 1 to 6.   (*b*) *g* to *h* is 2 to 1.

(c) *h* to *i* is 2 to 3.

Activity 11

Objective: To write a ratio for distance walked in a certain time.

1   Walk for 10 seconds. Count the number of steps. Write the ratio of the number of steps to the number of seconds. ＿＿.

2   If you keep going at this rate you would be going ＿＿ steps every 10 seconds. How far would you go in:

    (*a*) 20 seconds? ＿＿ steps in 20 seconds is ＿＿ to 20. The ratio is ＿＿.

    (*b*) 60 seconds? ＿＿ steps in 60 seconds is ＿＿ to 60. The ratio is ＿＿.

3   Speed is often shown by ratios. In most cases the second term of the ratio is 1. The ratio 4 to 1 could mean 4 meters in 1 second. Write these ratios to show speed.

    (*a*) 5 meters in 1 second ＿＿.

    (*b*) 64 kilometers in 1 hour ＿＿.

4   Write these speeds as ratios with the second term as 1.

    (*a*) 60 meters in 10 seconds ＿＿ to 1.

    (*b*) 45 meters in 5 seconds ＿＿ to 1.

QUESTIONS AND EXERCISES

1 Pupils learn the meaning of 0.4 as they illustrate it with many different materials. Show 0.4 with as many different kinds of materials as possible.

2 In developing the concept of a decimal, how is understanding of fractions used as a background? How is the concept related to that of whole numbers?

3 Some of your fifth-grade pupils need experiences to extend their understanding of the concept of decimals from hundredths to thousandths. Describe some suitable experiences.

4 List experiences for pupils through which they relate addition of numbers expressed with decimals to the following: (a) addition of whole numbers; (b) addition of fractional

numbers; (c) subtraction of numbers expressed by decimals.

5 (a) Draw a picture of a rectangular region to show 2 X 3.46. Label the regions to indicate the three multiplications performed. (b) Follow the instructions in (a) to show the four multiplications for 2.4 X 3.3.

6 One of your sixth-grade pupils asks, "Why, in multiplying 3.7 X 4.8, for example, do you add the number of decimal places instead of multiplying them in order to place the decimal in the product?" What would you have him do to help him answer his own question?

7 What is wrong with this teaching: The teacher wrote on the board 3.2 X 5.6. She said, "Multiply as if they named whole numbers,

and count off in the product the number of decimal places in the multiplier and multiplicand. Now practice this rule."

8 Summarize ways of obtaining a reasonable answer to 8.92 X 3.06.

9 Describe how to objectify $6\overline{)15.6}$ and $4\overline{)7.6}$, using place-value charts.

10 Describe ways in which a pupil could improvise the results for the following: (a) 3 X 5.1; (b) $3\overline{)6.9}$; (c) $0.2\overline{)1.2}$.

11 What are the different forms for expressing a ratio? Illustrate by giving an example of a situation described by a ratio and expressing it in each form.

12 What is meant by the statement "Percent is not a new idea to the pupil, but rather is an old idea expressed in a different language"?

13 The paper said, "Fifty percent of the student body of 1,000 attended the operetta." Does this mean that 500 students were in attendence? If 400 of the 1,000 students were girls, did 200 girls attend? If 200 of the 1,000 students were seniors, how many of them attended?

14 Summarize the difficulties that arise from the language used in percent problems.

15 Describe some concrete experiences through which pupils may learn the concept of percent.

16 What computational skills are used in dealing with situations expressed by percent?

17 Describe some things that a pupil should be able to tell or show if he understands the meaning of 13%.

18 If a pupil consistently makes mistakes, such as 1/2% of 600 = 300, or 1/3% X 1,200 = 400, what would you as his teacher have him do?

PROJECTS

1 Study a series of recent mathematics textbooks and teacher's manuals for grades K-8 and answer the following for decimals: (a) List the major topics and important concepts that are introduced at each grade. (b) What concrete materials are suggested for use, and what concept does each help to develop? (c) What experiences are given to help pupils understand placing the decimal point in products and quotients? (d) What activities are suggested for the mathematics laboratory? (e) What are suggestions for individualizing the program with decimals?

2 Demonstrate to the class: (a) The meaning of 12%, 125%, and 1/2%, using models and pictures. (b) How to find n in as many ways as possible if 15% of n is 12. (c) The meaning of the ratio 3 to 5, using concrete materials and pictures. (d) The use of place-value charts or the 18-bead abacus for developing the concept of decimals, adding with decimals, or subtracting with decimals. (e) The use of the number line in picturing operations with decimals.

3 Plan a lesson and describe it to the class. Possible topics are: expressing a percent as a decimal, learning to express problems in the form of proportion, or learning the meaning of percents greater than 100%.

4 Examine a series of elementary school mathematics texts and teacher's manuals, and report to the class answers for the following: (a) Describe pupil experiences for introducing the topic of percent and helping pupils understand the idea of percent. (b) What experiences are provided to help pupils understand and solve problems with percent?

5 Write an Activity card with an objective for each of the following: (a) concept of hundredths using cardboard regions; (b) subtraction with decimals using place-value charts; (c) estimating products with factors as decimals; (d) relationship of multiplication and division with decimals; (e) idea of a ratio using concrete materials; (f) meaning of percent.

6 (a) Complete Activities 1, 3, 4, 5, 6, 7, and 10. (b) Write an Activity Card the objective

of which is learning to solve percent problems.

7 What materials are especially useful in learning the concept of percent? Describe specific experiences using these materials through which pupils explore the meaning of percent.

Bibliography

1 Henry, B.: "Do We Need Separate Rules to Compute in Decimal Notation?" *The Arithmetic Teacher*, vol. 18, pp. 40-42, Jan., 1971. A plea to compute with fractions using the same algorithm whether the numbers are in common or decimal notation.

2 Jencks, S. M., and D. M. Peck: "Mental Imagery in Mathematics," *The Arithmetic Teacher*, vol. 19, pp. 642-644, Dec., 1972. Ideas to support the thesis that the problem of teaching addition of fractions reduces to one of finding suitable objects to portray the fractions.

3 Kennedy, L. M.: *Guilding Children to Mathematical Discovery*, Wadsworth Belmont, Calif., 1970. Chap. 11 outlines experiences for learning decimals and percent.

4 Kidd, K., S. Myers, and D. Cilley: *The Laboratory Approach to Mathematics*, Science Research Associates, Chicago, 1970. Excellent set of experiments and investigations for ratio.

5 Major, J. R.: "Science and Mathematics in the Elementary School," *The Arithmetic Teacher*, vol. 14, pp. 629-635, Dec., 1967. Description of AAAS program, "Science—a Process Approach, "of which mathematics is an integral part.

6 Major, J. R.: "Science and Mathematics—A Decade of Change," *The Arithmetic Teacher*, vol. 17, pp. 293-297, April, 1970. Recommends with illustrations how decimal fractions should be taught before common fractions.

7 Nelson, J.: "Percent: A Rational Number or a Ratio," *The Arithmetic Teacher*, vol. 16, pp. 105-109, Feb., 1969. Fine models using sets for helping pupils understand ratio and percent.

8 Nuffield Foundation: *The Nuffield Mathematics Project: Computation and Structure*, John Wiley, New York, 1969. This teacher's guide (Book 4) has activities for extending the numeration system to decimals.

9 Schmenke, C. W., N. Maertens, and W. R. Arnold: *Teaching the Child Mathematics*. Dryden, Hendale, Ill., 1973. Chapter 9 is a discussion of teaching decimals, ratio and percent.

10 Wilson, G. H.: "Decimal-Common Fraction Sequence Versus Conventional Sequence," *School Science and Mathematics*, vol. 72, pp. 589-592, Oct., 1972. Pupils can learn decimal fractions before learning common fractions.

9
MEASURES AND MEASURING

It is essential that pupils understand measurement and be able to measure. This is clearly revealed by studies of the mathematics needed by people in all walks of life. But the concept of measurement is a very subtle one, difficult to understand and teach effectively. Thus, while refined concepts of measurement are being developed, it is necessary for the teacher not only to select appropriate experiences, but also to use and teach the vocabulary that precisely conveys the concepts.

It seems paradoxical that the learning of measurement has traditionally been started in the early grades, with many of its subtle ideas completely neglected. Because these concepts are now being emphasized, every teacher must learn or review such material as is presented under Mathematical Understanding in this chapter. The major topics discussed in that section are measurement as a comparison, the arbitrary nature of measuring units, the approximate nature of the measuring process, and precision and accuracy. With this background, the section on Directing Learning of Measuring focuses on ways for the effective teacher to:

● Select meaningful experiences that illuminate the many subtle ideas (all measurements are approximate, units for measuring are arbitrary) involved in learning measurement concepts.
● Help pupils discover appropriate units for measuring segments, regions, angles, capacity, and so on.
● Guide pupils to explore and understand the role of formulas in determining size.
● Choose from available activities those which provide for individual differences in learning measurement.

MATHEMATICAL UNDERSTANDING

One line segment may be longer, just as long as, or shorter than another line segment. In a similar manner, one angle may be larger, just as large as, or smaller than another angle. A tentative decision as to which of these possibilities exists in any given instance may be made by an intuitive judgment or by a physical comparison of the two objects.

On a more sophisticated level, if one desires to know the length of a room, he may use a meterstick as his measuring unit and count the number of times it is applied; to find the weight of an object, he determines the number of grams, kilograms, or pounds required to *balance* it; to measure liquids, he compares with fixed units of volume, such as the gallon or liter; to determine time, he measures it by comparison with such standards as seconds, minutes, or hours. The process of measuring, regardless of what is being measured, consists of choosing the proper unit and comparing with that unit; comparison is normally made with some known or accepted reference unit. For practical purposes and for teaching in the elementary school, the last sentence may be considered a definition of measuring.

Measurement by Nonstandardized Units

There is a tendency to think of the present age as one precise measurement, as opposed to past centuries, which were characterized by inexact and varying units of measure. However, even today, nonstandardized or crude units are often adequate for purposes of comparison or decision or description: "Use a pinch of salt in the cookie batter"; "We live a half-hour's drive from the city"; "The job will take all afternoon."

It may be supposed that early man used measurement only for making rough comparisons. He judged relative lengths, compared two weights by placing one in each hand, and developed a general feeling or sensitivity for more, less, larger, smaller, or heavier. Having no specifically defined units with which objects might be compared, he was content to use whatever was available as a reference unit for comparison, judging an object to be "longer than a spear" or "heavier than a rock." Although he lacked precise measuring instruments, his basic approach of establishing the measuring unit and comparing this unit with the item being measured was identical to present practice.

As the need for more precise measurement increased, a variety of measuring units or referents were developed. Most of these were readily available parts of the human body, such as the length of a finger joint, the breadth of a finger or hand, the distance from elbow to tip of finger or from nose to finger tips (arm extended), the human foot, and the length of a pace. Other units were derived from daily activities: an acre was the amount of land that could be plowed during a day, and a furlong was the length of a plowed furrow in a field.

Measurement by Standardized Units

As transfer of commodities between men increased, differences in the manner of measuring objects that were being exchanged created serious difficulties. To remedy this, it became necessary to standardize units of length, weight, or bulk that could be known and accepted by both parties in the trade. Sometimes it even became necessary to define the process of measuring. With the growth of commerce and industry, measures were more and more carefully defined and standardized.

A standard unit of measure is one that is precisely defined and legally established. For example, the meter was defined in 1960 at the Eleventh General (International) Conference on Weights and Measures in terms of wavelengths of krypton 86 under specified conditions. The meter, not the yard, has been the standard of length in the United States since an act of Congress in 1893. The United States Metric Study performed in 1968-1971 has recommended that metric units be adopted for all sectors of our economy within ten years. It would seem that metric units will soon predominate in our lives but may not be exclusively used. A football field, for example may possibly remain 100 yards long.

Units of measure, then, have been established for us and measuring devices produced in the form of rulers, protractors, watches, thermometers, and so on. We apply these instruments so automatically that we tend to ignore some of the subtle concepts of measurement that should be recognized.

Units of Measurement Are Arbitrary

The fact that a length of 1 inch is used derives more from historical or physiological reasons than reasons of convenience. The choice of the standard length of 1 inch was an arbitrary one; segments such as $\overline{AB}$, $\overline{CD}$, or $\overline{EF}$, shown in Fig. 9-1, could serve equally well as a unit length. In a similar manner, standard weights of 1 pound or 1 ton were established not because they have any special advantage, but because over a period of time people became accustomed to them and they were finally standardized. Other units for measuring areas, volumes, angles and time are similarly arbitrary.

The development of the metric system is an exception to the procedure of standardizing arbitrary and unrelated units of measure. It is the rational characteristic of the system and its decimal form that make it so useful for scientific work.

Units Are of the Same Nature as the Object Measured

Units have the same nature as the object measured, a fact that is often overlooked. This is evident from the fact that teachers often

Figure 9-1
$\overline{AB}$, $\overline{CD}$, and $\overline{EF}$ are three of many possible unit segments.

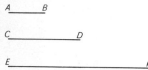

get answers such as, "The area of the rectangle is 12 centimeters." Figures 9-2a, b, and c may be considered as unit measures, each of which is appropriate for measuring an aspect of rectangle *PQRS* (Fig. 9-2d). The unit segment (a) could be compared with segment QR and the length of $\overline{QR}$ described as a number of such unit segments. The unit region (b) could be used to measure the area of the rectangular region *PQRS*. The unit angle (c) could be used to measure any angle of *PQRS*. Segment (a) is obviously of no use for measuring either the area or the angle, and a similar statement could be made about unit area (b) and unit angle (c). In general, then, to measure a segment a unit segment is needed; to measure a volume a unit volume is needed; or to measure a time a unit time is needed.

Figure 9-2
(a), (b), and (c) are for measuring properties of (d).

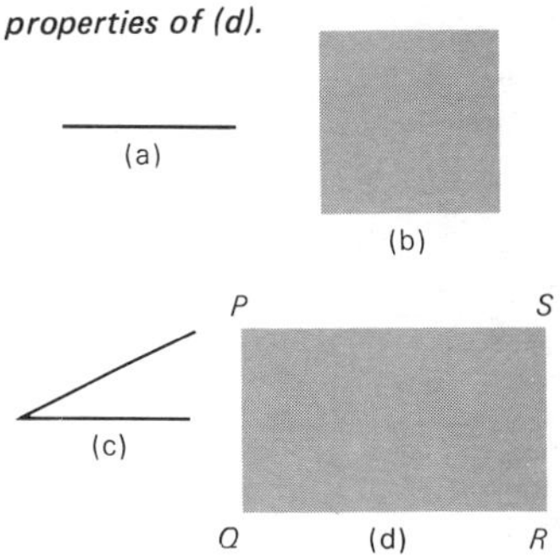

All Measurements Are Approximate

The counting numbers were invented to describe a certain property of finite sets. They actually describe how many separate or discrete elements are contained in a given collection. Hence, correct counting of the members of a finite set always supplies the same result in the form of a counting number.

However, there are no natural breaks or separate entities in a line segment, a volume of water, an angle, or a period of time. These are continuous quantities and are not composed of discrete members. The distance across a classroom does not suggest a number in the same way that set $A = \{\bigcirc \; \ominus, \; \oslash\}$ does. There is nothing in the area of a playground, the length of a piece of string, or the temperature at noon that suggests the application of the same procedure that determines how many children are in the classroom.

When one measures the length of a legal envelope with a centimeter as the unit, the measure is expressed as 22. With a smaller unit, such as 0.1 centimeter, the length may be stated more precisely as 22.3 centimeters. In other words, by using increasingly smaller units, one can express the measurement with increasing precision. But there is always a still smaller unit by means of which a more precise measurement could be attained. Any measurement is, therefore, approximate.

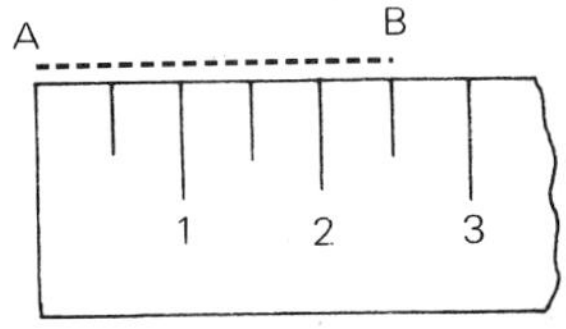

Instructions for making a measurement should take into account and clarify this idea—for example: "Measure segment AB (Fig. 9-3) to the nearest centimeter" (*answer:* 2 centimeters); Measure $\overline{AB}$ to the nearest 0.1 centimeter" (*answer:* 2.5 centimeters). One should bear in mind that an exact measure of any length, area, time, or weight cannot be determined by the process of measuring.

Figure 9-3

Figure 9-4

∠ABC measures 2 in unit angles.

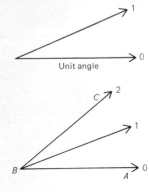

Measure and Measurement

Think about a line segment AB whose length is exactly 25 centimeters. (Remember, such a segment exists as an idea, even though it cannot be exactly reproduced.) Strictly speaking, it is not correct to write $\overline{AB}$ = 25 centimeters because the equals sign is reserved for use between different names for the same number or different names for the same set. Here $\overline{AB}$ is not a name for a number but for a set of points.

Since we must communicate and record measurements, the following convention is used when correct terminology is desired: $m(\overline{AB})$ = 25 (in centimeters).

In a similar manner, $\angle ABC$ has a measurement of 2 unit angles, where the unit angle is defined as shown in Fig. 9-4. This may be recorded as $m(\angle ABC)$ = 2 (in unit angles).

A statement such as $m(\overline{AB})$ = 25 does not convey the needed information because the unit of measurement is not known. To provide all information, the unit of measurement as well as the number of those units must be named.

Although such precise language and notation may seem unduly technical and the distinctions seem very subtle, there are good reasons for this approach. When mathematical terms or symbols such as = are used, their definitions should be made carefully and they should be applied according to those definitions. The language and symbolism of mathematics must be unambiguous and able to convey precise meanings. To use them loosely is to destroy their efficiency.

Precision in Measurement

Ms. Peterson, an eighth-grade teacher, asked Joe and Bill to measure the width of the playground. A steel tape marked off in meters and tenths of a meter was available. Bill and Joe said the width was 20.3 meters to the nearest tenth of a meter. From Fig. 9-5 it may be seen that while it was a little less than 20.4 meters, it was closer to 20.3 than to 20.4. If the width had been measured as in Fig. 9-6, it would have been greater than 20.4 meters but still would have been 20.4 meters to the nearest tenth of a meter. That is, to the nearest tenth of a meter, any measurement between 20.35 meters and 20.45 meters is reported as 20.4 meters. Ms. Peterson knew that the measurement was approximate, or about right—the error was not greater than 0.05 meter.

Error in this sense does not imply a mistake. It merely tells how precisely the measurement was performed. With more careful application of more refined measuring devices, a measurement can be made to almost any degree of precision that is desired. There

Figure 9-5

Steel tape marked in tenths of a meter.

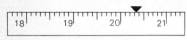

Figure 9-6

is, however, always some error present in any measurement. Measuring, of necessity, is an inexact process.

In general, the use for which a measurement is made determines the degree of precision required. For example, the length of a highway measured to the nearest kilometer may be sufficiently precise for recording on maps or locating markers along the road; however, a contractor, when submitting a bid for a construction of the road, which may cost as much as 1 million dollars a kilometer, must measure the distance with greater precision. Similarly, decidedly greater precision is needed by the pharmacist in weighing ingredients for a prescription than by the coal dealer in weighing a load of coal, or the butcher in weighing a roast.

In using reported measures, one may not know the degree of precision to which a measurement was performed or reported. For example, if the statement is made that "Jimmy weighs 49 pounds," the average adult thinks of this as if it were exact, although some error must exist. In the absence of qualifying statements on which to base a judgment of exactness, we tend to ignore inexactness of measurements in the practical affairs of everyday life, with few or no resulting difficulties.

For purposes of avoiding ambiguity, scientists and mathematicians have established a convention to specify how precisely a measurement was made or reported. That convention may be stated: "If a measurement is recorded with no indication of how it was obtained, it will be assumed correct to the smallest unit shown." Using this principle, the meaning of certain recorded measures is shown in Fig. 9-7. Hence, 8 centimeters and 8.5 centimeters indicate measurements of different precision. The first is correct to the nearest centimeter, the other to the nearest 0.1 centimeter.

Correct use of the equals sign (=) The equals sign (=) has been used to indicate names for the same number. To avoid over elaborate terminology and because of accepted usage, = is also permitted in statements such as "10 decimeters = 1 meter" or "1 square meter = 100 square decimeters." It is understood that

Figure 9-7
Errors in measurements.

Recorded measurement	Meaning	Error	How the error is computed
48 liters	Closer to 48 liters than to 47 liters or 49 liters	0.5 liters	½ of 1
37.4 kilometers	Closer to 37.4 kilometers than to 37.3 or 37.5 kilometers	0.05 kilometers	½ of 0.1
8.75 centimeters	Closer to 8,75 centimeters than to 8.74 or 8.76 centimeters	0.005 centimeters	½ of 0.01
0.453 grams	Closer to 0.453 grams than to 0.452 or 0.454 grams	0.0005 grams	½ of 0.001

Figure 9-8
6 square centimeters in each of 4 rows.

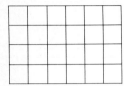

the meaning here is that the measure of the length of a certain segment is 10 (in decimeters) and is also 1 (in meters), or the measure of area of a region is 1 (in square meters) and is also 100 (in square decimeters).

At the same time, expressions such as "area = 6 centimeters × 4 centimeters" for finding the area of a rectangular region 6 centimeters long and 4 centimeters wide, while commonly used, are not correct in the strictest sense. In this case neither 6 centimeters nor 4 centimeters is a number; each is a measurement. An alternate form for finding the area of a rectangular region and one that imparts correct ideas is to think of the region shown in Fig. 9-8 as 4 rows with 6 square centimeters in each row. The area is 24 square centimeters from 4 × 6. Some teachers prefer to think of 4 × 6 (square centimeters), including the unit of measurement parenthetically.

Since there does exist a line segment AB, that is 6 centimeters in length even though it cannot be drawn, it is correct to write $m(\overline{AB}) = 6$ (in centimeters). If line segment AB is measured to the nearest whole number of centimeters, then $m(\overline{AB}) = 6$ to the nearest centimeter. Similarly, $m(\overline{CD}) = 6.5$ to the nearest tenth of a centimeter means a unit of precision of 0.1 centimeter. These units of precision are understood when the measurements are reported as "The length of $\overline{AB}$ is approximately 6 centimeters" or "The length of $\overline{CD}$ is approximately 6.5 centimeters."

In a similar manner, if the length and width of a rectangle are *given* as 6.5 and 4.5 centimeters, the area is 6.5 × 4.5 square centimeters. However, if the length and width are *measured* correct to the nearest half-centimeter, then the area is approximately 6.5 × 4.5 square centimeters. Obviously, such distinctions are only made after the pupil has had many varied learning experiences.

DIRECTING LEARNING OF MEASURING

The study of measures on the primary level was described in Chap. 3. However, few if any of these concepts or skills are fully learned in those grades. A systematic study of measures in grades 3-8 includes the following: refining concepts of measures such as the approximate nature of measurement; introducing and using new metric units as well as those English units still being employed; discovering how to display data in the form of graphs for the purpose of communicating; increasing skill in measuring for more technical situations with an appreciation of the use of formulas for perimeter, area and volume.

Refining Concepts of Common Measures

The pupils' introduction to the basic concepts of measurement is best accomplished in the mathematics laboratory. Only through

continued and varied experiences therein can they mature and refine those ideas, with discussion and completion of textbook exercises necessary for the required understanding and skill.

The arbitrary nature of units of measurement may be introduced
by having pupils measure the length of the front of the room by
their steps. In a laboratory setting, a group of pupils discussed
the necessity of having each pupil make each of his steps as
nearly the same length as possible; they also decided to measure
to the nearest whole number of steps. As each pupil walked across
the room, the results were recorded on the Activity Card in the
form shown in Fig. 9-9. Pupils also wrote the name of the child
who took the most and the fewest steps and answered these
questions: "Who took the longest step?" "Who took the shortest
step?" "Tom takes longer steps than Bob. Guess how many steps
he will take." "Pam takes shorter steps than anybody in the room.
Will she take more steps than Georgia? Why?" Pupils or the teacher
should originate the question "Whose answer for the length of the
room is correct?" It should be agreed that all answers are correct,
but that for the measurement to be understood, the number of
steps must always be accompanied with a knowledge of *how long
the step is.*

Similar experiments may be carried out, with pupils inventing
the units. For measuring the length of the top of a pupil's desk,
many different units are possible, as indicated in Fig. 9-10. Pupils
may also invent units other than the step for measuring the front
of the room, some of which may be Mary's shoe, Barbara's string,
Paul's strip of paper, Walter's strip of paper (which is two of Paul's),
Carol's umbrella, or Len's stick.

Throughout all of these experiences, certain emphases are
continually made:

There is an error in measuring. Pupils see this as they apply their
units and agree to a precision such as "Measure to the nearest whole
number of steps."

To measure a segment, a unit segment must be used. Pupils think
of the front of the room or the edge of a desk as a segment. Likewise,
they visualize the unit used as a segment, whether it be a step, a
stick, or the edge of a book.

Not only must the measurement of an object be given by a number,
but also the unit must be identified.

The measure depends on the unit used. If the measure is a certain
number for a given unit, it will be less for a larger unit.

Need for and accuracy in measurement Pupils develop an appreciation of the importance of measurement in modern life as
they measure, describe objects in terms of units of measure, and

Figure 9-9

Front of room	
Measure	Unit
20	Ellen's step
18	Bill's step
21	Georgia's step
16	Bob's step

Figure 9-10

Top of desk	
Measure	Unit
11	Len's hand
43	Joe's thumb
7	Marcia's pencil
15	Tom's eraser
4	Edge of mathematics book

identify situations in which measured quantities are used. For example, they describe themselves as carefully as possible using measurements: they find linear units needed to indicate height, distance around hips, waist, chest, or biceps, length of arm, foot, or finger; they find weight in pounds. Later, as additional concepts are developed, they may think of their skin surface as a number of square units and volume occupied as a number of cubic units.

Pupils compile lists of objects and situations described by measurements. This inventory may be classified under headings of measurements used at home, in school subjects, or on the playground (Fig. 9-11); another possible classification is the use of measurement in recreation, sports, or travel. An investigation of the difficulties that would arise if certain measurements were discontinued or outlawed is an example of the thought-provoking questions that lead pupils to sense the dependence of our present culture on measurement. The class may then try to improvise units of measurement to replace those discontinued in this imaginary situation.

Understanding the degree of accuracy desirable in measuring develops simultaneously with investigation of the needs for measures. Pupils do research to determine the accuracy that the law requires for scales and other measuring instruments used by merchants; they consider differences in the degree of accuracy used in reporting results of sports events—the length of the pass in the football game and the height cleared by the pole vaulter. They list items, such as ordinary loose-leaf paper, for which a size of 8 1/2 inches by 11 inches is more or less standard, and other items, such as books, which are found in varying sizes. This is followed by a discussion of reasons for uniformity or lack of uniformity of sizes and the precision of measurement needed for different situations.

Developing the concept of new units To develop an accurate concept of a unit of measure, most pupils need experiences beyond hearing or reading about it. They require first-hand experience in applying each new measuring unit and comparing it with things with which they are familiar. The importance of this *intuitive feel* for a unit of measure is indicated when situations such as the following are considered: "The room temperature is 30°C. Is this too warm?" "Jim drove down the street at 50 kilometers per hour. Should he be arrested?" Familiar referents are needed if the statements are to be understood. For this reason many teachers have found it useful during early stages of instruction to have pupils visualize the inch, foot, and yard in terms of the human body—the *finger-inch* (Fig. 9-12a) as the distance between two knuckles, the

Figure 9-11
Measurements at the playground.

Measuring a distance for the race.
Measuring the court for the volleyball games.
Measuring the size of the basketball court.
Comparison of a basketball and a baseball.
Measuring the circle for kickball.
Measuring to partition a field for games.

Figure 9-12
Human measuring units.

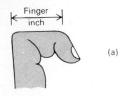

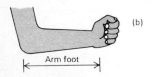

arm-foot (Fig. 9-12*b*) as the distance from the elbow to the fist and the *arm-yard* (Fig. 9-12*c*) as the distance from the tip of the nose to the tip of the fingers. For the metric system, too, pupils can identify human units, showing the width of a fingernail as about 1 centimeter or noting that the finger-inch is about 3 centimeters and even inventing a name such as tri-centimeter. An understanding of the relative accuracy of the ruler develops as pupils compare the results from using a ruler to those obtained from using their human units. Discussion of the reliability of answers and sources of error serves to summarize the experience.

The concept of a unit of weight is refined as pupils lift butter, cheese, or nails, and other materials bought by the pound. A stone or pail of water weighing 1 kilogram may be handled and compared to the weight of other objects. The concept of liquid and dry-volume measure is extended as pupils experiment with containers of different shapes which measure various materials.

The concepts of longer periods of time such as month, season, or year mature as experiences are provided to give these units meaning. Experiences are designed so that pupils comprehend shorter periods of time, as well as the number of these shorter periods making up the larger units. For example, they gain understanding of a week as the time from Sunday to Sunday. The month is perceived as about four of these weeks, or about 30 days; or the month is the time until Christmas, the time since a birthday, or the time between allowance payments. Out of these referents and through repeated attention to periods of a month in a child's life, the concept of the month is built. In a like manner, the notion of a year develops. Periods such as a decade, generation, or century are sensed principally as the time between two numbers in the sequence of years.

Figure 9-13

Certain laboratory experiences with lengths of segments which help the learner develop more mature concepts while developing his intuition can be done on a geoboard. For example:

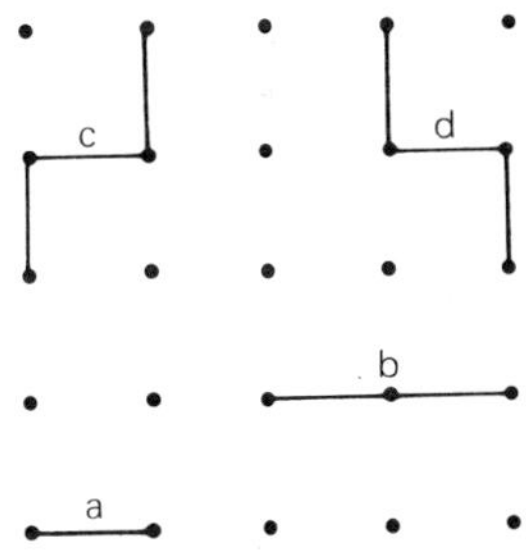

Segment *a*, Fig. 9-13, is 1 unit long. With elastics show segments that are 2, 3, and 4 units long. Can you show a segment 6 units long? Why?

Segment *b*, is a unit segment. Try to show segments 1/2, 1 1/2, 2, 2 1/2, and 3 units long. Which one cannot be shown?

Segment *a* is a unit segment. Show all shapes that are 3 units long. Should *c* and *d* be considered different shapes? Draw your pictures on dot paper. (See page 390 for construction of dot paper.) Have a contest with a friend using lengths of 2, 4, 5, (or any length) to see who can find the most shapes. How many shapes are closed? Put the most original ones on the bulletin board.

Measuring and reporting results In the primary grades pupils use rulers, scales, various sized containers, and clocks as measuring instruments. They have a preliminary introduction to concepts and develop some ability to use linear, weight, volume, and time measure. In the beginning their rulers have marks that indicate only whole numbers of centimeters or inches. Such instructions are given as "Measure the length of the pencil to the nearest centimeter." Pupils report results of their measurements in the form "The length of the pencil is 10 cm to the nearest cm." Later, they explain the meaning of such statements as "The length of the pencil is closer to 10 cm than 11 cm and closer to 10 cm than 9 cm." When fractions are understood, pupils learn to measure to the nearest half-centimeter, tenth-centimeter, and so on.

Pupils often encounter difficulty in measuring to a given fraction of a unit. It is not as easy to learn this skill as is generally supposed. One source of difficulty lies in the fact that only the unit marks have numbers to help in reading the scale. The marks indicating smaller subdivisions must be identified by counting. Further, different rulers have different subdivisions, and mistakes are likely to occur unless the pupil carefully examines the graduation before measuring.

Caution is necessary so that pupils learn to interpret the 1/10 on a metric ruler as a *length* from the beginning of the scale to the 1/10 mark, rather than as a point on the ruler. When this is understood, the idea that a centimeter is separated into ten congruent parts by nine marks is clarified. Pupils must learn, also, to select the correct starting point when measuring. On rulers, this point may be at the left end, or it may be a mark near the end. Similarly, the bathroom or balance scale must be adjusted to show a zero weight when not in use.

Refinement of ability to read and interpret measuring scales develops simultaneously with the use of fractions. Thus with the presently used English units the pupil can show 1/8 inch as one of the eight congruent parts of an inch and can illustrate 2 1/2 with 2 pints plus 1/2 of another pint. With the metric system much of the work with measurements involving fractions will be simplified since the pupil will deal with subdivisions of tenths, hundredths, etc.

In the study of fractions, relationships are objectified and problems are solved by means of a clock, ruler, scales, or gallon, quart, and pint containers. These experimental verifications give pupils confidence in their answers, help them formulate a mental picture of the fractional number, and motivate them to study fractions as they see the relation to their surroundings. Some examples are as follows:

Problem	Objectification
1/8s in 2	Find how many 1/8 pounds (2 ounces) are contained in 2 pounds (32 ounces).
1/3 of 3/4	Separate 3/4 inch on the ruler into three congruent parts, finding 1/4 inch.
1/4 = 2/8	1/4 on the ruler corresponds to 2/8.

The following experiments help the pupil learn to measure and understand the need for units of measurement as well as their approximate nature.

Make your own personal body chart:

Little finger: about _____ centimeters long

Front tooth: about _____ centimeters wide

Foot: about _____ centimeters long

Height: about _____ meters and _____ centimeters

Weight: about _____ kilograms and _____ grams

Waist: about _____ centimeters

Pulse rate: about _____ beats per minute

Temperature: about _____ degrees centigrade

Age: _____ years _____ months _____ days

_____ hours _____ minutes _____ seconds

Each group of three or four pupils is given a length such as 1 cm, 2 cm, 5 cm, and so on. They are to locate items of about this length and show them to the class. A few examples are:

1 cm: Joe showed one of his fingernails. Mary had a paperclip about 1 cm wide and about 3 cm long. Ellen held up a pen a little less than 1 cm across.

5 cm: Henry had an old glasses case about 5 cm across. Gary brought the headlines of a newspaper with letters almost 5 cm high.

10 cm: A comb, each side of the bottom of a milk carton, and the short side of an envelope were shown to illustrate lengths of about 10 cm.

It should be recognized that most items mentioned above vary in size and therefore each must be shown to the class as a pupil tells its length. Further, pupils should emphasize the approximate nature of measurements by reporting, "It is a little less than 5 cm long," or "It is between 9 and 10 cm but closer to 10 cm."

Measure and describe objects in the classroom:

My mathematics book is about _____ millimeters or about _____ centimeters long. It weighs about _____ grams or about _____ kilograms.

Figure 9-14

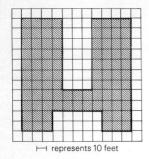

Figure 9-15
Micometer calipers.

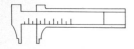

The basketball hoop is about ___ meters above the ground. This is about ___ centimeters.

The milk carton we get at school has about ___ liters of milk and weighs about ___ grams when full.

In learning to measure and report results, the number of relevant experiences for pupils is almost endless. For linear and weight measure, the pupil:

Measures with a 5- or 25-meter tape to determine longer lengths, and uses the results to make scale drawings. A scaled plan of the school plant (Fig. 9-14) may be an attractive project.

Uses a micrometer caliper (Fig. 9-15) for measuring thickness of cardboard, fingernail, and hair.

Measures a plot of ground for laying out the school garden. Later measures growth of plants.

Measures how far pupils jump or throw a ball.

Weighs textbooks, notebooks, erasers, pencils, overshoes, clothes.

Weighs the same volume of different substances—a jar of water, sand, dirt, and beans.

Weighs different letters and determines the cost of mailing them first class or air mail.

Weighs bags of candy for a candy sale.

Compares the weights of a dozen large, medium, and small eggs.

Estimating measurements helps pupils develop concepts of units and their relations as well as facility in a process that is highly important in life. Some examples of such experiences are as follows:

Point to positions on the back of a ruler that are estimated as 3 centimeters or 30 centimeters, and then check by turning the ruler over.

Estimate the height, length, and width of the schoolroom, and then check by measuring.

Lift various articles, estimate their weights, and check by weighing.

Pupils stand beside their chairs, sitting down when they think 1 minute has elapsed. The teacher reports the actual times that were judged by various pupils as 1 minute.

In all of these experiences the idea of precision must be continually emphasized, along with correct use of terms and proper recording of the results of measuring. Besides the suggestions listed above, pupils may complete a table like the one shown in Fig. 9-7 for their measurements in order to concentrate on precision and to learn the conventions established for reporting measurements.

Finding Perimeters The idea of perimeter is introduced in an experimental setting using its meaning of "measure around." The variety of activities is illustrated by the following:

> Segment *a*, Fig. 9-16, is 1 unit long. Find the distance around each figure.
>
> On your geoboard show rectangles whose perimeters are:
> a. 4 units   b. 6 units   c. 8 units
>
> On your geoboard make as many different shapes as you can each with a perimeter of 12 units.
>
> Find the perimeter of the triangle, Fig. 9-17, in:
> a. *J*-units   b. *K*-units   c. *L*-units   d. *M*-units

To avoid difficulties that may arise from precise but complex language, the teacher makes some modification in wording. "The length of the segment" is often used instead of "the measure of the length of the segment." Frequently, this simplification of language avoids long, involved sentences which distract the listener or the speaker from the idea. On certain days, a game may be played when everybody must use precise language. Here, "the area of the circle" would be replaced by "the area of the circular region" or "the area of the region enclosed by the circle."

Introducing the Metric System

Because the metric system, which has furnished the basic units for technical and scientific work for years, is finally to be used in industry and everyday life in the United States, this special section of experiences for teaching is provided.

The changeover to the metric system will be difficult and will take considerable time; yet the conclusion of many citizens that it will be a traumatic one is based on their own school experiences with the metric system, which in many cases involved only changing English units to metric units and vice versa. The changeover, in addition to the passage of needed legislation, must be accompanied by effective programs of adult education for citizens and of inservice work for teachers.

Every elementary school teacher can provide a set of experiences for his pupils through which they can learn to use the metric system and discover its convenience. At present, few pupils in any grade can measure with or use metric units with a satisfactory degree of accuracy or understanding; hence, teachers at all levels must initiate the study of the metric system. This program is based on

Figure 9-16
Find the perimeter if segment a is 1 unit.

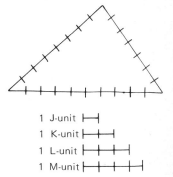

Figure 9-17
Find the perimeter of the triangle.

1 J-unit
1 K-unit
1 L-unit
1 M-unit

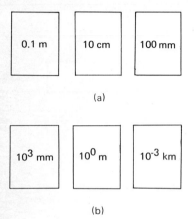

Figure 9-18
Cards showing metric equivalents.

0.1 m	10 cm	100 mm

(a)

10^3 mm	10^0 m	10^{-3} km

(b)

the use of scales for weighing, containers for measuring liquid, and rulers and tapes for measuring length. Obviously the mathematics laboratory will provide for many effective activities. In the following, experiences designed for familiarization with the metric system, pupils:

Make their own rulers. Each pupil is given a strip 1 cm long. He makes marks 1 cm apart on his strip of tagboard and labels these marks 1 cm, 2 cm, and so on. To make a tape for measuring distances in the schoolyard, pupils tie pieces of string one meter apart around a piece of rope.

Make posters for the bulletin board showing segments of length 1 cm, 2 cm, 3 cm, and so on.

Study the metric prefixes. Lengths for example are expressed in terms of millimeter (1/1,000 meter), centimeter (1/100 meter), decimeter (1/10 meter), meter (1 meter), decameter (10 meters), hectometer (100 meters), and kilometer (1,000 meters). Pupils find the meaning of a mill as .001 dollar and cent as .01 dollar and note the prefixes *milli* and *centi* have similar interpretations as part of a meter. The analogy is continued comparing a $1 bill to 1 meter, a $10 bill to a decameter, a $100 bill to a hectometer, and a $1,000 bill to a kilometer. (It should be recognized that some of the prefixes are less important than others. It seems probable for example, that 1 hectometer will be used seldom because equivalences such as 100 meters or 1/10 kilometer are more readily recognized.)

Sort cards with measurements written on them. Cards are prepared so that three or four have equivalent measurements written on them (Fig. 9-18a). Pupils are to sort them so each member of a set of cards represents the same measurement. When exponents have been introduced, the cards may be prepared as in Fig. 9-18b. These cards may be used to play a game of rummy with rules adapted so that three or more cards showing the same measurement may be placed on the table.

Play the game "Guess What I'm Thinking Of." While pupils cover their eyes, a leader measures an object in the room. The leader describes the object by saying, "I'm thinking of an object whose length is 120 cm." Pupils look about the room and try to guess the object measured. As a guess is made, the object is measured to see if its length is close to 120 cm. The pupil who identifies the object becomes the leader.

List the advantages of the metric system.

Discuss and list problems that will arise in the changeover to the metric system.

Solve problems such as "Does the world record for 1,500 meters represent a faster rate of running than the world record for 1 mile."

Experiences in the above list can be described as those for developing the concepts of metric units. Learning to use these concepts effectively is one of the most important aspects of the program along with developing specific skills such as measuring precisely and determining error in measuring.

Directing Learning of Measures of Area

The sequence for learning about the area of plane regions is the same as that followed in learning about other measurements. First, pupils compare regions by making physical comparisons of models of each. Then they choose a suitable unit for measuring area and determine the area of differently shaped regions by applying the unit. Finally, they select appropriate units and generalize formulas as substitutes for physical application of the unit.

Physical comparison of models of regions The comparison of models of two plane regions to determine whether the measure of area of the first is less than, equal to, or greater than the measure of area of the second may be relatively simple, as shown for regions S and T in Fig. 9-19a. Here the pupil finds that because region S "fits into" region T (Fig. 9-19b), its measure of area is less than that for T. In the case of regions Q and P (Fig. 9-19c), the pupil finds that neither will "fit into" the other. By cutting paper models (Fig. 9-19d), he shows region P larger than region Q. Similar experiments in which pupils make crude comparisons of the areas of two regions may be performed with regions of many shapes and sizes.

The concept of area In studying measurement of segments, the pupil learned that he must choose a suitable segment and name it 1 (a unit segment). In a similar manner, when studying the areas of regions, he must select a unit, in this case a region whose area is agreed to be 1 (a unit region). The important idea is that the unit regions are to be placed so that they touch, but do not overlap, and yet cover the region to be measured. Pupils need to experiment with unit regions of various shapes and sizes. In Fig. 9-20 square and circular unit regions are shown "covering" triangular region ABC. After trying rectangular unit regions as well, pupils discover that circular unit regions do not completely cover a given region but any given region can be completely covered with square or rectangular unit regions.

In developing the concept of area and its measure, pupils need a variety of concrete experiences using unit regions such as are shown in Fig. 9-21. They discover the area of the regions in Fig. 9-21a, b, and c quite readily because the pattern for covering can

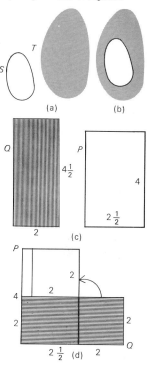

Figure 9-19
Comparing the size of regions.

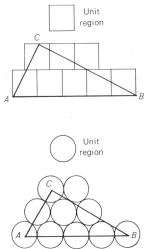

Figure 9-20
Covering a region with unit regions.

Figure 9-21
Using unit regions to find area.

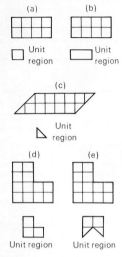

Figure 9-22
Area is approximately 125 unit regions.

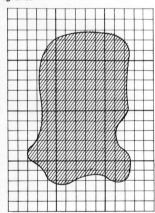

be found with minimum experimentation. Covering the region is Fig. 9-21*d* requires some exploration before four of the unit regions are fitted to cover the region. For Fig. 9-21*e* pupils find the region cannot be covered by unit regions without overlapping. They should however, discover a way to cut the unit regions, cover the region to be measured and be reasonably sure that the measure is four unit regions.

Using his geoboard the pupil performs experiments such as the following as he continues to mature his concept of area.

> Use the small square on the geoboard as enclosing a 1-unit region. Make some "strange shapes" on your geoboard. Draw each shape on dot paper. Write the area enclosed by each. Make a bulletin board display of the "strange shapes" which are not found in mathematics books.

> Show each tangram piece on your geoboard. Decide which tangram piece is 1 unit of area. What is the measure of area of each other tangram piece? What is the area of all tangram pieces together?

When pupils use graph paper to estimate area, they count each small square region as a unit region. For Fig. 9-22 they find that 100 unit regions are completely in the interior and that 49 other regions are partially included. They conclude that the area is between 100 and 149 unit regions, and they may make an estimate of about 125 unit regions as its area. Many pupils may appreciate the logic of this answer. They observe that some of the 49 partial unit regions are almost entirely in the interior, some are about half in the interior, some have only a small portion in the interior, and so on. The best guess for these 49 regions is that on the average each is one-half a unit region. Hence, $1/2 \times 49 = 24 \ 1/2$ should be the best guess for their area. This is an excellent approximation and the procedure provides a best answer in some cases.

The understanding of measure such as square centimeter, square decimeter, and square meter begins with pupils cutting models of these regions out of paper. These are placed on the interior of various rectangles, and the number of these units required to cover the region is called the *measure of the area*. Through actual handling of these units and using them to measure regions, pupils see why areas are labeled in square units rather than in centimeters, decimeters, or meters.

The term *area*, while it eventually becomes a part of the vocabulary of all pupils, may be omitted from early instruction; problems are stated as "Find the number of square meters or square feet" within certain boundaries. The phrase "Find the area" as an abbreviation for "Find the number of square units" is introduced later. When basic understanding develops through experiences such as those described above, the common mistake of confusing area and perimeter is avoided. Determining length, width, perimeter, and area of the same rectangular region and recording the answers with proper units help pupils see the appropriate uses for linear and surface measures.

Area of rectangular regions　For the following experiences pupils are supplied with 18 models of square tri-cm regions.[1] They are told to fit the unit regions together without overlapping so that the boundary is rectangular. They find all possible rectangular regions and list their results in a chart (Fig. 9-23). The exercise may be repeated by distributing a different number of square tri-cm to pupils.

Next pupils are provided with models of several rectangular regions. They determine the area of a rectangular region 5 centimeters by 4 centimeters by finding how many of the square centimeters can be placed on the region, drawing a square around each (Fig. 9-24). The relationship between the total of these regions and the product of the number of rows and the number in each row is examined. They find the number of square centimeters is the same as the number of rows of square centimeters times the number of square centimeters in each row. Specifically, for the example, the pupils find four horizontal rows of 5 square centimeters each and record the area in square centimeters as 4 × 5, or 20. Referring to columns rather than rows, they see five vertical columns of 4 square centimeters each; they find the area of the rectangular region by multiplying 5 × 4 and record the area as 20 square centimeters.

Progressing to a more mature solution, pupils explore methods for finding the number of square centimeters in each row without fitting the square regions. They verify the fact that since each unit region is 1 centimeter long, there are as many square centimeters in one row as there are centimeters in the length or base; also since each row is 1 centimeter high, there are as many rows as there are centimeters in the width or altitude (Fig. 9-25).

Thus pupils can generalize that the length as a number of linear units is equal to the number of square units in a row and the width is the number of rows. Then they can discover and understand the following rule: "The area of a rectangular region is found by multiplying the number of squares in each row by the number of rows." Applying this rule, the written solution to "Find the number of square centimeters for a rectangular region 6 centimeters by 5 centimeters" is:

$$\text{Area} = 5 \times 6 = 30 \text{ square centimeters}$$
$$\text{or}$$
$$\text{Area} = 6 \times 5 = 30 \text{ square centimeters}$$

[1]The tri-cm region is a square 3 cm on a side. It is more convenient for manipulating because of its size than a square region 1 cm on a side.

Figure 9-23
Shapes for area of 18 tri-cm.

Length	Width	Area
18 tri-cm	1 tri-cm	18 sq. tri-cm
9 tri-cm	2 tri-cm	18 sq. tri-cm
6 tri-cm	3 tri-cm	18 sq. tri-cm

Figure 9-24
Covering a 5 by 4 region with unit regions.

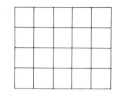

Figure 9-25
Four rows of 5 unit regions each.

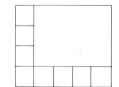

Pupils should gradually abandon sketching the squares (returning to this practice for review or to refresh the concept of area) when they really understand that the *number* of rows is equal to the measure of one side, and that the *number* of squares in a row is equal to the measure of the other side. Pupils need this more mature idea so that they will understand how to determine areas of rectangular regions with measures other than counting numbers for length and width.

A solution written as area = 6 meters × 5 meters = 30 square meters is to be avoided. The solution in the form 6 × 5 (square meters) clarifies the idea of area; during the stages of learning when understanding the concept of area is the primary object, this form is preferred. However, the rule "To find the *number* of square units in the area, multiply the *number* of units in the length times the *number* of units in the width" is valid and useful.

As a final step in learning to find the areas of rectangular regions, the pupil expresses and uses the formula $A = lw$.

Through investigation, the pupil sees the square region as a special rectangular region with four congruent sides. Therefore, the measures of length (s) and of width (s) are equal, and the measure of the area in square units is $A = s \times s$. This is later expressed by the formula $A = s^2$.

Figure 9-26
Determining the area of region ABCD.

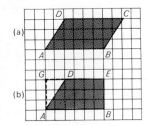

Area of the interior of a parallelogram Through examination of a variety of parallelograms, such as $ABCD$ (Fig. 9-26a), the pupil comes to recognize the interesting properties of a parallelogram as a four-sided closed figure in which the opposite sides are congruent, the opposite sides are parallel, and the opposite angles are congruent.

The pupil discovers that the exact area of a region whose boundary is a parallelogram (i.e., a parallelogram region) is difficult to find by counting since partial unit square regions are formed by the boundaries $\overline{AD}$ and $\overline{BC}$ (Fig. 9-26a).

Most pupils are able to discover a procedure for finding the area of the interior of a parallelogram, such as $ABCD$ (Fig. 9-26a), some with no guidance, and others after the hint is given that it can be converted to a rectangular region. Each pupil actually obtains the rectangular region by cutting along $\overline{BE}$ and placing region BEC on the opposite side of the parallelogram to complete the change in shape to a rectangular region $ABEG$ (Fig. 9-26b).

Pupils find that the rectangular region $ABEG$ and the parallelogram region $ABCD$ are made up of the same regions and therefore have the same area. They note that sides $\overline{AB}$ and $\overline{BE}$ of the rectangular region are, respectively, a base and altitude of the parallelogram region. On the basis of this experience, pupils conclude,

"The number of square units in the area of a parallelogram region is the number of linear units in the base times the number of linear units in the altitude to this base."

Either side of a parallelogram region may be thought of as the base, as in Fig. 9-27. Thus, if A is used to represent the measure of the area of parallelogram region $EFGH$, then

$$A = m(\overline{EF}) \times m(\overline{JH}) \text{ or } A = m(\overline{FG}) \times m(\overline{KH})$$

With b and h representing, respectively, the measures of the lengths of a base and altitude, the formula $A = bh$ is used to determine the number of square units for a parallelogram region.

Area of triangular regions Before developing a generalization for the area of a triangular region, pupils review some important properties of a triangle, e.g., that a triangle has exactly three angles and it is a simple closed curve that is the union of three segments. Further, the pupils discover that it is possible to separate a parallelogram region into two triangular regions by cutting along a segment connecting opposite vertices. They discover that the two triangular regions seem to be congruent by placing one on top of the other. Reversing the process, they start with two congruent triangular regions and see that they can be placed so as to form a parallelogram region.

To determine the area of a triangular region, such as ABC (Fig. 9-28a), the pupils take another region congruent to it and arrange them as in Fig. 9-28b. The measure of the area of the resulting parallelogram region is the product of $m(\overline{AB})$ and $m(\overline{EC})$. Since this product is equal to the measure of area of two of the original triangular regions, the pupils can derive the idea and may make the statement, "The area of a triangular region is one-half the product of the number of linear units in a base and its altitude."

Since any side of the triangle may be thought of as its base, there are three ways to find the area of triangular region ABC, shown in Fig. 9-29. Pupils should verify that the measure of the area of triangular region ABC is

$\frac{1}{2} \cdot m(\overline{AB}) \cdot m(\overline{DC})$, as in Fig. 9-29$a$

$\frac{1}{2} \cdot m(\overline{BC}) \cdot m(\overline{EA})$, as in Fig. 9-29$b$

$\frac{1}{2} \cdot m(\overline{AC}) \cdot m(\overline{BF})$, as in Fig. 9-29$c$

Finally, pupils learn to use A, b, and h, respectively, as measures of the area, base, and height of the triangular region and obtain the familiar formula $A = \frac{1}{2}bh$.

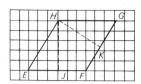

Figure 9-27
Altitudes of EFGH are $\overline{JH}$ or $\overline{KH}$.

Figure 9-28
Determining the area of $\triangle ABC$.

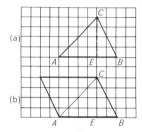

Figure 9-29
Bases and altitudes of $\triangle ABC$.

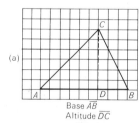

Base $\overline{AB}$
Altitude $\overline{DC}$

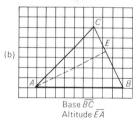

Base $\overline{BC}$
Altitude $\overline{EA}$

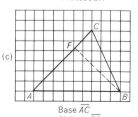

Base $\overline{AC}$
Altitude $\overline{BF}$

Directing Learning of Circles

As he studies models of circles, the pupil observes that if the center of a circle is called O, then every point on the circle is the same distance from O. The teacher and pupils discuss properties of circles and develop and illustrate important concepts and vocabulary. Experiences include drawing circles, measuring radius, diameter, and chords, estimating arc lengths, and comparing the radius and diameter of circles of varying size.

The ratio of measures of circumference to diameter. The pupil invents ways to measure the circumference and diameter of a number of circular objects, such as wastepaper baskets, washers, and cylindrical cans. He discovers the circumference is measured with a tape or by rolling the object on a ruler, making sure it does not slip. In measuring the diameter, if the center is not known, he places the zero point of the ruler on the circle and reads the distance to other points on the circle; the longest of these distances is the diameter. The diameter may also be measured accurately by setting the circular object between two rectangular blocks placed along the edge of a ruler, as shown in Fig. 9-30.

Data obtained by measuring diameters and circumferences are assembled in chart form, and the calculations in the last column are performed:

Figure 9-30
Measuring the diameter of a circle.

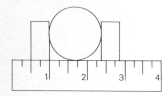

Object	Measure of circumference, c	Measure of diameter, d	Ratio of c to d	$\frac{c}{d}$
Roll of tape	10.25 centimeters	32 centimeters	$\frac{32}{10.25}$	3.12
Wastebasket	1.50 feet	4.75 feet	$\frac{4.75}{1.50}$	3.17

Measuring other circular objects, pupils continue the chart until they see that, for each circle, the measure of the circumference divided by the measure of the diameter seems to yield approximately the same number. After these experiences, pupils are ready to accept the fact that this ratio for all circles is the same. This ratio is expressed by the symbol π, read "pie" and spelled *pi*. The teacher explains that this number has been calculated to a high degree of accuracy, but that useful approximations are 22/7, 3.142, or 3.1416. These numbers seem reasonable to the pupil since they conform rather closely with the numbers that he obtained in his experiments.

Some upper-grade pupils may be able to understand that π cannot be expressed exactly as the ratio of two counting numbers. All pupils will be interested to learn that π has been calculated correct to thousands of decimal places.

Since $c/d = \pi$, pupils apply the relationship of division and multiplication and write $c = \pi d$. Further, since $d = 2r$, the other commonly used formula, $c = 2\pi r$, is obtained by substituting for d. Some experiments that demonstrate the plausibility of these formulas are found in the Activities at the end of the chapter.

Area of circular regions By definition, the area of a circular region is the number of unit square regions required to cover it. To reinforce this idea, pupils draw circles on graph paper and approximate the number of unit regions inside the circle. The curved boundary, however, creates a difficulty in finding the area by counting. But pupils make a good approximation by counting the number of square regions (Fig. 9-31) inside the circle and adding to this number one-half the number of square regions partially inside the circle. They recognize the need for a formula for the area of a circular region because they find this technique of estimating tedious and see the advantage in having a generalized procedure which will apply to all circular regions.

Figure 9-31
Approximate area of circular region by counting unit square regions.

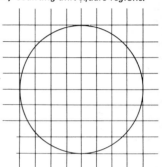

Pupils are now helped to formulate $A = \pi r^2$ through analogy with the area of a parallelogram region. Each pupil is furnished with cardboard on which a circle is drawn, and, while the teacher describes the experiment, the pupils carry it out at their seats:

1 Rule the region into eight congruent parts (Fig. 9-32*a*).

2 Cut along a diameter to form two semicircular regions (Fig. 9-32*b*).

3 Cut from the center along each radius, leaving a small distance uncut, and spread the sectors, as in Fig. 9-32*c*.

4 Fit the sectors together to form a figure like a parallelogram region, as in Fig. 9-32*d*.

5 Observe that the figure resembles a parallelogram region; the individual sectors resemble triangular regions; the height of each sector is the radius of the circle; both top and bottom bases are made up of four arcs, with total length one-half the circumference of the circle; the area of this region is the same as the circular region because each is made up of the same pieces.

6 Apply the formula for the area of parallelogram region to this new region. The length of the base is one-half the circumference or $\frac{1}{2}(2\pi r)$ units, or πr units, while the altitude is r units. Hence, by analogy to the parallelogram region, $A = (\pi r)(r) = \pi r^2$.

While improvising this solution, pupils investigate such questions as the following:

Figure 9-32
Area of a circular region is πr^2.

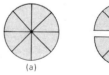

(a)

(b)

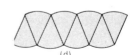
(c)

(d)

Is there any restriction on the number of congruent parts into which the circular region is partitioned for purposes of the experiment? Could 12 parts be used? 13? 25?

If each semicircular region were partitioned into 36 congruent parts, would the figure be more like a parallelogram than if partitioned into 4 parts?

Can the same conclusion be reached considering each sector as if it were a triangle, applying the formula for the measure of the area of a triangular region, and totaling the measures?

The teacher should recognize that conclusions drawn through reasoning by analogy may lack validity unless unusual precautions are taken. In this case, the reasoning is sound because the area of a triangular region is found by taking 1/2 × base × altitude, and the area of a sector of a circle is found by taking 1/2 × arc length × radius (Fig. 9-33). The method used here can be extended into a formal proof later in mathematics when the idea of a limit is developed.

Pupils may investigate the product πr^2 (in the form $3.14r^2$, for example) by further experimentation to determine whether it is reasonable. They may inscribe a square in a circle of radius r and observe that the area of the circular region is larger than the area of the square region, as in Fig. 9-34a. The area of the square region is $2r^2$—the sum of the areas of four triangular regions of $\frac{1}{2}r^2$ each. Hence the area of the circular region is greater than $2r^2$. Next, a square is circumscribed about a circular region, as in Fig. 9-34b. Since the square region has a side of $2r$, its area is $(2r)^2$, or $4r^2$. This is greater than the area of the circular region. It may now be concluded that the area of a circular region of radius r is greater than $2r^2$, but less than $4r^2$, and thus that $3.14r^2$ seems plausible.

When the pupil has gained confidence in the formula for the area of a circular region through intuitive investigations, he is ready to practice using the formula to determine areas of a variety of circular regions. Continued emphasis should be placed on the fact that the number used for π will vary with the requirements of the situation and the accuracy with which the radius has been determined.

Directing Learning of Measures of Volume

In the primary grades, the pupil becomes familiar with some standard measures of volume through experience with pints, quarts, gallons, and liters used in measuring milk, gasoline, or soft drinks. In later grades, he must develop an understanding of cubic units

Figure 9-33
Area of a sector is arc length times radius.

Figure 9-34
$2r^2 < A < 4r^2$.

(a)   (b)

for measuring volumes of space figures and develop some appreciation in terms of cubic units for the definition of previously encountered standard units, such as quarts and gallons.

The generalized concept of the volume of space figures is developed through experiences similar to those described for learning the concept of area. These are designed to provide answers to these questions: "Why must we measure volume?" "Why are linear and square units not used for this purpose?" "Why are cubic units suitable?" Following this, pupils experiment to discover methods for measuring volume, generalize their conclusions as a rule and formula, and develop facility in their use.

Developing the concept of volume measure   The need for measuring volume is seen by pupils as they examine situations described by, or materials bought by, cubic units. These items, which may be listed on the bulletin board, include topsoil, fertilizer, ready-mix concrete, some kinds of fuel, and dirt from an excavation. Discussion of the purposes for such measurement leads naturally to the conclusion that a new "space-occupying" unit is required. The need for some standardization of the space-occupying unit can be clarified through discussion of measures, such as the volume of a carton—the number of packages of breakfast food that it contains and the fact that breakfast-food boxes differ in size. Some uniform units of measurement are clearly needed to avoid ambiguity. Pupils readily sense the convenience of standard units in the shape of cubes.

The pupil develops a mental picture of a unit cube as he actually constructs and handles standard cubes. He may build cubic inches and cubic centimeters by cutting and folding cardboard, using as a guide a form such as the one shown in Fig. 9-35. Cubes of wood can also be constructed or purchased. A number of these cubes may be arranged in the form of prisms with various dimensions, so that the concept of volume as a number of cubic units is developed. For example, the pupil may use 24 cubes and show that a rectangular prism 2 by 4 by 3 (Fig. 9-36a), or 2 by 2 by 6 (Fig. 9-36b), or 8 by 3 by 1 (Fig. 9-36c) has a volume of 24 cubic units.

Finding volumes   After first counting each cube, pupils are encouraged to seek shortcut methods for determining the number of cubic units in a given rectangular prism. Referring to cubic units piled as shown in Fig. 9-37, pupils are assisted in discovering a formula for the volume of this prism by answering questions such as:

Figure 9-35
Model for a cube.

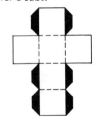

Figure 9-36
Prisms of volume 24 cubic units.

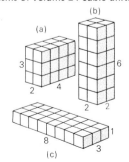

Figure 9-37
Rectangular prism of 4 X 5 X 3 cubic units.

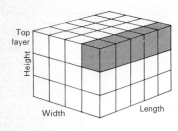

Top layer

Height

Width   Length

Figure 9-38
Studying length, area, and volume together.

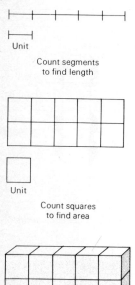

Unit

Count segments
to find length

Unit

Count squares
to find area

Unit

Count cube units
to find volume

How many cubic units are there in one row of the top layer? (*Answer:* 5)

How long is the prism? (*Answer:* 5 units.)

How many rows of cubes are there in the top layer? (*Answer:* 4.)

How wide is the prism? (*Answer:* 4 units.)

How many cubes are there in the top layer? (*Answer:* 20.)

What do you obtain if you multiply the number of rows times the number in each row? (*Answer:* $4 \times 5 = 20$.)

What is a quick way for finding the number of cubes in one layer? (*Answer:* Multiply the number of cubes along the length and the number of cubes along the width.)

How many layers of cubes are there? (*Answer:* 3.)

What is a quick way of finding the entire number of cubes? (*Answer:* Multiply the number of layers [3] times the number of cubes in each layer [20] giving 60.)

If you multiply the measures of the length, width, and height, what number do you obtain? (*Answer:* $5 \times 4 \times 3 = 60$.)

Does this suggest a rule for finding the volume of a box? (*Answer:* Yes. Multiply the number of linear units in the length, width, and height.)

As a result of experiences such as these, pupils develop a formula for the volume of a rectangular prism. With V as the number of cubic units in the volume, and l, w, and h, respectively, as the number of linear units in the length, width, and height, they write $V = lwh$. Facility in the use of the formula results from application to a variety of problems. Models are used frequently to check answers.

Studying Length, Area, and Volume Together

Some teachers have found that teaching length, area, and volume together in the early middle grades is an effective procedure. Each of these concepts is introduced with concrete and pictorial experiences (Fig. 9-38). Then pupils study various situations and decide whether they should find the length, area, or volume to answer questions such as the following [for the box (Fig. 9-39)]:

How wide is it?
How large is the dark side of the box?
How much can I put inside the box?

Similar questions can be asked about a swimming pool. For example, do you find the length, area, or volume to answer these questions?

How deep is the pool?

How large must the cover of the pool be?

How much water does it hold?

Figure 9-39
Box has properties of length, area, and and volume.

There are many everyday situations for which the pupil can differentiate between the use of one of the three measurements. For example, do you use length, area, or volume to decide the following?

The height of the door.

The amount of canvas needed to cover the baseball field.

How much room is inside the space capsule.

The size of a leaf.

How much water the jar holds.

Teachers who have taught these ideas together feel that their pupils tend to make fewer mistakes, such as the statements "The area of the paper is 8 *centimeters*" or "The box holds 10 *square decimeters*." There is no valid evidence to completely substantiate this view. However, it can be safely concluded that one key to pupils' understanding these measurement concepts is the extent to which they have had many rich experiences in actually measuring length with many different linear units, measuring a variety of regions using different unit regions, and physically measuring volumes by different unit cubes.

EVALUATION OF THE MEASUREMENT PROGRAM

The program for developing competence with measures and measuring, starting in grade one and continuing to grade eight and beyond, has as a focus the use and importance of measurement in everyday life. Its success will be judged by the number of affirmative answers that can be given to questions such as the following:

Can the pupil measure accurately?

Can he select the appropriate units for use?

Can he translate between different units as needed?

Does the pupil recognize measurement as a powerful tool of scientists?

Does he recognize the role of measurement in the development of the automobile, airplane, rockets, satellites, and other technical inventions?

Does he understand the relation between the development of measurement and that of civilization in general?

Does he think of measurement as a comparison to a suitable unit of measure?

Does he understand why all measurements are approximate?

Does he know the difference between a measure and a measurement and why the distinction is made?

Does he know the difference between a precise and an accurate measurement?

The extent to which pupils can demonstrate, explain, or illustrate competencies such as these is the means of determining the effectiveness of instruction in measuring and measurement. There is no topic in mathematics that lends itself more to and prospers more from an abundance of laboratory experience.

Graphs

The ability to read and interpret graphs is a requirement for effective citizenship today. Pictorial representation of data is found extensively in newspapers, magazines, and almost all forms of written communication. The study of graphs, then, can contribute to attaining the social aim of mathematics. In addition, the curriculum in graphing aids in achieving such other major objectives as the abilities to organize, present, and critically evaluate data as well as to design experiments to collect and present data to solve a problem. With these important outcomes possible it is strange that graphing has not usually received sufficient attention in recent years. Too often it has been neglected in the early school years and presented formally in the middle and upper grades, resulting in a lack of high-level achievement in this topic and often a dislike for it.

The discussion of teaching graphing in the following pages emphasizes experimentation with active participation by pupils. In most cases the experiences can be adapted for use on many grade levels. They are designed so that individualization of the program can be at least partially achieved.

Early Experiences in Graphing Early experiences in graphing are concerned with displaying individual characteristics of children. The primary teacher, for example, may have pupils pile small boxes with their names on them in two columns—those that wear glasses and those that do not wear glasses (Fig. 9-40). The opportunities for the separation of children into disjoint subsets and displaying the distribution by means of a bar graph are almost endless. A few that have been used by creative teachers are: like baseball, do not like baseball; girls wearing dresses, girls not wearing dresses; like television program A, do not like television program A.

For the graphing of wearing glasses there are a number of related problem-solving activities. Some of them are the following:

Children stand by the appropriate "wear glasses" and "do not wear glasses" signs. They compare this representation of the data to the graph.

Figure 9-40
Bar graph shown with boxes.

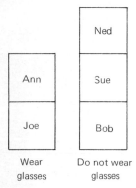

Wear glasses

Do not wear glasses

They determine how many wear glasses both by using the graph and without it.

They discover the concept of one-to-one correspondence as one box in the graph for each pupil.

As pupils mature, bar graphs may be built for more than two categories. For example, each pupil places his box above one of twelve signs indicating the month of his birth (Fig. 9-41). The analysis of the resulting graph can highlight many mathematical ideas: "In which month do we have the most birthdays?" "The fewest birthdays?" "For which months do we have the same number of birthdays?"

Collecting and Organizing Data The collection and organization of data may be instituted as pupils find their shoe sizes and, using both a horizontal and a vertical scale, display the data as shown in Fig. 9-42. Such activities can constitute readiness experiences for dropping the use of boxes to show how many and merely drawing a bar to represent the number in a certain category.

There are many opportunities to collect data from interesting situations in the child's environment. Some pupils may collect data on how many hours each pupil watches television for each day of the week. Here specific agreements must be made on how to determine the length of time so the data will not be biased. Others may determine and compare the number and duration of commercials for certain television programs by using a bar graph. Still others may make a study of television programming by finding how many half-hour periods for a certain afternoon or evening may be classified as comedy, game show, news, and so on. Before collecting this information and completing the graph, decisions concerning the classification of certain shows must be made and agreed upon.

Graphing Requiring Decision Making There are graphing activities to interest every pupil, and these activities may be developed so that pupils have an opportunity to critically examine the situation, then make decisions on the best method for collecting data and the best graph for displaying the data. Categorized examples of these problem solving activities follow.

Sports. One sports-related problem may be to show how fast each pupil can run 50 meters. This seemingly simple problem requires some nontrivial decisions. If pupils decide to make two bars on their graph, one for "runs 50 meters in less than 4 seconds" and one for "runs 50 meters in more than 4 seconds," they will find that the first bar contains no entries. They must decide how many bars will best display the data, and this in turn may depend on

Figure 9-41
Bar graph showing birth months.

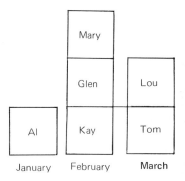

Figure 9-42
Bar graph showing shoe size.

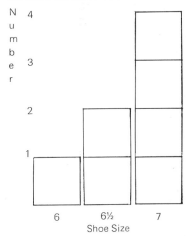

Figure 9-43
Data showing growth of a plant.

Age in weeks	Height in centimeters
1	
2	3.6
3	8.2
4	10.9
5	13.2
6	15.4
7	17.1

how accurately they can determine the time required to run 50 meters.

Gardening. The class may plant and observe growing flowers and vegetables, collecting, analyzing, and graphing numerical data about them. If the data on the growth of a plant is as shown in Fig. 9-43, pupils may make a bar graph and a broken-line graph and decide which best represents the information. Various questions requiring computation may be answered: "During which week did the plant grow fastest?" "When did it grow the least?" They may also predict its height for the eighth week and compare this to the measured height. For this prediction procedure pupils must be very critical. A discussion of the question "If this plant has grown an average of 2.5 cm per week, what will its height be after 30 weeks?" should bring out serious consideration of a number of important ideas: "Will this plant continue to grow for 30 weeks?" "Is its growth slowing down?" "Why should we be careful in predicting growth for times not shown on the graph?"

Science. Even though many experimental programs in science have developed science activities that require mathematical concepts, especially graphing, such activities are not commonly used by the average teacher. While there are many reasons for this, those most often given are the lack of equipment and inability to handle a laboratory situation with a class. Both the experiment with leaves in Chapter 8 and the one below require little apparatus, are interesting to pupils and may be organized by most teachers.

The purpose of this experiment is to determine how high a ball will bounce. Small groups of pupils are told to sit down and devise an experiment toward this end. The individual groups must first define the problem. They wonder if they are to throw the ball and measure the height of the bounce. This does not seem a good idea because of the variable force given to the ball on each throw. They may wonder too if the ball should be bounced off a wood floor, a cement walk, or other material.

In some cases the teacher must aid in setting up the experiment by saying, "You must drop the ball from various heights and measure how high it bounces. Now invent a way to do this." Most pupils will now see that holding a meterstick perpendicular to the landing surface will allow them to measure the height from which the ball is dropped and approximate the height of the bounce. Even with the experiment defined, certain plans and decisions are necessary by the experimenters:

From what heights shall we drop the ball? Should we drop from 10 cm, 20 cm, 30 cm, and so on up to 100 cm?

From what minimum height should we drop the ball? Can we measure the height of the bounce for a drop of 10 cm?

How do we measure the height of the drop? The height of the bounce? Should these measurements be made from the bottom of the ball to the landing surface?

Measuring the height of the bounce will not be easy. Should more then one pupil estimate these heights?

One group of pupils decided to have two of their members determine the height of the bounce while the other dropped the ball. They were to make four trials for each "dropping height" and measure the height of the bounce to the nearest centimeter. If Maude and Ken "agreed closely" on the height of the bounce, the result was retained. If they disagreed, the trial was discarded. In Fig. 9-44 Trial 2 was discarded. They then took an average of Maude's and Ken's observations for each trial. These are 32 cm, 31.5 cm, and 33 cm, as shown in Fig. 9-44. Then for a final number for the height of the bounce they found the average of 32, 31.5, and 33. This was about 32.2, which rounded off to 32. Their data was organized as in Fig. 9-45.

They then graphed the data they had collected as in Fig. 9-46. With information on the height of the bounce for each 10 cm from 50 cm to 100 cm, they tried to predict the height of the bounce when the ball is dropped from heights less than 50 cm. They checked their predictions by actually conducting the necessary experiments.

Traffic. At the request of the school parents' organization a class undertook a traffic survey to determine the number of cars passing the school. When the teacher described the project to the class, a number of questions arose which had to be answered in order to present accurate, nonbiased data. Some of these questions were:

Figure 9-44
Height of bounce of a ball for a 50 cm drop

Height of drop 50 cm

Trial	1	2	3	4
Maude	34 cm	36 cm	30 cm	32 cm
Ken	30 cm	31 cm	33 cm	34 cm
Average	32 cm	33.5 cm	31.5 cm	33 cm

Figure 9-45
Height of bounce for drops of various heights

Height of

Drop	Bounce
50	32
60	38
70	45
80	52
90	60
100	67

Figure 9-46
Graph of height of bounce of a ball.

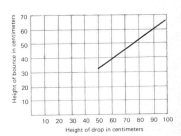

At what time or times should the survey be made? (It was decided to collect and organize data for each one-hour period from 8 AM to 4 PM.)

Do we count all vehicles for a single total, or should we classify them in some way and report for each classification?

Where do we count the vehicles? In front of the main entrance to the school is one possibility. A corner of the schoolyard is at the intersection of two streets. Should we collect our data there?

In what form should we deliver the results of the survey?

If a car stops at the school should it be counted?

The final report included three parts:

1   A description of how, when, and where the data were collected.

2   A compilation of the raw data including the numbers of various vehicles for each hour and the total number for each hour.

3   Graphs: (a) bar graphs showing the number of various kinds of vehicles for each hour period; (b) a broken-line graph showing the total number of vehicles during each hour period; (c) a circle graph showing the percent of each kind of vehicle (truck, bus, passenger car, etc.) that passed in front of the school each day.

There are a number of reasons why graphing experiences such as the foregoing should be incorporated into the curriculum. For example:

Pupils practice a number of skills in situations that are, for them, practical applications of mathematics.

Pupils actively participate in illustrating mathematical ideas in concrete and pictorial as well as in symbolic ways.

Pupils practice the designing of experiments in order to solve a problem in an efficient manner.

Pupils tend to be more motivated to a task when it involves recording or describing data in which they have a personal interest.

EXPERIMENTS FOR PUPILS

On the following pages are a number of Activities designed to develop concepts and skills in measurement. For each Activity there are many adaptations and extensions. In Activity 1, for example, the unit of measure may be changed to a pencil, a popsicle stick, or a ruler. Upper-grade pupils may measure the boundaries of certain regions and make scale drawings. Further, pupils may compare the results of their measuring by deciding which measuring device—a piece of string, a pace, or a pencil—gives the "best" answer for certain objects.

ACTIVITY 1

Apparatus needed: string, trundle wheel   *Objective:* To develop the idea of unit measure.

1   Guess the length of each item in the chart, then measure it with your string. Fill in the chart. A sample answer is given for a door.

2   Measure the items again using a pencil as your unit. Write your results in a chart.

3   Compare your answers with those of a friend. Why aren't your answers the same?

4   Why do you get different answers for the length of the desk using a piece of string and a pencil?

5   *Brainbuster:* Make a map of the playground. Use a trundel wheel to find distances.

Unit of measurement used: string

Item	Guess	Measurement
door	5	between 6 and 7
desk		
window		

ACTIVITY 2

Apparatus needed: 25 square tiles   *Objective:* To compare perimeters of regions with the same area.

1   Here are two ways to make a rectangular figure from 6 tiles. Each tile is 1 unit long and 1 unit wide. Each tile has an area of 1 square unit.

2   Take 12 tiles. Make as many rectangular shapes as you can. Find the area and perimeter and write your results in the chart.

3   Do Ex. 2 with 9 tiles. Do Ex. 2 with 16 tiles. Do Ex. 2 with 25 tiles.

4   For which shapes do you find the greatest perimeter?

5   *Brainbuster:* For what rectangular shape of a given area is the perimeter the smallest? Place tiles in rectangular shapes to help in answering the question.

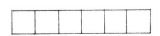

Size	Area	Perimeter
2 by 3	6 sq. units	10 units
1 by 6	6 sq. units	14 units

ACTIVITY 3

Apparatus needed: graph paper, leaves   *Objective:* To develop the idea of area as "covering."

1   Put your hand on your graph paper. Draw an outline of your hand up to your wrist.

2   About how many square units does your hand cover?

3   Draw a leaf on graph paper. About how many square units does the leaf cover?

4   *Brainbuster:* Suppose you used different sized graph paper to measure the area of your hand. Would your answer be different? Explain.

ACTIVITY 4

Objective: To develop library research and reporting skills.

1   Look up the history of the number π. Report your results on a time line. What symbol for π did the Chinese use?

ACTIVITY 5

Apparatus needed: 64 cubes

Objective: To explore the relationship between volume and surface area.

1   With 64 cubes make a one-story building 8 blocks long and 8 blocks wide. What is its volume? What is its surface area? Check your answers in the chart.

2   Make a one-story building 16 blocks long and 4 blocks wide. Fill in the chart.

3   Make a one-story building 64 blocks long and 1 block wide. Fill in the chart.

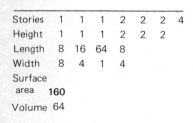

Stories	1	1	1	2	2	2	4
Height	1	1	1	2	2	2	
Length	8	16	64	8			
Width	8	4	1	4			
Surface area	160						
Volume	64						

4   Make all the two-story buildings you can. Fill in the chart.

5   Make all the four-story buildings you can. Fill in the chart.

6   Which building has the largest surface area?

7   Which building has the smallest surface area?

8   *Brainbuster:* How would you design a building to use the least material and have the greatest volume?

ACTIVITY 6

Objective: To find the weight of stacks of blocks.

1   The weight of each block is 3 grams. Find the weight of each stack.

ACTIVITY 7

Apparatus needed: inch and centimeter rulers   *Objective*: To measure the length of a path.

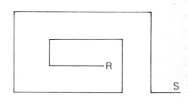

1   Measure the path R to S to the nearest (*a*) inch, and (*b*) centimeter.

2   How could you measure the length of the path R to S with a piece of string?

ACTIVITY 8

Apparatus needed: geoboard, graph paper   *Objective*: To find different shapes of the same area.

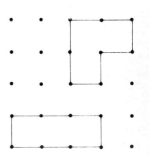

1   There are two different shapes of area 3 shown.

2   Find all shapes of area 4 on your geoboard. Draw a picture of each on graph paper.

3   Do Ex. 2 for an area of 5.

4   Have a contest with your friend. Who can show on a geoboard the most different shapes of area 8?

ACTIVITY 9

Apparatus needed: geoboard   *Objective*: To find all segments of different length on a geoboard.

1   Find all segments each a different length on your geoboard.

2   Check your answer with your partner.

3   *Brainbuster*: Invent a way to be sure you have all segments.

ACTIVITY 10

Apparatus needed: geoboard   *Objective*: To follow directions and discover a pattern.

1   Here are two figures each with 3 nails on the boundary and 0 nails inside.

2   Make three different figures, A, B, and C, on your geoboard with 4 nails on the boundary and 0 nails inside. Find the area of each figure. Fill in the chart. What can you say about the areas of each of the three figures?

3   Do Ex. 2 for 5 nails on the boundary and 0 nails inside. Name your figures D, E, and F. Fill in the chart. What can

Figure	Area
A	——
B	——
C	——
D	——
E	——
F	——

you say about the areas of each of the three figures?

4 *Brainbuster:* Repeat your experiment for 6 nails on the boundary and 0 nails inside. What is the area of each figure? Guess the area of a figure with 7 nails on the boundary and 0 nails inside. Check your answer by making figures on the geoboard. Guess the area of a figure with 10 nails on the boundary and 0 nails inside.

ACTIVITY 11

Apparatus needed: geoboard

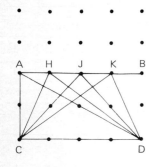

Objective: To investigate the areas of triangular regions.

1 In the figure $\overline{CD}$ is parallel to $\overline{AB}$. Look at triangles CAD, CHD, CJD, CKD.

2 Show triangles like this on your geoboard. What is the area of each triangle?

3 Make more different triangles but like those in Ex. 2. What is the area of each triangle?

4 Tell your friend what you have discovered.

ACTIVITY 12

Objective: To establish limits for the circumference of a circle.

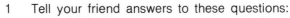

1 Tell your friend answers to these questions:

   (a) Why in Fig. a is the circumference greater than 4 radii?

   (b) Why in Fig. b is the circumference less than 8 radii?

   (c) Why in Fig. c is the circumference greater than 6 radii?

2 If C stands for the circumference and r for the radius then ___ $r < C <$ ___ r.

3 Tell your friend why the circumference is closer to $6r$ than to $8r$.

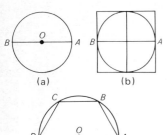

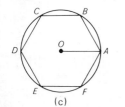

QUESTIONS AND EXERCISES

1 For what purposes do pupils use pencils, steps, etc. to approximate lengths?

2 Make a list of experiences through which pupils may come to sense the great need for measurement in their lives.

3 What is meant by "All measurements are approximate"? What experiences help pupils learn this idea?

4 Summarize some important things a pupil should be able to do if he is "skillful in meas-

uring the length of a segment."

5 A fifth-grade pupil who understands the concept and has ability to use the unit *centimeter,* can spell the word and recognize the abbreviation *cm,* and knows 10 centimeters = 1 decimeter. List other things he should know or be able to do.

6 What is meant by "Units of measurement are arbitrary"? What experiences help pupils recognize this idea?

7 A parent says to you, "My son told me he studied the concept of a kilogram today. What is meant by the concept of a kilogram?" Answer her.

8 List some concrete and pictorial experiences that may be provided for pupils as they develop the concept of area.

9 List a sequence of experiences for finding the area of a rectangular region, starting with the counting of square regions and concluding with the use of the formula $A = lw$.

10 What objectives are accomplished by having a pupil complete his own "body chart"?

11 What experiences are effective in helping a pupil understand the concept of perimeter?

12 Describe experiences with a geoboard for learning about the area of regions.

13 In what ways may a pupil measure the circumference of a circle?

14 Describe how $A = \pi r^2$, the area of a circular region, may be discovered in the mathematics laboratory.

15 What experiences may be helpful to a pupil in developing the concept of a unit of volume?

16 Describe how the formula for the volume of a right rectangular prism may be discovered.

17 A pupil asks, "How are cubic feet changed to square feet?" How would you help him answer his own question?

18 Why should pupils, at the appropriate time, study units of length, area, and volume together?

19 Write one purpose for each experiment on pages 235, 238, and 240.

20 *Brainbuster*: How many segments of different lengths can be made on a 6-by-6 (36-nail) geoboard?

PROJECTS

1 Look through a series of recently published textbooks and teacher's manuals and answer the following about measurement: (a) Determine the grade level at which important topics of measurement are introduced. (b) To what extent are geometric (nonmeasurement) and measurement topics taught together? (c) List experiences through which pupils sense the fact that all measurements they make are approximate. (d) List experiences through which pupils are guided to discover concepts and formulas.

2 Consult a school supply catalog and make out an order for the materials that would be useful for teaching measurement in a grade of your choice.

3 Demonstrate to the class: (a) How to find the area of a parallelogram region using at least three concrete models. (*Hint*: geoboard, graph paper, tangrams.) (b) Invent a concrete model for showing that area of a trapezoid region is its height times the average of the bases. (*Hint*: Adapt the method of finding the area of a triangular region.)

4 Describe changes in the measurement program in the last 20 years. Secure your information by contrasting the program in present-day texts with texts published 20 years ago. Look for new topics that have been introduced and others that have been discarded or receive less attention.

5 Prepare a report entitled "A Day Without

Measurement," discussing the problems that would arise if no measurements were available for a twenty-four hour period.

6   Throughout the chapter many experiments were described but not written as such. Choose some of these, determine the objectives, and write them as Activity Cards.

7   Write Activity Cards for use in the mathematics laboratory for: (a) contrasting the idea of area and perimeter; (b) discovering the area of the interior of a trapezoid; (c) measuring and computing the area of a triangular region in three ways.

8   Complete the following supplementary experiments for Activities given in this chapter: (a) *Activity 2.* For what rectangular shape of a given area is the perimeter the greatest? The least? (b) *Activity 3.* Discuss with other members of the class the best method to find an estimation for the area of your hand or a leaf. (c) *Activity 5.* Use 72 blocks to find the buildings with the largest and least surface areas. Do your results agree with those you found with 64 blocks? (d) *Activity 10.* Write an Activity card for figures with a certain number of nails on the boundary and 1 nail in the interior.

Bibliography

1   Biggs, E. E., and J. R. MacLean: *Freedom to Learn,* Addison-Wesley Ltd., Ontario, 1967. Many excellent experiences for measuring and graphing.

2   Bourne, H. N.: "The Concept of Area," *The Arithmetic Teacher,* vol. 15, pp. 233-243, March, 1968. Many practical suggestions for introducing the idea of area following the introduction of the concept of volume.

3   Brougher, J. J.: "Discovery Activities with Area and Perimeter," *The Arithmetic Teacher,* vol. 20, pp. 382-385, May, 1973. Experiences whereby pupils distinguish area and perimeter of polygons.

4   Copeland, R. W.: *How Children Learn Mathematics,* The MacMillan Co., London, 1974. Chapters 10 and 11 are about teaching measurement based on some of Piaget's research.

5   Davis, P. J.: *The Lore of Large Numbers,* Random House, Inc. New York, 1960. Sections 17 and 18 provide an interesting account of the history of *pi* and some of its uses.

6   Hallerberg, A. E.: "The Metric System: Past-Present-Future," *The Arithmetic Teacher,* vol. 20, pp. 247-255, April, 1973. History of the metric system in the United States and its advantages. This issue has six articles on the metric system.

7   Harne, S.: *Learning About Measurement,* Franklin Publications, Inc., Chicago, 1968. Interesting activities for learning about measurement.

8   Nuffield Foundation: *The Nuffield Mathematics Project: Pictorial Representation,* John Wiley, New York, 1967. Introduces graphs as a way of recording data and making pictures of it.

9   Pincus, M., and F. Morgenstein: "Graphs in the Primary Grades," *The Arithmetic Teacher,* vol. 17, pp. 499-501, Oct., 1970. Suggestion of graphing experiences for young children.

10 Steffe, L.P: "Thinking About Measurement," *The Arithmetic Teacher,* vol. 18, pp. 332-338, May, 1971. Experiences with linear measurement that give the teacher an opportunity to assess the thinking of pupils.

11 Walter, M.: "A Common Misconception About Area," *The Arithmetic Teacher,* vol. 17, pp. 286-289, April, 1970. Clever treatment of area and perimeter with many activities to help children learn the relationship between various perimeters and fixed areas.

10

TEACHING SPECIAL TOPICS

Certain mathematical topics previously reserved for study in high school or college are presently being introduced in the elementary school. Some of these, such as topics from algebra and geometry, have been examined already. Other topics, including integers, probability, other bases, prime numbers, ordered pairs of numbers, and functions are discussed from an intuitive and experimental approach in this chapter. The emphasis is on providing experiences for pupils through which they may discover ideas, organize data, and draw and test conclusions. A formal approach to these concepts ordinarily is not taught prior to the eighth or ninth grade, and so is omitted here.

There are a number of reasons for including these topics in the elementary school. Among them are:

● Research psychologists and teachers agree that learning a concept over a period of years is more effective than teaching it in its entirety in a short period of time.
● The study of these topics offers the opportunity for pupils to practice many computations of arithmetic in a novel and interesting setting.
● The simple basic ideas of all these topics can be understood by most elementary school pupils.
● Such a study affords pupils many opportunities for investigation, problem solving, and discovery experiences.

THE INTEGERS

Historically, negative numbers were introduced in order to solve equations such as:

$$n + 5 = 2 \quad \text{or} \quad 10 - 14 = x \quad \text{or} \quad 3 - y = 5$$

Two thousand years ago such equations were called absurd, and as late as the seventeenth century they were referred to as false or fictitious. Later in that century meaning was given to negative numbers.

The set of negative integers is symbolized as:

$$\{\dots, \,^{-}4, \,^{-}3, \,^{-}2, \,^{-}1\}$$

The raised dash ($^{-}$) is used initially rather than (-) in order to avoid confusion with subtraction. It should be recognized that the symbol for a negative number has two parts, the dash and the numeral.

The set of integers is the union of the set of negative integers and the whole numbers:

$$\{\dots\,^{-}3, ^{-}2, ^{-}1\}\cup\{0,1,2,3,\dots\} = \{\dots,^{-}3,^{-}2,^{-}1,0,1,2,\dots\}$$

While on a strict mathematical basis there is objection to the statement "A whole number such as 4 is equal to the positive number $^{+}4$," $^{+}4$ and 4 will be used here as different names for the same number. The subtle differences between them are discussed when the integers are restudied in algebra.

A Novel Introduction

In an "Information Sheet"[1] describing the University of Illinois Arithmetic Project, David Page gives an example of an interesting and understandable approach to directed numbers. Here the pupil thinks about a cricket, located at a particular spot on a number line, and gives him jumping instructions. For example, if the cricket is at 2 (Fig 10-1a) and is told, "Plus 3," he would make the jump shown in Fig. 10-1b. After numerous exercises with "plus" crickets, the pupil may tell the cricket at 2, "Minus 3." The cricket would jump as shown in Fig. 10-1c.

Now the pupil has no difficulty in describing where the cricket lands. Possible answers are: "He is 3 below 2," or "He is at 3 less than 2," or "He is at 1 to the left of 0." The only problem remaining is to name this location in some way. A meaningful name to one child was $b1$ (meaning 1 below 0). It would be possible to develop the entire topic, including operations with integers using $b1$, $b2$, and so on. Or pupils can be shown the usually accepted symbols ($^{-}1$, $^{-}2$, etc.). They learn to use this notation without difficulty.

Using Social Situations

Pupils are encouraged to bring in examples of the integers from everyday life and list them on the bulletin board. Some that they will find readily are:

The temperature 10° above zero is $^{+}10$, and 10° below zero is $^{-}10$.

The elevation of Mt. Whitney is 14,495 feet above sea level ($^{+}14,495$),

Figure 10-1
Picturing positive and negative jumps.

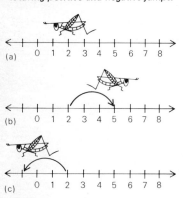

[1]D.A. Page, "Information Sheet," University of Illinois Arithmetic Project, Urbana, Ill., July 24, 1961.

and the elevation of Death Valley is 282 feet below sea level ($^-282$).

A gain of 4 yards on the football field is $^+4$, and a loss of 4 yards is $^-4$. On a time line for history, A.D. 1000 is $^+1000$, and 1000 B.C. is $^-1000$.

Stock A gains 2 points ($^+2$), and stock B loses 2 points ($^-2$).

They may also make a list of the possible uses of negative numbers such as:

lose $2	$^-2$
three days ago	$^-3$
owe $5	$^-5$
debt of $4	$^-4$

Throughout all of these experiences, the correct words to be used are *negative 1* for $^-1$, *negative 2* for $^-2$, and so on. The expressions *minus 1, minus 2,* and so on are to be avoided; the word *minus* will continue to indicate a subtraction. Similarly, 3 or $^+3$ will be called *positive 3* and not *plus 3,* and the word *plus* will be used to indicate the operation of addition.

Using the Number Line

The most useful device for a concrete representation of the integers is the number line. It is constructed as an extension of the number line for whole numbers (page 57). After 0 is located on a straight line (Fig. 10-2), 1 is located an arbitrary unit distance to the right of 0, with 2 the unit distance to the right of 1, and so on. Now $^-1$ is a unit distance to the left of 0, with $^-2$ a unit distance to the left of $^-1$, and so on.

Experiences with the number line for integers are similar to those for whole numbers. In one such initial experience, for example, each of several pupils is given a numbered card (Fig. 10-3). After marking a number of equally spaced dots on the floor in front of the classroom, the teacher asks a pupil having the card with zero to stand on a dot. Then other pupils with cards arrange themselves in order, as in Fig. 10-4. This activity is varied, as a pupil with a card other than zero is asked to be first to position himself.

For seatwork, pupils may be given papers each having number lines with unlabeled points. They complete the labeling with different instructions, such as: "Label the point at the right with 0 (Fig. 10-5). Now finish the naming of other points."

Through questions from the teacher and studying the number line, pupils make generalizations such as: "7 is greater than 5 because 7 is to the right of 5 on this number line"; or "2 is greater than $^-5$ because it is to the right of $^-5$." Similar statements are

Figure 10-2
Number line showing integers.

Figure 10-3
Cards showing integers.

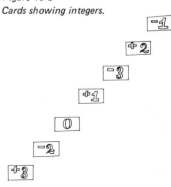

Figure 10-4
Placing cards in order.

Figure 10-5
Complete the labeling.

Figure 10-6
An integer and its opposite.

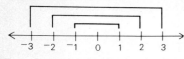

made, using the expression *less than*.

Some teachers have found it very helpful to have pupils name ⁻1 as "the opposite of 1," ⁻2 as "the opposite of 2," and so on. The rationale for this usage is shown in Fig. 10-6, where ⁻1 is located the same distance from 0 as 1 but in an opposite direction. Similarly, 1 is the opposite of ⁻1. One advantage of this method is that a seemingly complicated but useful expression ⁻(⁻1) is readily interpreted as "the opposite of negative 1." This is 1, the simplest name for ⁻(⁻1).

Integers Represented by Vectors

Figure 10-7
Vectors representing + 2.

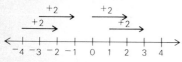

Figure 10-8
Vectors representing ⁻ 1.

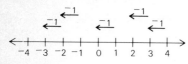

Often the integers are called *directed numbers* because they seem to indicate a direction as well as a magnitude. All of the vectors (or arrows) in Fig. 10-7, as well as many others, represent 2 because their length is two units and they point toward the right (the positive direction). Similarly, all of the arrows in Fig. 10-8 represent ⁻1 because they are one unit in length and point toward the left (the negative direction).

Experiences that may be provided for pupils include picturing vectors for ⁻3, 4, or ⁻5; a vector for ⁻4 starting at ⁻2; a vector for ⁺3 ending at ⁻1; a vector for 1 less than ⁻3; and so on. This second representation of an integer is important for objectifying operations with integers.

Addition of Integers

Figure 10-9
2 + 3 = n.

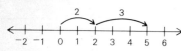

For beginning instruction, an intuitive definition of addition of integers is used. For addition of whole numbers, such as 2 + 3, young children may say, "2," and then count on their fingers, "3, 4, 5." Here addition means *count on*. The number line picture for the addition of whole numbers 2 and 3 (Fig. 10-9) seems to indicate *count on* also. It shows an arrow starting at 0 and ending at 2, followed by an arrow starting at 2 and extending three units to the right. This idea of addition as counting on is used for early instruction and no rules for computing the results for additions are generalized, although many pupils may discover them. Some appropriate experiences for this early stage of learning are described below.

Figure 10-10
-2 +⁻3 = n.

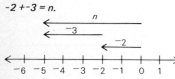

Drawing number line pictures Using the idea of addition as counting on, pupils draw vector (arrow) pictures to show addition and read the diagram to obtain answers.

For ⁻2 + ⁻3 = n, the pupil draws (Fig. 10-10) an arrow for ⁻2 starting at 0, followed by an arrow for ⁻3 starting at ⁻2. The single arrow for *n* starts at 0 and ends at the terminal point for the ⁻3 arrow. Hence *n* = ⁻5.

For $^+4 + {}^-6 = n$, the pupil draws (Fig. 10-11) the arrow for 4 starting at 0, followed by an arrow for $^-6$ starting at 4. The vector for the sum starts at 0 and ends at the terminal point of the arrow for $^-6$, the second addend.

Pupils are encouraged to generalize their results with statements such as:

The arrow for the first addend always starts at zero.

The arrow for the second addend always starts at the end of the arrow for the first addend.

The arrow for the sum starts at zero and ends where the arrow for the second addend ends.

Pupils may study patterns, as in Fig. 10-12. They observe the results shown in the table, and write logical answers in place of the question marks. Then they may draw number line pictures to verify their results.

Many teachers have found that reference to money situations is useful in helping pupils reason answers to additions. A few of these are:

For $3 + 4 = n$, the pupil thinks, "I earned $3 and then I earned $4. I have $7."

For $^-3 + {}^-4 = n$, the pupil reasons, "I owe Joe 3 dimes and I owe Bill 4 dimes. So I owe 7 dimes. This means $n = {}^-7$.

For $^-5 + 3 = n$, the pupil thinks, "I owed $5 for my radio. I just paid $3 so that I still owe $2. This is $^-2$."

Practice in developing skill is not recommended when addition of integers is first introduced, but many pupils on their own may find and intelligently use the correct rules. This should be encouraged. However, the important outcome for this stage of the learning sequence is the development of the concept of addition.

Special attention should be given to solutions for examples such as $^-4 + 4 = n$, $5 + {}^-5 = n$, $^-7 + 7 = n$ and so on. The answer to each of these is 0. The pupil will meet this more formally later, as $^+a + {}^-a = 0$, where a is an integer.

The relationship between addition of whole numbers and addition of integers can be discovered by pupils. By examining a number of examples, they can find that the closure, commutative and associative properties hold also for addition of integers, and that 0 is the identity element.

Subtraction of Integers

The formal definition of subtraction of integers is:

If a, b, and c are integers and $a - b = c$, then $a = c + b$.

Figure 10-11

$^+4 + {}^-6 = n$.

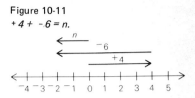

Figure 10-12

Pattern for discovering results for addition.

Add

4	4	4	4	4	4
3	2	1	0	$^-1$	$^-2$
7	6	5	4	?	?

Add

$^-2$	$^-2$	$^-2$	$^-2$	$^-2$	$^-2$
$^-3$	$^-2$	$^-1$	0	1	2
$^-5$	$^-4$	$^-3$	$^-2$	?	?

This is recognized as the definition of subtraction used with whole numbers. So once again a relationship between integers and whole numbers is observed.

Readiness as preparation for subtraction of integers Pupils read subtractions with whole numbers emphasizing the relationship to addition:

13 – 6 = n means what number added to 6 is 13?

9 – 4 = n means what number added to 4 is 9?

Then they rewrite subtractions in an equivalent addition form:

$$13 - 6 = n \qquad \text{means} \qquad 13 = 6 + n$$
$$9 - 4 = n \qquad \text{means} \qquad 9 = 4 + n$$

Next pupils apply the above ideas to relationships with integers. They write, for example:

$$^-6 - 2 = n \qquad \text{means} \qquad ^-6 = 2 + n$$
$$8 - {}^-2 = n \qquad \text{means} \qquad 8 = {}^-2 + n$$

It should be noted that securing answers is not the purpose of these experiences, but that they are intended to help pupils discover the meaning of subtraction and progress toward meaningful ways of obtaining solutions.

Thinking about subtraction If a class is asked, "How can we show the subtraction $5 - {}^-3 = n$?" many students will suggest possibilities:

A pupil may think, "What added to $^-3$ is 5?" On a number line on the floor he may step off eight steps from $^-3$ to 5 (Fig. 10-13). He steps to the right, and so the result is 8.

Another may think, "What added to $^-3$ is 5?" and draw a picture similar to Fig. 10-14. Here, too, the answer is 8, as the arrow points to the right.

Or another may think, "It is 3 from $^-3$ to 0 and 5 more to 5, and so the result is 8."

Studying patterns As with addition, pupils may discover relationships and possibly create rules for subtraction, as they fill in answers for patterns such as those in Fig. 10-15.

Not included here are a number of other experiences with subtraction which lead to the rule "To subtract a number, add its opposite." These include drawing number-line pictures with three arrows clearly demonstrating the relationship between addition and subtraction, comparing the properties for subtraction with integers to subtraction of whole numbers, and studying situations that illustrate subtraction. One of the most interesting of the latter is found in Ref. 1 in the bibliography at the end of this chapter.

Figure 10-13
Stepping from $^-3$ to 5.

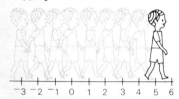

Figure 10-14

What added to -3 is 5?

Figure 10-15
Pattern for discovering results for subtraction.

Subtract						
4	4	4	4	4	4	4
3	2	1	0	$^-1$	$^-2$	$^-3$
1	2	3	4	?	?	?

Subtract						
$^-4$	$^-4$	$^-4$	$^-4$	$^-4$	$^-4$	$^-4$
$^-4$	$^-3$	$^-2$	$^-1$	0	1	2
0	$^-1$	$^-2$	$^-3$	?	?	?

Figure 10-16
Pattern for discovering results for multiplication.

Multiply						
4	4	4	4	4	4	4
3	2	1	0	$^-1$	$^-2$	$^-3$
12	8	4	?	?	?	?

Multiplication of Integers

In teaching the integers it should continually be emphasized that any conclusion concerning operations with integers should not violate conclusions concerning operations with whole numbers. With this in mind, pupils try to complete a pattern for multiplication, as in Fig. 10-16. As they discover that the results for 3 × 4, 2 × 4, 1 × 4 and 0 × 4 are the numbers for counting by fours backward (12, 8, 4, 0), they reason that the results for ⁻1 × 4, ⁻2 × 4, and ⁻3 × 4 should be ⁻4, ⁻8, and ⁻12, respectively.

Another pattern is displayed in Fig. 10-17. Pupils obtain the answer to 3 × ⁻4 by thinking, "Three negative 4s," or, in terms of a social situation, "Three debts of $4 is a debt of $12 (⁻12)." Thus they find that 3 × ⁻4 = ⁻12, 2 × ⁻4 = ⁻8, 1 × ⁻4 = ⁻4, and a sequence of ⁻12, ⁻8, ⁻4 is observed. This they see is counting by 4s. Then they conclude that 0 × ⁻4 = 0 and ⁻1 × ⁻4 is four more than 0. Hence, it is ⁺4.

A class discussion brings out the fact that studying patterns and determining plausible results is not proof but does give considerable confidence that the results are valid.

Completing a table Each student is given a table, as in Fig. 10-18. This is in form of the multiplication tables already studied with whole numbers, with factors listed in the left column and top row and each result to be recorded in the table.

Pupils first are asked to fill in the part of the table for which "there would be no arguments." Through discussion pupils will generally agree on the entries in Fig. 10-19. The results with 0 as a factor should be emphasized, with pupils once again noting that this agrees with products of 0 and any whole number as factors.

Next a pupil studies row *a* (Fig. 10-19), and, reading from left to right, he sees 9, 6, 3, and 0. He recognizes this as counting by threes backward, and deduces that row *a* should read:

$$9, 6, 3, 0, -3, -6, -9$$

Similarly, he observes row *b* as 6, 4, 2, and 0, which is counting by twos backward, and reasons that row *b* should read:

$$6, 4, 2, 0, -2, -4, -6$$

Likewise, row *c* is concluded to be

$$3, 2, 1, 0, -1, -2, -3$$

In a similar manner, columns *d*, *e*, and *f* are seen as counting by 3, 2, and 1 backward, and with these entries the table is as shown in Fig. 10-20.

Again looking for patterns, the pupil sees in Fig. 10-21 that

Figure 10-17
Pattern for discovering results for multiplication.

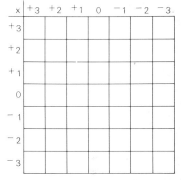

Figure 10-18
Extending the multiplication table.

Figure 10-19

Figure 10-20

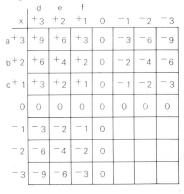

Figure 10-21

Multiplication table completed by examining patterns.

x	d +3	e +2	f +1	0	l −1	k −2	j −3
a +3	+9	+6	+3	0	−3	−6	−9
b +2	+6	+4	+2	0	−2	−4	−6
c +1	+3	+2	+1	0	−1	−2	−3
0	0	0	0	0	0	0	0
i −1	−3	−2	−1	0	+1	+2	+3
h −2	−6	−4	−2	0	+2	+4	+6
g −3	−9	−6	−3	0	+3	+6	+9

row *g* is counting by threes forward, row *h* is counting by twos forward, and row *i* is counting by ones forward. The table is completed, as in Fig. 10-21. Entries in the lower-right corner can be checked by observing that (from top to bottom) column *j* is counting by threes, column *k* is counting by twos, and column *l* is counting by ones.

Now pupils observe results, such as −3 × −3 = 9, −2 × −1 = 2, −2 × −3 = 6. It seems, then, that a negative number times a negative number is a positive number. Pupils should discuss once again that these results have not been proved. However, because of the observed patterns and the reasonableness of the answers, the results are plausible.

Studying a social situation There are a number of social situations which can be used to justify results for multiplication of signed numbers. Some of these are:

Pumping water into a tank and letting it out over a period of time.

Gaining and losing yards for a number of downs in a football game.

People dying and children being born over a period of days.

In a situation concerning trains moving at a constant rate of speed, for example, the following assumptions are agreed to:

Future time or time hence is given as +1, +2, +3, etc., meaning, respectively, one hour hence, two hours hence, three hours hence, and so on.

Time "ago" is given as −1 for one hour ago and as −2 for two hours ago.

The speed of the train is +50 mph moving to the right and −50 mph moving to the left. Points to the right of 0 (Fig. 10-22) are associated with positive numbers and points to the left of 0 with negative numbers.

Figure 10-22

Train movement illustrating multiplication.

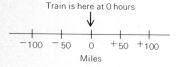

Train is here at 0 hours

−100 −50 0 +50 +100

Miles

Now for each of the following cases the train is at position 0 at a time zero (0) hours:

Case 1: (+2)(+50) = ? If the train is at 0 now and is going +50 mph, where is it two hours hence (+2)? It is at +100 (Fig. 10-23), and so (+2)(+50) = +100.

Case 2: (+2)(−50) = ? If the train is at 0 now and is going −50 mph, where is it two hours hence (+2)? It is at −100 (Fig. 10-23), and so (+2)(−50) = −100.

Case 3: (−2)(+50) = ? If the train is at 0 now and is going +50 mph, where was it two hours ago (−2)? It was at −100 (Fig. 10-23), and so (−2)(+50) = −100.

Case 4: (−2)(−50) = ? If the train is at 0 now and is going −50

Figure 10-23

Products interpreted through motion of trains.

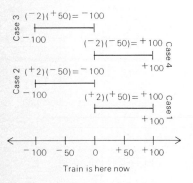

Case 3 (−2)(+50) = −100
−100

(−2)(−50) = +100 Case 4
+100

Case 2 (+2)(−50) = −100
−100

(+2)(+50) = +100 Case 1
+100

−100 −50 0 +50 +100

Train is here now

mph, where was it two hours ago ($^-$2)? It was at $^+$100 (Fig. 10-23), and so ($^-$2)($^-$50) = $^+$100.

This intuitive procedure helps clarify the case which seems to cause difficulty—a negative number times a negative number is a positive number. Here, once again, there is no proof of any of the four cases, but the experiences are designed to make results plausible.

Division of Integers

Through a discussion of the meaning of division of whole numbers and emphasizing the desire to have the definition for division of integers consistent with that for division of whole numbers, pupils can discover the results for the four possible cases of division of two integers:

$$\frac{^-15}{^-3} = n \qquad \frac{^-15}{^+3} = n \qquad \frac{^+15}{^-3} = n \qquad \frac{^-15}{^-3} = n$$

For $^-15 \div {}^+3 = n$, the pupil rewrites the equation in the form $^-15 = (^+3)(n)$ because he is familiar with procedures for handling multiplication but not division. He now argues that since $(^+3)(n)$ must be $^-15$, n must be $^-5$. The other three cases are handled in a similar manner.

When introducing for the first time the concept of and operations with integers, the teacher must keep in mind the objectives to be accomplished. These will be stated specifically in the teacher's manual and in most cases will indicate that experiences will be intuitive and that skill in the operations is not expected. Too much detail and mathematical justification of procedures at this time may confuse pupils.

PROBABILITY

Most pupils use one or more of the following expressions in everyday conversation:

It is *likely* to rain.

There is *not much chance* we will win the game.

Mike will *probably* ask me to the dance.

In each case, the speaker is concerned with an event about which he is not sure. The use of the words *likely, not much chance,* and *probably* give some indication of the expected outcome. In mathematics the theory of probability was developed to provide numbers which help *predict* the probable outcomes of events in which chance plays a part. Probability has been used by gamblers to predict, with some certainty, that particular events would occur

Figure 10-24

Recording results for tossing a coin.

Outcome	H	T
First 10 tosses		
Second 10 tosses		
Third 10 tosses		
etc		

Figure 10-25

Analyzing results of coin tossing.

The Coin Experiment

	10	20		100
Total number of tosses	10	20		100
Total number of heads				
Total number of tails				
Ratio of heads to tosses				
Ratio of tails to tosses				

Figure 10-26

Outcomes (last digit of page numeral)	Result after 100 openings
0	
1	
2	
3	
4	
5	
6	
7	
8	
9	

"in the long run." Today it is a respectable and useful branch of mathematics. This theory, for example, helps predict the outcome of an election when only 5 percent or less of the votes have been counted. It is used by insurance companies to determine premiums that they charge for protection against death or accident. Further, most branches of science are concerned with the chances that certain events will occur with predicted frequencies.

In the following section only the basic elementary concepts of probability are introduced. Although even simple formulas are not stated specifically, they will be discovered by many pupils and often may be expressed in algebraic form.

Experimenting

In readiness for the study of probability, pupils perform experiments, collect the data, organize them in suitable form, and make predictions. Two such experiments follow.

The coin experiment

1   Toss a penny 10 times. Each time the outcome is a head (H) or a tail (T). Record your results in the table (Fig. 10-24).

2   Toss the penny 10 more times. Record your data.

3   Repeat tossing the penny 10 times until you have 100 tosses. Record your data.

4   Record all of your results in the table (Fig. 10-25).

5   Suppose a penny is tossed 10,000 times. Answer probably true or probably false:

(a)   The number of heads and the number of tails will be about equal.

(b)   The ratio of heads to tosses will be about 1/2.

The book experiment

1   Open a book. Choose the last digit of the numeral for the page. Record your results in the table (Fig. 10-26).

2   Do this experiment 100 times.

3   Combine your results with other pupils so you have 1,000 openings of the book.

4   (a)   List the 10 possible outcomes for this experiment.

(b)   The last digit was 6 in ____ out of ____ trials.

(c)   The ratio of the number of 6s to the total number of trials was ____.

(d) Each outcome of this experiment was equally likely. What is meant by this?

Counting

The following are some more elementary experiments, situations, and problems for which pupils discover how to list all possible outcomes in a slightly more formal manner than for the two foregoing experiments.

Tossing coins   As a pupil tosses a coin, he observes that it may land head up, which he records as H; or it may land tail up, which he records as T. There are no other outcomes. He may show this as a tree diagram (Fig. 10-27) and record the set of outcomes as $\{H,T\}$.

Next he tosses a coin twice and lists all possible outcomes. If the first toss is a head and the second a tail, he writes HT. Similarly, a tail first and then a head is written TH. Next he draws a tree diagram, such as Fig. 10-28. Here path 1 is HH, path 2 is HT, and so on. He records the set of possible outcomes as $\{HH,HT,TH,TT\}$.

Choosing an outfit   A girl has two dresses (a and b), two hats (c and d), and three pairs of shoes (e, f, and g). If she may wear any combination of these, in how many different ways can she dress? The pupil once again draws a tree diagram (Fig. 10-29), noting that there are two choices for a dress, two choices for a hat, and for each selection of a dress and a hat there are three choices for shoes. There are 12 possible outfits. Pupils may note that $12 = 2 \times 2 \times 3$.

Pupils will be interested in completing a tree diagram if the shoes are selected first. They find the same 12 different outfits. It should be noted that in this problem *ace* and *eca*, as well as other orders of *a, c,* and *e,* mean the same outfit (outcome). However, in coin tossing HT and TH are different if the order of occurrence is important.

Choosing a route   Joe can go from Boston to Portland in three different ways, named 1, 2, and 3. He can go from Portland to Seattle in four different ways, named 4, 5, 6, and 7. In how many ways can he go to Seattle from Boston by way of Portland? The pupil may draw a tree diagram to determine the answer. He also learns to find the solution by means of a chart (Fig. 10-30). Here the routes are listed, as shown, to the left and above the chart. (It is similar to an addition or multiplication table.) The chart is filled in by recording an ordered pair of numbers, such as (1,4) in the row opposite 1 and the column under 4 (Fig. 10-31). This

Figure 10-27
Outcomes for tossing a coin.

$\{H,T\}$

Figure 10-28
Outcomes for tossing a coin twice.

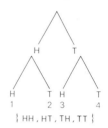

$\{HH,HT,TH,TT\}$

Figure 10-29
Choosing outfits from among two dresses, two hats, and three pairs of shoes.

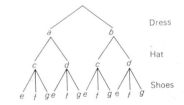

Figure 10-30
Choosing a route from Boston to Portland to Seattle.

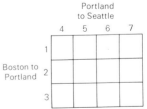

Figure 10-31
Number of routes from Boston to Portland to Seattle.

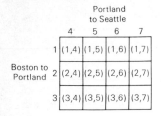

means route 1 to Portland and route 4 to Seattle. There are 12 number pairs and hence 12 routes. Here the pupil may note that $12 = 3 \times 4$.

The meaning of probability Most pupils know that if a coin is tossed there is a "50-50" chance of a head and a "50-50" chance of a tail. This can form the basis of a class discussion, with the teacher asking questions such as the following concerning one toss of a coin:

Which should you expect more often—a head or a tail?

What does 50-50 mean?

How often should you expect a head? A tail?

What is the set of possible outcomes from tossing a coin once? (*Answer:* $\{H,T\}$.) How many different outcomes are there? (*Answer:* 2.)

How many of the outcomes are H? (*Answer:* 1.)

What fraction tells the chances for a head? (*Answer:* 1/2.) For a tail? (*Answer:* 1/2.)

Another example of an experiment on the intuitive level that helps pupils discover the meaning of probability is the following:

Each pupil is given a wooden hexagonal pencil. He writes 1, 2, 3, 4, 5, and 6, one numeral on each side of the pencil. The pencil is rolled and the side that comes up when it stops is observed. To vary instructional procedures the teacher may prepare a plate with the following questions for the overhead projector (have pupils write on the plate):

List all possible outcomes. (*Answer:* $\{1,2,3,4,5,6\}$.)

How many possible outcomes are there? (*Answer:* 6.)

If success means that side 3 is up, what are the chances of success? (*Answer:* 1 out of 6 or 1/6.)

What is the probability that side 3 will be up? (*Answer:* 1/6.)

What is the probability that side 3 will not be up? (*Answer:* There are 5 out of 6 sides without 3; thus 5/6.)

If success means that side 1, 2, or 3 is up, what is the probability of success? (*Answer:* 3 out of 6, or 3/6.)

Other questions that may be used are variations of the last question: "What is the probability that side 1, 2, 3, 4, 5, or 6 will be up?" (*Answer:* 6 out of 6, or 1.) "What is the probability that the side that is up is numbered greater than 4?" (*Answer:* 2 out of 6, or 2/6.)

Still building the concept of probability, the teacher may make a top, such as the one shown in Fig. 10-32. If spun, it will come to rest on one of its edges, each of which is numbered as shown. Once again, a series of questions will aid the pupils' understanding:

Figure 10-32
Top or spinner.

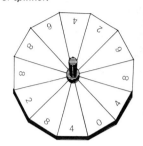

The top may stop on what numerals? (*Answer:* {0,2,4,6,8}.)

On which numeral is it most likely to stop? (*Answer:* 8.) Why?

On which numeral is it least likely to stop? (*Answer:* 0.) Why?

In how many different positions may the top stop? (*Answer:* 12.)

In how many different positions will it stop on 8? (*Answer:* 4.)

What is the probability of stopping on 8? (*Answer:* 4/12.) On 6? (*Answer:* 2/12.) On 4? (*Answer:* 3/12.) On 2? (*Answer:* 2/12.) On 0? (*Answer:* 1/12.)

Devising an Experiment

The creative teacher is always searching for experiences for pupils that not only contribute to the attaining of many of the objectives of instruction but also arouse their interest. One such experience concerned with probability is described below. It is recognized that as pupils devise the experiment, make fundamental decisions, and carry out their procedures they are attaining not only important mathematical objectives but many others that may be classified as needed to be "generally educated."

The teacher separates the class into groups of two, three, or four pupils, then poses this problem:

You have a sheet of paper. It is half shaded and half white. You are to drop a penny on the paper. What is the probability that it will land on the white part? On the shaded part?

At first the problem seems trivial. The immediate and intuitive answer is that the probability is 1/2 for landing on each part. However, for this answer a number of not necessarily valid assumptions have been made. One of these is that the paper has been separated into two parts as in Fig. 10-33a. This is not the only possible separation and was not necessarily implied in the statement of the problem.

In devising the experiment a group of pupils must have plans so that the bias of their own results will be a minimum. Further, if results of two or more groups are to be combined, each must conduct the experiment under the same conditions. Making these decisions gives pupils the opportunity to critically examine possible procedures and select those that will give valid results. A few of the problems for which decisions are necessary are the following:

How should the paper be shaded? Eight possible ways of separating

Figure 10-33

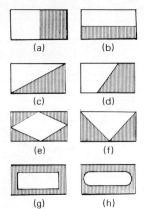

the paper are shown in Fig. 10-33, and there are many others. If results are to be combined, should each group use the same design? If one group used design *a*, another *b*, another *c*, and another *d* in Fig. 10-33 and we combined results, would we have a bias?

Are there any problems concerned with dropping the coin? Should the coin be dropped from the same height each time? Should we try to hit the middle of the sheet of paper and have it land flat each time? Do we need to be specific about these to have a fair experiment?

Can the paper be placed anywhere? Should it be on the floor or a table? Would it be best to have padding under the paper to reduce bouncing of the penny? Can answers to these questions influence results?

What is to be done when the penny stops at certain positions? What is to be done if we can't decide if the penny is on white or shaded? What is to be done if it is half on the sheet and half off, or rolls off the paper?

In addition to examining the problem from many viewpoints, making decisions, and carrying out the experiment, interested pupils may vary the experiment by changing the sheet of paper to one that is circular or triangular and compare results to those found with the rectangular sheet. Or they may change the object dropped to a pencil or a marble.

PRIME NUMBERS

The study of prime numbers was once called a "fascinating adventure," an activity "for those who like climbing intellectual mountains." Indeed, the primes inherently generate a good deal of interest and curiosity. Beyond their basic elementary uses in finding greatest common factor and least common multiple, statements about them stimulate many pupils to enthusiastic investigation. Further, they provide many opportunities for computational practice in a novel and interesting setting. These purposes for studying primes can be identified in the following experiments.

These experiments have been classroom tested and found effective. They strongly emphasize pupil discovery. To conduct them, pupils must know the set of prime numbers and know that each prime number has exactly two factors (1 and itself).

ACTIVITY I

Apparatus needed: 30 objects or counters

Objective: To discover how prime numbers are shown by arrays.

1   Take 6 counters. Can you arrange the 6 counters so:

(a) There are 2 or more rows and

(b) 2 or more in a row?

You should find two ways to do this.

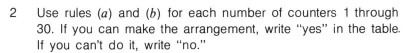

2 Use rules (a) and (b) for each number of counters 1 through 30. If you can make the arrangement, write "yes" in the table. If you can't do it, write "no."

Number 2 3 4 5 6 7 8 9 10 11

Yes/No

3 List the numbers for which you wrote "no" in Ex. 2. These are the prime numbers.

4 Explain to a friend how you could tell if 31 is a prime.

ACTIVITY II

Objective: To guess the meaning of "twin primes" and then to list twin primes.

The set of primes less than 100 is:

2, 3, 5, 7, 11, 13, 17, 19, 23, 29, 31, 37, 41, 43, 47, 53, 59, 61, 67, 71, 73, 79, 83, 89, 97

Some students tried to guess what twin primes were. They were told that twin primes were a pair of primes and twins were close together.

1 Would 2 and 3 be a good guess? Why?

2 One pupil guessed 23 and 29, 31 and 37, 53 and 59 as twin primes. How are his twin primes alike?

3 Why could 17 and 71, 37 and 73, 13 and 31 be called twin primes?

4 None of the above happen to be twin primes. Twin primes are two primes whose difference is 2. List the twin primes less than 100.

ACTIVITY III

Objective: To list numbers with certain numbers of factors.

1 For each number 1 through 30 list all factors in the table below.

Number 1 2 3 4 5 6 7 8 9 10 11 12 13 14 15...

Factors								
				1	1			
				2	7			
				3				
				6				

2 Study your table and write members of these sets:

(a) Exactly one factor:

(b) Exactly two factors:

(c) Exactly four factors:

(d) Exactly five factors:

(e) Exactly six factors:

3 Write more numbers with:

(a) Exactly three factors:

(b) Exactly four factors:

ACTIVITY IV

Apparatus needed: hundreds chart

Objective: To follow directions in order to determine the set of prime numbers.

On your hundreds chart:

```
✶  2  3  ④  5  [6]  7  ⑧  [9][10]
11 12 13 14 15 16 17 18 19 20
21 22 23 24 25 26 27 28 29 30
```

1 Cross out 1.

2 Circle all multiples of 2 except 2.

3 Draw a box around multiples of 3 except 3.

4 Draw a triangle around multiples of 5 except 5.

5 Draw a rectangle around multiples of 7 except 7.

6 The numbers that are not crossed out are primes. List them.

ACTIVITY V

Objective: To explore the famous Goldbach conjecture.

1 Do you think this statement is true or false?

Every even number greater than 2 can be expressed as the sum of two primes.

2 Try a few cases.

$$4 = 2 + 2 \qquad 6 = \quad + \qquad 8 = \quad +$$
$$10 = \quad + \qquad 12 = \quad + \qquad 14 = \quad +$$

3 Express each of the following as the sum of 2 primes:

26 in three ways
$$26 = \quad + \qquad 26 = \quad +$$
$$26 = \quad +$$

34 in four ways
$$34 = \quad + \qquad 34 = \quad +$$
$$34 = \quad + \qquad 34 = \quad +$$

4   Choose some even numbers. Express them as the sum of two primes.

5   What is your guess about the statement in Ex. 1? Your best guess should be yes. For 200 years mathematicians have been trying to prove or disprove this statement. So far they have failed. It is known as the Goldbach conjecture. You could be famous if you could prove or disprove this conjecture.

ACTIVITY VI

Objective: To express even numbers as the sum of 3 or 4 primes.

1   Try to express every even number greater than 4 as the sum of three primes.

   (*a*) $6 = 2 + 2 + 2$ (*e*) $24 =\ \ +\ \ +$
   (*b*) $8 =\ \ +\ \ +$ (*f*) $38 =\ \ +\ \ +$
   (*c*) $10 =\ \ +\ \ +$ (*g*) $50 =\ \ +\ \ +$
   (*d*) $12 =\ \ +\ \ +$ (*h*) $66 =\ \ +\ \ +$

2   Try to express every even number greater than 6 as the sum of four primes.

   (*a*) $8 =\ \ +\ \ +\ \ +$ (*e*) $20 =\ \ +\ \ +\ \ +$

   (*b*) $10 =\ \ +\ \ +\ \ +$ (*f*) $28 =\ \ +\ \ +\ \ +$

   (*c*) $12 = 2 + 2 + 3 + 5$ (*g*) $52 =\ \ +\ \ +\ \ +$

   (*d*) $16 =\ \ +\ \ +\ \ +$ (*h*) $74 =\ \ +\ \ +\ \ +$

3   Choose some even numbers. See if you can express each as the sum of three primes and as the sum of four primes.

4   *Brainbuster:* Investigate this theorem and try to determine if it is true or false: If Goldbach's conjecture is true, then every even number greater than 6 can be expressed as the sum of four primes.

ACTIVITY VII

Objective: To study special cases of the Goldbach conjecture.

1   Is the Goldbach conjecture (see Activity V) true if you cannot use 2 as one of the primes? How many counterexamples do you need to disprove a statement? Can you express 4 as the sum of two primes if you cannot use 2?

2   What is the smallest odd number you cannot express as the sum of two primes?

3   Is the Goldbach conjecture true if you cannot use 3 as one of the primes?

ACTIVITY VIII

Objective: To discover the number of factors of 2^n and 3^n.

1   Fill in this chart.

Number	$2^1 = 2$	$2^2 = 4$	$2^3 = 8$	$2^4 = 16$	$2^5 = 32$
Factors	1, 2				
Number of Factors	2				

2   Study your chart. How many factors for 2^6? For 2^7?

3   Guess the number of factors for 2^n, n a counting number.

4   Try to find the number of factors for 3^n n a counting number.

ACTIVITY IX

Objective: To determine which digits may be in ones place of numerals representing primes.

1   Write the set of primes less than 100.

2   What numerals are in the ones place if the number is prime?

3   Except for 2 and 5, all primes have a ____ , ____ , ____ , or ____ in the ones place.

4   Why can no prime have a 0, 4, 6, or 8 in the ones place?

ACTIVITY X

Objective: To determine the prime numbers among members of a set.

1   In the country of Triad the only numbers are 1, 4, 7, 10, 13, 16, 19, 22,... In Triad as here, 1 is not a prime.

2   4 is a prime in Triad. Its only factors are 1 and itself. Don't forget that in Triad 2 is not a number and so cannot be a factor of 4.

3   7 is prime and so is 13. 16 is composite. It has factors of 4, 1 and 16.

4   Write all Triad numbers through 100. Write prime or composite next to each.

ACTIVITY XI

Objective: To locate prime numbers in a certain pattern.

For these charts circle all prime numbers.

```
 1  2  3  4
 5  6  7  8
 9 10 11 12
13 14 15 16
```

```
 1  2  3  4  5  6
 7  8  9 10 11 12
13 14 15 16 17 18
```

Except for 2, in which columns are all primes?

Except for 2 and 3 in which columns are all primes?

Continue the chart. Why will all primes, except 2 be in these columns?

Continue the chart. Why will all primes except 2 and 3 be in these columns?

OTHER BASES

Many mathematics educators have indicated that learning numeration systems with bases other than ten has been overemphasized. They say further that from such study no deeper understanding of our base ten system has been accomplished. The validity of these statements may be debated. However, many teachers will verify that the curriculum in other bases has been too strongly oriented toward symbolic representation, and the necessary experiences to provide for a conceptual understanding of basic ideas have been minimized or neglected entirely.

The experiences described below are illustrative of what creative teachers can do to help pupils discover ideas through experimentation and learn approaches to problem solving as they study numeration systems of bases other than ten. The suggestions do not constitute a sequence of activities, nor do they cover the entire content as presently found in most textbooks.

The Game of One or No Blocks

Pupils are furnished with one block each that has 1 dot, 2 dots, 4 dots, and 8 dots (Fig. 10-34). These can be made from a ditto and printed on heavy paper.

After pupils have become acquainted with the blocks, they are given rules of the game of "one or no blocks": Show each counting number with your blocks, using any of your blocks or none.

In the beginning each pupil merely shows how each number is represented with his blocks. If he makes a mistake, there is no written record of it. Later he is provided with a form such as that in Fig. 10-35 on which to record his results. If he uses a block, he writes "yes" in the correct column. For example, for

Figure 10-34
1, 2, 4, and 8 blocks for game.

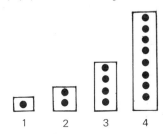

1 2 3 4

Figure 10-35
Form for recording blocks used for each number.

Number	8	4	2	1
1				
2				
3				
4				
5				

Blocks Used

5 he writes "yes" under 4 and "yes" under 1. For 11, he writes "yes" under 8, 2, and 1.

As the study is expanded, pupils may use numerals to express their results. When dealing with 9, the pupil finds he uses an 8-block and a 1-block. He writes $9 = 8 + 1$. When experimenting with 7, he finds $7 = 4 + 2 + 1$.

Without knowing it, pupils have been dealing with a base-two system. When they are ready to record results with numerals in base two, they may write 1 instead of yes and 0 instead of no in the proper cells of their chart. A few sample answers are shown in Fig. 10-36. It should be noted that 11, 110, and 1010 are, respectively, the base-two numerals without the subscript "two" for 3, 6, and 10.

Figure 10-36
Blocks used for each number.

Blocks Used

Number	8	4	2	1
3			1	1
6		1	1	0
10	1	0	1	0

Social Situations

The idea of other bases is merely one of grouping or packaging. The most famous speech in our history groups a number of years into sets of twenty: "Four score and seven years ago...." We most often group years as single years, 10 years (decade), and 100 years (century).

So that pupils appreciate and understand this concept of grouping, they are encouraged to hunt for examples, bring them to class for sharing, and place them on the bulletin board. They will readily find, for example, that eggs are packaged as dozens and grosses (a dozen dozen), and that many food items such as hot dog-buns or soft drinks are packaged in sets of six or eight.

They investigate which way a baker groups his loaves of bread for baking or how the delivery man groups the wrapped bread in his truck. Candy bars are often packaged 10 bars to a box and 20 boxes to a carton.

One interesting packaging is when the "things" are grouped in sets of 31, 30, 29, 28, 7 and 1. For example, 143 is packaged as two 31s, one 30, one 29, three 7s, and one 1 as shown in Fig. 10-37. Pupils are given other examples of this grouping and urged to guess the situation. The hint that everybody lives with this packaging often brings about the discovery that the grouping is done by a yearly calendar. The first 143 days of a leap year are arranged as in Fig. 10-37.

Figure 10-37
Where is 143 "packaged like this"?

31	30	29	28	7	1
2	1	1		3	1

Expressing Base-Ten Numerals in Base Five

There are shortcut algorithms available for expressing base-ten numerals in any other base. These should be reserved for the upper grades or high school when base systems are studied in detail.

For beginning instruction stories and games can be invented to help pupils visualize the operation as they move through a series of experiences designed to lay a strong foundation for dealing later with the ideas in the abstract.

The following story-game concerns the country of Penta where there are a few peculiar rules.

There are four coins. Their names are penny, nickel, quarter, and buck-and-a-quarter. Their values are shown in Fig. 10-38.

No item in Penta costs more than 624 pennies.

You must always pay exactly for any item with the fewest number of coins.

First pupils may be given play money of Penta. They will need four of each coin. They use this play money to pay for various items in various combinations: a 35-penny tablet with 1 quarter and 2 nickels, for example, or a 252-penny show ticket with 2 buck-and-a-quarters and 2 pennies. They recognize there are possibly other ways to "pay" for these items. The 35-penny tablet, they discover, has the same value as 7 nickels. But since the rules of Penta state that an item must be paid for with the fewest number of coins, the clerk will not accept 7 nickels for the tablet.

In order to avoid long statements such as "4-buck-and-a-quarters, 3 quarters, 1 nickel, and 3 pennies pay for a 583-penny item." pupils may be urged to invent abbreviations for the name of each. The following was suggested by a sixth grader: *baq* for buck-and-a-quarter, and *q, n,* and *p* for the three smaller coins. Then the cost of the 583-penny item is written as 4 *baq*, 3 *q*, 1 *n*, 3 *p*. Later they may also invent ways to indicate the meaning of the numeral 4313 in this game. To avoid confusion with the base-ten numeral, pupils have suggested drawing a bar above or below 4313 or a box around it. This, of course, brings them very close to dealing with the usual representation of a base-five numeral.

If one of the outcomes of any curriculum is the study of other bases, learning it can be made meaningful by experiences such as the foregoing.

Figure 10-38
The coins of Penta.

Coin in penta	Value of coin in U.S.
Penny	1 cent
Nickel	5 cents
Quarter	25 cents
Buck and a quarter	125 cents

NUMBER PAIRS

The idea and use of number pairs written in the form (3,5) is being incorporated more extensively in the mathematics curriculum starting about grade 3. The early study of this concept is related to display of data such as for the height of a child at certain ages. Here the pairs (age in years, height in inches) provide information in a compact form and from it a bar or line graph could be plotted easily. Gradually, attention is shifted to plotting points in the coordinate plane with experiences emphasizing the graphing of geometric figures.

While the use of number pairs may not be extensive in everyday life, it is a convenient way to express data and will probably have expanded application because it can be easily given to and retrieved from a computer.

Introducing Number Pairs

A novel way of beginning the study of number pairs is examining the classroom (if chairs are arranged in rows) or an arrangement such as that in Fig. 10-39 of how the class kickball team sat for a picture. For this picture pupils gave answers to such questions as:

Who sat in row 2 and seat 1?

Name all who sat in row 3.

Where did Jane sit?

Give the name of the player in row 2, seat 3. Here, the notational form offers no difficulty.

Fill in the blanks (row ____, seat ____) for Sue.

Pupils are urged to invent a shorter form for the position of a player. They may try $(R1,S2)$ and find it identifies Ray. They see, too, that $(S2,R1)$ is an alternate way to locate Ray.

With encouragement, pupils try to name players if the R and S are discarded in a pair such as $(R3,S1)$. They discover that $(3,1)$ would be Sue if we agree to always state the row number first. They find, too, that an agreement of seat number first would be equally satisfactory. In either case, the emphasis is on mutual agreement so that pupils may learn the importance of definition.

Next each pupil may be given a card with a number pair such as $(3,4)$ with the agreement that this is an *ordered pair* with the row number first. After finding their seats (Fig. 10-40), pupils are told they are to be identified not by name but by an ordered pair in the form (row, seat). The pupil is asked to raise his hand if:

He is $(4,3)$. [The teacher writes $(4,3)$ on the chalkboard.]

He is in Row 2.

His row number equals his seat number.

His row number plus his seat number equals 5.

His row number is 1 more than his seat number.

The last four activities may be extended further. For the instruction "Raise your hand if you are in Row 2," pupils may:

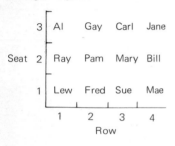

Figure 10-39
Seating arrangement for team.

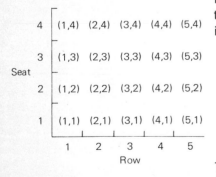

Figure 10-40
Number pairs show seating arrangement.

List the ordered pairs. (2,1), (2,2), (2,3), (2,4).

List the other ordered pairs if the class were larger. (2,5), (2,6), etc.

Discuss how the ordered pairs are alike and how they are different.

The teacher may even say, "Raise your hand if you are in the position $R = 2$." Pupils discover that this means "all pupils in Row 2" or even "all pupils with a first number of 2." A further extension may be to investigate $R + S = 5$. Here the interpretation is that row number plus seat number equals five. The variety of interesting discoveries that can be made by pupils is later extended to a study of equations and graphs of straight lines.

Collecting and Organizing Data

The use of number pairs can help make every subject studied in school more relevant. A few of the many investigations that pupils may complete to further important objectives of the total school program are the following.

Pupils collect and organize data concerning themselves. For their class, they may get information on (age in months, number of children) or (weight in pounds, number of children) or (number of brothers and sisters, number of pupils). They may display the data as number pairs, in a table, and in the form of graphs. They decide which is the best way to show this information.

They study the speed of a jet airplane before and after takeoff. For this problem they must search for a source to obtain the information. One class secured this data with speeds given approximately in miles per hour and negative numbers indicating seconds before takeoff:

(-40,0), (-30,10), (-20,50), (-10,100), (0,180), (10,185), (20,195), (30,205), (40,215)

They set up a coordinate system and graphed the ordered pairs. They decided during which 10-second period the plane "speeded up" the most and the least. They collected similar data on other jets and even compared jets and propellor crafts.

One class studied a newspaper with the objective of finding as many situations as possible that could be described by ordered pairs. Some of these were:

1   Sports—(number of games won, number of games lost). This they wrote as, Giants: (47,42).

2   Stocks—(gain or loss, number of stocks). Here (1/2,23) would mean that 23 stocks each gained 1/2.

3   Telephone numbers. One creative pupil invented an intriguing number pair concerning telephone numbers found in the newspaper. His ordered pair was (sum, number of cases). For the telephone

number (no area code) 287-3863, for example, he first added $2 + 8 + 7 + 3 + 8 + 6 + 3 = 37$; then he added $3 + 7 = 10$; then he added $1 + 0 = 1$. This gave him the first number of the ordered pair. The second number of the ordered pair was the number of telephone numbers with this "sum."

Interesting Practice With Number Pairs

The creative teacher can devise many interesting drill activities requiring experimentation rather than a memorized response. Examples of two such activities follow.

What's My Rule? Pupils are given pairs of "starting numbers" and answers for a few of the pairs. In Fig. 10-41*a* starting with (2,6) the answer is 12 and starting with (9,3) the answer is 27. From the examples given the pupil is to discover the rule and use the rule to find other answers. In Fig. 10-41*a* the rule, Multiply the numbers, is relatively easy to discover. The rule in Fig. 10-41*b* is considerably more difficult and pupils may need more examples to find it. Can the reader discover the rule?

The variety of rules is almost endless and their difficulty ranges from very simple to very complex.

What am I thinking? The teacher may state a problem such as "I'm thinking of two whole numbers whose product is 10. Write all answers as number pairs." Pupils write (1,10), (2,5), (5,2), (10,1).

Pupils may also state a problem. Here the opportunity to stress preciseness of language may arise. A pupil may give the problem "I'm thinking of two numbers whose quotient is 6. Write all answers as number pairs." Pupils may question if (6,1) and (1,6) are both correct. Further, if division with fractions has been studied, (3, 1/2) is a possible answer. Here too, pupils will note that the number of answers is infinite.

FUNCTION

The study of ordered pairs of numbers leads naturally to the concept of function, which prevades many mathematical and scientific ideas from the early grades through graduate level.

The idea of function, although possibly not the technical word itself, is understood by most people and used by them in many situations. This idea is:

For each member of a set of objects there is exactly one object to which it is related.

Some examples clarify this idea:

- There is *exactly one* number of days related to each month in any non-leap year. Thus we may write:

Figure 10-41
What's my rule?

(a)

Starting numbers	Answers
(2,6)	12
(9,3)	27
(4,8)	32
(5,9)	

(b)

Starting numbers	Answers
(3,4)	14
(2,3)	8
(5,9)	47
(6,7)	

                    January →31   or   (January, 31)
                    February →28   or   (February, 28)
                    March →31   or   (March, 31)

Here exactly one number, 31, is related to January, exactly one number, 28, is related to February, and so on. Order is most important. Where each month is related to the number of days a function is defined. However, if the set of ordered pairs is (number of days, month) where the number of days is related to the month, a function is not defined. In this case (31, January) and (31, March) show that more than one item is related to 31.

- For each child there is exactly one natural mother. Here the set of ordered pairs (child, mother) constitutes a function. The set of ordered pairs (mother, child) is not a function because a mother may have more than one child.

- The set of ordered pairs (word, number of letters in that word) is a function because for each word there is exactly one number which describes correctly its number of letters. Thus the set

$$\{(a, 1), (function, 8), (in, 2), (of, 2)\}$$

is a function. If the order of writing members of these ordered pairs is reversed to obtain

$$\{(1, a), (8, function), (2, in), (2, of)\}$$

a function is not illustrated. However,

$$\{(1, a), (8, function), (2, in)\}$$

is an example of a function because for each first member—1, 8, and 2—there is exactly one second member.

The foregoing illustrations along with other examples—some of them social situations that are part of the pupils' lives and others more mathematical in nature—may be supplied by the teacher and pupils to introduce the concept of function. Examples are:

(Name of football player, his average gain per play)

(Name of candidate, number of votes he received)

(Number of members in a set, number of subsets)

(Name of pupil, number of times he "jumped rope")

Another experience sometimes used in early stages of instruction to develop the idea of function is the "function machine." In most cases this is an imaginary machine constructed so that it relates an *object* or *input* to a unique *related object* or *output* (Fig. 10-42). If the function rule is "multiply by 2" then for an input of 1 there is an output of 2, (Fig. 10-43) and for an input of 10 there is an output of 20. Pupils may organize results from this function machine in various ways:

Figure 10-42
Function machine.

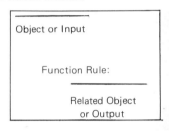

Figure 10-43
Function machine in operation.

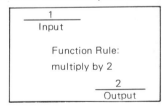

Figure 10-44
Data from rule "multiply by 2".

Input	Output
0	0
1	2
2	4
3	6

A set of ordered pairs: $\{(0,0), (1,2), (2,4), (3,6),\dots\}$

Using an arrow: $0\rightarrow0$, $1\rightarrow2$, $2\rightarrow4$, $3\rightarrow6$, and so on.

As a table (Fig. 10-44).

As a formula: output = 2 × input; or, if 0 stands for output and I stands for input, the $0 = 2I$.

One ingenious teacher made an operational function machine. A pupil called the operator was placed inside a large box. He was told the function rule to be used, "Double and add 1." Another pupil put a card in the input slot with a numeral on it. The operator looked at the card, did the required computation, and passed the related number into the output slot. Thus if 3 was the input, 7 was the output from $(2 \times 3) + 1$. The set of ordered pairs generated was $\{(0,1), (1,3), (2,5), (3,7),\dots\}$. Another operator was chosen along with a new function rule, such as "The remainder when a number is divided by 3." Here, for example, an input of 5 yielded the output of 2 and an input of 12 gave an output of 0. In this situation pupils had the opportunity to practice simple mental calculations and check the answers of the operator.

These intuitive experiences, then, emphasize the idea of a function as a set of ordered pairs in which no two pairs have the same first member. As the concept of function is studied again and again, the pupil finds that functions are described by statements, equations, graphs, and tabulated data. Later he is able to look at a graph and determine if it represents a function. For this problem he merely looks to see if any vertical line touches the graph in more than one point when the graph is drawn on the x- and y-axes with their usual orientation. If it does, a function is not pictured.

With added maturity the pupil uses functional notation that inables him to deal symbolically with functions. He will find many mathematical ideas clarified if he grasps the concept of function early in his schooling and understands the concise notation associated with function.

EXPERIMENTS FOR PUPILS

The following activities deal with integers, probability, bases, number pairs, and functions. There are many adaptations and extensions for each. In Activity 1, for example, the expressions may be written horizontally, $4 + {}^+3$, for example. Or an addition such as $4 + {}^-3$ may be compared to the related subtraction $4 - {}^+3$, and pupils may again search for patterns.

ACTIVITY 1

Objective: To complete patterns for addition, subtraction, and multi-plication of integers.

1 Finish these patterns.

Add:

+4	+4	+4	+4	+4	+4		-4	-4	-4	-4	-4	-4
+3	+2	+1	+0	+1	+2		-3	-2	-1	0	+1	+2
+7	+6	+5					-7	-6				

Subtract:

+4	+4	+4	+4	+4	+4		-4	-4	-4	-4	-4	-4
-3	-2	-1	0	+1	+2		+3	+2	+1	0	-1	-2
				+3	+2						-3	-2

Multiply:

+4	+4	+4	+4	+4	+4		-2	-2	-2	-2	-2	-2
+3	+2	+1	0	-1	-2		+3	+2	+1	0	-1	-2
+12	+8						-6	-4				

2 Tell your partner any patterns you see.

3 Make up some patterns like these.

ACTIVITY 2

Objective: To compute a person's birthday and to discover when the computation results in a negative number.

1 Here is a way to discover a person's birthday. Months are numbered as 1 for January, 2 for February, and so on until December is 12.

(a) Tell your friend to write his birth month as a numeral. Suppose it is May. He writes 5.
(b) Multiply by 2.
(c) Add 5.
(d) Multiply by 50.
(e) Add birth date. Suppose it is 12.
(f) Subtract 365.
(g) Ask for his result. He tells you 397.
(h) You now add 115 to 397. The sum is 512. The 5 represents the month May and the 12 is the day.

$$
\begin{array}{r}
5 \\
\times 2 \\
\hline
10 \\
+5 \\
\hline
15 \\
\times 50 \\
\hline
750 \\
+12 \quad \text{birth date} \\
\hline
762 \\
-365 \\
\hline
397
\end{array}
$$

2 Try this on other friends in your class.

3 Suppose a person's birthday was January 1. What number would he tell you? Would your trick still work?

4 For what birthdays will the result be a number less than 0?

ACTIVITY 3

Objective: To discover the order relation of integers using a number line.

1 Complete the labeling on this number line.

2 Write $>$ or $<$ in each blank so each sentence is true.

(a) $^-6$ __ 4 (b) $^+3$ __ $^-3$ (c) $^-1$ __ $^+4$

The number n is greater than the number x if n is to the ____ of x on this number line.

3 Arrange in order with the smallest on the left. The first is done for you.

(a) $^-4$, $^-1$, $^-5$ (b) $^+3$, $^-1$, 0 (c) $^-3$, $^+5$, $^+1$, $^-5$
$^-5 < ^-4 < ^-1$

4 Make up some examples like these. Give them to a friend to solve.

ACTIVITY 4

Objective: To discover a number pair as identifying a point.

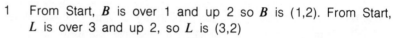

1 From Start, B is over 1 and up 2 so B is (1,2). From Start, L is over 3 and up 2, so L is (3,2)

2 Fill in the blanks. From Start
(a) H is over ____ and up ____ . So H is ____ .
(b) T is over ____ and up ____ . So T is ____ .

3 Name the letter for each number pair.

(a) (3,1) ____   (c) (5,2) ____

(b) (1,4) ____   (d) (2,2) ____

ACTIVITY 5

Objective: To practice using number pairs by playing a spelling game.

Look at the figure in Activity 4.

1 You are to play a spelling game. A number pair is used in place of a letter. For example, the number pairs (2,2), (2,4), (4,3), and (3,2) spell G I R L.

2 Most of you have heard of this place. Find its name.
(1,4), (2,4), (4,4), (3,4), (1,5), (5,5), (3,2), (1,1), (3,4), (1,4)

ACTIVITY 6

Objective: To write a number pair with each member a prime number and the sum of the members a given number.

Complete the number pairs. The members of each pair are prime numbers and their sum is shown at the left.

1   26: (23,3), (19,), (,   )

2   34: (31,), (29,), (23,), (,   )

3   40: (37,), (29,), (,   )

ACTIVITY 7

Apparatus needed: bean sticks   *Objective:* To use bean sticks to picture numerals in base-three.

1   You need 2 each of these bean sticks: 1-stick, 3-stick, 9-stick for this bean-stick game.

2   With your sticks you are to show each number 1 through 26. There is only one rule: For each number you can use 1, 2, or 0 of each stick. The sticks for 7 and 11 are shown.

3   In the table show with tallies the number of sticks you need. The tallies are shown for 4. Extend the table to 30.

No.	9-sticks	3-sticks	1-stick
1			
2			
3			
4		1	1

Activity 8

Objective: To show how 13 dots may be grouped as a certain number of disjoint subsets.

1   There are 13 dots in each picture. In the first, 1 set of ten has been grouped to show 1 ten and 3 ones. The second set of 13 has been grouped to show 1 set of nine and 4 ones.

2   Draw rings to show the grouping of other sets of 13.

1 ten and 3 ones
1 nine and 4 ones
1 seven and 6 ones
2 sixes and 1 one
2 fives and 3 ones
3 fours and 1 one

ACTIVITY 9

Objective: To group a set of items as singles, dozens, gross, and great gross.

1   You work for the Ace Pencil Company. They sell pencils as:
        single: 1 pencil
        dozen: 12 single pencils
        gross: 12 dozen = 12 × 12 = 144
        great gross: 12 gross = 12 × 144 = 1728

2. How many pencils would be in each of these orders?

    (*a*) 3 gross and 7 dozen.
    (*b*) 2 great gross, 5 gross and 6 singles.
    (*c*) 1 great gross and 9 dozen.
    (*d*) 10 gross, 11 dozen and 8 singles.

3   They write orders like this: 2, 8, 3, 4. This means 2 great gross, 8 gross, 3 dozen, and 4 singles. The total number of pencils in this order is shown at the left.

$$2 \times 1{,}728 = 3{,}456$$
$$8 \times 144 = 1{,}152$$
$$3 \times 12 = 36$$
$$4 = 4$$
$$\text{Total} = 4{,}648$$

4   How many pencils are in these orders?

    (*a*) 1, 10, 6, 5   (*b*) 3, 7, 11, 6   (*c*) 4, 9, 8, 7

5   *Brainbuster:* How would you write an order for 2,500 pencils? You cannot have more than 11 of any of singles, dozens, gross, or great gross.

ACTIVITY 10

Apparatus needed: 10 thumbtacks

Objective: To determine experimentally the probability that a thumbtack lands "point up."

Number of tacks dropped, n	Number with points up, u	Ratio, $\frac{u}{n}$
10		
20		
30		
40		
.		
.		
.		
100		

1   Drop 10 thumbtacks onto a table.

2   Count the number of tacks with points up. Record this number on the chart.

3   Find the ratio $\frac{u}{n}$ (number of points up to number tossed). Record this number on the chart.

4   Repeat steps 1 through 4 until 100 tacks have been dropped.

5   What is your best estimate of the number of tacks with points up in 1,000 tosses?

6   What is your $\frac{u}{n}$ for 1,000 tosses?

7   What things must you do so this experiment will be fair?

ACTIVITY 11

Objective: To determine experimentally the probability that two or more people out of four have the same birth month.

At least two have the same birth month	
Yes	No

1   Ask each of four friends his birth month. If at least two of them have the same birth month, tally a "yes." If not, tally a "no."

2   Repeat this with ten different sets of four friends.

3   There were ___ yes out of 10. There were ___ no out of 10.

4   What is your best guess for the chances of finding at least two people out of four with the same birth month? The probability is 41/96. This is slightly more than 4/10.

ACTIVITY 12

Objective: To determine the number of "words" that can be formed from a given set of letters.

1   How many two-letter "words" can be formed from the letters $\{x,y\}$ if each letter is used exactly once? The answer is two. They are xy and yx.

2   (a) List the three-letter words that can be formed from the letters $\{a,b,c\}$ if each letter can be used exactly once?

    (b) If a three-letter word is chosen at random, what are the chances that it:

            Starts with a?
            Has c in the middle?
            Has a and b next to each other?

3   *Brainbuster:* How many four-letter "words" can be formed from $\{r,s,t,u\}$ if each letter is used exactly once?

QUESTIONS AND EXERCISES

1   Many teachers feel that situations with signed numbers are easy to recognize and rules are reasonably easy to memorize, but teaching of these operations in not easy. Give reasons for this.

2   A pupil asks, "Why, when I subtract -2 from 5, do I get a number larger than 5?" Answer him.

3   The table below summarizes signs for multiplying positive and negative integers. Explain how the same table can be used to summarize signs for *division* of integers.

×	−	+
+	−	+
−	+	−

4   It has been stated that if two coins are tossed out on the table, there are three outcomes— (a) two heads, (b) one head and one tail, or (c) two tails—and each outcome is equally likely. You have several different committees of pupils toss two coins 100 times and compile the data. Will the results necessarily conform to the statement given above? Suppose one result is 20 of $2H$, 35 of $1H$ and $1T$, and 45 of $2T$. What is the important idea to be learned from such a result?

5   What are important objectives that are accomplished when pupils devise an experiment like the one described on page 275?

6   A parent asks at a conference with you, "Why should my child have to study probability?" Answer him.

7   A pupil asks, "Why isn't 1 a prime? It has factors of 1 and itself." Answer him.

8 The shapes of the arrangement of objects to show a prime and a nonprime number are different. Describe that difference.

9 How could the experiment with blocks on pages 281-282 be used to help pupils write numerals in base two?

10 Make a list of items from your environment in sets other than ten. A partial list is on page 282.

11 Considerable data in everyday could be expressed by number pairs. One example would be from a survey of cars passing a certain point in a day. It would be (name of car, number of cars.) List other possibilities.

12 Under what conditions can pairs of numbers be used and when is it necessary to use ordered pairs of numbers in discussing situations or data?

13 Why is it important to introduce the topic of number pairs in familiar situations?

PROJECTS

1 Study a series of recently published textbooks and answer the following questions about each of the five major topics of this chapter. (a) At what grade level is each introduced? (b) What experiments for individual pupils or groups of pupils are suggested? (c) What are some interesting drill experiences? (d) What concrete materials are used?

2 Demonstrate to the class: (a) How to determine the prime numbers using a hundreds chart. (b) How to justify that $(-2)(-3) = +6$. (c) How to count in base two. (d) How to picture and solve this problem: You can go to a town by car, bus, train, or plane. A friend will then pick you up and drive you by way of the Dumbarton, San Mateo, or Bay Bridge. How many possible ways can you make the trip? (e) How the idea of an ordered pair of numbers can be introduced.

3 Choose any concept discussed in the chapter. Write an experiment that could be given to a pupil so he could discover the concept upon completion of the experiment.

4 List the most important materials, concrete and pictorial, for introducing each of the five topics in the chapter.

5 No reasons for the study of bases other than base ten were given in the text. Find reasons and report to the class.

6 Complete each Activity for primes pages 276-281. (a) Make some guesses for the meaning of "prime triplet" similar to those suggested for twin primes in Activity II. Find the definitions of prime triplet. (b) As an extension of Activity VI prove the following statement: "If Goldbach's conjecture is true, every even number greater than 4 can be expressed as the sum of three primes." (c) Experiment as suggested in Activity VIII to discover the number of factors for 5^n, 7^n. Make a general statement. How many factors for 4^n?

7 Choose concepts for which the study was described as a class situation in this chapter and write laboratory experiments for use by small groups or individual pupils.

8 Consult a series textbooks. Trace all experiences from first grade on which lead to an understanding of the idea of ordered pairs of numbers.

Bibliography

1 Cohen, L. S.: "A Rationale in Working with Signed Numbers," *The Arithmetic Teacher*, vol. 12, pp. 563-567, Nov., 1965. Very interesting make-believe situation which illustrates addition and subtraction of signed numbers.

2 Johnson, D. C., and L. S. Cohen: "Functions," *The Arithmetic Teacher*, vol. 17, pp. 305-315, April, 1970. Experiences for relating real-world situations to the formal idea of function.

3 Lath, L. M.: "A Model for Arithmetic of Signed Numbers," *The Arithmetic Teacher*, vol. 14, pp. 220-222, March, 1967. Interesting visual aid for

developing the concept of, and operations with, integers.

4 Niman, J., and R. Postman: "Probability on the Geoboard," *The Arithmetic Teacher*, vol. 20, pp. 167-170, March, 1973. An interesting set of problems concerned with the probability of an imaginary parachutist landing on a given region of the geoboard.

5 Nuffield Foundation: *The Nuffield Mathematics Project: Probability and Statistics*, John Wiley, New York, 1969. English program in which graphs are used to analyze data from games and activities involving chance.

6 Omejic, E.: "A Different Approach to the Sieve of Eratosthenes," *The Arithmetic Teacher*, vol. 19, pp. 192-196, March, 1972. Shortcut to the well-known procedure for generating the set of primes.

7 Oliver, C.: "Gus's Magic Numbers: A Key to the Divisibility Test for Primes," *The Arithmetic Teacher*, vol. 19, pp. 183-189, March, 1972. Fascinating account of a young boy's discovery.

8 Peterson, J. C.: "Fourteen Different Strategies for Multiplication of Integers or why $(-1)(-1) = +1$," *The Arithmetic Teacher*, vol. 19, pp. 396-403, May, 1972. A number of different ways to illustrate multiplication with integers.

9 Stenger, D. J. L.: "Prime Numbers from the Multiplication Table," *The Arithmetic Teacher*, vol. 16, pp. 617-620, Dec., 1969. Discovering primes, making conjectures, and generalizing while studying a multiplication table.

10 Wardrap, R. F.: "Divisibility Rules for Numbers Expressed in Other Bases," *The Arithmetic Teacher*, vol. 19, pp. 218-220, March, 1972. More capable upper-grade pupils can discover these rules.

11
LEARNING TO SOLVE WORD PROBLEMS

Many crucial problems will be encountered in the future by pupils who are in school today. What these problems will be we cannot say; but we do know that they will arise in the personal, vocational, and public lives of those who will hold the responsibility for the future, and that they will require original methods of solution and answers. Those who will solve them must know how to define and analyze the problems, secure information they do not have, and draw sound inferences from the data at hand.

To prepare people who are able to solve problems is a primary responsibility of the organized curriculum in the school. It is the ultimate outcome of learning and the real challenge to teachers. While mathematics does not have a monopoly on this responsibility, it does have two contributions to make. First, many important problems in everyday life are quantitative or geometric and require analysis of quantitative data and spatial relations. This is becoming increasingly true as the activities in our society are becoming more and more mathematical. Second, mathematics provides a pattern for the techniques required in problem solving. The problem-solving structure, although it is not a stereotyped procedure, is more clearcut in mathematics than in other fields, and is more readily studied with quantitative data than with any other kind of data. Yet the general structure is equally applicable in problem situations which are not primarily quantitative.

A problem is a task which the learner can understand but for which he has no immediate solution. Problem solving, accordingly, involves exploration and discovery. Inherent in every problem is a difficulty which requires that the pupil develop new insights, if not new procedures. From this point of view, when the pupil improvises a solution to a problem that demands a procedure which he has not mastered, he is solving a problem.

This chapter provides a set of experiences on which an effective program of problem solving may be developed by:

- Reviewing and extending methods by which pupils explore a problem and discover possible ways to attack it.
- Outlining ways in which teachers may help pupils read and understand the setting of word problems.
- Illustrating mathematical models most useful for translating data from a word statement to a numerical statement.
- Outlining a sensible way to guide pupils to check and verify answers.
- Listing experiments for pupils through which the problem-solving program may be individualized.

EXPLORATION AND DISCOVERY

Exploration and discovery have been emphasized in every previous chapter. Now with problem solving identified as developing and learning ways to attack problems, the pupil who has had a rich experience in experimenting and who has had opportunities to discover ideas for himself can use such procedures in solving problems. Some attitudes and techniques needed for this problem solving are:

> When confronted with a problem, the pupil has an experimental attitude that leads him to investigate the data and organize them for study.

> He has sufficient confidence to embark on a study of the data and to continue after encountering dead ends.

> He has techniques for finding and testing clues leading to a solution of the problem.

For several reasons these attitudes and techniques are most readily acquired in group activities. The interchange of ideas in such situations provides a stimulus to explore the data and the realization that such exploration is a trial-and-error process. It is natural for each pupil to assume that everyone else proceeds systematically to a solution while he alone fumbles in a trial-and-error manner, encountering a dead end with the resulting frustration. He must learn that dead ends are part of the process of learning about the relationships that exist, and he must acquire for himself procedures for exploring relationships. Hence, he must learn through experience the importance of *trying something* if there is no obvious clue. He should recognize that by trying something, even if he reaches a dead end, he has learned more about the relationships and is brought closer to the clue that will lead to the solution.

Toward this end the puzzle type of problem is useful. It has two advantages: first, its very triviality makes the procedure in its solution more important than the answer; and second, it usually

Figure 11-1
"Missing digits" puzzle.

```
        XX8XX
  XX )XXXXXXX
     XXX
       XX
       XX
      XXX
      XXX
```

Figure 11-2

```
      3X8X
  3X )X8XXX
     XX
     XXX
     XX6
      6X
      XX
```

Figure 11-3

```
    A E C
  x   E 2
    8 D 8
  A E C
  5 P N 8
```

Figure 11-4
How many rectangles?

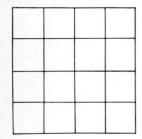

appears impossible at the outset but yields readily to exploration.

The *missing-digits* puzzles have both of these qualities. The extreme example of Fig. 11-1 makes a good classroom exercise. Each *x* represents a missing digit. At first examination, it appears hopeless to reinstate the original exercise. However, if the class starts to examine it, in response to the question "What can you find out?" a number of bits of information begin to appear. These can be put together to yield a solution. Careful questions by the teacher can lead pupils to discover that:

The product of the divisor and the first digit is a three-digit number. *Then the divisor must be 12 or greater.*

The second and fourth digits in the quotient are zeros. (How do you know this?)

When multiplied by 8, the divisor gives a two-digit product. *Then it cannot be greater than 12,* and, from conclusion 1, *it must be 12.*

Then *the first and last digits in the quotient must be 9.*

Since we have recovered the divisor and quotient, we can restore the dividend by taking their product.

Having worked this puzzle orally in class, the pupils may be ready for individual work on a less forbidding one, Fig. 11-2. Missing-digits puzzles are possible with every operation. Another type is Fig. 11-3. Each letter represents a specific digit.

Another interesting problem for which the procedure is more important than the answer is "How many rectangles can you trace with your finger for Fig. 11-4?" Here again the solution at first may seem very complex, but class or group discussion of ways to attack the problem can bring out the needed exploration:

We need to find a way to count the rectangles.

We need to find a way to count so we are sure we have counted all rectangles.

We must be sure we know what a rectangle is. (Is a square a rectangle?)

Maybe we can do a simpler but comparable problem.

This last suggestion is one that must be practiced and is used often by effective problem solvers. As pupils count the rectangles in Fig. 11-5 *a, b,* and then *c,* they develop a plan for counting and a way of recording their results that may be applied to the more difficult original problem.

Experiences in guided discovery need not be limited to story problems. One very profitable type of exercise is "Find the Rule." Starting in the early grades with simple activities asking pupils to "state the next numbers," these may become progressively more difficult:

        2,4,6,8,...   1,2,4,8,...   1,3,6,10,...

The role of the teacher during the activities of exploration is very important in guiding the thinking of the pupil without giving him the answers. It is useful for the teacher to keep these principles in mind:

> The emphasis of the activity is on the method of analysis, rather than on the answer.

> The pupil should develop an experimental attitude that allows him to try new leads and to abandon them without being discouraged when they appear fruitless.

> The pupil must discover the solution for himself. The teacher's role is to orient attention toward discovery, to encourage the pupil to try whatever appears promising and plausible, and to teach him to recognize dead ends.

> The ability to solve problems develops progressively as information and techniques, in addition to experimental attitudes, are developed.

The teacher should:

> Ask questions that help the pupils focus on the elements necessary for a solution.

> Check the pupils' understanding of vocabulary, what is to be found, and the meaning of the data.

> Suggest plans for organizing the data so that relationships will be revealed.

> Give careful attention to pupils' attitudes as well as their understanding.

PROMOTING PROBLEM-SOLVING ABILITY

As soon as the pupil begins the study of mathematics, he is given verbal problems which help him understand the situations that call for the operation he is learning. He must be guided to understand that he is not just solving a particular problem but that he is learning to solve problems in general. This attitude is necessary to focus attention on the *process* as well as answers to the problems.

Every teacher has heard "I don't understand the problem." While the reasons for this statement are different for different pupils, many difficulties result from lack of familiarity with the setting or the vocabulary of the problem. Some of these difficulties may be isolated and dealt with separately. Experiences related to exploring a problem and understanding it are described on the following pages.

Understanding the Problem

When a problem is presented in a setting unfamiliar to the pupil, the mathematical relationships that otherwise would be apparent

Figure 11-5
How many rectangles for each figure?

(a)

(b)

(c)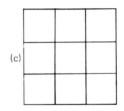

to him may be obscured. The difficulty can be removed by first translating the problem into a familiar setting in which the relationships become clear and then exploring the original setting. For instance, if the original problem dealt with the time required for a rocket to travel to Venus, many pupils might have difficulty in visualizing the data. Restatement of the problem in terms of a car traveling between two cities or a pedestrian intercepting a friend would clarify the relationships. These same relationships could then be found in the original problem.

When a sixth-grade teacher found her class was having difficulty in solving problems dealing with the retail stores, she developed an original topic on the problems encountered by Henry and Joe when they set up a fruit stand on the highway. In this setting, such things as overhead and various other expenses were readily comprehended, as was the difference between margin and profit. More important, perhaps, was the fact that the pupils realized the need to establish the selling price of commodities in order to allow for expenses and profit as well as the original cost. The topic was useful in preparing the class for a successful study of the retail store. The teacher also learned from the experience. In the following year, before undertaking the study of the retail store with her class, she prepared a short topic on the problems Martin experienced when he set up a hot-dog concession at a football game.

Trips and other firsthand experiences An effective procedure to help establish an understanding of some types of problems is that of visiting places of business or government where the problem setting can be observed at firsthand. For example, problems dealing with cost, discount, overhead, list price, and depreciation were clarified for a class as Mr. Kryder, a local merchant, took the pupils through his store. He explained the following: the price that he paid for 10 electric frying pans; the discount that he received for paying within 30 days; how the cost of light, water, heat, rent, salaries, and other expenses made up his overhead; and how the selling price was established to allow for a profit. Mr. Kryder also explained that the price of certain articles was reduced in order to decrease his stock and secure money which he could reinvest in Christmas goods.

Similarly, trips to the bank, a stock brokerage or exchange, the assessor's office, or a building under construction, as well as experience running a school store, school bank, or classroom insurance firm, have served to clarify situations, vocabulary, and relations for many pupils.

Informal dramatization Many problems have words and ideas that are obscure to pupils, but which cannot be clarified by any of the methods listed above. Frequently these are made clear through informal dramatization of the situation. For example, Ms. Hand's seventh-grade class was studying perpendiculars, bisectors, and other topics in intuitive geometry. One problem required a description of the set of all points that separate an angle into two congruent angles. To dramatize this, pupils stood in positions that satisfied the conditions of the problem, using a corner of the floor to represent the vertex of the angle and the two adjacent sides of the floor to indicate the rays forming the angle. Each pupil was asked to show how his position satisfied the stated conditions; those that were out of position were corrected by class criticism. The concepts thus illustrated formed a basis for the successful solution of problems requiring bisection of angles.

Concrete materials A lesson conducted by Ms. Lindquist with her sixth-grade class illustrates how the meaning of problems may be clarified through reference to concrete materials. Her class was ready to work on a series of problems dealing with cotton raising that contained terms such as *length of fiber, seed cotton, cotton seed, staple cotton,* and *lint.* Ms. Lindquist realized that few of her pupils were familiar with these terms. To introduce the lesson, she brought a cotton boll into the classroom and had the pupils measure the length of the fibers and extract some of the seeds. The class talked about the length of the fibers and learned from reference to the encyclopedia that seed cotton is raised to produce seeds and that lint is what is left after the seeds are removed. After this introduction they had little trouble understanding the situations and vocabulary in the problems.

Similarly, other teachers have used such things as egg cartons, butter cartons, tin cans, gallon containers, ribbons, price tags, thermometers, and checks and other business forms to help pupils visualize problems.

Pictures, films, filmstrips, and resource personnel Frequently, problems that would otherwise be vague to the pupil are clarified for him through the use of pictures. These may be illustrations in a book or pictures cut from a magazine or projected from a filmstrip or a motion-picture film. For example, a class was solving a set of problems dealing with Christmas shopping. From a mail-order catalog the pupils cut pictures of articles mentioned in the problems. The pictures were mounted on a posterboard, and pupils inserted the prices mentioned in the textbook. As problems were read, pupils referred to the pictures. The result was that many who had previously encountered difficulty with similar problems were now able to do them with little help from the teacher.

An eighth-grade class was to solve a number of problems dealing with banking forms and procedures. Before working problems from the textbook, they viewed and discussed a film on banking supplied by a local bank. The teacher reported that the class had far greater success in understanding the problems than previous classes that had not seen the film.

Another class was undertaking a study of life insurance. One of the parents who was in the insurance business spoke briefly to the pupils on insurance and answered their questions. Again, a marked increase in ability to understand problems was observed.

The need for pictures to help them visualize the setting for problems varies considerably among pupils, as does the need to use concrete materials. While these needs should decrease as pupils mature, pictures and concrete materials are still useful in the upper grades, particularly for problems placed in less familiar settings.

The effective teacher selects a variety of experiences to help pupils understand the vocabulary and situations of problems. The pupil who has profited from such experience has a wide range of information that permits him to understand many of his problems immediately. When he encounters a problem that is not clear to him, he follows a systematic procedure to help him clarify it. He may use reference books, tangible materials, or pictures, restate in his own words, or apply other procedures that he has learned. When he has the setting of the problem clearly in mind, he has eliminated the first of these difficulties that could block the successful solution of his problem.

Specific Instruction in Reading

Mathematical material calls for a different kind of reading skill than does fiction or history; it is condensed and concise, and it requires concentrated attention to obtain all the important details. The pupil accustomed to skimming often needs to be taught how to read mathematical material carefully for content and how to pay careful attention in order to obtain all the data.

The skills required for reading mathematical material with understanding may be improved if part of the time allotted for instruction in problem solving is devoted to testing the level of reading ability and providing experiences in reading mathematics problems.

Reading text that contains quantitative information A variety of procedures may be used to provide special practice in reading and interpreting textual material that contains quantitative data. Mr. Desoto conducted such a lesson which emphasized both science and mathematics with an opaque projector showing information concerning the Apollo flights to the moon:

The actual surface [of the moon] is everywhere pocket-marked by craters of various sizes. The smallest craters known are less than 1/1000 inch across; the largest exceed 50 miles. Most craters are very old. Some may be several billion years old. But some were produced during the past few million years when objects from space struck the moon. At velocities of 8 to 20 miles per second, these objects possess very high energy—even more than an equivalent mass of TNT.[1]

Electrical power for the experiments on the lunar surface [for Apollo 17] is provided by a device termed a Radioisotope Thermoelectric Generator. A total of roughly 70 watts is delivered....It is truly incredible that all of the experiments together, and including the radio that sends the scientific information over a quarter million miles of space to us, use no more power than is consumed by an ordinary 75 watt light bulb.[2]

All lunar rocks are very, very old. Their ages range from 3 to 4 billion years. The oldest known terrestial rock is about 3 1/2 billion years and rocks older than 2 billion years are extremely rare.

An inventory of lunar rock returned by the first five Apollo missions is shown below.[3]

Lunar Sample Inventory

Apollo Missions:	A-11	A-12	A-14	A-15	A-16
Amount returned	21,694	34,369	42,927	77,380	95,476
Used for biotesting	702	538	589	158	72
Destructive analysis	4,225	2,681	2,823	3,010	2,933
On display	2,113	1,925	247	660	20
Processing loss at MSC	650	600	200	200	40
Available for future generation experiments	15,218	29,669	39,315	74,012	92,431

All amounts shown are grams of material.

The pupils answered the following and other mathematical questions by reference to the article:

How many more grams of rock were returned by Apollo 16 than by Apollo 11?

In comparing the weight of lunar rocks returned, which mission brought back about 2 times that of another mission?

About how many pounds of rock were returned by the first five missions?

[1] Simmons, G., "On the Moon with Apollo 17," *National Aeronautics and Space Administration*, December, 1972, p. 1.
[2] Ibid, pp. 24-25.
[3] Ibid., pp. 82-83.

What percent (to the nearest 1%) of the rock returned for the five missions has been lost due to processing?

Similar experiences in reading and answering questions about articles presenting data on space travel, conservation, sports, and other topics of interest is a useful means for increasing pupils' ability to read quantitative text.

Reading instruction in the mathematics class   When pupils tend to read problems carelessly or give other evidence of difficulty with reading, an effective procedure is to have them read sets of problems on each of several days before they attempt to solve them. As they read aloud and discuss the problems, the teacher can judge the degree of understanding that has been achieved. Words and phrases that cause difficulty can be studied and illustrated. During supervised study, when a pupil asks how to work a particular problem, the teacher may reply, "Read it aloud to me." Next he will ask, "What does this word mean?" and, "State the problem in your own words." Then he may direct the pupil to tell what the problem is about. Such a set of questions frequently helps the pupil to locate and correct the source of his difficulty.

Oral lessons, in which the pupils first read and then restate the problem in their own words, help them to read with understanding. Nonverbal pupils may have difficulty in substituting their own statements for those in the textbook. This may be overcome by phrasing the instructions, "Tell what the problem is about." Here the pupil understands that an informal description of the setting and action in the problem is what he is to present. Through constructive criticism by the class, the pupil develops his ability to interpret what he reads.

Vocabulary building requires special attention in mathematics. Textbooks frequently recognize this and provide lists of key words to be used in the topic; they also provide vocabulary tests made up of matching, short-answer, or completion questions.

Pupils frequently accumulate lists of new words for review and ready reference. These lists may be kept on a special part of the bulletin board during work on a topic, with more words and brief definitions added as they are encountered. Pupils in the upper grades may keep such a list in their notebooks.

Mr. Murphy devised a vocabulary game that proved effective with his eighth-grade class when they studied the business uses of percent. On a number of 6- by 9-inch cards he printed words such as *discount, commission, interest, margin, overhead, cost, selling price,* and *profit,* and printed short definitions on a second set of cards (Fig. 11-6). After shuffling the cards, he passed them

Figure 11-6
Cards for a vocabulary game.

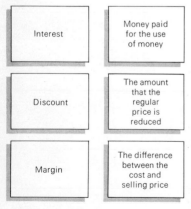

to pupils. Then he asked one pupil to come to the front of the room and hold up his card showing either a word or a definition. The pupil who held the corresponding card then came up and stood beside the first pupil, and the class verified the matching.

Television quiz shows also suggest procedures for a change of pace. One teacher, for example, used a "64 peanuts" game. The contestant started with one peanut and could double his earnings up to 64 if he could correctly answer six consecutive questions. These questions ranged in difficulty as seen by these two examples: (1) "A bank pays for the use of money that you deposit in a savings account. What do we call the money paid to you?" (2) "A merchant paid $100,000 for the furniture that he plans to sell. Expenses of doing business are $35,000. The furniture is sold for $160,000. If we subtract the cost from the selling price and then subtract the overhead from that result, what name do we give to the final difference?" Some fanfare that simulates the atmosphere of a television quiz program adds to the pupils' enthusiasm for the game.

Any experience that helps a child form a mental picture of the situation described in a word problem will increase his ability to comprehend that problem. Successful teachers have found a number of techniques such as the foregoing effective in assisting pupils to "bring to life" situations described in words.

CONSTRUCTING MATHEMATICAL MODELS TO REPRESENT RELATIONSHIPS

Recognizing relationships that exist among numbers calls for the development of specific mathematical insights. When a pupil directs his efforts solely toward finding answers, he seriously hinders this development. Thus, experiences at every level of instruction and dealing with every topic should be designed to develop the pupil's ability to build a mathematical model that relates the given data. This is a long-term program. Detailed activities directed to this end have been described throughout previous chapters. One important factor contributing to ability to relate data in problems is a well-directed sequence of experiences whereby each pupil acquires a full understanding of the kinds of situations to which each operation of arithmetic applies.

Through grouping materials, drawing and examining pictures, improvising solutions, discovering relations among various operations, and searching his environment for appropriate places to apply what he has learned, the pupil is increasingly able:

To recognize addition as the operation called for when two or more disjoint sets are combined and recognize that multiplication is illustrated when equivalent disjoint sets are joined.

To form conclusions such as "I divide to find the amount for each when sharing equally" and "I subtract to find how many more are in one set than in another."

To recognize that the solution of the equation $8 \div 1/3 = n$ answers a variety of questions: "1/3 of what number is 8?" "1/3 times what number is 8?" "8 is 1/3 of what number?" "What is the number if 1/3 of it is 8?" "How many 1/3s are in 8?"

An operation is mastered only when the pupil recognizes the situations that call for its use. The basis for recognizing the correct operation to answer a particular type of question is also the basis for proper selection of the numbers to use in the algorithm.

Increasing attention is given in current textbooks to exercises that develop the ability of pupils to relate the data in problems. While this material is very useful, the teacher will most often need to augment it with additional experiences. Some of the techniques successfully used by teachers illustrate the possibilities.

Drawing Pictures

Most people have found from experience that drawing a sketch or picture helps to clarify the situation, build the mathematical model, and state the relations in a problem. Learning to draw pictures for problems starts in the early grades. For example, Ms. Harper and her second-grade class talked about an appropriate picture for the following problem: "There were five apples on the table. If two apples fell off, how many are left?" After several pupils tried drawing a picture on paper mounted on an easel, the pupils selected Joe's picture (similar to Fig. 11-7) as best. Next Ms. Harper gave the pupils a mimeographed set of problems, with directions to draw a picture to represent each problem. When a particularly suitable picture was found, she gave the artist a blank plastic slide and had him draw his picture on the slide. It was then projected for the class.

This practice can be continued, with modifications, throughout the school years. The shift from pictures to line, rectangle, or circle diagrams was encouraged by a sixth-grade teacher, using problems that he made up for that purpose. The first of these problems, selected from pamphlets used in the study of conservation in social studies, was as follows: "The elevation of Mt. Whitney is 4393 meters above sea level, while the bottom of Death Valley is 85 meters below sea level. By how much do these two elevations differ?" Pupils were directed to draw a picture to represent the conditions in the problem. The teacher walked about the classroom,

Figure 11-7
Picturing "There were 5 apples and 2 fell off".

Figure 11-8
Simplifying the picture of a problem.

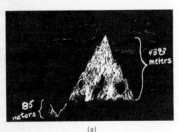

(a)

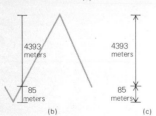

(b)   (c)

observing progress on the pictures; when they were completed, he asked one pupil to put his picture on the blackboard. That picture is shown in Fig. 11-8*a*. When the pupils had discussed the picture briefly, another pupil drew a picture, as in Fig. 11-8*b*, and the pupils agreed that this would be another way to picture the problem. Next, the mountain and valley were erased, leaving only the segment with appropriate arrows to show directions, as shown in Fig. 11-8*c*. After the same procedure had been followed for two more problems, the pupils were asked to complete, independently, drawings for the rest of the problems. Examples of the diagrams drawn by pupils at different grade levels illustrate some of the many possibilities of this technique:

Figure 11-9
Picturing a hiking problem.

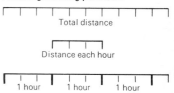

> The Boy Scouts plan to average 3 kilometers per hour on the hike. How much time will be required to hike 10 kilometers? (Fig. 11-9.)

> A certain paint contains 40 percent white lead. How much white lead is required for 10 gallons of this paint? (Fig. 11-10.)

> Bicycles cost Mr. Stewart $30, and the margin is 40 percent of the selling price. What is the selling price? (Fig. 11-11.)

Such diagrams bring out more clearly than words what the known and unknown data are and the relations which exist among them.

Making up Problems

As pupils formulate, criticize, and refine problems from situations familiar to them, they frequently discover for the first time that all problems supply data and ask a question, the answer to which can be obtained by the appropriate manipulation of that data. Ms. Reese, for example, wrote the following information on the blackboard and asked members of her third-grade class to write a *problem* for any one of the sets of data:

> One child has eight marbles, another has five marbles, and another has three marbles.

> Number of children at a party: four; cost of soda pop: 15 cents a bottle.

> A pupil has 40 cents. He wants to treat himself and three friends.

After a little time had passed, Ms. Reese collected the papers and wrote some of the pupils' "problems" on the blackboard. Examples were: "I have eight marbles, Bill has five marbles, and Ted has three marbles." "How much will the party cost?" "I have 40 cents. I want to treat Mary, Helen, Jane, and myself. How many candy bars can we each have?"

Figure 11-10
How much white lead?

Figure 11-11
What is the selling price?

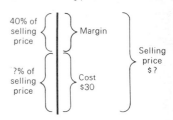

Through discussion the children pointed out what was lacking in each "problem." Marie said that the first problem didn't ask a question. The children agreed that asking you to find or do something is an important part of every problem. Where questions were lacking, they were supplied through suggestions by the class. Someone noted that the second "problem" asked a question but failed to give the information that was needed for its solution. The class agreed and supplied the needed information in the statement of the problem, and also supplied it in other problems in which it was missing. Similarly, pupils criticized the third "problem" on the grounds that it didn't say what price the candy bars were. Ted, who formulated the problems, said that he meant 10-cent candy bars. Others suggested that some candy bars cost 15 cents and that some can be purchased at the supermarket at three for 29 cents.

From the discussions in refining problems, Ms. Reese guided the class to generalize that a problem must always give data and must always ask a question. Furthermore, the data must be related to the question in some way so that the question can be answered from the given information.

At other times, assignments call for making up problems to be solved by a specific operation. To vary these lessons it is sometimes required that the numbers in the problem be expressed as fractions or decimals or be based on a situation from aviation, industry, or recreation.

Analyzing Model Solutions

When problems in books or on the blackboard are presented with accompanying solutions, they often suggest a good method of developing and recording a solution. They may furnish the basis for discussions of mathematical ideas, order of performing computations, usefulness of labeling, and alternate solutions. The discussion questions for the following problem illustrate one effective procedure: "When Bill's family started their vacation trip of 1,218 kilometers to Yellowstone Park, the odometer of the car read 11,420.7. They traveled 543 kilometers the first day. If they planned to average 75 kilometers per hour, how many hours should it take them to finish the trip?" Pupils study a model solution, Fig. 11-12 and then discuss answers to questions such as the following:

Figure 11-12
Model solution.

$1,218 - 543 = n$

1218 kilometers for the entire trip
−543 kilometers traveled first day
  675 kilometers yet to travel

$$675 \div 75 = x$$

$$\begin{array}{r} 9 \\ 75\overline{)675} \\ 675 \\ \hline 0 \end{array}$$

It would take 9 hours to travel 675 km at 75 km per hour.

What is the hidden question?

Why was the 11,420.7 not used in the computations? Would the answer have been the same if the odometer had read 12,000.0?

Ask questions that would have required using the 11,420.7. For each of the questions, identify the extra data.

What relationship of distance, rate, and time is applied in this problem?

Why were the numerals labeled in the first computation?

Suppose in this car car the odometer was set to show miles (1 kilometer ≈ 5/8 of a mile). If all other data remained unchanged, but kilometers were replaced by miles, would the answer be smaller, larger, or the same?

How could you estimate the answer to this problem?

Make a sketch for this problem.

While model solutions may be useful as a basis for analysis of techniques, it must be understood that they should not be followed mechanically.

Restating a Problem with other Numbers

Often very large whole numbers or fractional numbers tend to obscure the relations among the data. This is seen in the following examples:

How thick is a book of 200 pages if each page is 1/120 centimeter thick?

The sun is about 149 million kilometers from the earth, while the moon is about 389,000 kilometers away. The sun is how many times as far away as the moon?

What would otherwise be relatively simple problems are complicated in the first problem by the fractional number and in the second by the large numbers. Attempts to sketch either situation would lead to added difficulties for any but the most skilled pupil. However, the substitution of numbers, even though they may make the problem unrealistic, may lead the student to discover which operation to use. For example, the statement "Find the combined thickness of four pages, each 1/2 centimeter thick" gives sufficient data to make an answer of 2 centimeters (4 × 1/2) easily obtainable. Hence, the thickness of the real book is 200 (number of pages) × 1/120 (thickness of one page).

This very powerful tool for solving problems may be used even in more advanced mathematics and can be stated as a rule: "If you can't solve a problem as it is given, try solving it after substituting 'simpler' numbers."

Critical Examination of the Data

In life, problems do not come in a neatly organized form, with all the relevant data provided and no extraneous data given. If genuine problem-solving ability is to be developed, the practice of critical examination of data is required. For this purpose, problems with too many or too few data such as the following may readily be constructed by both teacher and pupils:

> A dress pattern calls for 4.5 meters of cloth. The pattern is for a size-12 dress. At $2.39 a meter how much would the cloth cost?

> Ms. Grey's class consists of two-thirds girls and one-third boys. How many boys and how many girls are in the class?

The teacher informs his class that one of the problems contains more than enough information to answer the question, while the other does not contain enough. He instructs them to write "Too much" or "Not enough" by the appropriate problem, and tells if in the case of "Too much," what the extra information is, and what else one would need to know in order to solve the problem in the case of "Not enough."

Using Mathematical Sentences

If it were necessary to choose the one method used in elementary school mathematics programs that contributes most to the more effective solution of verbal problems it would be the use of mathematical sentences as a means of expressing mathematical models. This procedure has been emphasized in previous chapters and is reviewed here because of evidence that pupils who have used this method have made substantial gains in their ability to solve problems. The following examples illustrate how mathematical sentences are used in the problem-solving program.

> Project Mercury, which placed our first astronauts in orbit around the earth, had about 19,300 people on the job during a flight. Of these about 15,600 were associated with the recovery effort. How many were not associated with the recovery?

(a) Once he understands the question, the pupil makes a statement or draws a picture that can be considered the first stage in developing the mathematical model for the problem. The pupil's picture may be like that in Fig. 11-13, with the outer closed curve indicating the joining of the two sets of people performing the mission. He may think of a word statement and express it orally or in some cases write it:

> The number of people associated with recovery plus the number not associated with recovery equals the total number associated with the mission.

(b) The pupil writes the equation. He replaces the words in the statement with numerals and letters: If n represents the number not associated with recovery, then $15,600 + n = 19,300$.

Figure 11-13

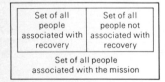

Set of all people associated with recovery	Set of all people not associated with recovery
Set of all people associated with the mission	

Some pupils may express the equation using subtraction:

$$n = 19{,}300 - 15{,}600$$

(*c*) The pupil performs the computation mentally or when necessary uses pencil and paper: $19{,}300 - 15{,}600 = 3{,}700$.

(*d*) The pupil answers the problem with a sentence: "There were about 3,700 people not associated with the recovery effort."

The city parking lot at Booneville has 25 parking rows, with 16 spaces for cars in each. At 11:00 A.M. exactly 11 of the rows were completely filled. How many more cars can be parked?

(*a*) The pupils may think, "The total number of parking spaces minus the number filled equals the number unfilled."

(*b*) If *n* represents the number of unfilled parking spaces,

$$(25)(16) - (11)(16) = n$$

(*c*) The pupil performs the computations, as in Fig. 11-14 *a*. He may or may not write all steps for finding *n*, as in Fig. 11-14 *b*. The pupil who understands the distributive property may perform the computations, as in Fig. 11-14*c*.

(*d*) The pupil completes the solution by making a statement, "There are 224 empty parking spaces."

One difference between examples 1 and 2 is that 1 is a *one-step* problem and 2 is a *three-step* problem. This merely means that only one computation is necessary in example 1, whereas in example 2, three are required. In some cases, a pupil may perceive hidden questions in 2, which must be answered before the problem can be solved. Examples are: "How many spaces are there in the parking lot?" and "How many spaces are filled?" The stress on breaking problems up into one, two, or more steps and finding and answering hidden questions is unnecessary if the pupil learns to make the mathematical statement and then express the relations by means of a mathematical sentence.

There are 13 books on a shelf. Each is either red or blue. If there are more than 10 red books, how many are blue?

(*a*) Mathematical statement: "The number of red books plus the number of blue books equals 13."

(*b*) Mathematical sentence: If *x* represents the number of red books and *y* represents the number of blue books, then

$$x + y = 13$$

There is, however, another condition: the number of red books is more than 10. This can be expressed in a number of ways:

   (1) Because *x* represents a whole number more than 10, and because there are only 13 books in all, *x* must be 11, 12, or 13.

Figure 11-14

Three ways of finding (25) (16) − (11) (16).

(a)

```
  25        11       400
x 16      x 16     - 176
-----     -----    -----
 150        66       224
  25        11
-----     -----
 400       176
```

(b)

$$(25)(16) - (11)(16) = n$$
$$400 - 176 = n$$
$$224 = n$$

(c)

$$(25)(16) - (11)(16) = n$$
$$16(25 - 11) = n$$
$$(16)(14) = n$$
$$224 = n$$

(2) $x > 10$ and $x < 14$

(3) $|10 < x < 14$.

One way of writing the mathematical sentences is: $x + y = 13$ and $10 < x < 14$; x represents a whole number.

(c) The solution may be recorded in different ways:

(1) By a table. First, all possible values for x are recorded by $10 < x < 14$ in Fig. 11-15a. The pupil thinks $11 + 2 = 13$ and writes 2 for y under the 11 for x. He continues with $12 + 1 = 13$ and $13 + 0 = 13$, completing the table as in Fig. 11-15b.

(2) The pupil writes three equations, as in Fig. 11-15c, one each for $x = 11$, $x = 12$, and $x = 13$, and determines y so that each mathematical sentence is true. He pairs values for x and y as in Fig. 11-15d, obtaining three possible answers.

(d) The pupil answers the question in the problem in the following way: "There are 11 red books and 2 blue books, or there are 12 red books and 1 blue book, or there are 13 red books and 0 blue books."

The teacher often finds pupils who object to writing mathematical sentences and to answering a simple question by a statement in words rather than symbols because they can find answers without doing this. Good judgment should be used in such cases. The intuitive pupil with considerable insight should not be forced to do busy work. However, the less skilled student must be taught to apply the procedures described above to simple problems, so that he may later use them to solve more difficult ones. Further, it should be remembered that finding answers to verbal problems constitutes only one of the objectives of the problem-solving program. The methods of attacking problems in general must be learned in order that problems dealing with unfamiliar situations can be solved.

CHECKING COMPUTATIONS

While he has been analyzing the data and arriving at a solution, we have been taking for granted that the computations will be accurately performed by the pupil. However, this is an assumption that can never be safely made. In the business world those who are in positions in which a computational error will cost money or customers are sure to check each computation carefully, regardless of time consumed. The habit of checking computations is an important one to develop, and it is one that the pupil will avoid developing if possible.

Figure 11-15

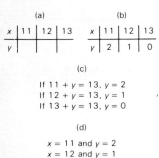

(a)

x	11	12	13
y			

(b)

x	11	12	13
y	2	1	0

(c)

If $11 + y = 13$, $y = 2$
If $12 + y = 13$, $y = 1$
If $13 + y = 13$, $y = 0$

(d)

$x = 11$ and $y = 2$
$x = 12$ and $y = 1$
$x = 13$ and $y = 0$

The pupil is expected to use the formal check that he learned along with each algorithm to assure the correctness of each of his computations. For the final solution, the best procedure for checking is to estimate an answer and compare this to his computed answer.

There are several reasons why it is important for the pupil to learn to arrive at an approximate answer to a problem without use of pencil and paper. One is that in adult life we frequently find ourselves in the position of needing an approximate answer when pencil and paper are not available. Another is that a major proportion of the problems we encounter in everyday life do not need precise answers:

How many liters of gasoline can I buy with the money I have?

How long will it take to type 23 pages if I can type 6 pages an hour?

Since, an approximate answer is the best method of checking the computed answer to a problem, the teacher will do well to provide special practice in estimating answers to problems. For a set of problems pupils are asked to describe procedures for finding approximate answers. As the different methods are presented, the class decides which one seems most appropriate.

● In his 4-H project, Bill gathered over five days the following number of eggs: 68, 94, 55, 54, and 83. In all, how many eggs did he collect?

One pupil may describe his thinking as, "The sum of the two numbers in the fifties is about 100, the 94 is about 100, and the 83 plus 68 is about 150, making about 350 in all." Or another may say, "The number of tens adds to 33. and it looks as if about 2 more tens are carried from the ones, or about 35 tens (350) in all."

● The bus fare to the capital is $8.15 per pupil. How much will it cost for our class of 38 pupils?

The thinking may be, "The solution is about 40×8. Therefore the cost is about $320." Or, "The cost for three pupils is about $25, so the cost for 12 pupils is about $100. Hence, the cost for 38 pupils is about $325."

Multiple-choice questions, such as those illustrated in Chapter 13, provide practice in estimating correct answers. Brief sessions of oral exercises provide more practice. The teacher states the problems orally, with pupils using paper and pencil only to record answers. Suitable questions are:

One-half of 198 is ____. (Estimated as 100 from 1/2 of 200.)

Three-fourths of what number is 72? (Estimated as 100 because 75 is 3/4 of 100.)

Bob swam across a 35-meter pool six times. How far did he swim? (Estimated as 200 from thinking, "Three 35s are about 100, so that six 35s are about 200.")

Pupils may be kept alert and their interest maintained through the interjection of "sleeper" problems, such as:

If one broad jumper can jump a ditch 2 meters wide, how wide a ditch can seven broad jumpers jump?

A rooster weighs 2.6 kilograms when standing on both feet. How much does he weigh if he stands on one foot?

Here the wording of the first question suggests multiplication, while wording of the second question suggests division.

The practice of rereading the problem with the answer filled in can also reveal the reasonableness or absurdity of an answer. For example, to solve the following problem a pupil multiplied (2/3) × 3 and obtained an answer of $2. "At a sale, a girl bought a kiln for making copper jewelry. She paid $3 for the kiln. The salesman said this was two-thirds of the usual price. What was the usual price?" To check her answer, the pupil read the problem with her answer of $2 substituted for "the usual price," and the absurdity of the answer was revealed.

Solving in Other Ways

Seeking other methods of solution is an excellent way to verify answers. At the same time, it provides further insight into relations among data and improves ability to choose the most economical method of solving a problem.

For example, pupils obtained a solution for the problem "Canine brand dog food costs 77 cents for three cans. What is the cost of six cans?" The class, urged to seek alternative solutions, came up with the following:

- I need to find the cost of two sets of three cans each. One set of three costs 77 cents; therefore two sets cost twice 77 cents, or 154 cents. Some pupils, using n to represent the cost of six cans, wrote the equation $(2)(77) = n$.

- $77 \div 3 = 25 \ 2/3$. Then the cost of one can is 25 2/3 cents.
  $$6 \times 25 \ 2/3 = 154$$
  Hence the cost of six cans is $1.54. Using n to represent the cost of six cans, some pupils wrote $(77/3)(6) = n$.

- The ratio of price for three cans to number of cans at three cans for 77 cents can be expressed as 77/3. At the same rate, n cents will buy six cans, expressed by the ratio $n/6$. The two ratios are equal. Therefore $77/3 = n/6$. Because 6 is twice 3, n is twice 77, or 154. The cost of six cans is 154 cents.

Each time a pupil reexamines a problem and finds a different way to relate the data, he gains added insight into the relations among the elements of the problem and increases his ability to analyze and solve problems.

GENERALIZATION OF SOLUTIONS

Out of the total problem-solving program, there emerge certain generalizations that form the basis for the mature solution of problems. The variety of situations in which a person encounters problems is unlimited. If he had to remember each as a separate entity with separate vocabulary, data, and relations, he would be engulfed by detail. Instead, he draws generalizations that classify the relations that repeatedly recur in problems.

Postsolution Analysis

Generalizations of relations are developed out of concrete illustrations in problem solving. For example, a mature understanding of the relationship between distance, rate, and time develops out of problems such as:

How far did Jimmy and his Dad hike if they walked for 2 hours and covered 3 kilometers each hour?

On the second day of their vacation, Joe's family averaged 80 kilometers per hour for each of the 7 hours they drove. How far did they travel?

The coach said his runner could run at the rate of 8 meters per second. If he maintained this rate for 2 minutes, how far would he run?

How far would a boat travel if it went for 4 1/2 days at 332 nautical miles per day?

How far did the racing car travel if it averaged 203.82 kilometers per hour for 1/6 of an hour?

Many situations, such as hiking, bicycle riding, and racing, or a trip in a car, plane, or boat, afford examples of a steady rate of movement maintained for a specific period of time. The pupil begins to sense the similarity of the problems; furthermore, he finds that the same device—a number line—may be used to represent the data of each problem. Different kinds of numbers, such as whole numbers or fractional numbers, are used to express the data, and various units of measure, such as time in seconds or days, rate in meters per second or kilometers per day, and distance in meters or kilometers, are encountered. Yet, regardless of these variations, a common relationship becomes apparent:

$$\text{rate} \times \text{time} = \text{distance}$$

(with each element expressed as a number of proper units).

The pupil who has generalized the connection between rate, time, and distance understands a relationship that he can apply to a large number of different yet related situations. He finds the relationship is valid for all objects and also for many types of motion. Eventually, when he expresses the relationships as a formula, $d = rt$, he has a compact yet powerful tool for solving certain kinds of problems. Continued experiences in postsolution analysis lead to similar generalizations of relations among many other kinds of data:

> We wish to find the total cost, c cents, knowing the cost of one item, p cents, and the number of those items n at that cost. The formula is $c = np$.

> We wish to find the area of a rectangle, A square meters knowing the length, l meters and the width, w meters. The formula is $A = lw$.

> We wish to find the interest, I dollars, for one year, knowing the principal, p dollars, and the interest rate r percent. The formula is $I = pr$.

In all of these, the number to be found is the product of two factors. The pupil sees that the general formula $a = bc$ expresses the relationship common to all problems of this type.

The pupil should be encouraged to find the most economical of the variety of solutions possible. It should be emphasized that he is not acquiring a rule of thumb through the postsolution analysis. He is developing the ability to disregard the irrelevant and superficial facts in the problem situation in order to identify the key relationships that will lead to a solution. Once he acquires confidence that these relationships are there, and that he can find them, he will also acquire the positive attitudes that make the problem a challenge rather than a threat.

EXPERIMENTS FOR PUPILS

Each of the following Activities is designed to provide pupils with an opportunity to explore a process rather than merely solve a "word problem." As in previous Activities, many adaptions and extensions are possible. In Activity 1, for example, one of the rules may be changed so as to have one nail inside the triangle, or pupils might be asked to compare answers for a 25-nail and a 36-nail geoboard.

ACTIVITY 1

Apparatus needed: graph paper and geoboard   *Objective:* To discover the number of different triangles formed by following certain rules.

1   On your geoboard form as many different triangles as you

can. Here are the rules:

(*a*) There can be no nails inside the triangle.

(*b*) Two triangles are different if they are of different size or shape.

(*c*) Draw a picture of each of your triangles on graph paper.

2 *Brainbuster:* Do Ex. 1 for quadrilaterals instead of triangles.

ACTIVITY 2

Objective: To discover patterns in an array of numbers.

1 Write more rows of numerals in the array at the right.

2 Fill in the blanks as you discover patterns in the array.

1	2	3	4	5	6
7	8	9	10	11	12
13	14	15	16	17	18
19	20	21	22	23	24

(*a*) There are ____ numerals in each row.

(*b*) In the last column are ____ of 6.

(*c*) The diagonal line with 1, 8, 15, 22, and so on lists numbers that increase by ____ .

(*d*) Each left-to-right diagonal line lists numbers that increase by ____ .

3 Write other statements about patterns you see. Think about factors, multiples, primes, even numbers, and so on.

4 *Brainbuster:* Write the counting numbers seven to a row. Write statements about patterns or tell a friend the patterns you see. Repeat with the counting numbers five to a row.

ACTIVITY 3

Objective: To select needed data to solve problems.

1 Use only this information to find the products shown below.

$$6 \times 7 = 42 \qquad 9 \times 42 = 378 \qquad 9 \times 7 = 63$$
$$9 \times 6 = 54 \qquad 11 \times 54 = 594 \qquad 63 \times 11 = 693$$

$$9 \times 7 \times 6 = \qquad 11 \times 9 \times 6 = \qquad 7 \times 11 \times 9 =$$

2 Make up a problem like this and have a friend solve it.

ACTIVITY 4

Apparatus needed: graph paper and 9 square regions

Objective: To find the region with a given area which has the smallest perimeter.

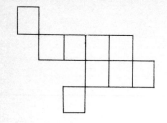

1 The figure on the left has an area of 9 square regions. Its perimeter is 22 units.

2 With your 9 square regions form other figures. Draw each figure on graph paper. Write its perimeter near each figure.

3 Which region has the greatest perimeter?

4 What is the name of the region with the smallest perimeter?

5 See if your answers to Ex. 3 and 4 agree with those of your friends.

ACTIVITY 5

Objective: To find numbers that can be expressed by using certain numbers.

1 For this game you are to name numbers. Here are the rules:

(*a*) You can use only the numbers 2, 3, and 4.

(*b*) You can name numbers with one of 2, 3, or 4, or as the sum of two or more of them.

(*c*) No number can be used more than once in a sum. Two numbers you can name are 2 and 7. $7 = 3 + 4$. There are five other numbers. They are:

2 Try this game again using 1, 2, 5, and 7 instead of 2, 3, and 4.

3 Try the game again. Use the rules of Ex. 1 except replace the word "sum" by the word "product."

4 Make up a game like this. Have a friend solve it.

ACTIVITY 6

Apparatus needed: play money

Objective: To discover in how many ways a certain purchase can be paid for with exact change.

Way	10¢	5¢	1¢
first	1	1	0
second	1	0	5
third	0	3	0
fourth	0	–	5
fifth	0	1	–
sixth	0	0	–

1 You must pay for a 15-cent candy bar with the exact change. There are 6 ways to do it. Fill in the blanks in the table on the left to show those six ways.

2 Make tables to show the number of ways you can pay exactly for purchases of: (*a*) 10 cents; (*b*) 20 cents. Use your play money if you need to.

3   What amounts less than 30 cents can you pay for exactly with 4 coins?

4   *Brainbuster:*
    (*a*) In how many ways can you pay exactly for a 25-cent purchase?

    (*b*) In how many ways can you make change for a quarter?

ACTIVITY 7

Objective: To make up problems from the given data.

1   Make up questions that can be answered from this data: a kite costs 35 cents and a ball of string costs 21 cents. Some sample questions are:

    (*a*) Which costs more, 3 kites or 5 balls of string?

    (*b*) What could you buy for 91 cents?

    (*c*) How much change would you get if you paid for 1 kite and 1 ball of string with $1.00.

2   Make up questions from this data: 2 tablets cost 32 cents and 3 pencils cost 15 cents.

ACTIVITY 8

Apparatus needed: newspaper   *Objective:* To make up number stories from a newspaper.

Read your newspaper. Then make up some story problems about numbers you find there. Give your friend the problems to solve. Here is one example: The headlines of the newspaper had four words. The words had 5, 4, 7, and 3 letters. How many letters were in the headlines?

ACTIVITY 9

Objective: To express numbers using the digits in 1976.

1   Use each of the digits in 1976 once to express as many counting numbers as you can. You may use place value, addition, subtraction, multiplication, and division. Here are some examples:

$$9 = (9 - 6) + (7 - 1)$$
$$57 = 76 - 19$$
$$16 = (97 - 1) \div 6$$

2.   Follow the directions of Ex. 1 for 1776. Did you express more counting numbers for 1976 or 1776?

ACTIVITY 10

Objective: To discover the missing digits.

```
 B 4     B 4      14
+B A    +B 2    + 12
-----   -----   -----
 A 6     2 6     26
```

1 In these problems a letter may be 0, 1, 2, 3, 4, 5, 6, 7, 8, or 9. Study the example at the left. A must be 2 because $4 + 2 = 6$. Then B must be 1.

```
  4 2
 +4 7
 -----
  8 9
```

2 Solve each of the following. The first is done for you.

```
 A 2     2 A     A B     6 A     A 6
+A 7    +3 A    +9 3    -A B    -B B
----    ----    ----    ----    ----
 8 C     B C    C4 7     1 2     B 5
```

```
  B C
 +C C
 -----
  C C
```

3 Explain to your friend why the example at the left cannot be done.

4 *Brainbuster:* Fill in the blanks.

```
           6 __ __                          5 __ __
    __ )_____              8 )_____
    __ __ __ __ __                  __  3 __ __
      __ 6                          ====
      5   3                              __  6
      __ 8                                =====
      -----                                  __     0
      __ __                                  ======
      5   4                                          0
          0
```

5 Make up problems like this and give them to a friend to solve.

QUESTIONS AND EXERCISES

1 What purposes are served by having pupils use concrete materials to represent word problems?

2 Describe some special techniques that help pupils learn to read mathematical materials.

3 Why are pupils who have had a program of many experiences with objects in learning concepts and algorithms more likely to be able to determine the process to be used in solving a word problem than pupils who have not had such experiences?

4 Answer *true* or *false* and defend your answer: "Before solving a problem, pupils should be required to draw a picture of it."

5 If a pupil meets an unfamiliar problem in mathematics, what should he do to try to solve it?

6 How can a teacher use magazine and newspaper articles that are numerical in nature to provide special practice in reading?

7 Why should some pupils be encouraged to search for alternate solutions for word problems?

8 What is a problem? Why does problem solving involve exploration and discovery? Why is exploring a problem a trial-and-error process?

9 In what way does the suggestion "try something" aid in problem solving?

10 What is the role of the teacher in guiding exploration of a problem by pupils.

11 Why is securing the answer not the final step in the solution of a problem?

12 What is the purpose of having pupils make up problems from a given set of data?

13 How may the study of model solutions contribute to increasing pupils' success in solving word problems? What precautions must be taken when using this technique?

14 Why can difficulties in computation be identified more readily than those in solving verbal problems?

15 Why should the goal of teaching pupils problem solving be as important as teaching them basic skills?

PROJECTS

1 From a series of textbooks and teacher's manuals for grades 1-8, secure answers to the following: (a) For a grade level (3 or above) list special techniques which are included to help pupils solve word problems. (b) For a given grade list sets of word problems that are concerned with a certain situation (scouting, space exploration, etc.). To what extent do you think these are of special interest to pupils? (c) What experiences do you find for helping pupils estimate reasonable answers for problems? (d) Locate problems which you believe contain unfamiliar situations or difficult vocabulary. (e) Find examples of problems which can be represented by a picture or sketch and others you think are difficult or impossible to picture.

2 One objective of the problem-solving program is to help pupils develop abilities to explore and discover. Many experiences toward this end have been discussed in this and previous chapters. Summarize five such experiences and locate others in a text for elementary school mathematics.

3 In a newspaper or magazine find an article containing quantative text, such as that on page 303 and write appropriate questions for testing the ability of pupils to read it.

4 Look through a series of texts for grades three to eight published ten years ago and another series published less than three years ago. What difference for any grade level do you find in the kinds of word problems in the texts and in suggestions for solving them?

5 Some teachers have found that rewriting textbook word problems so there are fewer words aids pupils who have reading difficulties. One example is: "Had 12 cents. Lost 3 cents. Spent 5 cents. How much left?" Find a set of word problems in a textbook. Rewrite them with fewer words.

6 (a) Solve the missing-digit puzzles in Fig. 11-2, Fig. 11-3 and Activity 10. (b) Solve the problem in Fig. 11-4.

7 Complete Activities 1 and 4. For each organize your pictures on the graph paper so that you have found all solutions and have no duplication. Discuss in a small group the best procedures for exploring the results.

8 (a) Complete Activity 5. (b) Make up a game as suggested in Ex. 4 of Activity 5. Give it to a friend to solve. Discuss with him the effectiveness of his plan for solving and of his organization of his solution.

Bibliography

1 Earp, N. W.: "Procedures for Teaching Reading in Mathematics," *The Arithmetic Teacher*, vol. 17, pp. 575-580, Nov., 1970. Practical suggestions that every teacher can follow for helping pupils read.

2 Eisenberg, T. A., and J. G. Van Beynen: "Mathematics Through Visual Problems," *The Arithmetic Teacher*, vol. 20, pp. 85-90, Feb., 1973. Contains useful problems to teach students to generalize.

3 Grossman, R.: "Problem-Solving Activities Observed in British Primary Schools," *The Arithmetic Teacher*, vol. 16, pp. 34-38, Jan., 1969. Activities in English schools which promote creativity in pupils' problem solving.

4 Henney, M.: "Improving Mathematics Verbal Problem-Solving Ability Through Reading Instruction," *The Arithmetic Teacher*, vol. 18, pp. 223-229, April, 1971. Suggestions for helping pupils read and analyze word problems.

5 Riedesel, C. A.: "Problem Solving: Some Suggestions from Research," *The Arithmetic Teacher*, vol. 16, pp. 54-58, Jan., 1969. Suggestions from researchers which aid in the improvement of problem solving.

6 Scandura, J. M.: "Algorithm Learning and Problem Solving," *The Journal of Experimental Education*, vol. 34, pp. 1-6, Summer, 1966. Interesting report of research concerning successful problem solving and understanding the problem.

7 Scandura, J. M.: *Mathematics—Concrete Behavioral Foundations*, Harper and Row, New York, 1971. Chapter 1 is a clear description of mathematical thinking.

8 Schaefer, A. W., and A. H. Mauthe: "Problem Solving with Enthusiasm in the Mathematics Laboratory," *The Arithmetic Teacher*, vol. 17, pp. 7-14, Jan., 1970. Examples of activities through which pupils explore problems in the mathematics laboratory.

9 Sims, J.: "Improving Problem-Solving Skills," *The Arithmetic Teacher*, vol. 16, pp. 17-20, Jan., 1969. Practical suggestions for improving problem-solving ability.

12
INDIVIDUAL DIFFERENCES IN LEARNING

Learning is an active process engaged in by the individual student. The competent teacher may set the stage, provide effective learning experiences, and give assistance when needed, but it is the student who does the learning.

Moreover, individual students in the same class learn different things at the same time and learn the same things at different rates. For this reason, we do not find that the whole class moves through the steps in the learning process together, but rather singly, as individuals. It is necessary, in any given class activity, to recognize the level that each pupil has reached and to adjust the activity to make it effective at that level.

To plan effectively a program that meets the needs of pupils with varying backgrounds of interest, skill, understanding, and ability to investigate mathematical situations, the teacher needs to:

• Know how school organization and classroom procedures may be adapted to care for individual differences.
• Have available instructional materials and methods especially appropriate for slow and fast learners.[1]
• Be acquainted with the wealth of textbooks and materials available for the mathematics laboratory which can enrich the program of all pupils.

THE TEACHER AND INDIVIDUAL DIFFERENCES

A variety of procedures has been used to adjust instruction to individual differences among pupils. In general, these procedures

[1] If all pupils fitted one or the other of these stereotypes, the problem of adapting to individual differences would be simpler. But, within either category, there are many variations. The slower pupil, for example, may be achieving below grade level in general, he may be underachieving in mathematics only, he may be handicapped because of his environment, and so on.

may be classified in two categories.

One approach affects school organization because it requires administrative readjustment in schedule or assignment of personnel. Examples include the provision of a special room for exceptional children, special teachers for especially slow or accelerated pupils, special laboratory rooms for slow or fast pupils, and grouping of pupils to secure more nearly homogeneous abilities in some cases or heterogeneous abilities in other cases.

The other approach calls for specialized classroom procedures wherein each teacher adapts his teaching methods to care for individual differences within a heterogeneous group. Some teachers section their classes into fast, average, and slow groups and help each group proceed at a pace best suited to its ability. Other teachers try to start the class together on a new topic and then let the more rapid learners move faster and study the topic more thoroughly with enrichment, while the slower pupils complete a minimum course.

Whatever approach is used, the experiences should be adapted to the pupils' abilities, and extensive use should be made of the mathematics laboratory. The following sections provide the teacher with a source of methods and activities for both slower and more capable pupils. The experiences are characteristic of those that creative teachers have used in adapting to different administrative organizations and groups of different pupils.

Experiences for Slow Pupils

Some of the numerous modifications of instructional materials, content, and methods that recognize the characteristics of slow pupils and that have proved effective for raising their understanding and their levels of achievement are described and illustrated in the following section. The various categories are interrelated, but they are listed separately in order to emphasize each.

Adjusting the program to ensure success All approaches for helping slower pupils learn mathematics imply adjusting experiences to ensure a large measure of success. This is necessary to improve attitudes and self-confidence and to progressively build new concepts and abilities on familiar and understood bases.

To provide successful experiences, teachers make suggestions such as:

Make liberal use of concrete, manipulative, investigative experiences.

Make the course easy at first for these pupils.

Make initial problems in each assignment easy to assure some measure of success.

Pay more attention to readiness by providing liberal review of needed concepts and skills.

Introduce one difficulty at a time.

The principle of working with each child at the level of his development is generally accepted in the home. Here, for example, when the child is learning to eat with a spoon and fork instead of fingers, small-size implements and large bibs are provided, foods easy to put on a spoon are used, and all aspects of the situation are arranged to help the child succeed. Adult performance is neither demanded nor expected at the outset.

The teacher of mathematics must apply the same principle in the classroom—in fact, he has no other choice. The primary teacher cannot expect his pupils to succeed in identifying situations where addition is used unless they have had a rich background in combining sets of materials and drawing pictures of combined sets. The fifth-grade teacher cannot expect his pupils to learn addition of fractional numbers with different denominators if they do not comprehend how to add them when they have the same denominator, or if they do not know what the equality of fractions means. The same is true in problem solving. "The goal for our school in the Red Cross Drive is $300, and we have $210. What percent of our goal has been reached?" A thoughtful approach to this problem cannot be made without previously learning how to express comparisons of two different weights, lengths, or sets of objects, and without learning that a fraction, such as 1/2, when interpreted as a ratio, represents a comparison of 1 to 2, and that percent is an expression of comparison of a number to 100.

This is merely a recognition of the need for readiness. In each of these cases, those pupils who lack adequate backgrounds are likely to fail. Common sense dictates that experiences must be provided which are profitable to the pupil. One criterion of readiness is: "Can the pupil achieve a reasonable degree of success if he exerts a reasonable effort?"

Mr. Harris, a sixth-grade teacher, recognized this principle. His class was about to begin the study of multiplication with decimals. He had observed some of his pupils having considerable difficulty with the multiplication algorithm (first introduced in grade 4), especially in remembering the numbers to be "carried" in the short-cut form. Instead of reviewing expanded algorithms (see page 112), he decided to help the class discover an historic algorithm called lattice multiplication. He told the class, "Do you know that years ago people had a different way of multiplying? I want you to find out how they did it. The product for 6 × 28 is 168. Here's how it was done in the past."

Figure 12-1

Lattice multiplication for 6 X 28.

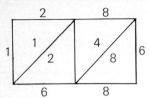

He wrote as shown in Fig. 12-1 on the overhead projector. "This is called lattice multiplication." He then asked these questions:

Where are the factors 6 and 28 found?

Where is the product 168 found?

Find 48. In this problem how do you get 48?

Find 12. In this problem how do you get 12?

How do you get the 1, the 6 and the 8 in 168?

Instead of having pupils say answers out loud, Mr. Harris had them come to the overhead projector and point to answers. To show how the 48 was determined, a pupil put his finger on 6, then on 8, and then on 48.

Mr. Harris then had pairs of pupils work on this Activity Card. (Notice how the examples increase slightly in difficulty.)

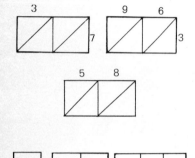

ACTIVITY I

Objective: To discover how to multiply on a lattice.

1   Use lattice multiplication to do these multiplications.

2   Draw a lattice. Multiply.
   (a) 3 × 47   (b) 6 × 78   (c) 5 × 49

3   Which lattice would you use to find 6 × 347?

As pairs of pupils finished and checked their answers, they were given Activities concerned with further examples of lattice multiplication such as 2 × 678, 4 × 3,562, and 6 × 21,076, and then 23 × 46 and 47 × 236. In each case they had to experiment to determine the lattice of the correct shape. Finally they compared their lattice multiplications to expanded forms such as in Fig. 12-2. They listed ways in which lattice multiplication and the expanded form were alike and ways in which they were different.

Procedures such as those of Mr. Harris are effective because pupils:

Actively participate rather than merely listen.

Do not simply review, but review in a new and interesting setting.

Are able to discover how the procedure can be adapted to more difficult multiplications.

Practice a way of organizing their work.

Mr. Harris had pupils who tended not to keep the numerals in vertical columns when they were computing turn their ruled paper

Figure 12-2

Expanded forms for multiplication.

32	347
X7	X 6
14 = 7 X 2	42 = 6 X 7
210 = 7 X 30	240 = 6 X 40
224 = 7 X 32	1800 = 6 X 300
	2082 = 6 X 347

"sideways" as shown in Fig. 12-3 for 8 × 27. This forced them to write the numbers of ones underneath one another, the numbers of tens under each other and so on.

Figure 12-3
Keeping numerals "in line".

		2	7
X			8
		5	6
	1	6	0
	2	1	6

Using specially designed textbooks Many publishers have completed or are preparing textbooks designed for underachievers. Procuring and using such books for one section of a regular class or for special classes under homogeneous groupings can be a desirable first step in adjusting instruction.

These special texts generally reduce the content studied in a year to an essential minimum, introduce material at a slower pace, provide for more frequent review, reteaching, and practice, and keep required reading to a minimum by careful selection of vocabulary and by increased utilization of diagrams and pictures. Teacher's manuals accompanying these texts suggest extensive manipulative and experimental activities.

Reducing the amount of material At every grade level it is possible to omit or postpone certain less essential topics found in textbooks and to modify the levels at which other topics are studied. This does not grossly disturb the progression of the fundamental material that every pupil must learn, and it leaves time for more experiences that promote understanding and mastery of essential material.

Examples of topics that can be omitted or postponed are the following: formal symbolization of operations with sets; topics from number theory, such as prime numbers, tests for divisibility, and formal study of greatest common factor and least common multiple; study of historic numeration systems and systems with bases other than ten; operations with great numbers (such as those greater than a million), additions with many addends, and computations in fraction form with seldom-used fractional numbers (expressed with denominators other than 2, 3, 4, 8, 10, and 16, for example).

In reducing the amount of material, certain precautions and procedures should be followed:

Decisions on deletions should be made by a group of teachers in conjunction with the mathematics supervisor, in order that correct choices are made.

Too often, pages of drill are retained and those that promote understanding are omitted. Such a policy can lead only to a dull, sterile curriculum.

Even though wise choices are made on material to postpone or delete, it is absolutely essential to provide extensive mathematics laboratory experiences for low achievers.

A principle, then, to be observed in planning activities for slower pupils is to make sure that the experiences for each pupil are at an appropriate level. This does not imply a "watered-down" program, which both teachers and parents fear. It is rather a realistic program that recognizes the futility of teaching every child sixth-grade mathematics because he happens to be in the sixth grade. If he has not learned many of the basic ideas assigned to the "average" fourth- or fifth-grade program, the child may be entirely helpless when exposed to certain topics in the sixth-grade curriculum.

Using relevant problems In order to generate interests of slower pupils, motivational problems in the introductory stages and problems providing for transfer should be *relevant* to their environment and interests. In cases where relevance may be questionable, care must be taken to dramatize, illustrate, and talk about the problems to develop some feeling of relevance.

Examples of a few of the numerous sources for relevant problems are:

Classes in such subjects as art, cooking, woodworking, science, geography, and social science.

School data, such as attendance and causes of absence.

School affairs, such as distributing supplies, collecting lunch money, financing parties, and the like.

School trips, for example, to the airport or the bank.

Experiments, such as weighing, measuring, comparing various fractional parts, or determining the number of beans in a jar.

Sports data, such as team standings, records of individuals, and school, state, national, and world records.

Mail-order catalogs, advertisements, student weekly papers, and newspaper articles.

Out-of-school experiences, such as scouting, paper routes, selling cards or candy, camping, vacations, and charity drives.

Mr. Griffin, a seventh-grade teacher, to dramatize to his class the prevalence of mathematical ideas, often used the newspaper for mathematical problems and experiments. Here are three activities he developed from five consecutive daily copies of the local newspaper:

Sets of three pupils underlined in red all numerals on the front page and ringed all expressions associated with mathematics, such as many, circle, above, speed, and so on. The group with the most marks and rings won the contest.

Pupils compared the prices of food items in the various advertisements.

Each pupil was given an imaginary $1,000 with which to buy shares of stocks from the listings in the Tuesday paper. He found the daily loss or gain of each of his stocks and determined his net loss or gain at the end of the week. The pupil with the greatest gain (or least loss) was crowned "The Best Investor" with appropriate ceremonies.

Obviously, sources for relevant problems vary according to the ages of the pupils and the nature of the community in which the school is located. It is the teacher's responsibility to know the interests of his pupils and to select experiences accordingly.

Substituting reason for rote   The pupil who has forgotten or never really learned a mathematics concept or operation must be provided with remedial experiences that offer some assurance of permanent mastery of skills. In many cases, investigation will reveal that the pupil never understood the process or concept. During his first exposures to the topic, he may have memorized a mechanical algorithm or "learned" some facts and definitions without actually grasping their significance, the underlying relations, and the mathematical meanings. Once a pupil has lost a skill that was temporarily achieved in previous grades, it is pointless to limit his remedial experiences to refreshing skills. His *reason* must be brought into play with new experiences to provide for refreshing, or learning for the first time, the rationale of the process. Procedures for encouraging pupils to substitute reason for rote operation may be illustrated by the practices of skillful teachers.

Concrete and pictorial experiences.   The importance of concrete materials as an aid to all children in developing concepts, rationalizing processes, and solving problems has been emphasized in previous chapters. The slow pupil needs a larger number and variety of such experiences, spread over a longer period of time. His progress will be slow, and even after he is able to work on a symbolic level, he will need to return periodically to the use of materials in order to reinforce meanings.

Figure 12-4

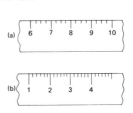

When some of Ms. Gould's eighth-grade pupils were having trouble subtracting fractional numbers expressed in mixed form, she divided them into pairs, giving each pair of pupils a set of number-line rulers she had dittoed. Each pupil had to choose the correct ruler for a given problem and describe to his partner how to get answers. For 9 1/4 – 6 3/4 a pupil selected the ruler in Fig. 12-4*a* and found the distance from 6 3/4 to 9 1/4. His thinking was 1/4 to 7, 2 more to 9, and 1/4 to 9 1/4—answer 2 2/4." For 3 1/6 – 1 5/6, he chose the ruler in Fig. 12-4 *b* and did similar thinking. Later, when the class restudied the algorithm, they were able to check their answers by reference to number-line rulers.

A field trip. Ms. Garcia's class had been studying units for measuring length. After designing a field trip around the school grounds with the help of a committee of pupils, she handed out the ditto sheet shown in Fig. 12-5. Each pupil decided on and recorded his "best guess" to the nearest meter for each item. Then the class measured to see which pupil was the "best guesser." After some trouble with the first item because of the height of the basketball hoop and because they had only one meterstick, they finally invented a way to find the height. They had the janitor climb on his stepladder and cut a piece of string with one end touching the ground and the other touching the hoop. When they stretched this string tight, they found it to be about 3 meters.

Later, during recess, two boys measured objects in the room and wrote their measurements on the board:

About 60 centimeters

About 10 centimeters

When they returned, pupils looked around the room and tried to locate the objects measured.

Thinking through problems. Another teacher, Mr. Seymour, told a slow section of his sixth-grade class a story about Marty, who lived on a farm. Marty had told his teacher that he used arithmetic while helping his father load sacks of grain. As his father threw the sacks on the truck, Marty counted 41 sacks. His father said each sack weighed 75 pounds. As his father drove off, Marty multiplied 41×75 and mistakenly obtained 285, performing as in Fig. 12-6. Since the truck had a 1-ton capacity, Marty said his father would have no trouble with too much weight. Marty had, of course, multiplied 1×5 and 4×7 to secure his answer. Mr. Seymour, whose class was grouped in sets of three pupils for work and lab experiments, said, "Could you talk about this problem, apply some common sense, and show Marty the unreasonableness of his anwer?" After a while, the following suggestions were reported to the class.

Four 75s = $75 + 75 + 75 + 75$, which is more than Marty's answer, so that he made a "bad mistake."

Forty 75s and forty-one 75s are about the same. Forty 75s = ten 75s + ten 75s + ten 75s + ten 75s, or $750 + 750 + 750 + 750 = 3,000$.

If forty 75s are 3,000, then forty-one 75s should be $3,000 + 75$, or 3,075.

Figure 12-5

Guess

Height of basketball hoop	__ meters
Length of seat on the swing	__ meters
Width of volleyball court	__ meters
Height of school yard fence	__ meters

Figure 12-6
A mistake in 41×75.

$$\begin{array}{r} 75 \\ \times 41 \\ \hline 285 \end{array}$$

Forty 100s would be 4,000. This answer is too big, but does give an indication of an approximate answer.

Mr. Seymour recognized that this kind of reasoning would not be developed quickly by his slower pupils. However, periodically he planned lessons which emphasized methods such as those described and found the pupils making progress. He realized that every pupil who was able to do such thinking had more confidence in his computational methods and also developed as an independent worker.

Creating interest   It has been said that the study of mathematics should be an exciting adventure. To expect it to be such for everybody is an almost impossible dream. Negative attitudes toward mathematics are quite firmly fixed even in the lower grades with some pupils, especially low achievers. However, changes in attitude are possible. Too often the most interesting experiences and explorations with numbers and geometry have been reserved for the above-average classes based on the stereotyped thought "My slow pupils wouldn't enjoy that and couldn't learn it anyhow." However, it is possible to stimulate slower pupils. Besides the use of relevant situations and provision for successful experiences and activities that develop understanding, creative teachers have introduced games, tricks, and recreations for motivation.

Tricks and recreations.   Tricks and recreations are appealing to practically all children. The work of solving the trick becomes fun when their thinking powers are challenged. With careful planning, the interest fostered by puzzles often stimulates pupils to greater effort in mathematics.

The experiences of Ms. Marcy, a seventh-grade teacher, affords an excellent illustration of the effectiveness of recreational material. She had been placing on the bulletin board a "Problem of the Week" (to be solved in leisure time) with a number of the brighter pupils solving and explaining to the class. In an effort to secure more participation, she began posting an easy problem along with a more difficult problem each week. Some of the simpler type were: "Separate 1-,2-,3-,4-,5-,6-,7-,8-, and 9-pound weights into three piles so that each pile weighs the same." "Ms. Valdez has ten very rare exotic trees that she wants to plant so that there are five rows, each containing four trees. How can the trees be planted?" "Using pennies, nickels, and dimes, assemble 21 coins whose value is $1."

Each week, more pupils were attempting the problems and more were arriving at successful solutions. One morning before school, Joe came running into the classroom yelling, "I got it. I got it."

Figure 12-7
How many triangles?

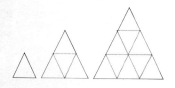

Figure 12-8

	Number left
Start	10
A removes 1 bean	9
B removes 1 bean	8
A removes 2 beans	6
B removes 2 beans	4
A removes 1 bean	3

In view of Joe's previous attitude in refusing to try to learn mathematics, spelling, or reading, and showing no interest in anything at school except physical education, Ms. Marcy wondered about his enthusiasm. Joe repeated, "I got the problem. I did it. I found the answer by myself." He did have the correct solution to separating the nine different weights into three piles of equal weight. The pride Joe displayed while assuring the teacher and fellow pupils that the work was completely his own and his satisfaction in solving a problem with numbers were new experiences for him. He then began to "try" during the mathematics period, and the effects of this were soon noticeable in terms of progress.

The game of "How Many."   Children, from the time they are very young, have been fascinated in determining how many toys, fingers, animals and so on. They enjoy counting. Creative teachers take advantage of this by phrasing problems in that language.

How many triangles? (See Fig. 12-7.) Be sure to count them all. Discuss with your partner a way to find them all.

How many ways can you name 6 as a sum of two numbers? You can use any two of 0, 1, 2, 3, 4, 5, 6.

How many true sentences can you write using 7, 9, and 15 each once? Have a contest with your partner.

Suppose the headline of a newspaper is $7 = 3 + 4$. How many stories can you make up about it? Report your stories to the class.

A game of strategy.   A game which not only provides interesting practice but also provides an opportunity to develop a strategy for winning has the following rules:

1   Two players place a number of beans between them.

2   They are to take turns in removing 1 or 2 beans.

3   The player who removed the last bean wins.

An example of this game, with players A and B starting with 10 beans, is shown in Fig. 12-8. With 3 beans left and B's turn, A must win the game. In fact, starting with 10 beans and removing either 1 or 2 beans per turn, the player who goes first can always win! What is the strategy?

This game is especially interesting because of its many variations and the fact that the strategy changes with rule changes:

In the early grades it is played with materials such as beans. In later grades these are dropped and a running score is kept.

The starting number may be varied. Starting with 12 beans and removing 1 or 2, the player who goes second can always win.

For more mature pupils the rules can be varied to start, for example, with 50 and remove any counting number 1 through 10.

Instead of subtraction a change in rules provides practice in addition. For example, players choose in turn any counting number 1 through 4. A running total is kept with the winner being the player who makes the total 22.

Bingo. Among the various methods illustrated in previous chapters, games such as dominoes, sorry, time-track, and relay races are particularly effective with slower pupils. For example, Ms. Anders, a first-grade teacher, used bingo in teaching children to read and recognize two-digit numerals. Each child was given a card, as shown in Fig. 12-9. A leader drew tags, numbered 1 to 75, from a box and read them to the class. If a child found the numeral on his card, he placed a bean on it. The first child who had beans covering a row, column, or diagonal won the game.

Magic squares. Too often an activity is devised which initially interests the pupil and yet the method used leads the slow pupil to failure. One such topic is magic squares. For Fig. 12-10a the pupil finds the sum of each row, column, and diagonal is 15. There are many variations, such as Fig. 12-10b, where he must rearrange two numerals to make a magic square. In Fig. 12-10c he must insert 3, 4, 8, 9, 10, and 11 in the blank cells so all eight sums are 21. The pupil often tries to complete the magic square in Fig. 12-10c by writing numerals in the cells and is not immediately successful. He may erase and try again. If he fails, he continually sees a written record of his mistake and often quits.

One ingenious teacher gave his pupils tiles with numerals written on them and told them to move the tiles around until they made magic squares. Then they wrote the numerals in the blank cells. Here any record of failure was avoided and pupils worked until they were successful.

Experiences for More Capable Pupils

Rapid pupils require special programs and experiences in order to maintain their interest and help them learn to the maximum of their capabilities. Because of the unsatisfied demands in the sciences for persons who demonstrate insight into mathematics, society requires that the school provide for these pupils. In general, effective programs for more capable pupils consist of acceleration, enrichment, or a combination of both.

Acceleration Many variations of accelerated programs are in use. However, the general effect is that faster pupils in the fourth grade,

Figure 12-9
Bingo card for learning place value.

B	I	N	G	O
12	23	32	47	64
5	24	42	54	68
14	19	■	48	63
13	27	43	50	66
7	21	40	60	61

Figure 12-10
Magic squares.

4	3	8
9	5	1
2	7	6
(a)

8	2	4
1	5	9
6	7	3
(b)

6	5	
	7	
(c)

for example, complete all the work of that grade and some or all of fifth-grade mathematics. Thus they become one or more grade levels ahead of their classmates in mathematics. The merits of acceleration are often debated without reaching an uncontested conclusion. Acceleration is one way to develop a challenging program for more capable pupils, and the fact that such a program is needed is accepted by all. Its administration, however, becomes very complex, as individual differences become greater each year.

One of the most common forms of acceleration is teaching algebra in grade 8. This has proved quite successful, especially in districts organized to include a junior high school (grades 7-9), where teachers generally have a stronger background in mathematics. For this plan, the mathematics of grade 8 is learned in grade 7 or plans are initiated to teach the content of grades 6, 7, and 8 in grades 6 and 7.

Another recent attempt at acceleration is the teaching of high school plane geometry except for proof prior to grade 9. This program has proved successful because of topics that are interesting to pupils: ruler and compass constructions, measurement, and discovery of properties of geometric figures. Such a program offers also a great opportunity to individualize instruction with experiences in the mathematics laboratory and the chance to study mathematics outdoors when topics such as similar triangles are introduced.

Enrichment The most common interpretation of enrichment is a set of organized experiences beyond the normal program that are suitable for more capable pupils. From this point of view, the fast learner studies the content of his grade level and is provided with optional topics that are challenging and interesting, but that may be omitted by slower pupils without interrupting the sequence. The more capable pupil, for example, rationalizes the processes more carefully, studies alternate algorithms and historic patterns of solution, explores relevant abstractions, investigates complex applications, and in general increases his understanding of mathematics beyond that expected of the average child.

Enrichment exercises for all pupils, as well as for special groups, are found in any effective mathematics program. The techniques described for extending understanding of the various concepts and algorithms (discussed in previous chapters) can be used as enrichment experiences for many pupils. The following are suggestive of the many other enrichment experiences that have proved successful. This list can be expanded by reference to books or through the ingenuity of the teacher. It should be recognized that any one suggestion can be used at different grade levels. That is, a certain experience may be appropriate for some sixth graders and some fourth graders. Further, any suggestion may be simplified or its difficulty increased by changing the wording, asking for a single solution or a generalized solution, using fewer or more symbols, and so on.

Discovering patterns and rules The importance of exploration leading to the discovery of theorems and procedures has been emphasized in previous chapters. This exploration, which often takes the form of examining a number of cases, organizing the data, and looking for a pattern, should not be reserved for more capable pupils. However, they are able to carry such investigations further and see deeper relationships.

Two experiments in geometry illustrate how individuals or groups may search for patterns. In the first problem, pupils are to study the pictures and fill in the blanks in Fig. 12-11. They try to predict the maximum number of regions for six segments, seven segments, and eight segments. They verify their guesses by drawing pictures, and some pupils try to write a formula from which the number of regions for *n* segments is determined. Can the reader discover this formula?

The second problem, similar to the first, may act as a deterrent to "jumping to a conclusion too fast." First, two points on a circle are connected with a segment (Fig. 12-12). There are two regions. Then, for three points on the circle, each pair of points is connected with segments (Fig.12-12), and four regions result. As the number of points on the circle is increased, the maximum number of regions is determined. There seems to be a pattern for the number of regions when the number of points is 2, 3, 4, and 5. Is the number of predicted regions for 6 points and 7 points the actual number that can be counted? Can the reader answer this question?

Studying proofs In general, the study or completion of a proof for a mathematical theorem or procedure has been avoided in the traditional elementary school program. Pupils were considered to be too immature either to understand the proof or to appreciate its nature. While this conclusion has not been completely refuted, currently there seems to be a trend toward having young pupils work on the inductive level with very simple proofs, while more mature pupils develop carefully recorded proofs, writing logical steps to reach conclusions. In general, the study of proofs has been more successful when tried with more capable pupils. An illustration of the levels at which pupils may be successful is illustrated by the following example, in which the teacher helps pupils discover the answers to the questions concerning the addition of even and odd numbers:

Figure 12-11
Partitioning a circular region with segments.

Number of segments drawn in circle	Picture	Number of regions in interior of circle
1		2
2		4
3		?
4		?
5		?

Figure 12-12
How many regions?

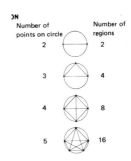

Number of points on circle		Number of regions
2		2
3		4
4		8
5		16

Figure 12-13
Patterns for even and odd numbers.

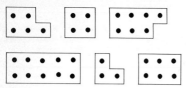

any even number + any even number = ?
any odd number + any odd number = ?
any odd number + any even number = ?

The teacher had prepared dittoes on which a number of dots were arranged as shown in Fig. 12-13. These were cut out by some pupils who volunteered to do the job after school. When the experiment started (the part of this lesson using dot pictures was described in Chapter 2 as an example of teaching for discovery), the teacher gave a number of dot cards to each pupil and reviewed the meaning of *even* and *odd* with the entire class as the pupils illustrated even and odd numbers with their dot cards. Next pupils were asked to choose two cards showing odd numbers and fit them together. As various pupils did this, they were asked to show their results (Fig. 12-14). In every case, the sum of two odd numbers was an even number. Slower and average pupils continued using the cards and the beam balance to find answers for the two other cases, even added to even and odd added to even, while the teacher took the more capable pupils to the side of the room to help them verify deductively that "If two numbers are odd, their sum is even." The *direct proof* that they eventually completed follows:

Figure 12-14
Odd number + odd number is an even number.

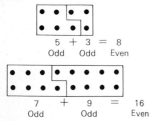

Let the two odd numbers be $2n + 1$ and $2l + 1$, where n and l are any whole numbers, and let S be the sum of two odd numbers. Then:

$S = (2n + 1) + (2l + 1)$

$S = (2n + 2l) + (1 + 1)$ Associative and commutative properties for addition.

$S = 2(n + l) + 2$ Distributive property.

Now, $n + l$ is a whole number   The whole numbers are closed under addition.

$2(n + l)$ is an even number   Two times any whole number is an even number.

$2(n + l) + 2$ is an even number   Two more than any even number is an even number.

Figure 12-15

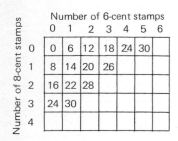

Tabulating all possible cases is another way to prove a statement. Suppose Joe had a supply of 6- and 8-cent stamps and had to place exactly 36 cents in stamps on a letter. In how many different ways could he do this? Pupils prepare a table as in Fig. 12-15. The numerals in the body of the table show the costs of numbers of 8- and 6-cent stamps. The 28 in the table, for example, is the value of two 8-cent and two 6-cent stamps. Not all blanks in the body of the table need be filled since the numbers would be greater than 36. As the pupils study their compilations they find that there are exactly two ways to solve the problem.

Whenever the truth of a statement is uncertain, it is wise to test it. It may be that one example can be found for which the statement is false. This is called a *counterexample*. Only one counterexample is needed to prove a theorem false. Is this true or false? "Every whole number greater than 3 can be expressed as the sum of two primes." Making some trials, we find that $4 = 2 + 2$, $5 = 2 + 3$, $6 = 3 + 3$, $7 = 2 + 5$, and $8 = 3 + 5$. For these five cases the theorem is true. What is the smallest number for which the theorem is false?

Studying historic methods As they study ancient ways of performing mathematical operations, pupils not only discover certain properties, but develop some appreciation of the ingenious yet often crude procedures formerly used:

- At one time, multiplication tables with products greater than 25 were not used. Then 7×8 was performed as

$$
\begin{aligned}
7 \times (5 + 3) &= (7 \times 5) + (7 \times 3) \\
&= [(5 + 2) \times 5] + (7 \times 3) \\
&= (5 \times 5) + (2 \times 5) + (7 \times 3) \\
&= 25 + 10 + 21 = 56
\end{aligned}
$$

Figure 12-16
Find 22 × 31 from this table.

$1 \times 31 = 31$
$2 \times 31 = 62$
$4 \times 31 = 124$
$8 \times 31 = 248$
$16 \times 31 = 496$

- Multiply by doubling. This is illustrated for 22×31 in Fig. 12-16. Successive products are obtained by doubling the previous product. The answer to twenty-two 31s is found by adding sixteen 31s, four 31s, and two 31s, or $496 + 124 + 62$. Pupils may try to use this method with an abacus and see one way to multiply when facts are not memorized.

- Use the Russian peasant's method, which is illustrated for 39×63 in Fig. 12-17. Either factor is multiplied by 2 and the other divided by 2, discarding 1/2 when it occurs in the quotient. The operation is continued until the number in the column being halved is 1. Then every number in the column being doubled is discarded if it is opposite an even number and the remaining numbers are added. In this case, $39 \times 63 = 63 + 126 + 252 + 2,016 = 2,457$

Figure 12-17
Why is 39 × 63 = 63 + 126 + 252 + 2,016?

39	63
19	126
9	252
4	~~504~~
2	~~1,008~~
1	2,016

- Pupils should compare this solution with the method of successive doubling. They will see that 32×63, 4×63, 2×63, and 1×63 are added to make 39×63. Pupils may also try to discover why the procedure works.

Extending understanding of computation The variety of experiences for promoting deeper understanding of computational procedures is indicated by the following samples:
- Demonstrate how regrouping in addition or subtraction is performed

on a 10-bead abacus. Find the product of 8 and 124 on this abacus.

- Investigate shortcut methods of multiplication, discovering, if possible, why they work.

  (a) Multiplying a whole number by 25 is performed mentally by annexing two zeros and dividing by 4. Similar procedures are possible for multiplying by 50, 12 1/2, 16 2/3, 33 1/3, and other numbers.

  (b) Multiplying a two-place number by 11 is done as follows: If the sum of the digits is 9 or less, the product is formed by placing the sum of the digits between the digits. Examples: 11 × 63 = 693; 11 × 42 = 462. Pupils may extend this process to the case where the sum of the digits is greater than 9 and also to the multiplication of any number by 11.

- Explain the following method for multiplying: To find 8 × 9, write 8 under 9, subtract each from 10 and record the result to the right of each (Fig. 12-18). In the answer, 72, a number of tens (7) are found by performing either 8 – 1 or 9 – 2. To this is added the product of the numbers shown in the righthand column (2) to obtain the product.

- Try this interesting method of division on other examples with divisors close to 100 or 1,000. It is illustrated for $98\overline{)52,904}$ in Fig. 12-19. Numerals in the quotient are obtained in the usual way.

- Pupils may test numbers for divisibility by such numbers as 2, 3, 4, 5, 6, 7, 8, 9, 10, 11, and 12 and may, in some cases, rationalize the process or intuitively verify it. A few examples of tests for divisibility are:

  (a) A number is divisible by 3 if the sum of its digits is divisible by 3: 1,854 is divisible by 3 since $1 + 8 + 5 + 4 = 18$ and 18 is divisible by 3.

  (b) A number is divisible by 4 if the number shown by its last two digits is divisible by 4: 2,824 is divisible by 4 since 24 is divisible by 4.

  (c) A number is divisible by 12 if it is divisible by both 3 and 4: 2,736 is divisible by 12 since $2 + 7 + 3 + 6$ is divisible by 3 and 36 is divisible by 4.

- Compute with a numeration system founded on base four and using different symbols. Pupils may be given addition and multiplication tables, as in Fig. 12-20, and then asked to compute $\beta\gamma + \gamma\gamma$, $\gamma\alpha\beta - \beta\beta\delta$, $\gamma\beta \times \delta\alpha$, $\beta\delta\delta \div \delta$.

Having fun with recreations While the major purpose in solving puzzles is entertainment, insight may be developed and attitudes improved as well. One good way to use puzzles is to write them

Figure 12-18
What is 8 × 9 from this table?

9 1
8 2

Figure 12-19
An algorithm for 52,904 ÷ 98.

$$
\begin{array}{r}
539 \\
(100-2)\overline{)52904} \\
\text{Add five 2s to 29} \quad 10 \\
\hline
390 \\
\text{Add three 2s to 90} \quad 6 \\
\hline
964 \\
\text{Add nine 2s to 64} \quad 18 \\
\hline
82
\end{array}
$$

Figure 12-20
Addition and multiplication tables, base four.

+	α	β	γ	δ
α	α	β	γ	δ
β	β	γ	δ	βα
γ	γ	δ	βα	ββ
δ	δ	βα	ββ	βγ

×	α	β	γ	δ
α	α	α	α	α
β	α	β	γ	δ
γ	α	γ	βα	βγ
δ	α	δ	βγ	γβ

on cards and have pupils who solve a puzzle write their names on the backs of the cards. Some examples of puzzles are:

Change 64 to 65. Start with an 8-by-8 square (Fig. 12-21a). Cut it into three parts, *A, B,* and *C.* Fit these together as in Fig. 12-21b to form a rectangle 13 by 5. Thus, the original 64 squares has been changed to 65. Explain.

Letter-arithmetic was studied as long ago as 1000 A.D. in India and China. The problem is to replace letters in a given computation by the digits 0 through 9. A story is told that a son wrote home for money. His father replied, "Solve this letter-arithmetic problem (Fig. 12-22) and I'll send you money."

Magic squares can be invented of increasing difficulty. Fast learners may try to insert numbers 1 through 9 in Fig. 12-23 so the sum is 15 horizontally, vertically, and diagonally. The 1 in Fig. 12-23a must be in the upper-right corner and the 4 in Fig. 12-23b must be in the center cell.

THE MATHEMATICS LABORATORY

While the mathematics laboratory has not been specifically emphasized in the previous sections, it has great contributions to make in implementing the suggestions made. Certainly, the lab offers an opportunity for slow pupils to succeed at appropriate levels and improve their self-image. It can provide for more relevant and interesting experiences and a variety that is impossible from the exclusive "class presentation by the teacher and then practice" routine. Also it encourages stimulating participation—a special need for slow learners. The lessons of Mr. Harris and Mr. Griffin described earlier in the chapter contain many elements of a mathematics lab situation. Their lessons can be organized so that even more individualization is accomplished and greater use made of a lab if the physical facilities and personnel are available.

For fast learners too the mathematics lab provides an opportunity to work on challenging problems. These pupils may be given Activity Cards, from which they read the instructions and investigate the situation given. Working alone or in small groups, they have the opportunity to progress at a rate commensurate with their ability, learn to explore a problem, and avoid the boredom of unnecessary practice.

EXPERIMENTS FOR PUPILS

On the following pages are a number of Activities for slow and fast learners. As in previously given Activities, there are many adaptions and extensions.

Figure 12-21
Why is the area of (a) 64 and of (b) 65 square units?

Figure 12-22
Replace the letters with numerals.

```
  S E N D
+ M O R E
M O N E Y
```

Figure 12-23
Make magic squares with 1-9, if possible.

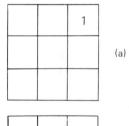

ACTIVITY 1

Objective: To form 5-digit numbers, divide each by 9, and make a discovery.

1 This is called the 9s game. It has rules:

(*a*) Use the digits 1, 2, 3, 4, and 8 each once.

(*b*) Write a 5-digit numeral.

(*c*) Divide by 9 and record your remainder.

2 Suppose you choose 34,128. If you divide by 9, the quotient is 3,792 and the remainder is 0. These results are in the table. Follow the rules with other numbers to fill in the table.

Number	34,128
Quotient when divided by 9	3,792
Remainder	0

3 Tell your friend what you see in the table.

4 *Brainbuster:* Form a number shown with the five digits 1, 2, 3, 4, and 8 so the remainder is not 0 when divided by 9.

ACTIVITY 2

Apparatus needed: 16 toothpicks   *Objective:* To form geometric figures with toothpicks.

1 Use your toothpicks to make these figures.

Number of toothpicks	Figure	Drawing of your figure	Number of toothpicks	Figure	Drawing of your figure
4	one square		12	three squares	
8	two squares		11	three squares	
7	two squares		10	three squares	

2 *Brainbuster:* Make four squares with:

(*a*) 16 toothpicks   (*c*) 14 toothpicks

(*b*) 15 toothpicks   (*d*) 13 toothpicks

3 Find a way to make four squares with less than 13 toothpicks.

ACTIVITY 3

Objective: To practice addition in an interesting way.

1 Cut out this rectangular region.

2 Place it on the clock face so it covers four numerals. The

picture shows the rectangular region covering a total of 28 from $10 + 9 + 5 + 4$.

3   Cover a sum of (*a*) 26; (*b*) 16; (*c*) 14.

ACTIVITY 4

Objective: To discover which counting numbers can be expressed as the sum of consecutive counting numbers.

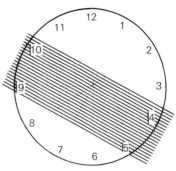

1   Here are examples of sets of consecutive counting numbers: {1,2}, {5,6,7}, {13,14,15,16}.

2   Express each counting number as the sum of consecutive counting numbers. Some are done for you.

3   It is impossible to do what numbers?

4   Guess the next number that should be on your list for Ex. 3. Continue your table to check your answer.

3 =	10 =
4 =	11 =
5 =	12 =
6 = 1 + 2 + 3	13 = 6 + 7
7 =	14 =
8 =	15 =
9 =	16 =

ACTIVITY 5

Objective: To check and prove, if possible, Ramanujan's statement.

1   It was said of Ramanujan, an Indian mathematician, that every counting number was one of his personal friends. Once when in the hospital, he was visited by G. H. Hardy who said, "I rode here today in cab No. 1,729. That is such a dull number. I hope it is not a bad omen." "On the contrary," replied Ramanujan, "It is a very interesting number. It is the smallest number that can be expressed as the sum of two cubes in two different ways."

2   Express 1,729 as the sum of cubes in two different ways. *Hint:* $8^3 + 9^3$ is not a correct answer because $8^3 = 512$ and $9^3 = 729$. $512 + 729 \neq 1,729$. Try to prove there are *exactly* two ways to do this.ql

ACTIVITY 6

Objective: To describe the classroom with numbers.

1   Describe your classroom using numbers. Some examples are 31 pupils, 12 windows, and 2 doors.

2   Describe your classroom without using numbers. Is this an easy or difficult task?

ACTIVITY 7

Objective: To prepare a bulletin-board display to show the wide use of numbers.

1   Choose a topic such as sports, television, travel, or one of your choice.

2   Prepare a bulletin board to show how numbers are used in your topic.

ACTIVITY 8

Apparatus needed: brads, cardboard strips

Objective: To determine the minimum number of diagonals to make a polygon rigid.

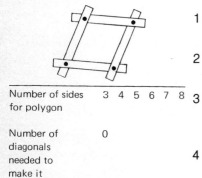

Number of sides for polygon	3	4	5	6	7	8
Number of diagonals needed to make it rigid	0					

1   Make a parallelogram as shown at the left. Make your parallelogram a different shape. This 4-sided polygon is not rigid.

2   Make 3-, 4-, 5-, 6-, 7- and 8-sided polygons. Which are rigid? That is which can have only one shape?

3   Insert cardboard strips to form diagonals for your polygons. Find the minimum number of diagonals needed to make each polygon rigid. Write your results in this table.

4   Guess the minimum number of diagonals needed to make these polygons rigid: (*a*) 9 sides; (*b*) 12 sides; (*c*) 20 sides.

5   Explain to a friend how to make a polygon rigid. Why is your explanation correct?

ACTIVITY 9

Apparatus needed: 16 toothpicks

Objective: To follow directions and make geometric figures.

Starting figure	Toothpicks removed	Final figure
a	3	2 squares
b	2	2 squares
c	3	3 squares
d	2	3 squares
e	3	4 squares
f	2	4 squares
g	1	4 squares

Make each *starting figure*. Remove the number of toothpicks you are told to get the *final figure*.

(a)

(b)

(c)

(d)

(e)

(f)

(g)

ACTIVITY 10

Objective: To name as many numbers a possible.

1   Cut out these tiles. They should suggest 1, 4, 9 and 16 to you.

2   Put any two together. How many numbers can you make? The example shows you can make 25 as 9 + 16.

3   *Brainbuster:* Put any three tiles together. How many numbers can you make?

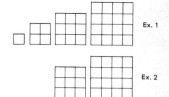

Ex. 1

Ex. 2

QUESTIONS AND EXERCISES

1   Two general plans for facilitating adjustment to pupils' individual differences are school organization and special classroom procedures. Summarize ways in whcih each of these may be implemented.

2   For slower pupils, how should use of manipulative materials, such as sets of objects, paper folding, and the like, differ from their use with average pupils? Accelerated pupils?

3   Why are firsthand, familiar (relevant) problems particularly important in mathematics programs for underachievers?

4   Describe criteria to be used in reducing the amount of material to be studied by slow learners at a certain grade level.

5   Why is a review that consists only of practice not considered to be a satisfactory teaching procedure?

6   In what ways should the mathematics teacher administer the program of practice for slower pupils so that it is most effective?

7   If the teacher finds certain pupils need special review before proceeding to a new topic, what can he ask the more capable pupils to do while he teaches this review lesson?

8   What methods may the mathematics teacher use to help slow pupils succeed?

9   Describe and illustrate procedures through which slow pupils may be motivated to want to learn mathematics?

10   Describe some specific things that can be done to adjust a mathematics program so that each pupil has opportunity for "optimum growth."

11   Explain briefly what is meant by these two approaches to programming for more capable pupils: (a) enrichment; (b) acceleration.

12   What areas of study are suitable for enrichment of the mathematics program for more capable pupils?

13   Illustrate how pupils may discover rules and patterns by examining cases and drawing tentative conclusions.

14   State a rule for multiplying a number mentally by each of the following: 50, 25, 12 1/2, 16 2/3, 33 1/3.

15   Tell how studying and completing proofs may contribute to the mathematics education of more capable pupils.

16   Explain this statement: "Experiences that are enriching for one pupil may not be suitable for another pupil."

PROJECTS

1 Examine an up-to-date textbook for a grade of your choice. (a) List topics that might be omitted for slower pupils. (b) List topics that should be included only for more capable pupils. (c) Make a summary of methods designed for individualizing instruction. (d) Describe enrichment activities that are extensions of the basic content of the book. (e) Do the activities suggested for the mathematics laboratory seem to be most appropriate for slow or fast learners?

2 Examine the textbook for a grade level of your choice of a series especially designed for the "lower track." What are special characteristics of this book? Place bookmarks in the text to show and tell the class.

3 Most series of texts have accompanying workbooks. Study one of these for a grade level of your choice. List experiences that can be used to: (a) reinforce understanding; (b) provide extra practice; (c) develop problem solving ability. How may a workbook be used in caring for individual differences?

4 Locate mathematical recreations appropriate for elementary school pupils at a grade level of your choice. Describe them to the class.

5 Your class is studying volume and surface area. Each pair of pupils has 24 sugar cubes. (a) Write an experiment with the objective for all pupils. (b) Write an experiment as an enrichment activity for fast pupils.

6 (a) Do Activities 1, 2, 3, 4, 8, 9, and 10. (b) Which seem most appropriate for slow pupils? For fast pupils? (c) Choose one Activity that you think is appropriate for either group and rewrite it so it is appropriate for the other group.

7 (a) Finish the exploration for the two geometric examples on page 335. (b) Study the Russian peasant method on page 337. Try to discover why it "works." (c) Where did the extra square region "come from" in the example on page 339? (d) Complete, if possible, the magic squares in Fig. 12-23.

Bibliography

1 Biggs, E. E.: "Mathematics Laboratories and Teachers' Centre—the Mathematics Revolution in Britain," *The Arithmetic Teacher*, vol. 15, pp. 400-408, May, 1968. Illustrations of how pupils discover mathematics in British schools.

2 Clark, H. C.: "Before You Individualize Your Elementary Math," *School Science and Mathematics*, vol. 71, pp. 676-680, Nov., 1971. Discussion of needed planning to tailor instruction to individual needs.

3 Dienes, F. P.: *Mathematics in the Primary School*, Macmillan, Ltd., Toronto, 1966. Chapter 9 embodies a philosophy for organizing the classroom effectively.

4 De Vault, M. V., and T. E. Kriewall: *Differentiation of Mathematics Instruction* in Chapter 11, Sixty-ninth Yearbook, National Society for the Study of Education, NSSE, Chicago, 1970. Many suggestions and evaluation of four parameters—content, learner, teacher, and instruction—as they contribute to individualization of instruction.

5 Henderson, G. L.: "Individualized Instruction: Sweet in Theory, Sour in Practice," *The Arithmetic Teacher*, vol. 19, pp. 17-22, Jan., 1972. Important objectives of mathematics education cannot be met if self-study is the only means of instruction.

6 Kevra, B., R. Brey, and B. Schimmel, "Success for Slower Learners or Rx: Relax—and Play," *The Arithmetic Teacher*, vol. 19, pp. 335-343, May, 1972. Excellent suggestions of experiences for slower learners.

7 Kidd, K., S. Myers, and D. Cilley: *The Laboratory Approach to Mathematics*, Science Research Associates, Inc., Chicago, 1970. Chapter 6 describes laboratory experiences for the low achiever.

8 National Council of Teachers of Mathematics, *Instructional Aids in Mathematics*, Thirty-fourth Yearbook, Washington, D.C., 1973. Extensive discussion of individualization including classroom organization, use of texts and other materials.

9 National Council of Teachers of Mathematics: *Enrichment Mathematics for the Grades*, Twenty-seventh Yearbook, Washington, D.C., 1963. Excellent source of enrichment experiences for all

grades through nine, as well as annotated biblio-graphies of books and articles.

10   National Council of Teachers of Mathematics: *The Slow Learner in Mathematics,* Thirty-fifth Year-book Washington, D.C., 1972. Comprehensive book on the slow learner with extensive aids to the teach-er concerning adjustment of instruction activities, promising programs, and so on.

11   Trafton, P. R.: "Individualized Instruction: Develop-ing Broadened Perspectives," *The Arithmetic Teach-er,* vol. 19, pp. 7-12, January, 1972. Clear view of the scope of individualized instruction with specific ways of providing it.

13
EVALUATING PUPIL PROGRESS

Which experiences were effective in promoting learning? Have pupils developed adequate skill? Are the attitudes of my pupils favorable? How is John progressing in problem solving? Do the pupils in my class understand the meaning of common denominator? Do they really understand the procedure for determining a common denominator or do they do it purely mechanically? These are the kinds of questions that continually confront the conscientious teacher as he plans and guides learning for each individual in his class.

This chapter provides the teacher with guidance for evaluation by:

- Outlining the purposes for evaluation.
- Describing how to plan an effective program of evaluation.
- Illustrating a sample program for evaluation.
- Establishing procedures for observing and interviewing pupils.
- Suggesting ways of improving teacher-made tests.

PURPOSES OF EVALUATION

Current trends and social pressures are making the evaluation of the instructional program in elementary school mathematics increasingly important. An examination of some of the more significant developments in teaching reveals why this is so. Consider, for example, the following:

- In order that the pupil may learn more mathematics with better understanding in a shorter time:

    More effective direction of learning with better application of principles of learning is being required.

    New devices and materials for instruction are continually being developed and recommended.

    New mathematics curricula and content are being developed for all grades.

- Since more attention is being directed to the progress of individual pupils:

    There is greater need to discover and capitalize on the abilities of all pupils, including both the gifted and the slower.

    Parents and pupils require adequate information on the progress that is being made by each one.

It is worthwhile to examine some of the implications of each of these developments.

Directing Learning Activities

The classroom activities need to be continually adjusted to the progress of the class in terms of the steps in the learning sequence. When a topic is introduced, readiness to begin study of the new subject and motivational readiness must be seriously considered. Subject-matter readiness can be determined by a formal or informal test. Motivational readiness is more difficult to assess. By observing each pupil's degree of attention and the nature of his response, the teacher can obtain important information about the interest and attention of individual class members as well as the class as a whole. In this way he can decide upon those procedures that will best engage the interest of the class and help to motivate each pupil.

With experience every teacher develops favorite procedures for each stage of the learning sequence—encouraging exploration and discovery, organizing drill, teaching for transfer, etc. Yet he should still be alert to the possibility of finding new and more effective methods. The teacher who continually evaluates his procedures never ceases to improve. Before comparing a new procedure with an older one, an intelligent basis for comparison must be established. Subject-matter outcomes, as well as abilities and attitudes essential for exploration, verification, and generalization, must be taken into account.

Appraising Instructional Materials

Current attention to mathematics has created a new market for instructional materials, ranging from textbooks and a multitude of concrete manipulative devices including games to computers and television. While the teacher should be ready to utilize what is valuable, he should also require evidence of effectiveness before adopting the newer materials.

Many factors enter into a learning situation and it is difficult to isolate the most important one. Moreover, what is useful to one teacher may not be useful to another. Only by trying different materials in teaching the same topic on several occasions can a teacher reach a tentative conclusion as to their relative values. Even this is possible only by deciding in advance what benefit is to be expected and what evidence is needed in order to make a careful appraisal. Such a careful procedure usually reveals that, if it is expertly administered, almost any instructional material is useful at least for some specialized purpose.

Determining Effectiveness of the Curriculum

Because sweeping changes are still occurring, the evaluation of the curriculum has become especially important today. It is to be kept in mind that no matter how carefully a program is planned, it must be tried out in practice before we can be certain it will work. But before it can be tried out experimentally, decisions must be made defining precisely what results are expected and what kind of evidence will be sufficient to show that these results have been obtained. Whether or not the curriculum is effective is determined by the rate at which the pupils progress toward the desired goal.

Moreover, it is necessary to have detailed information on the progress of each pupil in order to determine whether the level of difficulty suits the class as a whole or is appropriate only to the upper or lower levels of it. The subject matter should interest and stimulate the entire class rather than merely a part of it. Measurement should reveal continued progress at all levels. If this is not the case, more revision is needed.

Pupil Placement

A continual appraisal of the achievement level and rate of progress of each pupil must be available at all times. It was noted in Chapter 12 that programs to provide for individual differences may be organized within a given classroom, or may be so designed as to require administrative adjustments. In either case, adequate operation of the program depends on abundant information on the status of the individual pupil.

Reporting Pupil Progress

Ideally, information on pupil progress includes many aspects of learning besides the pupil's degree of information and skill. His attitude toward mathematics, his achievement as it relates to his aptitude, his work habits, his understanding, and his problem-solving abilities should be part of the record. The teacher should be prepared to point out to each pupil his strengths and weaknesses and to help him analyze the sources of his difficulties. The teacher's recommendations for means of improvement should be based on data which reveal the causes of success and failure as well as the areas in which they occur.

Such information is increasingly important in the eventual determination of the career of the pupil and should be used in reporting to parents and advising them. Some of these data may also be included in the pupil's records so that they will accompany him if he moves to another school.

From what has been said of the purposes of evaluation, it is apparent that it must be a continuous procedure. It is designed as an operational control to guide the learning sequence, as well as a quality control to test results.

The evaluation procedures to be used depend on the kind of information needed. Tests are used when appropriate, but much of the data comes from observation during learning activities, when the teacher may raise provocative questions to elicit revealing comments and discussions.

The purpose of evaluation is not merely to check on pupil achievement. Another purpose, equally as important, is that it provides a means of determining the effectiveness of the curriculum, the instructional materials, and the classroom activities. In each instance, the evaluation is designed to determine whether and to what extent they promote progress toward the established objectives. Evaluation, accordingly, must be based on a clear statement of objectives.

THREE ASPECTS OF PLANNING

Evaluation is an integral part of teaching. In elementary school mathematics, as in other areas, the overall planning of classroom activities must take into account three things:

The definition of objectives: What results are desired?

The planning of learning activities: How are these objectives to be achieved?

The evaluation of results: How well were the objectives achieved?

Securing the answer to each of these questions calls for professional skill and understanding.

Definition of Objectives

The objectives provide the frame of reference for both the planning of activities and the evaluation of results. Those set up for each topic must fit into the outline of objectives for the year's work, and those for each class period must fit into the objectives for the topic. Thus the definition of objectives controls the sequence and flow of activities.

Objectives are most useful when they are stated in terms of what the pupil is expected to learn, including the development of interests, attitudes, comprehension, and skills. What is to be learned is defined by describing the behavior of a pupil who has achieved the objectives. It will be readily seen that in describing the desired behavior the teacher has specified the evidence needed for evaluation. Such a definition becomes a useful starting point in planning learning activities, as well as evaluation.

The objectives set up by Ms. Green in planning a topic on the addition of fractional numbers illustrate how the desired pupil behavior may be described:

Vocabulary:

(*a*) The pupil uses the technical vocabulary associated with fractional numbers in such a way as to demonstrate his understanding of the basic concepts.

Interest:

(*a*) His immediate interest in the topic: He demonstrates a desire to explore situations that call for addition of fractional numbers.

(*b*) His general interest in mathematics: He demonstrates an increased desire to participate in the class activities and pursue the study of mathematics.

Meaning of the operation:

(*a*) He explains and otherwise demonstrates an understanding of the properties basic to renaming fractional numbers.

(*b*) He describes and illustrates the relationship of addition of whole numbers to addition of fractional numbers.

(*c*) He pictures addition of fractional numbers using a number line, and circular and rectangular regions.

Skills:

(*a*) He demonstrates speed and accuracy in the addition of fractional numbers.

(*b*) He solves verbal problems that involve fractional numbers.

Generalizations:

(*a*) He identifies real situations calling for addition of fractional numbers.

(b) He applies what is learned to new situations.

(c) He can explain and illustrate the relationship between addition and subtraction of fractional numbers.

(d) For the set of fractional numbers under addition, he explains and illustrates properties, such as the commutative property or the identity element.

(e) He explains how the algorithm for addition is an illustration of the use of the distributive property.

Planning of Learning Activities

The five categories of outcomes, as classified and given by Ms. Green, are directly related to the steps used by effective teachers. Her next step in planning the topic was to list the major learning activities through which pupils might achieve the objectives. Some of these were:

Vocabulary:

(a) A study including a discussion of concepts and a list of words to be related to them, such as different names for the same number, and terms, such as *mixed form, addend,* and *sum.*

Interest:

(a) Providing a stimulating situation to introduce the topic, with a workshop example.

(b) Maintaining interest in class activities through:

(1) A variety of problem situations, some of which involve measurement.

(2) A variety of activities—experiments in the mathematics laboratory, discussion of procedures by groups of pupils, practice with paper and pencil, oral reports by pupils—to provide for individual differences.

(c) Promoting general interest in mathematics by means of:

(1) Studies of how mathematics (particularly fractions) is used in adult life.

(2) Historical background of fractions including the clumsy yet ingenious methods used by the Romans and other ancient peoples.

Meaning of the operation:

(a) Using a ruler, paper folding, egg cartons, chips, etc. to verify the result of 1/8 + 3/8.

(b) Exploration leading from ruler and other materials to abstract manipulation of numerals.

(c) Exploration leading to discussions of: What characteristics of this situation indicate that the operation called for is addition?

(d) Contrasting the properties of the set of whole numbers under addition and the set of fractional numbers under addition.

(e) Picturing an addition such as 1/4 + 2/4 on a number line and comparing it to the number-line picture for 1 + 2.

Skills:

(a) Practice in renaming a fractional number using a greater or a smaller denominator.

(b) Practice in expressing members of a set of fractional numbers so that each member of the set has the same denominator.

(c) Practice in addition with and without expressing results in simplest form.

(d) Practice in solving problems requiring addition of fractional numbers.

Generalizations:

(a) Summaries arising out of discussion and exploration lead to such generalizations as:

   (1) If numerator and denominator are both divided by the same number (not 0), the fractional number is renamed.

   (2) Every fractional number has an infinite number of names.

   (3) If a, b, and c represent fractional numbers and if $a + b = c$, then $a = c - b$.

   (4) If a and b represent fractional numbers and $a + b = a$, then $b = 0$.

(b) Summary arising out of discussions of: Why is this an addition situation?

Following this outline, Ms. Green moved to the detailed planning of classroom activities. The selection of these experiences at each level was determined by the stage the pupil had reached in the learning sequence. Those useful for fixing skills, for example, may not be suitable for developing generalizations. Activities must also be suited to the purposes for which mathematics is taught; those designed to promote interest may differ from those used to develop understanding of meanings. Since classroom resources vary, every skillful teacher has at hand a variety of procedures for each purpose. Another teacher might have selected different activities to achieve each outcome.

Evaluation of Results

Even the most expert teacher continuously appraises his success in adapting techniques to a particular situation. Their effectiveness is determined by the progress which pupils have made. Procedures are adjusted according to the interests and abilities of the pupils, the resources of the school and community, and the characteristics of the teacher himself. It is necessary to determine not only how well the plans are working for the class as a whole, but also how they are working for the individual pupil. For these reasons, all classroom activities must be conducted on an experimental basis and continuously adjusted to pupil progress.

A TYPICAL PROGRAM FOR EVALUATION

Planning detailed procedures for evaluation requires a precise definition of what each outcome means in terms of pupil behavior. Situations are then planned to bring about and record the desired behavior. Regardless of the purposes and nature of the evaluation, the key questions are: What kinds of pupil behavior would indicate learning or failure to learn? Where and in what situations will such behavior occur? How can a record of such behavior be obtained? While most kinds of behavior can be observed in routine class activities, some kinds may need to be brought out in specially planned activities; others will require the construction of tests or the use of commercial tests.

The program of evaluation planned by Ms. Green depended in part on tests, but more extensively on observation of the pupils' work. This is shown in Table 13-1. It may readily be seen that evaluation is a time-consuming procedure. Without adequate assistance no teacher would have time to devise the checklists, construct the tests, or plan the discussions to collect the data, to say nothing of the time required to analyze the data and use the results to improve the program. The general rule is each year to evaluate the part of the program in which a weakness is suspected and hope to cover the total program over several years. This should be understood as Ms. Green's evaluation program is described.

A Sample Program

Following are some samples from Ms. Green's procedures, with the question each is intended to answer. They are keyed to the items in Table 13-1.

TABLE 13-1 PLAN FOR EVALUATION

| Objectives | Information for Evaluation Secured by Means of | |
	Observation	Instrument
Vocabulary	Ability to express ideas and use the technical terms correctly	Vocabulary test
Interest	Immediate: Does the pupil manifest a desire to pursue the topic? General: As defined on checklist	Checklist
Meanings		
Principles	Ability to apply principles that he has learned	Test on understanding basic to addition with fractions
Application of the concept of addition to fractional numbers	Verification of the properties for the set of fractional numbers under addition	
Skills		
In the operations	As demonstrated in classwork, during supervised study, and in written assignments	Computational tests
Verbal problems	Ability to analyze and solve problems during class discussions and in written assignments	Problem tests
Generalizations	Ability to state in class why addition applies to a given situation	Later: Tests on ability to differentiate addition from subtraction
Identifies addition situations with fractions		
Applies what is learned to life situations	Ability to handle concepts and operations in new situations during class discussions	
Illustrates and uses the properties for the set of fractional numbers under addition	Ability to explain and use the properties in algorithms	Class discussion and test on generalizations

Vocabulary Do the pupils have the special vocabulary necessary to pursue the topic? Here Ms. Green devised tests with questions, such as:

In each equation, circle all numerals or letters that are addends.

a. $7/8 + 1\ 2/3 = n$ b. $2/3 - 1/6 = 1/2$ c. $n + 3/4 = 11/12$

Circle all numerals that are in mixed form.

a. 12/7   b. 1 7/9   c. 1/19   d. 13 1/2

Find the one member of each set that is not a name for the same fractional number as the other members of the set.

$\{7/10 + 1/10,\ (7-3)/(4+1),\ 5/6 - 1/30,\ 20/16\}$

$\{1\ 2/3 + 3/4,\ 30/12 - 1/12,\ (57-28)/(15+14),\ 2\ 1/2 - 1/12]$

Ms. Green had each pupil correct his own test. Then sets of three pupils discussed their errors, decided on ways to determine the correct answer, and reported to the class.

Interest Because so many important vocations require mathematical ability and because so many pupils in the upper grades come to dislike mathematics, Ms. Green was especially concerned with developing interest in it. Knowing that no test could measure interest, she devised a checklist of the kinds of behavior she felt would indicate its presence. By keeping the list on her desk, she could readily enter the name of any pupil who exhibited the desired behavior.

Are pupils willing to do work beyond what is required?

Do pupils tend to resist distractions in class activities?

Do pupils demonstrate pleasure in their own or others' mathematical activities?

Do pupils voluntarily seek information on mathematical questions?

Do pupils voluntarily bring items of mathematical interest to class?

Do pupils volunteer relevant suggestions in group discussions?

Do pupils volunteer reasonable generalizations?

Do pupils show pleasure in analyzing problems?

Ms. Green recognized that another teacher might have assembled a different list. However, since this list included the kinds of behavior she was interested in developing in her pupils, she felt that by using it she would not only collect information on interest, but, at the same time, would direct her own efforts toward encouraging its development.

Meaning of the operation Do pupils understand how to express every member of a set of fractions so that each has the same denominator and how to express them in simplest form? Tests such as the following were used to obtain evidence.

Directions: Each statement is correctly completed with *larger than, smaller than,* or *equal to.* Write one of these phrases in each blank.

1   Both numerator and denominator of a fraction are multiplied by the same counting number. The resulting fraction is ____ the original fraction.

2   Several fractions have the same numerator and different denominators. The fraction having the largest denominator is ____ the others.

3   Several fractions have the same denominator and different numerators. The fraction having the largest numerator is ____ the others.

4   Both numerator and denominator of a fraction are divided by the same counting number. The resulting fraction names a number that is ____ the original fraction.

To test for ability to apply the principles basic to renaming fractions:

Express each of the following fractions as a fraction with the denominator as designated: 1/2 = ?/4; 3/5 = ?/15.

For which of these sets of fractions can the denominator of any one member be used as a common denominator?
{3/4,5/6,7/8}; {1/2,2/3,5/6}; {3/8,5/6,9/4}

For each of the following sets of fractions, express the fractions so that each member has the same denominator:
{2/3,5/6,11/12}; {1/4,1/3,1/6}; {3/8,1/2,3/4}.

Express these fractions in their simplest form and, if possible, name them in mixed form: 9/12; 15/4; 30/12.

Write a numeral in each frame so that the result is a true mathematical sentence.

$$\frac{\square}{6} = \frac{12}{\triangle} = \frac{4}{3} = \frac{\bigcirc}{27} = \frac{32}{\square} = \frac{\square}{31+5} = \frac{\triangledown + 1}{\bigcirc}$$

Can pupils apply the concept of addition to fractional numbers? To answer this question, the teacher engaged the pupils in discussions of problems which can be solved through experimenting with materials. For example:

If John glues a 6/10 cm board to another 6/10 cm board, how thick will the resulting board be?

If I pour 3/4 of a cup of milk into a container with 1/2 cup of water in it, how much will I have?

The teacher gave the pupils opportunities to improvise solutions by using a ruler or measuring bowl.

Skills   Do pupils have the computational skill required for addition with fractions? To determine this, Ms. Green used a test and observed the pupils while they worked on it. When there was serious doubt about the ability of a pupil, he was given an individual test and was encouraged to think aloud while he worked.

The test was designed to cover many types of addition with fractions, so that mistakes on the test would indicate the level of difficulty. The simplest exercise was fraction plus fraction, same denominator, and one of the most difficult was fraction in mixed form plus fraction, common denominator to be found.

In order to determine whether or not pupils could solve problems requiring addition of fractional numbers, Ms. Green prepared a test of verbal problems that called for such addition. The questions dealt with measurement in situations familiar to the pupils. The emphasis was upon ability to solve problems, rather than on computational ability.

Generalizations Can pupils apply properties for addition of fractional numbers to the solution of mathematical sentences? The following set of questions for the sentences below may form the basis for a class discussion or may be adapted for use as a test:

Find n so that each mathematical sentence is true.

Which sentences can be quickly solved for n by applying the commutative property for addition?

Which can be solved by applying the associative property for addition?

Which can be solved by applying the identity element for addition?

$$2 \ 9/16 + n = 7/8 + 2 \ 9/16$$
$$(7/12 + 5/6) + 8/3 = 7/12 + (5/6 + n)$$
$$(2/3 + 1/2) + n = 7/16 + (2/3 + 1/2)$$
$$4 \ 7/8 + n = 39/8$$

Characteristics of the Program

It will be seen that the evaluation program is designed, insofar as possible, to cover all the important outcomes. It includes a variety of methods for securing and recording the evidence needed to provide information on pupil progress. For the teacher who is completely aware of what he is looking for, practically all learning activities afford an opportunity for collecting this evidence. Through observation during class discussion, individual and committee reports, and supervised study, the teacher learns a great deal about each pupil.

Yet the more concrete and detailed evidence provided by tests is still necessary. No other source yields evidence so economically and in such convenient form. The important thing to recognize is that tests should be used to supplement, rather than to supplant, the evidence collected through observation. Accordingly, an important aspect of teaching skill is the ability to devise suitable tests for specific outcomes and to integrate the use of tests into the sequence of learning activities.

Tests are useful for measuring achievement in fundamental skills and ability to solve verbal problems; they can also aid appraisal of the pupil's understanding. It is important, however, that those outcomes which cannot be appraised through tests should not be neglected. Whether a pupil has ability to think critically about a mathematical situation is best determined in an informal class discussion of a problem that has immediate significance to him. This is true also of the ability to apply what he has learned to life situations, and of the development of interest in mathematics.

The following generalizations may be drawn from Ms. Green's program:

Both the learning activities and the appraisal procedures are based on the definition of outcomes   Most of the learning situations provided opportunities for useful observations. Some of these situations were especially designed to reveal understanding, critical thinking, and ability to apply what had been learned. On the other hand, the tests were designed primarily as a means of evaluation but some of them were utilized to stimulate class discussion.

Although tests provide a great deal of important evidence, they must be supplemented by observation, sometimes in planned situations situations   Ms. Green had a carefully planned procedure for observing the degree of interest in mathematics. The same kind of procedure could be designed to secure information on ability to think critically or ability to use mathematics in life situations. Stated in more general terms, the procedures used are those required to obtain evidence of pupils' progress toward the most crucial objectives.

The ability to design simple tests for a variety of purposes is important in teaching elementary school mathematics   Each of the items in the tests used by Ms. Green was a modification of one of a few standard types that have proved their usefulness in the classroom. They are simple to construct when the teacher understands a few elementary techniques of construction and avoids a few obvious pitfalls. These will be considered below.

Ms. Green did not have occasion to use any of the commercial tests, which also have their place in an evaluation program. It is useful for the teacher to be familiar with these in order to choose those best suited to his purposes.

OBSERVATIONAL PROCEDURES

In his daily contacts with his pupils, the teacher is continually collecting information on their progress as it is revealed in discussions and other situations. Such information is very valuable— perhaps the most valuable of all the kinds of information available. It has, however, two possible weaknesses: (1) there is apt to be no record available when the teacher needs it, and (2) important behavior may be overlooked or forgotten.

Standard procedures have been developed to guard against these two weaknesses. The most commonly used of these are anecdotal records, checklists, and rating scales.

Anecdotal Records

Many teachers find it convenient to keep a pad on the desk ready for notetaking. Usually it is designed to provide for two kinds of entries: what happened, and what it probably means. Any interpretation of the meaning of behavior is tentative and subject to revision as more anecdotes are collected. For example:

What happened: In a discussion of how carpenters use instruments to make linear measurements, George offered to bring in his father's rule, which is calibrated to tenths of an inch.

Interpretation: This indication of interest is encouraging because George has not been cooperative in the past.

With practice, a teacher can become sufficiently skillful in keeping anecdotal records to make routine observation an effective evaluation procedure. The teacher will find that after he has become accustomed to using these records, his observations will be considerably more detailed and astute. Moreover, he will have a permanent and very useful record of pupils' behavior.

Checklist A checklist is a list of the kinds of behavior to look for, with provision for making notes. The checklist used by Ms. Green to evaluate interest is one example. A similar checklist could be made for "Ability to Apply Procedures to Life Problems" or for some other area in which the teacher desires information. With a little alteration, Ms. Green could have made her checklist apply to the individual pupil instead of the whole class. This would require having a separate sheet for each pupil. The notation would include a date and a concise description of what happened. By looking through the blanks at the end of the month, Ms. Green would know to what extent the interest of each pupil was increasing or decreasing.

Whether or not to devise a checklist for a particular outcome depends on how important the need is for special information. If the teacher feels that he may be neglecting certain outcomes or if he has any question as to the effectiveness of his procedures, he should use a checklist.

Rating scales In order to record an appraisal along with her behavioral observations, Ms. Green might have used a rating scale

A check is placed above the phrase most nearly descriptive of typical performance.

It is important to realize, of course, that specialized observational procedures are time-consuming. The choice of what data to collect depends on whether the information is really needed and whether it will be used. Ms. Green suspected that in her concern for pupil achievement she might be neglecting pupil interest. Clearly there is nothing to be gained in such achievement if the pupils lose interest—hence her desire for getting information on this particular outcome. She would continue to rely on informal observation for information on other important outcomes, however, until she had reason to suspect that more detailed information was needed.

INTERVIEWS TO DETERMINE UNDERSTANDING

Most of the present evaluating procedures provide information on whether or not a pupil knows the correct answer. Thus the teacher is informed of the product of his thinking and has no data on his process of obtaining the answer.

The renewed interest in the theories of Piaget has also brought a special study of his method of research, which is essentially that of interviewing children. His success in assessing the number knowledge of his subjects in face-to-face situations as they are solving problems and talking to him can be used effectively in the classroom.

It is generally accepted that the teacher has little time for personal interviews. However, the great worth of interviews should force a reexamination of the use of time by the teacher. Two examples indicate that the understanding possessed by a pupil can be determined to some extent by an interview.

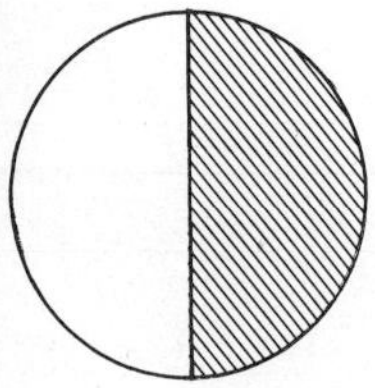

Tell Me All You Can

In talking to an individual child alone, the teacher may show two half-circular regions, one white and one black, and draw a picture of the same item (Fig. 13-1). The pupil is asked, "Tell me everything you can about this." The variety and sophistication of answers helps the teacher evaluate the level of understanding. A few sample answers are:

Figure 13-1

There are two things.

One is black. One is white.

They form a circle.

There is a line segment between the black and white.

The black is one-half of the whole.

The ratio of black to white is one to one.

The whole circle is one; the black is one-half.

It is readily recognized that answers such as the last two would indicate considerable understanding. At the same time, because a premium is being placed on the ability to verbalize, nontechnical language from the child should be accepted. Further some "coaxing" of answers from the quiet child may be necessary.

How Many Points?

Having a pupil talk while solving a series of problems of increasing difficulty not only supplies information on his reasoning but also may direct the teacher in planning the needed remedial experiences. A teacher interviewing a single pupil may show him, in order, *a* of Fig. 13-2, then *b,* and then *c.* For *a,* the questions are: "Which of points *X, Y,* and *Z* are inside one triangle?" "Which of points *X, Y* and *Z* are inside two triangles?" "Which of points *X, Y,* and *Z* are inside three triangles?" If answers are incorrect, the pupil may be asked to trace with his finger the triangles in the figure.

Similar questions are asked concerning Fig. 13-2*b* and *c.* Whereas there are three triangles in Fig. *a,* there are five in each of the other two drawings. Further, there is the added difficulty of points being on certain triangles in *c.* By analyzing the pupil's answers the teacher determines his understanding of the ideas of "inside" and "on" and also his ability to see triangles when they "overlap."

Skills remain very important in mathematics. A correct answer is respected. There are, however, other more important outcomes from learning mathematics. These are in the realm of learning to think mathematically. Only a beginning has been made in evaluating this aspect of learning. At present the best way to assess it is an interview.

EVALUATION AND RECORD-KEEPING BY PUPILS

The abilities to become independent learners, to organize data, and to draw conclusions from data are three important outcomes

Figure 13-2
Points inside, on and outside triangles.

(a)

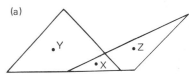

(b)

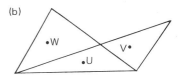

(c)

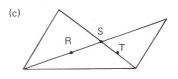

of all disciplines, including mathematics. The following is an illustration of one way to help pupils accomplish these as well as other objectives.

Mr. Jackson found his fifth-grade class having great difficulty with multiplication and division algorithms. One special deficiency of many pupils was that they did not know the multiplication facts. Because of this, they were trying to remember results for the facts when they should have been concentrating on computing. Recognizing that his pupils could not succeed under these conditions, Mr. Jackson initiated two plans. One was a short-term interim procedure to alleviate the problem temporarily; the other was designed to bring pupils "up to grade level" in knowledge of multiplication facts.

The Interim Plan

In order to avoid difficulties arising from incomplete knowledge of the multiplication facts, Mr. Jackson had each pupil make his own multiplication table to which he could refer readily. A larger copy of the table was placed on the bulletin board.

Using these tables for reference, the pupil no longer had to stop and try to remember certain facts when multiplying with the algorithm. He did, however, have to stop and look. Mr. Jackson recognized there would be little gain in really learning the facts although constant reference to the table might be of some help.

The Long-Range Plan

The purpose of the long-range plan was to help pupils know the facts, not only during fifth grade, but also in later grades and life situations.

The pretest   Mr. Jackson gave to all his pupils a test composed of the 100 multiplication facts. When he finished, each pupil recorded the time he required to take the test. Then he was given an answer key from which he corrected his test. Those pupils who did extremely well were excused from the review. Instead, they listened to tapes and did the required work or were given cards to complete lab experiments. The program for the remainder of the class is described below.

Record-keeping and evaluation   Each pupil who needed special help with the multiplication facts started his self-evaluation and progress chart by making a bar graph of his score with the data and time for the test (Fig. 13-3). As the test was repeated, he would record these results again. Next he made an analysis of his errors,

Figure 13-3
Bar graph for test score.

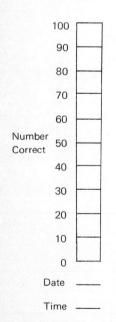

using a form like that in Fig. 13-4. The pupil who missed 9×7, for example, put a tally opposite 9 and a tally opposite 7. From this record, he was able to decide on which factors he needed to concentrate.

Reviewing for meaning First, all pupils reviewed some of the basic ideas about multiplication with Mr. Jackson. Some pupils demonstrated how to show a multiplication as an array; others showed 3×4, for example, as the number of intersections when 3 horizontal and 4 vertical lines are drawn; others illustrated the order property for multiplication; and still others told how facts with a 1 or a 0 could be remembered easily.

A prescribed program For each pair of pupils with similar difficulties—facts with a factor of 7, for example—Mr. Jackson outlined a program for remediation. In order to carry it out, he trained some seventh-graders as aides. Each aide worked with a pair of pupils for 15 minutes twice a week. Some of the variety of experiences directed by the aides were:

Learning to think answers. Pupils learned, as an intermediate step to immediate recall, to think, "I know 5 sevens are 35. So 6 sevens are 7 more, or 42."

Playing the rummy game. Each of two pupils was dealt five of the ten cards with a fact containing 7 as the first factor. No answers were on the cards. Each pupil played a card. If the one who played the card having the greatest product could name the products, he collected both cards.

Using flash cards. One pupil showed flash cards having the "troublesome" multiplications. The other pupils gave the products. A record was kept of mistakes.

Telling related facts. Mr. Jackson wanted pupils to know the relation between multiplication and division, so he had them practice telling related facts. For example, a pupil was told, "You know that $42 = 6 \times 7$. What else do you know about 42, 6, and 7?" Pupils replied, "$42 = 7 \times 6$, $42 \div 7 = 6$, and $42 \div 6 = 7$."

Pupils took the test of 100 multiplication facts again at the end of two weeks and continued their record-keeping. The challenge to all pupils was to make 95 or better for two consecutive tests and complete the test in less than five minutes. Then they qualified as aides to work with other pupils still needing help in learning the multiplication facts.

Figure 13-4
Form for analysis of errors.

Factor	Number of times missed
9	_____
8	_____
7	_____
6	_____
5	_____
4	_____
3	_____
2	_____
1	_____
0	_____

While Mr. Jackson's procedure may not be evaluation in the technical sense of the word, many features of it certainly exemplify effective teaching.

Student Folders

As each student is given more responsibility for his own learning, he should keep a folder of special assignments and those experiments he wants the teacher to review. One creative teacher had a golden folder in which students put only their best work. This permitted her to give only positive comments, which served to enhance the pupils' self-concept. Such informal evaluation is of great merit.

EVALUATION OF THE MATHEMATICS LABORATORY

Although numerous plans have been developed for organizing the mathematics laboratory and diverse materials are available for use in it, teachers and researchers, while recognizing the need, have not yet invented the means for objective evaluation of what is learned in it. Yet there are ways for the teacher who uses it as one of his methods to know if it is contributing to pupils' growth. Most of the following procedures may be thought of as subjective rather than objective. We have seen, however, that many experts believe observation and interviews with pupils to be a valuable means of evaluation, often neglected because of the extreme concentration on test results.

Evaluation of Objectives

There are a number of objectives accomplished in the mathematics laboratory that can be evaluated directly:

If the objective was for pupils to understand the idea of place value and they have performed experiments with a variety of materials, paper-and-pencil tests and demonstration on a piece of apparatus are appropriate evaluation procedures.

If the objective was for pupils to improve their skill in the use of the multiplication algorithm and they have experimented with lattice multiplication, any improvement in the skill can be determined by pretest vs. posttest scores.

If the objective was for pupils to sense the approximate nature of measurement, they may be asked to record answers to their measurement of segments. The use of "about 2 units" or "between 3 and 4 units" as answers would indicate at least partial accomplishment of the objective.

If the teacher thinks carefully of objectives for the various activities of the mathematics laboratory and uses the lab when it is the best method for accomplishing that objective, he will often find that conventional evaluation procedures can be applied.

Evaluation of Concepts

It has been emphasized that concepts are developed by pupils in the mathematics laboratory. It is also recognized that the possession of a concept is difficult to evaluate. Yet there are some possibilities for obtaining objective information.

> Most standardized tests in mathematics have a section on concepts. While these tests generally cover a number of concepts rather than the several in which a teacher might be interested, he may adapt their techniques to construct his own tests. For instance, if he wants to evaluate the effectiveness of a pupil's experiences with the idea of remainder in the mathematics lab, he may adapt toward this end many good matching, multiple-choice, or other questions found in standardized tests.

> Most textbooks currently in use have batteries of tests designed to evaluate concepts as well as skills. These tests cover a chapter and could be used or adapted to provide specific information on the worth of activities in the lab when coordinated with textbook activities.

Observation and Interviews

Techniques for observing pupils carefully and talking to them individually have been discussed. The value of this approach is illustrated by the following anecdotal records made concerning the understanding of one-half:

> Joe explained to his partner, "To show one-half you must first show what one is."

Figure 13-5
Is $\frac{1}{3}$ closer to $\frac{1}{2}$ or $\frac{1}{4}$?

> Marie reported to the class, "I cut a watermelon into two equal parts. Each is one-half. I cut a peach into two equal parts. Each is one-half. One-half a watermelon is bigger than one-half a peach, but each is one-half."

> Carole said, evincing significant progress, "Fifty cents is half a dollar because it takes two of them to make one."

> Rufus showed the class that one-third is closer to one-fourth than to one-half by putting pieces of circular regions next to each other (Fig. 13-5).

By observing and evaluating such pupil responses the teacher can determine the level on which a child is thinking and the extent to which he has understood a concept. Such subjective evaluation procedures provide reliable information about pupils that is available by no other means. It must be remembered that paper and pencil tests are only a sample of what a pupil has learned.

Attitudes of Pupils

A pupil's attitude toward mathematics is a strong factor in determining how much he learns. Whether the mathematics laboratory can change negative attitudes or even influence a neutral feeling about the subject has not been decided. Yet many teachers who have tried the lab and used it for the purpose intended report some favorable results from observing pupils work and talking to them. They find:

Many pupils meeting some success for the first time and trying harder.

A combination of concrete experiences, followed by or in conjunction with symbolic representation, helping pupils make progress.

Pupils discussing plans for exploring a problem with their partners and clarifying ideas.

Open-ended experiments permitting pupils to progress to varying degrees of attainment.

These and other reports are based on subjective evaluation and they do not represent a unanimous opinion. However, it is generally agreed that pupils like a well-organized laboratory experience. Reasons for this may vary from the thrill that comes from the discovery of an idea to the fact that the lab adds variety to the mathematics lesson. Most teachers want specific information on the attitude of their pupils toward mathematics and possible changes in that attitude because of use of the mathematics laboratory. Some of the procedures described under check lists and rating scales on page 359 may be used to collect such data. Perhaps anectodal records containing data about completion of all tasks would be more informative about attitudes than merely grades on tests.

If the mathematics laboratory is to attain any stature as one of the basic methods of instruction, ways for evaluating pupil progress and their motivation in the lab must be given careful attention.

TEACHER-MADE TESTS

Several types of test questions have proved their value in teacher-made tests of computational ability, vocabulary, information, understanding and other specific outcomes. These types are the short-answer, multiple-choice, matching, and true-false questions. A teacher who is to become competent in designing tests should know the purposes for which each type of question is best suited and the special techniques for constructing these questions.

Besides the directions and illustrations in this chapter, there are several sources to which the teacher can turn for further examples of good procedure. In any well-designed commercial test the items have been constructed by experts and are, therefore, examples of effective test construction. Some modern textbooks in mathematics contain expertly constructed tests to be used primarily for self-testing. They also serve as valuable models for the teacher who constructs his own tests.

The Short-answer Question

This type of question comes in a variety of forms and is known by a variety of names. There is the incomplete-sentence form: "A garden contains 72 square meters. If it is 9 meters long, then it is ___ meters wide." And there is the question form: "What geometric figure is formed by the intersection of a plane and a sphere?"

The various forms measure essentially the same thing. Experience indicates that the short-answer forms are more easily read and are less confusing than any other type of question. However, the range of outcomes to be measured by this type of question is limited, and other kinds of questions may be used to provide interest and variety and to serve special purposes.

The question form illustrated above is the most commonly used in mathematics. The illustrations given below differ from general classroom practice in that, as a convenience in scoring, a space is provided for filling in the answer. In general, short-answer questions are useful for measuring ability to perform an operation or to provide information. This is so because there is practically no way for the pupil to guess the correct answer; consequently, if he is able to supply it, there can be little doubt of his knowledge.

The short-answer type of question is limited, however, to questions that call for facts—who, what, when, where, or how many. Sample questions follow:

Directions: Write the correct answer in the blanks.

1 To estimate $83 + 29$, find the sum $80 +$ ___.

2 To estimate $61 - 38$, find the difference ___ $- 40$.

3 To estimate 6×57, find the product $6 \times$ ___.

4 To estimate $52 + 47$, find the sum ___ $+$ ___.

5 To estimate $397 + 502$, find the sum ___ $+$ ___.

6 To estimate 72×39, find the product ___ $\times$ ___.

If the answer can appear in more than one form, the pupil should be given specific directions about which to use. A problem like the following may have a number of acceptable alternative answers, depending on how the pupils are expected to perform operations: "The area of a room measured as 4.5 meters by 6.5 meters is _____ square meters." While 29 would be the generally accepted answer, most pupils would be inclined to carry the product to two decimal places.

Because of the possibility of alternative correct answers, the short-answer test is most useful when the teacher scores the papers. Even then, if there can be any question, the pupils should have directions as to how many decimal places are wanted, whether to express a fraction in simplest form, etc.

The Multiple-choice Question

The multiple-choice type is the best general-purpose question for testing outcomes other than computational skill and problem-solving ability. It is the most widely used type of question in standardized tests, largely because of its flexibility and the fact that it can be scored objectively—that is, anyone who scores it using the answer sheet will arrive at the same results. In teacher-made tests, the multiple-choice question is useful for measuring ability in:

Vocabulary.

Reading comprehension.

Interpretation of graphs, formulas, and tables.

Drawing inferences from a set of data.

Understanding of concepts and relationships.

This multiple-choice test is designed to measure understanding of sets and the symbols used with sets.

Directions: Read each question carefully, and select the response that answers the question. Underline the response and write the letter which indicates your choice in the blank to the left of the question.

_____ 1   In which of the following sets can the elements be placed in one-to-one correspondence with those in the set $A = \{1,2,3,4,\ldots,9\}$?
(a) $\{1,2,3,4,\ldots,14\}$ (c) $\{1,3,5,7,\ldots,23\}$
(b) $\{2,4,6,8,\ldots,18\}$ (d) $\{3,6,9,\ldots,30\}$

_____ 2   Which of the following is a subset of $A = \{2,4,6,8,\ldots,12\}$?

(a) $\{1,2,3,\ldots,9\}$　　　(c) $\{4,8,12\}$
(b) $\{3,6,9\}$　　　　　　(d) $\{0,2,4,\ldots,10\}$

___ 3　In a certain junior high school we have the following sets of pupils: A, the set of all seventh graders; B, the set of all eighth graders; C, the set of all ninth graders; and U, the set of all pupils in the school.

(a) $B \subset C$　　　　　(c) $(A \cap B) \cap C = \{\ \ \}$
(b) $B \cup C = A$　　　　(d) $A \cap (B \cup C) = U$

___ 4　If $A = \{1,3,5,7,9\}$ and $B = \{3,6,9\}$, which of the following represents $A \cap B$?

(a) $\{1,5,7\}$　　　　　(c) $\{3,9\}$
(b) $\{2,4,6,8\}$　　　　(d) $\{1,3,5,6,7,9\}$

___ 5　If $A = \{1,3,5,7,9\}$ and $B = \{3,6,9\}$, which of the following represents $A \cup B$?

(a) $\{2,4,6,8\}$　　　　(c) $\{3,9\}$
(b) $\{1,5,7\}$　　　　　(d) $\{1,3,5,6,7,9\}$

Direct questions were used in the illustration above. Sometimes an incomplete statement is used instead. For example:

___ 1　All factors of 18 are

(a) 1, 2, 3, 6, 9,　　　(c) 10 + 8 and 12 + 6
(b) 1, 2, 3, 6, 9, 18　(d)　2 × 9 and 3 × 6

It may be noted that the question form is more direct than the incomplete sentence. The latter becomes more confusing as it becomes longer.

The most critical feature of the multiple-choice test is the ability of the pupil to eliminate the distractors—the incorrect alternatives. The theory is that the pupil who is fully informed will recognize that each distractor is incorrect. Therefore the problem should be stated so that the pupil's knowledge determines his answer. The following example of a multiple-choice question is poorly constructed because it does not meet this specification:

___ 1　If, for a certain class, B is the set of all boys, G is the set of all girls, D is the set of all pupils who have dogs, and U is the set of all members of the class, which of the following is correct?

(a) $B \subset G$　　　　　(c) $B \subset D$
(b) $B \cup G = U$　　　　(d) $D \subset G$

Unless we know that not all the boys have dogs, we cannot be certain about (c). Unless we know whether any of the girls have dogs, we do not know if (d) is correct. The question is not designed to differentiate between well-informed and ill-informed pupils.

Distractors that are too obviously wrong should also be omitted:

___ 1 Which of the following is the formula for the area of a trapezoidal region?

(a) $\frac{1}{2}(hb)$ (c) $\frac{1}{2}(h)(a + b)$

(b) πr^2 (d) $(\frac{3}{4})\pi r^3$

If this question were included in a seventh-grade test, any good pupil would probably know that π does not belong in the formula for the area of a trapezoidal region. He would, accordingly, have a 50-50 chance to guess correctly even if he did not know the formula.

The multiple-choice question is limited as a measure of computational or problem-solving ability because it measures the ability to *recognize* the correct response rather than to *produce* it. However, because this is a characteristic of multiple-choice questions and because the modern curriculum is placing increased emphasis on the ability to estimate a reasonable answer, the multiple-choice question can be designed to aid in the development of this ability. Questions such as the following can serve both as a learning device and as an evaluation device if the time allotted for the test is limited so as to prevent the use of pencil and paper for computation.

Directions: Circle the most reasonable answer for each problem. You will not have time to use pencil and paper. Estimate mentally, using shortcuts.

1 If you bought 12 1/2 kilograms of grass seed at $2 per kilogram, how much would it cost?

(a) $2.10   (b $21   (c) $25   (d) $250

2 How much would a merchant pay for 34 dresses at $13 each?

(a) $38   (b) $380   (c) $44.20   (d) $442

1 Cone
2 Cube
3 Cylinder
4 Pyramid
5 Hemisphere
6 Rhombus
7 Sector
8 Square
9 Triangle

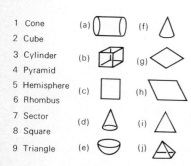

Matching Questions

An interesting variation of the multiple-choice question, and one which the teacher can use for a number of special purposes, is the matching question. Here is an example of it:

Directions: Copy the numerals 1 to 9 on a sheet of paper and after each numeral write a letter to indicate which picture is named.

This type of question is widely used in pairing up such things as definitions and words defined, and measurements and formulas. Three of the more important points to watch for in constructing questions of this type are:

The list on the right, from which selections are made, should contain more items than the list on the left.

To make it simpler for the pupil who knows the right answer to find it, possible answers should be arranged alphabetically, chronologically, or in some other systematic way, and each item should be short.

The questions should be homogeneous; that is, no item on the right should be logically excludable as an answer to any item on the left by a pupil who is uninformed.

Note how the following example violates the last-named condition in three ways. With one exception, the formulas given are for perimeters or areas, so that an alert pupil would limit his choice for any given formula to one beginning $p =$, or $A =$; the measure of the circumference of a circle could only be $C =$; and the formula for the area of a circular region must contain π and begin $A =$.

Directions: In the column at the left, you will find a number of measures of perimeter and area. Copy the letters on a sheet of paper. Find the formula at the right that fits each measure, and write its numeral beside the proper letter.

(a)	Area of a triangular region	1. $C = 2\pi r$
(b)	Perimeter of a rectangle	2. $A = \pi r^2$
(c)	Area of a circular region	3. $A = s^2$
(d)	Area of a trapezoidal region	4. $p = 4s$
(e)	Perimeter of a square	5. $A = \frac{1}{2} h(a + b)$
(f)	Area of a square region	6. $p = 2l + 2w$
(g)	Circumference of a circle	7. $p = 3s$
(h)	Area of a parallelogram region	8. $A = \frac{1}{2}hb$
		9. $A = hb$
		10. $A = 6s^2$

True-False Questions

While popular in other fields, the true-false question is not extensively used in mathematics. It has some properties, however, that justify its use in special cases. It can lend variety and interest to informal testing activities. It is easy to construct, interesting to the pupils, easily scored, and it arouses discussion. It is useful when performance of the pupil on any one item is not an important consideration—his success on any given item may be a result of a good guess, as he has a 50-50 chance. It should not be used for grading purposes since a true-false test does not yield a meaningful score unless it has 60 or more items, which is not usual in a mathematics test. In the following example, the true-false question was used because the exercise was designed as a learning activity as well as a test, and the true-false form, in itself, is of interest to pupils.

Figure 13-6

Directions: Refer to the graph (Fig. 13-6) to see if each of these statements is true. If it is, circle T; if not, circle F. Do not guess; if you cannot decide, omit the item.

T F 1. The stopping distance of a car increases rapidly at high speeds.

T F 2. If you double the speed of a car, you double the stopping distance.

T F 3. The stopping distance increases more between 45 and 60 kilometers per hour than between 90 and 105 kilometers per hour.

The teacher who designed the test also could have used multiple-choice questions to get a more precise idea of reading ability However, he knew that the pupils could cover a greater number of true-false questions than of any other type in the same amount of time, and that, furthermore, the true-false questions were more likely to stimulate discussion, which was desirable.

It is easy to make an ineffective true-false test. For this reason, four important precautions are worth keeping in mind.

Keep the items short. A long item becomes confusing to the pupil. Furthermore, he is likely to realize that the longer an item is the more likely it is to be true.

Check the items for ambiguities. Have another teacher go over them for you, or put the test aside for a day or two and then go over the items yourself.

Avoid easily recognizable clues, which tend to give the pupil an idea of whether the statement is true or false; sweeping modifiers. such as *always, never, only,* and *generally,* usually indicate false items.

The number of correct and incorrect items should be about the same, but they should not be alternated—the arrangement should be random.

Learning to Construct Tests

The interested teacher can readily become expert in test construction. Such expertness consists in deciding what is to be measured, selecting the type of item most appropriate for such measurement, constructing well-designed items, and giving proper directions.

While test items of the types illustrated here have been widely used in grades six, seven, and eight, not much reliable information about their usefulness in the lower grades is available. There is some indication that a multiple-choice item should have only two responses in grade four, but even here there is little evidence to support this conclusion. The teacher who is using items of any sort for the first time, at any level, should introduce them first as learning exercises for discussion, and through experience determine the inherent difficulty of the form of question before utilizing it in a test.

MEASUREMENT OF UNDERSTANDING

The current emphasis on development of pupil understanding has, of course, placed a corresponding emphasis on evaluation of that understanding. Unfortunately, development of effective techniques for direct measurement of understanding is difficult. Any well-designed test of other outcomes will incorporate some measurement of understanding. It is still true, however, that the level of a pupil's understanding can best be inferred from his behavior in class discussions and other activities. The teacher who is interested in developing his pupils' understanding will become skillful in recognizing the degree of that understanding. He will determine this from what the pupil says and does in improvising the solution to problems that confront him, and he will become skillful in planning activities that call for exploration, discovery, and generalization.

Attempts to devise tests that measure understanding directly are generally built around four major kinds of activities:

1 Questions about the meanings of whole numbers designed to reveal understanding of place value.

- To multiply a number by 10, which of these is correct?
  (*a*   Move each digit two places to the left.
  (*b*) Move each digit one place to the right.
  (*c*) Add 0 to the number.
  (*d*) The product is twice as large as five times the number.

- In 4,444 which of these statments is correct for the leftmost 4?
  (*a*) It represents 100 times the value of the 4 to its right.
  (*b*) It represents 10 times the value of the 4 to its right.
  (*c*) It is in the hundreds place.
  (*d*) It represents 4 × 100.

- In which of the following does 7 represent 7 tens?
  (*a*) 746   (*b*) 7,746   (*c*) 70   (*d*) 26,707

2 Questions on what procedure to use or on the correctness of procedures used in computations.

- In multiplying 22 × 34 you are doing which of the following?
  (*a*) (20 tens × 34) + (2 ones × 34)
  (*b*) (2 tens × 34) + (2 ones × 34)
  (*c*) 22 tens × 34 ones
  (*d*) 22 ones × 34 tens

- Which of the following are not correct? Give your reasons.

$$(a)\ 7\overline{)714}^{\,102} \qquad (b)\ 8\overline{)64}^{\,08} \qquad (c)\ 7\overline{)49}^{\,70} \qquad (d)\ 5\overline{)705}^{\,101} \qquad (e)\ 6\overline{)126}^{\,21}$$

- Which of the following are not true? Give your reasons.

  (a) 4 fourths + 2 fourths = 6 fourths.
  (b) 4 fourths ÷ 2 fourths = 2 fourths.
  (c) 4 fourths × 2 fourths = 8 fourths.
  (d) 4 fourths × 2 fourths = 6 sixteenths.
  (e) 4 fourths – 2 fourths = 2 fourths.

3 Questions calling for explanations of various operations.

- Which of these is the correct way to express a fraction in simplest form?

  (a) Divide the numerator by the denominator.
  (b) Divide the denominator by the numerator.
  (c) Divide numerator and denominator by the same number.
  (d) Subtract the same number from numerator and denominator.

- To find the average of some numbers, which of the following would you do?

  (a) Find their products and divide by the number of numbers.
  (b) Find their products and divide by their sum.
  (c) Find their sum and divide by their product.
  (d) Find their sum and divide by the number of numbers.

- Which of these can be only approximately determined?

  (a) The number of cars in a convoy.
  (b) The number of eggs in a container.
  (c) The time it takes to drive to town.
  (d) The cost of 5 liters of gasoline.

4 Questions calling for generalizations about operations.

- Which of the following operations should be used to find the average number of kilometers a car travels on a liter of gasoline?

  (a) Divide the number of liters used by the number of kilometers traveled.
  (b) Divide the total cost of gasoline by the cost per liter.

(c) Multiply the number of kilometers traveled by the number of liters used.

(d) Divide the number of kilometers traveled by the number of liters used.

- In front of each statement write T (always true), S (sometimes true), or F (always false).

    (a) ____ If the first factor is multiplied by four and the second factor is unchanged, the product is multiplied by four.

    (b) ____ If the first factor is increased and the second factor decreased, the product is increased.

    (c) ____ If the first factor is divided by two and the second factor is unchanged, the product is divided by two.

    (d) ____ If the first factor is halved and the second factor is unchanged, the product is divided by two.

    (e) ____ If the first factor is halved and the second factor is halved, the product is halved.

    (f) ____ If the first factor is increased by four and the second factor is increased by four, the product is increased by four.

    (g) ____ If the first factor is increased by four and the second factor is decreased by four, the product in unchanged.

These are intended only as samples of the informal attempts made by teachers to measure directly the level of the understanding of their pupils. Any teacher who is interested in the possibilities can improve and extend these techniques.

In addition to teacher-constructed tests, there are huge numbers and a larger variety of commercial tests. These include readiness, diagnostic, achievement, and others. While the mathematics teacher should know about these, their characteristics and limitations, their use is undoubtedly covered in other courses. Hence a discussion of them is omitted here.

ADEQUACY OF THE EVALUATION PROGRAM

The quality of the evaluation program is measured by its effectiveness in the operational control of classroom activities and the quality control of the product. There are, however, certain identifying marks of a good evaluation program which are apparent to an observer even without knowing its results. Important among these are the following:

Integration with learning activities: Evaluation is an integral part of the instructional program. Effective teaching is possible only if pupil progress is appraised in terms of each outcome. The various procedures for obtaining the required information are closely associated with the learning activities and, in the case of observational procedures, become a part of them.

Selectivity of outcomes evaluated: Evaluation is time consuming. It would be impossible to incorporate in an evaluation program a careful appraisal of all outcomes. Those to be omitted, however, should be determined only after careful consideration of priority. The term *comprehensive* is frequently used to describe a program of evaluation which has considered all the desired outcomes and selected the most important and critical for evaluation. The term *balanced* is frequently used to describe a program in which all of the high-priority objectives are formally evaluated and the emphasis is properly distributed among them. Both of these characteristics are required in a good program.

Systematic administration: The observational procedures are continuous and are made part of the learning activities. The more formal testing should take place at regular intervals, so that pupil progress may be systematically measured. To avoid neglect, a schedule for the formal testing should be set up in advance and rigorously adhered to.

Provision of information for effective records and reports: A properly designed evaluation program is commonly integrated with an effective system of records and reports. Pupils and parents should be continuously and fully informed with regard to pupil progress. The records that accompany pupils in their move to another school should be comprehensive and adequate. This is not a necessary consequence of a good evaluation program, but it would be impossible without such a program.

QUESTIONS AND EXERCISES

1 What are some major goals achieved by an effective evaluation program?

2 Why is it important to have a carefully developed set of objectives for the mathematics program before planning experiences and evaluation procedures?

3 What is meant by ". . . classroom activities must be conducted on an experimental basis. . ."?

4 Which of the following are most difficult to evaluate: attitude toward mathematics, skill in addition, understanding of properties,

vocabulary, ability to use precise language? Give reasons for your answer.

5 What are characteristics of an effective evaluation program?

6 Discuss the advantages and difficulties of using observational procedures in evaluating mathematical behavior.

7 Describe the kinds of evidence secured from tests and the kinds best obtained by procedures other than tests.

8 What precautions are to be kept in mind when writing matching, multiple-choice, incomplete-sentence, and true-false questions for mathematics?

9 Multiple-choice questions constructed by the teacher are especially useful in mathematics for measuring what abilities?

10 How are true-false questions used in mathematics classes? What precautions are to be used in constructing a true-false test?

11 How can a teacher secure information on whether pupils think critically about a mathematical situation?

12 What kinds of information can a teacher obtain about a pupil from a carefully planned interview with him?

13 How may the effectiveness of the mathematics laboratory be evaluated?

14 Why is determining a pupil's understanding of a mathematical idea difficult? For what topics has some progress been made in evaluating a pupil's understanding?

PROJECTS

1 Examine a current textbook for a grade level of your choice. (a) Identify the number and kinds of tests such as readiness, diagnostic, and achievement which you find. Do you find any kinds of tests that are neglected? (b) How many tests are included? To what extent are items in the test that evaluate a pupil's skill, understanding, ability to solve problems, and other abilities included? To what extent are the different kinds of test items listed in the chapter included in the tests?

2 Locate a readiness test in a textbook and identify the skills and concepts that the author identified as prerequisite to learning the topic.

3 For the division shown below, two questions are given to appraise the pupils' understanding of the mathematical meaning of the computation. Make up six other questions. (a) Why is the 5 in the quotient placed above the 8 in the dividend? (b) The 35 is actually 350 and is the result of multiplying _____ and _____ ?

$$\begin{array}{r} 54 \\ 7\overline{)381} \\ 35 \\ \hline 31 \\ 28 \\ \hline 3 \end{array}$$

4 Find in a newspaper a chart or article containing numerical ideas. Make up true-false, short-answer, and multiple-choice items to test understanding of the chart or text.

5 Select a topic other than percent and, under each heading below, list three types of behavior that pupils should demonstrate to show they have learned what they should. Remember that the question is, "What should they be able to do?" Topic: _____
(a) Vocabulary   (c) Meanings
(b) Interest   (d) Skills

6 Make ten true-false questions (with directions) to measure ability to read the bar graph pictured below.

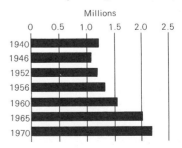

High school graduates

7 Write a set of short-answer questions to measure how well your fifth grade class understands the concept of simple closed curve.

8 Suppose $x \cdot y = r$, where x and y are non-zero rational numbers greater than zero. Below are some examples of true-false questions that can be used in a discussion of the relationship between x, y, and r. Write ten more true-false questions. (a) If x is less than 1, then r is less than y. (b) If y is equal to 1, then x is equal to r.

9 Write one experiment for pupils to complete in the mathematics laboratory for each of the Meaning of the Operation, Skills, and Generalizations in the Ms. Green example on page 351.

Bibliography

1 Biggs, E. E., and J. R. MacLean: *Freedom to Learn*, Addison-Wesley Ltd., Ontario, 1969. Chapter 10 is an excellent chapter on planning, assessing, and reporting students' progress.

2 Epstein, M. G.: "Testing in Mathematics: Why? What? How?" *The Arithmetic Teacher*, vol. 15, pp. 311-319, April, 1968. Description of criteria and considerations for use of various types of tests in mathematics.

3 Fellows, M. M.: "A Mathematics Attitudinal Device," *The Arithmetic Teacher*, vol. 20, pp. 222-223, March, 1973. Two short tests which every teacher can use to measure attitude toward mathematics.

4 Kidd, K., S. Myers, and D. Cilley: *The Laboratory Approach to Mathematics*, Science Research Associates, Inc., Chicago, 1970. Chapter 5 contains suggestions for evaluating the laboratory approach.

5 Maertens, N., and C. Schminke: "Teaching—for What?" *The Arithmetic Teacher*, vol. 18, pp. 449-456, Nov., 1971. Examples of assessing instructional procedures for learning concepts, principles and problem solving.

6 National Council of Teachers of Mathematics: *The Slow Learner in Mathematics*, Thirty-fifth Yearbook, Washington, D.C., 1972. Chapter 9 contains a short theorectical basis for evaluation and many practical suggestions for diagnosis and prescription.

7 O'Brien, T. C., and J. V. Richard: "Interviews to Assess Number Knowledge," *The Arithmetic Teacher*, vol. 18, pp. 322-326, May, 1971. Examples of a teacher giving a pupil a task, observing his strategies for solving, and interviewing him.

8 Romberg, T. A., and J. W. Wilson: "The Development of Mathematics Achievement Tests for the National Longitudinal Study of Mathematical Abilities," *Mathematics Teacher*, vol. 61, pp. 489-495, May, 1968. Brief description of how achievement tests for NLSMA were developed.

9 Weaver, F. W.: "Evaluation and the Mathematics Teacher," Chapter 9 in *Mathematics Education*, Sixty-ninth Yearbook, National Society for the Study of Education, NSSE, Chicago, 1970. Theory and examples of evaluation based on objectives and outcomes.

14

THE TEACHER AND THE MATHEMATICS CURRICULUM

In the preceding chapters, attention has been directed largely to current problems, goals, content, and methods in elementary mathematics. It has been seen that a great deal of thought, time, work, and money have been devoted to developing the current mathematical program in the elementary grades. Yet it would be a mistake to suppose that the result has been a completely satisfactory curriculum that needs only to be carefully implemented.

THE TEACHER AND EXPERIMENTATION

There are several reasons why we can never arrive at a final form for the elementary program in mathematics. Consider, for example, changing social and vocational needs. As only one example of this, demands for unskilled manpower are steadily decreasing. This requires a larger population with extensive technical preparation carefully planned by the school. Furthermore, mathematics itself is continuing to develop, with implications for the elementary program that must be identified and correlated with corresponding changes in the curriculum. Moreover, factors such as our position of world leadership, the prevalence of an ever-changing world, and domestic social problems and military and ideological conflicts mean that our educational program must be efficiently designed to develop fully all our human resources.

Adapting Materials and Methods

These requirements place a continuing responsibility on the teacher. Curriculum materials provided by educational leaders must be selected and adapted to classroom situations. New instructional materials and activities are required for a wide range of abilities. Thus, the teacher of elementary mathematics is confronted with a fluid and challenging situation. The inadequacies of some practices have become increasingly evident, and considerable work has been done in bringing together new and interesting materials. But how to select the best of these materials, how to adapt them for pupils of varying ability, and how to plan effective classroom procedures are problems that have not been completely solved. In the immediate classroom situation, the responsibility for solving these problems must rest with the teacher, who is in direct contact with pupils and parents, familiar with the interests and needs of his individual pupils, in a position to experiment both with materials and with procedures, and can keep parents informed of the nature and purposes of these new developments.

Increasing the pupil's understanding is considered to be the most important objective of all programs. This is especially true in the elementary school. The principle of meaningful teaching has been fashionable in the elementary school especially since about 1935. Its application to classroom procedures, however, has never been completely realized. Although it is generally agreed that pupils who understand can learn faster and with less repetition, have a stronger motivation to study, and transfer ideas more readily to related situations, the practical means of securing this understanding has never been made sufficiently clear, either in mathematics textbooks or in teacher training classes.

The need for a broader experimental attack on the question is highlighted by the conflict between various schools of thought on how understanding is best achieved. One example of conflicting viewpoints may be found in the question of degree of emphasis that should be given to the structure of the number system.

At one extreme are those who would introduce a concept such as the associative property for addition of whole numbers in the early grades, have pupils generalize it as soon as possible, identify it in certain manipulations, and use it for computations. For example, the detailed steps for adding 63 and 4 in Fig. 14-1 demonstrate an application of the associative property for addition. If this plan is successfully implemented, the pupil learns the properties on an increasingly abstract level as he matures.

At the opposite extreme are those who would have these properties studied intuitively in the elementary school and made explicit only when a number system is studied from a postulational viewpoint in high school and college. Those supporting this view say, for example, that the use of technical terminology, such as *commutative,* can only be verbiage for young children. They would rely more on intuition, on reasoning by analogy (63 + 4 = 67 because 3 + 4 = 7), and, in early instruction, on physical representation of the operation rather than on logic.

Figure 14-1

Applying the associative property.

$63 + 4 = (60 + 3) + 4$	63 renamed as $60 + 3$
$= 60 + (3 + 4)$	Associative property for addition
$= 60 + 7$	7 is common name for $3 + 4$
$= 67$	67 is common name for $60 + 7$

That neither extreme view is completely acceptable is obvious. However, such a controversy, even though possibly exaggerated, reveals the need for careful study and research to determine the best procedures for promoting understanding. If left at the level of abstract debate, the question only aggravates existing confusion. Many questions, such as the following, are related to the main issue: How long should a pupil be permitted to use an idea that is verified only by intuition? When should the deductive nature of mathematics be introduced to achieve maximum understanding? What are the purposes of mathematics education for a pupil of a specific maturity level with respect to mathematics?

The need for broad cooperation for any experimental attack on problems such as these is evident. Active participation by professional mathematicians is essential. So, too, is that of specialists in elementary education, who can design and direct the experimental attack so that the questions may be answered. We need to involve in the educational enterprise, also psychologists, especially those concerned with the learning of mathematics. Even more crucial, however, is the cooperation of the teacher, who can suggest the procedures that are worth testing and use them effectively in the classroom while the experimentation is in progress.

THE TEACHER IN THE SEVENTIES

One trend in the mathematics curriculum for at least the next few years certainly seems to be that improved facilities, materials, and methods for individualizing instruction will be incorporated into the mathematics laboratory. At present, however, this and other available procedures for individualized instruction require careful thought and some reorganization.

It would seem, too, that instruction in the years ahead will be based more and more on performance objectives. Such objectives, as previously stated, have made all mathematics educators more aware of those learnings that are important and those that are less important. While the writing of precise objectives in terms of behavior of pupils has had an affect in the mathematics curriculum and has clarified the thinking of some teachers, there is much yet to be done. It is easy to test the accomplishment of an objective such as "The pupil writes the correct answer for 2/4 + 1/4." Of more importance, however, is the cognitive level of response: Did the student memorize an algorithm? Did he discover a paper-folding algorithm? Has he reached an evaluative level of generalizing $a/b + c/b = (a + c)/b$?

Behavioral objectives help to specify the minimum levels of competence. These are usually at the skill level and much thought needs to be given to the higher-level cognitive processes, such as mathematical thinking or understanding, and methods of evaluating such objectives.

There are a number of plans, each claiming to individualize instruction, that are being used with varying degrees of success. Some are based on commercially developed materials, and other are teacher- school- or district-initiated with materials prepared locally. These are described in the following sections without detail or critical evaluation. One feature common to all programs seems to be that lessons in each are based on behavioral objectives. Another common feature is the use of the mathematics laboratory in some form or another.

Contracts

A series of lessons is ordinarily developed with an open-ended format in which pupils can contract to complete a number of lessons but may exceed this number. The contracts often contain objectives to be achieved, exercises, self-evaluation papers, textbook pages to which the pupils refer, and available concrete materials, tapes, and other audiovisual equipment.

Working in Pairs

In this plan, pupils work in pairs and at their own rates. Homework may or may not be collected. Partners may take tests together and receive the same grade. Teachers offer guidance and suggestions and often act as tutors. A variety of activities, exercises, and problems characterizes the program.

Individual Prescription

Each pupil is given a placement test from which the teacher decides where he should start on the given concept, skill, or problem set. From this diagnosis, his "course of study" is prescribed by carefully specified objectives, and he begins to work. When he is finished, a posttest is given to determine if he needs to do more on that topic or proceed to the next one. In many commercial programs the prescription of activities is quite varied to include individual tutoring by teacher or peer, working with concrete materials or from a workbook, and listening to tapes which explain a concept and then direct exercises relating to it.

Computer Assisted Instruction

Each child has access to a computer. In some lessons the computer asks a question to begin a lesson. In most cases, the pupil is asked a question or shown a picture to which he responds. There is relatively little computer-assisted instruction at present. One reason is that it was essentially unknown until the early 1960s. Further, programming lessons requires considerable time, and this expense added to the expense of the computers themselves makes the total cost high.

Performance Contacts

Some large companies have contracted with school districts with the agreement specifying that achievement levels of a group of pupils will be raised a certain amount in a given period of time.

There are many variations of the sample programs described above and many of similar nature under different titles. Some attempt to induce the pupil to interact with a computer, a classmate, or a small group; in many cases the pupil works alone. These methods replace interaction between teacher and class. Some of these programs will be improved, some may provide dramatic advances in individualizing instruction, and some will be discarded.

At the same time, it should be apparent that an effective teacher is a more important factor for most students than any type of class room management or any type of material. Hence the teacher must be alerted continuously to the kinds of programs being developed to meet the needs of each individual learner. Certainly, no panacea exists or ever will. Only by careful planning and evaluation as outlined in earlier chapters will children be assured of the best mathematics program possible.

All mathematics educators—maintaining constant emphasis on individualization—must keep *all* major outcomes for the mathematics curriculum in focus. In addition to finding better ways to provide for individual differences, we must find better ways to help pupils:

Learn to explore mathematical problems.

Understand algorithms more thoroughly.

Apply more mathematics and more mathematical concepts to life situations.

Understand concepts and then symbolize them in more and more precise ways.

Perhaps one final caution is in order. We must put forth every concerted effort to make schools and education more humane. This means meeting individual needs, societal needs, and the needs of specialized areas of study. Few discoveries have been made by individual effort. Therefore more classroom strategies should be developed that take advantage of individual talents, the talent of small groups, and the collected talents of large groups. Finally, all materials, methods, and classroom organizational patterns must work to supplement the textual materials developed for children.

THE TEACHER AND TEXTBOOKS

Even though a multimedia approach is being tried out successfully in some classrooms, the textbook remains a major source of experiences for pupils. During the last 25 years, a concerted and successful effort has been made to improve textbooks in elementary school mathematics. Some obvious features that have been incorporated are the emphasis on concepts, the writing of textbooks for the primary grades (for many years pupils had no mathematics texts prior to grade three), the use of functional pictures and sketches, the introduction of color, the use of readiness experiences prior to the introduction of new topics, systematic review of concepts as well as skills, and the inclusion of special experiences for both slow and fast learners.

A textbook is no longer considered to be merely a source of exercises and word problems. The effective teacher uses different sections of the book to help pupils discover ideas, learn the mathematics basic to various computations, read quantitative text, and review for a class discussion or test. Special features included in many texts are extra practice exercises near the back of the book, mathematical recreations to promote interest, and diagnostic tests to help teachers plan reteaching where needed.

Teacher's Manuals

A teacher's manual to accompany elementary school mathematics texts is a recent innovation. At present, all texts have a manual of some sort. One common type is a special, often enlarged book with a pupil's page reduced in size and printed with suggestions to the teacher alongside (Fig. 14-2). Although such a book may be bulky, it contains a wealth of suggestions. Some manuals include Pupil Objectives, Mathematical Background for the Teacher, Prebook Lessons, Book Lessons, and Suggestions to Care for Individual Differences. Another common type uses the margin of the pupil's book for suggestions to the teacher and a set of pages at the back of the book for mathematical background. These are often printed in a different color for easy reading.

The manual, whatever type, probably contains a description of the program for grades K-8 and a more detailed description for one grade. Other features found in many manuals are answers to all exercises, chapter and term tests, lists of commercially available teaching aids, and directions for constructing teaching aids.

Figure 14-2
One type of teacher's manual page.

Pupil's page

Suggestions for the teacher

Only by constant and careful reference to the manual can a textbook be used with full effectiveness. This is especially true for those pages where concepts are introduced and the rationale for procedures are explored. Further, the full effect of the program to develop understanding can be achieved only if the class activities designed to precede the practice exercises are used.

Some suggestions for using the manual effectively are:

Study the objectives of the lesson To be effective, the teacher must know the purpose of the lesson, which may not be clear even from careful examination of the pupil's page. For example, if the pupil's page is the study of certain addition facts, it may not be evident whether or not these are to be completely learned (memorized) when the page is finished.

Review the mathematical background thoroughly It may be located next to the pupil's page or in a special section where the mathematics for a chapter is presented. If the background is given individually for each page, the teacher may wish to study a number of consecutive pages in order to see how the mathematical ideas fit together.

Often the background is written in such a manner that the teacher will have studied the mathematics on a higher level than he is to teach. For example, if the class is investigating intuitively relationships, such as

$$\text{Because } 2/3 = 8/12, \text{ then } 2 \times 12 = 3 \times 8$$

$$\text{Because } 2/3 < 3/4, \text{ then } 2 \times 4 < 3 \times 3$$

the background would help the teacher see the truth of the generalizations

$$\text{If } a/b = c/d, \text{ then } a \times d = c \times b \ (b \neq 0 \text{ and } d \neq 0)$$
$$\text{If } a/b < c/d, \text{ then } a \times d < c \times b \ (b > 0, \ d > 0)$$

Thus, not only has he met the concept at a more mature level, but also he knows what the pupil will learn subsequently about the concept.

The background, too, is helpful with vocabulary. Now that many new words are being used, teachers often have more difficulty than pupils because they have to unlearn the older words as well as learn the newer ones. For example, *minuend, subtrahend,* and *difference* are being replaced by *sum, known addend,* and *unknown addend;* similarly, *multiplicative inverse* or *inverse under multiplication* is replacing *reciprocal.* Further, the vocabulary is not standardized. Often 4×3 is called a *product,* and such usage is correct. Yet in other books 4×3 is called a *product expression* and 12 is called the *product.* The teacher will use the vocabulary of the book (unless it is in error) in preference to that which he may have learned.

Use the "prebook" lessons faithfully This may include experiences for helping pupils discover an idea or procedure. Often it is a situation designed to motivate pupils, or it may describe concrete experiences to be used prior to the more abstract presentations of the text. Sometimes the pupil's page is worthless unless preceded by discussion, representation with objects, or manipulation of pictures.

Follow the recommendations for best use of the pupil's page There are many helpful suggestions, such as "Work through the entire page with the pupils," "Ask questions such as the following to help pupils understand the concept," "Avoid telling pupils by having them use the abacus," "Allow more capable pupils to study this page independently," "Before assigning written work be sure pupils know the correct form for recording their work," "If pupils are having difficulty, review pages 150-153."

It is a truism that the textbook determines the mathematics curriculum. However, there is more to the program than is found on the pages of the book. A program made up solely of experiences from the textbook would be sterile, and only a few of the objectives for teaching mathematics would be achieved. For best results the teacher's manual should be studied thoroughly. Experiences found there may be supplemented by selection from the extensive suggestions found in earlier chapters of this book and by effective practices developed by the ingenious teacher.

THE NEED FOR CONTINUING PREPARATION

Thus, the modern mathematics program, which represents the work of many scholars and researchers and the results of much classroom experimentation, is ineffectual unless the teacher can adapt it to the needs and interests of each of his pupils. To do this effectively, the teacher must know the program, know each of his pupils, and know how to make the adjustments that will produce the program that is of most value.

This is not the kind of expertness that can be mastered by merely earning a credential. It requires continuing study. Mathematics is changing in a changing society, within an advancing technology. It has often been observed how rapidly the content of mathematics is being developed—more mathematics has been invented in the past 50 years than had previously been invented since man learned to count. Advances in technology are equally striking—it has been stated that 90 percent of all scientists are still living.

Also, there is a correspondingly great change in our society and its physical environment. The rate of change has been accelerating, and there is every indication that it will continue to accelerate. Every technical advance has produced social problems—water pollution, traffic congestion, urban decay, and so on—none of which has been solved and all of which will probably be passed on for solution to the generation now in school. The competence needed by those who will inherit these problems defines a part of the outcomes sought in the mathematics program.

The fact that the program must be adapted to changing outcomes and changing needs of the pupils means that the teacher must be aware of current and future needs and of the procedures that must be used to meet them. It follows that in a changing society the preparation of the teacher is never completed. This is true of all professions—their members must continue to study to bring their preparation up to date and to keep abreast of changes. Eighty percent of the prescriptions currently written by a physician, as only one example, are for drugs that were not in existence 15 years ago.

How can the teacher acquire this continuing preparation after entering actively into his professional career? There are, of course, evening and summer programs for teachers offered by colleges and universities. Other agencies, too, are accepting the responsibility for this continuing education. Some governmental agencies, such as the U.S. Office of Education and State Departments of Education, are sponsoring inservice programs. Workshops and courses are also available to the teacher through participation in the activities of the various professional organizations. For the mathematics teacher, these are mainly the state and local chapters of the Classroom Teachers' Association of the National Education Association and the National Council of Teachers of Mathematics. The latter has national conventions throughout the country every year. The state and local affiliates of NCTM are also strong, active organizations at the grass-roots level. At their meetings, ranging in attendance up to 3,000, the teacher may learn about current problems, what is being done to solve them, and the degree of success with new content, procedures, and materials of instruction. In addition, college credit may be earned by attendance at most conferences.

Another source of continuing preparation is found in the professional literature, especially in the publications of the two organizations mentioned above. The National Council of Teachers of Mathematics publishes *The Arithmetic Teacher* (on a monthly basis), yearbooks, and many very practical supplementary booklets.

Equally important is the current literature of a general nature—popular periodicals and newspapers. The mathematics teacher should never forget his responsibility for being aware of the nature and significance of current social and technological developments. For example, a broad new field, which will probably become as important as the space sciences and industries, is now opening up in oceanography. This field will require scientists and technicians of a new kind: marine biologists, mineralogists, geologists, and so on. Pioneer industries are being developed to combat water and air pollution. Undoubtedly other social problems will give rise to other great industries that will broaden the vocational fields available to the pupil. The current literature provides the means for the teacher to keep informed of these developments.

The teacher is confronted with neither a static society nor a static field in mathematics. Rather, he encounters an opportunity and a challenge to keep abreast of a changing society and a dynamic field. The possibilities and responsibilities for leadership and guidance in development of pupil potential are clear and unmistakable. Equally clear are the requirements for keeping abreast of social change and technical advances.

The first requirement for the mathematics teacher is to understand the nature and potentialities of mathematics sufficiently well so that he may teach it meaningfully and profitably in the classroom.

Second is the responsibility to understand the developing goals of mathematics teaching, which must be consistent with the purposes of the elementary school and the individual needs of the pupils.

Third is to understand the learning process clearly enough to plan the procedures for adapting content to the needs of individual pupils and to evaluate the results in order to develop more effective procedures.

Finally, the mathematics teacher must appreciate the fundamental importance of mathematics in our culture and impart this appreciation to the pupils in order to establish a continuing interest and participation in the classroom activities.

APPENDIX A:
materials for the
mathematics laboratory

This appendix has two parts. In the first are instructions for the construction of materials that can be made inexpensively and are useful for pupils to manipulate as they discover and explore mathematical ideas. Included also are page numbers of this text on which reference has been made to a given device. The second part of this appendix is a short annotated bibliography containing descriptions of commercially available apparatus, addresses of firms distributing devices, and two references which indicate a means of evaluating materials for the mathematics laboratory.

TEACHER-MADE MATERIALS

Beads on a wire A number of beads are strung on a stiff wire such as the straight part of a coat hanger.

Uses: Studying sets and subsets and discovering relationships among addition facts. See pages 55, 62, and 106.

Beam balance A picture of a beam balance is shown. Washers are used as weights.

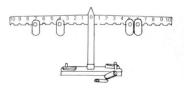

Uses: Discovering that = means balance, checking inequalities, and solving experimentally equations such as $2n + 3 = 5$. See pages 97 and 126.

Bean Sticks Red beans are glued to popsicle sticks and covered with acetate. For base ten, a supply of 1-bean, 2-bean, etc., through 10-bean sticks are needed. For base three, 1-bean, 2-bean, 3-bean, and 9-bean sticks are needed.

Uses: Studying place value in any base and the algorithms for adding and subtracting whole numbers. See page 291.

Circular geoboard On a square piece of wood draw a circle about 10 cm in radius. Equally spaced nails are driven into the circle. Some circular geoboards have 12 nails while others have 24 or 36 nails. Points for nails on the 12-nail geoboard are found

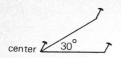
center

by making with a protractor a central angle of 30°; on the 24-nail geoboard the central angle is 15° and on the 36-nail board it is 10°. Available commercially.

Uses: Investigating the idea of fractions and making geometric figures. See pages 74 and 158.

Circular region for finding area of circular region Draw a circle about 15 cm in radius on a piece of cardboard. Cut it in half on a diameter. Draw radii so the central angle is 45°. Cut along each radius from the center almost to the circle. See picture on page 247. This makes an 8-piece region. For a 12-piece region use a central angle of 30°. Available commercially.

Uses: Showing area of a circular region. See page 247.

Circular sectors Draw circles about 10 cm in radius on tag board. With each circular region representing 1, sectors of the circle are cut to represent unit fractions. For various fractions make central angles with a protractor as follows (see pictures of 1/3 and 1/4). (*a*) 1/2. Cut on a diameter. (*b*) 1/3. Central angle, 120°. (*c*) 1/4. Central angle, 90°. (*d*) 1/5. Central angle, 72°. (*e*) 1/6. Central angle, 60°. (*f*) 1/8. Central angle, 45°. (*g*) 1/12, central angle, 30°. Sectors may also be cut for decimals and percent. 10% or 0.1 is cut with a central angle of 36°.

Uses: Exploring the concept of fractions, adding fractions and comparing fractions. See pages 164, 170, and 193.

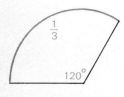

Cubes Wooden cubes of any size but commonly about 2 or 3 cm on a side are often made in the school woodshop. These can also be made from tagboard using the model on page 153.

Uses: Investigating sets, building towers by primary pupils and exploring the volume of rectangular prisms. May be used as dice when the six faces are numbered 1 through 6. See pages 154, 249, and 258.

Dot paper Like graph paper except that only dots which are intersections of segments show.

Uses: Drawing polygons and other geometric figures. See pages 145 and 235.

Geoboard On a piece of wood 2.5 cm thick and 15 cm square, drive 5 rows of 5 nails each. Adjacent nails in a row or column are 2.5 cm apart. May also be made with 16 or 36 nails. Colored elastics of various sizes are needed to form geometric figures. Available commercially along with many Activity Cards.

Uses: Exploring shapes and figures, perimeter, area and fractions. See pages 50, 145, 167, and 235 specifically as well as text and Activities in every chapter from 2 to 12.

Graph Paper   The squares on commercially available graph paper are ordinarily quite small. Draw squares of 1 cm on a side on a ditto.

Uses: Making bar and line graphs and pictures of geometric figures. See pages 163, 196, 208, and 317.

Hundreds Board   The construction is described on page 59.

Uses: Counting, investigating even and odd numbers, searching for patterns, and developing the meaning of percent. See pages 100, 207, and 278.

Number line   For use on the floor or blackboard, equally spaced marks are made on a roll of tape. The equal distance between each mark varies according to need.

Uses: As a model for showing the sequence of whole numbers or integers and adding and subtracting each. See pages 57, 108, 171, 195, and 265.

Pegboard   In a piece of wood 30 cm square 100 holes are bored in 10 rows, 10 holes to a row. The holes are started 1 1/2 cm from the side of the board and are 3 cm apart. Golf tees fit in the holes. If available, acoustical tile (with holes) may be used. See page 106 for a picture.

Uses: Showing place value and multiplication facts. See pages 64 and 127.

Place value or pocket chart   A picture of a chart with one pocket is on page 59 and one with three pockets is on page 85. They are made from pieces of tagboard sewed or stapled together.

Uses: Exploring the idea of place value, discovering the meanings of algorithms for addition, subtraction, and division with whole numbers and decimals. See pages 90, 120, 193, and 200.

Polygons and polyhedra   Drinking straws form the sides of figures and pipe cleaners fitted into the straws act as the vertices.

Uses: Constructing polygons and polyhedra. See pages 140 and 159.

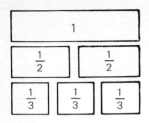

Rectangular regions Cut strips 3 cm wide and 30 cm long (this is a convenient, not a necessary size) to represent 1. Some strips are cut in halves, thirds, and fourths; the thirds and fourths are cut in half again to obtain sixths and eighths. There should be 2 halves, 3 thirds, 4 fourths and so on. Strips may also be labeled with decimals and percents.

Uses: Discovering the meaning of fractions and percent and adding of fractions. See pages 167, 169, and 193.

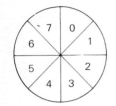

Spinner Use an empty margarine tub. The top of the tub is marked with the numerals needed. The figure shows the top separated into eight parts; a spinner is with a spinner fastened by a straight pin at the center.

Uses: Many primary grade activities and those concerned with probability and number pairs require a spinner. See pages 275 and 399.

Squares and strips Cut from tagboard or paper 3 cm-by-3 cm square regions, 3 cm-by-30 cm strips, and 30 cm-by-30 cm square regions representing 1, 10, and 100 respectively. Available in wood as Dienes Multibase Blocks for not only base ten but also for other bases.

Uses: Studying place value and addition and subtraction algorithms. See pages 60, 96, 125, and 194.

Strips Cut strips of tagboard or thin wood with small holes near the ends of each strip so its length in units is the distance between the holes. Fasteners are needed to hinge two strips.

Uses: Form and study polygons. See pages 140 and 342.

Tangram pieces The seven-piece tangram set made of tagboard is pictured at the right. The size of the square region may vary. The pieces are labeled *A, B, C, D, E, F,* and *G* to agree with the description of experiments in this text. Available commercially along with many Activity Cards.

Uses: Exploration cf pattern, shape, and area, and fractions. See pages 52, 186, and 221.

Tiles Square regions of varying size are cut from wood or cardboard.

Uses: Making geometric figures and covering regions to determine area. See pages 257, 317, and 333.

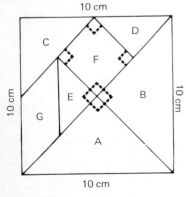

For Tangram Pieces

Trundel wheel A wooden wheel with a hole at the center is attached to a handle by an axle through the hole. Available commercially.

Uses: The length of a curve is determined by counting the number of revolutions of the wheel as it is rolled along the curve. See page 257.

Wood rods Rods are made from tagboard or strips of wood about the width of popsicle sticks. The size may vary but each unit should be a square. To be most useful a numeral is written on the rod as shown for the 1-,2-, and 3-rods. Coloring is optional. Available commercially in many forms with the best known being Cuisenaire Rods.

Uses: Studying the meaning of counting numbers and additon of counting numbers. See pages 58, 126, and 219.

BIBLIOGRAPHY ON MATERIALS FOR THE MATHEMATICS LABORATORY

This short bibliography contains readily available references to:

Commercially available materials for the mathematics laboratory.

Addresses of distributors of materials.

Topics for which materials are useful.

Ways of evaluating the worth of materials.

The teacher should recognize that, in addition to this bibliography, there are many sources for information about mathematics laboratories and the materials to be used. Some that are readily accessible to most teachers are the following:

The Arithmetic Teacher magazine. Published eight times a year by National Council Teachers of Mathematics (NCTM), it contains many articles on mathematics laboratories, descriptions of devices, and how to use them.

Professional meetings. Professional meetings of mathematics teachers are held throughout the United States with attendances ranging from a few dozen to a few thousand. At many meetings, publishers of textbooks and distributors of materials have their products on display. At many meetings, too, there are workshops and sections concerned with the descriptions of concrete aids and how they fit into an effective program.

In addition, inservice workshops at the school and district level are concentrating on aspects of the laboratory program. Further courses at the college level and inservice work through state departments of education, professional organizations, and the U.S. Office of Education provide up-to-date information.

1 Buckeye, D., W. Ewbank, and J. Ginther: *A Cloudburst of Math Lab Experiments,* Midwest Publications, Birmingham, Michigan, 1971. Four soft-cover booklets and a teachers' guide provide almost 1,000 experiments. Most apparatus needed can be made inexpensively.

2 Davidson, P. S.: "An Annotated Bibliography of Suggested Manipulative Devices," *The Arithmetic Teacher,* vol. 15, pp. 509-524, October, 1968. An excellent annotation of devices classified into fifteen categories with addresses of distributors.

3 Greenes, C., R. Willcutt, and M. Spikell: *Problem Solving in the Mathematics Laboratory: How To Do It,* Prindle, Weber and Schmidt, Inc., Boston, 1972. A fine collection of materials, games and how to make and use them.

4 Kelley, S. J.: *Learning Mathematics Through Activities,* James E. Freel and Associates, Inc., Cupertino, California, 1973. Manipulative materials to make, and activities using each.

5 Kennedy, L. M.: *Models for Mathematics in the Elementary School,* Wadsworth Publishing Co., Inc., Belmont, California, 1967. Models for teaching concepts with many pictures and where to get needed materials.

6 Laycock, M, and G. Watson: *The Fabric of Mathematics,* Activity Resources Company, Hayward, California, 1971. An excellent source book for materials, addresses of distributors of materials, where materials are useful, games, activities, references and other important topics concerned with mathematics laboratories.

7 Leeseberg, N. H.: "Evaluation Scale for a Teaching Aid in Modern Mathematics," *The Arithmetic Teacher,* vol. 18, pp. 592-594, December, 1971. Fifteen criteria to help a teacher evaluate a teaching aid.

8 National Council of Teachers of Mathematics, *Instructional Aids in Mathematics,* Thirty-fourth Yearbook, Washington, D.C., 1973. Many examples of manipulatives, games, puzzles, and so on, classified by concepts whose learning they promote.

9 Reys, R. E.: "Considerations for Teachers Using Manipulative Materials," *The Arithmetic Teacher,* vol. 18, pp. 551-558,

December, 1971. Pedagogical and physical criteria to be used in selecting manipulative materials.

10 Silverman, H.: "Teacher-made Materials for Teaching Number and Counting," *The Arithmetic Teacher,* vol. 19, pp. 431-433, October, 1972. Ideas for making needed materials for teaching primary mathematics at little expense.

APPENDIX B: games

This appendix has two parts. In the first is a set of games that were chosen because they have been effective in the classroom, little equipment is needed, and the teacher can use them with a minimum of preparation. Although they have been classified into a few general categories, changes in format are possible. Games for addition and subtraction, for example, may be used for multiplication with slight adaptions. Further changes in rules and numbers will make most games appropriate for either slow or fast learners. The second part of the appendix is a short bibliography of books containing games.

NUMBERS, NUMERALS, SETS

Three children have 3 pieces of paper, a dozen beans, the numerals 1,2,3,..., 9 cut from tagboard, and the number names one, two, three,..., nine each written on a card. The first child puts a number of beans on the first sheet of paper. The second child puts the corresponding numeral on the second sheet. The third child puts the corresponding name on the third sheet.

Place some counters in the desk. Each player tosses a die and removes as many counters as there are spots on the face of the die. Play continues until no more counters remain. The winner is the child with the most counters.

Pupils are in a circle. Leader says, "Three. Begin with Joe." They form sets of three, moving clockwise. This number of sets and the number left over are counted.

Children walk or jump as many spaces on a number line drawn on the floor as a thrown die or spinner indicates. The child who first reaches the end of the path wins.

The leader bounces a ball as the players count to themselves. A player is called on to bounce the ball the remaining number of times to reach a required number.

ADDITION AND SUBTRACTION

Two numbers on cards are held up. Among the competitors the winner is the one who gets the best approximation to their sum. For example, $173 + 436$ is approximately $200 + 400 = 600$. Rules of the game vary, with approximations required correct to within 100, 50, 10 and so on.

Such a game provides skill in estimating, a very practical skill often neglected in a program emphasizing accuracy.

Each of the two players has some beans, 10, for example. One player separates his beans, some in each hand. He shows how many in one hand. If the second player tells correctly how many beans are in the other hand, he takes one bean from the first player and then has his turn of partitioning the beans into his two hands and showing his opponent the beans in one hand.

The leader writes a numeral such as 6 on the chalkboard. Each player is to write all addition facts with a sum of 6. Younger children may show facts with wood rods (see page 393) instead of writing facts. The game is varied by writing subtraction facts with difference of 6.

The leader makes a statement such as, "If you subtract me from 10 you have three." The player naming the correct answer becomes the leader.

The leader in the center of a circle calls on a player in the circle to give the sum for a fact such as $7 + 4$. If the answer is incorrect, the player is "caught" and goes to the center of the circle. The leader calls another fact. The "caught player" can escape to the circle if he answers before the player on the circle.

An array of sixteen numbers is provided for two players. Two numbers are connected if a player can give their sum. Only adjacent numbers are connected. Pupils take turns. If one pupil gives an incorrect sum, his opponent has two turns. When a pupil completes a square, he puts his name on the square and receives one point.

2	8	1	7
5	3	9	8
6	2	4	5
4	3	6	7

Four players from each of two teams are at the chalkboard. The leader draws a flash card from a box, and tells the sum. Each player writes what he thinks the addition fact with that sum is. Each right answer scores a point. Players rotate after five sums are given. The game may be played also with subtraction.

MULTIPLICATION AND DIVISION

Each pupil has a card with a numeral on it. The leader makes a statement such as "Multiples of 4." Each pupil with a card that shows a multiple of 4 raises his card. A variety of statements can be made, "Factors of 18," "Common factors of 6 and 8," "Primes," "Greater than 6 and less than 11."

Duplicate a number of equations containing two or more operations with operations signs omitted: (8 3) $4 = 7$ for $(8 + 3) - 4 = 7$, or (2 8) $4 = 4$ for $(2 \times 8) \div 4 = 4$. Cards are held up and players search for correct answers. Competition may be with individuals or teams.

A telephone number such as 287-3863 is chosen. By addition or subtraction of two or more of the numbers, players are to make, for example,

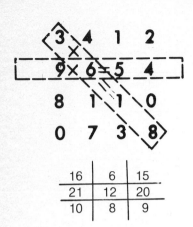

multiples of 5. Some answers are $8 + 7 = 15$, $8 - 3 = 5$, or $3 + 3 + 7 + 2 = 15$. A variation for more mature pupils is to allow multiplication and division. Here are some answers: $(8 \times 6) - 3 = 45$; $(8 \times 3) - (8 \div 2) = 20$. The team with the most correct answers wins.

Teams of pupils circle as many multiplication facts as possible, inserting $\times$ and $=$. Arrays may be larger. For younger children, replace multiplication by addition.

The leader writes a numeral such as 10 on the chalkboard. Players write as many equations in the form $5 \times 2 = 10$, $(3 \times 3) + 1 = 10$, or $(4 \times 5) \div (6 \div 3) = 10$ as possible.

Two players take turns writing a composite number in a tic-tac-toe design. The player who first has three in a row horizontally, vertically, or diagonally with a prime factor wins. In the figure shown, 2 is a factor of 6, 12, and 8.

Two teams or players compete. The leader calls a number such as 21. The first player who gives 21 as a product of two factors wins a point.

Each of nine players has a card with one of the numbers 1 through 9. The leader says, "Twelve." Players with factors of 12—which are 1, 2, 3, 4, and 6—hold up their cards. Cards are frequently interchanged.

Teams of two compete to see which can find the most factors of 820, 480, or some other "large" number in three minutes.

A number of pupils place themselves in any order. They count 1, 2, 3, and so on in turn except that "Buzz" must replace any multiple of 4 or a numeral with a 4 in it. In this case, the counting goes 1, 2, 3, buzz, and so on. Many variations are possible, such as "Say buzz for multiples of 7 or numerals with a 7 in the ones place" or "Say buzz in place of multiples of 2 and 3."

FRACTIONS

Each player has a supply of wood rods (see page 393). The leader says, for example, "Half of ten." Players show the rod or pairs of rods that measure half of ten. They show, in this case, the 5-rod, the 4- and 1-rods, or the 3- and 2-rods. As one of the many variations the leader says, "One third of twelve."

Each player has a card with a fraction written on it. The leader names a fraction. The player with that fraction on his card holds it up and names an equivalent fraction within a certain period of time. The game is varied by having the pupil hold up the card and name an equivalent decimal.

The leader names a fractional number such as 5/6. The player called names the number as a sum: 3/6 + 2/6 or 1/6 + 4/6, for example. For more mature pupils, addends with different denominations are required. One answer for 5/6 is 2/3 + 1/6.

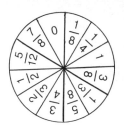

Teams of two compete to express as many counting numbers as possible in five minutes using four 4s. For example, $1 = \dfrac{4 + 4}{4 + 4}$, $2 = (4 \times 4)/(4 + 4)$, and $3 = (4 + 4 + 4)/4$.

Make a spinner (see page 392) with the disk as shown. Each player has a sheet of problems such as shown below. Players take turns spinning. Each writes the outcome of a spin in a □. First player to make 10 true statements wins.

$$\boxed{} < 1/2 \qquad \boxed{} + 1/4 = 1 \qquad 1/2 + \boxed{} = 3/4$$

$$\boxed{} + \boxed{} = 1 \qquad \boxed{} + \boxed{} = 0 \qquad \boxed{} + 0 = 3/8$$

The leader names a fractional number such as 1/2. He asks various questions of the players. "Name as many fractions equivalent to 1/2 as you can in five seconds." "What added to 1/2 is 3/4?" "Tell an equation for one-half times five eighths."

GAMES WITH A STRATEGY

Two players take turns choosing a number from 1, 2, 3, .., 10. A running total is kept. The player who gives the number to make the total 50 wins. Numbers may be chosen as often as desired. The first player may choose 6 and the second 7; the total is 13. If the first player now chooses 7, the total is 20. What is the strategy to always win? What are variations of the game?

For 122 the sum of the digits is 5: $1 + 2 + 2 = 5$. For 23 the sum of the digits is 5. What is the greatest number with 5 as the sum of its digits (no 0s allowed). What is the smallest number? What is the strategy to win? What variations in the rules are possible?

A number of counters are placed in each of three rows. Two players take turns in removing counters. At his turn a player may take any number of counters (from one to all) from a row. The object of the game is to leave one's opponent with the last marker.

The leader writes a number less than 100 on a piece of paper. Pupils try to guess the number with a minimum number of questions. Of these three questions the last is the best: "Is it 62?" "Is it in the thirties?" "Is it less than 50?" Is it possible to guess any number less than 100 in at most 6 guesses? What is the best strategy?

Each pupil chooses one of the numbers 6, 7, 8, 9, 10, 11, or 12. The leader says, "Multiply the number you have chosen by 2. Now add 10. Take one half of the sum. Subtract the number you selected. Show me your answer with your fingers." This problem is a "self-checking" one. What is the answer for any chosen number?

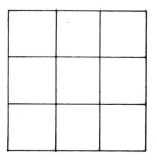

One player has 1, 3, 5, 7, 9. The second player has 0, 2, 4, 6, 8. Players take turns in writing one digit in a square. A digit can be

used only once. Winner is the player who writes the third number in a row or column or on a diagonal so the sum is 15.

Use a spinner with the disk having the numbers 0 through 9. A player spins twice to get a number pair (x, y). He plots this on his graph paper. The first player to plot four points in a straight line wins.

A starting number such as 24 is chosen by two players. The first player can subtract any factor of 24 except 1 and 24. Suppose he subtracts 4. Now since $24 - 4 = 20$, the next player can subtract any factor of 20 except 1 and 20. The game continues until a player is unable to subtract a factor that is not 1 or the number itself, and he loses. What is the strategy to win?

BIBLIOGRAPHY OF GAMES

There are many commercially available books of games and activities. The teacher can locate these in professional magazines and see them in bookstores and on display at professional meetings. With the huge variety of such books that have been published the teacher has the responsibility of choosing those games which meet the objectives he is trying to accomplish. A few books of games that many teachers have found useful are the following:

1   Allen, C.: *Daily Chores,* Creative Publications, Palo Alto, California, 1970. A collection of games and activities with masters for transparencies and pupils' worksheets.

2   Crescimbeni, J.: *Treasury of Classroom Arithmetic Activities,* Parker Publishing Co., West Nyack, New Jersey, 1969. Games, tricks, and puzzles for motivating interest and developing concepts.

3   Dumas, E.: *Math Activities for Child Involvement,* Allyn and Bacon, Inc., Boston, 1971. Games, puzzles, and riddles to spark children's learning.

4   Haugaard, J. C., and D. W. Horlock: *Fun and Games with Mathematics,* Contemporary Ideas, Los Gatos, California, 1972. A resource book of games, patterns and activities with permission to reproduce pages.

5   Henderson, G. L., and A. Walter: *Let's Play Games in Mathematics,* National Textbook Co., Skokie, Illinois, 1970. Eight books of games and activities, one for each of grades 1-8.

6   National Council of Teachers of Mathematics: *The Slow Learner in Mathematics,* Thirty-fifth Yearbook, Washington, D.C., 1972.

Appendix A has samples of good games and a bibliography of books and articles on games.

7   Read, R.: *Tangrams: 330 Puzzles,* Dover Publications, New York, 1965. This book will capture the imagination of all children.

8   Seymour, D., M. Laycock, V. Holmberg, R. Haller and B. Larsen: *Aftermath,* Creative Publications, Palo Alto, 1970. Four volumes of games, puzzles and stories.

INDEX

Point, 135-136, 157
Polygon, 24, 49-50, 66, 139-140, 158, 342
Practice (*See* Drill)
Precise language, 43, 135, 152, 166, 231, 231-232, 239
Precision in measuring, 230-232
Preschool number experience, 39-40
Primary grade teaching:
  activities for mathematics laboratory, 73-75
  addition and subtraction, 61-64
  in classroom affairs, 44-47
  counting members of sets, 54-55
    by 2s, 3s, 5s or 10s, 60-61
    rote, 52-53
  fractional numbers, 64-66
  geometry, 43, 48-50
  measure, 66-69
  metric system, 68-69
  money, 41, 69
  names for numbers, 55-57
  place value, 41, 43-44, 57-60
  problem solving, 70-72
  sets in, 47-48, 53-55
    counting, 54-55
    experimenting with, 48, 72-75
    related to addition and subtraction, 62-64
    vocabulary development, 51-52
    time, 69-70
    typical experiences, 40-50
Prime numbers, laboratory experiences with, 276-281
Prism, 150-155
Probability, 271-276, 292-293
Problem solving:
  activity cards for mathematics laboratory, 316-320
  acquiring background information, 299-305
  in addition and subtraction, 70-72
  as aims for teaching mathematics, 9
  clarifying problems, 297-305
  diagraming, 306
  in division, 122-123
  exploration, 297-299

  generalizing results, 315-316
  mathematical models, 305-312
  mathematical sentences, 310-312
  meaning of, 9, 296
  model solutions, 308-309
  in primary grades, 70-72
  reading in, 302-305
  simplifying problems, 297-299, 309
  using percent, 211-215
  verifying answers, 309-310, 312-315
Proof:
  deductive, 335-336
  plausible conclusions compared to, 24, 142, 143, 270, 335
Proportion, 213-215

Rapid Learners, 333-339 (*See also* Individual differences)
Ratio, 204-207, 211, 214, 222
Ray, 137-143
Readiness, 18-19, 30-32
Reciprocal, 176
Recreations, 331-333, 338-339
Rectangle, 49, 139-140, 243
Region, 52, 65, 141, 156, 241, 247
Regrouping in:
  addition, 83-85
  division, 117-121
  multiplication, 112-115
  subtraction, 89-91
Remainder in division, 31-37, 115-117
Remedial programs, 94-96, 124-126, 181-183, 324-333, 361-364 (*See also* Individual differences)

Science, correlation with mathematics, 215-219
Scope and sequence, 3-6
Sets:
  counting members of, 40-42, 54
  disjoint, 61
  empty, 53
  intersection of, 7, 27-28, 139, 172
  number of members of, 7, 54, 56
  subset, 54-55
  union of, 7, 8, 62, 64, 139

Skill fixing (*See* Drill)
Sphere, 150
Square, 43, 49, 340, 342
Structure:
  in learning, 19, 21
  in number systems, 5-6
Subtraction:
  activity cards for mathematics laboratory, 97-100
  addition relation, 62-64, 80-81
  algorithm, 89-91, 96
  borrowing, 89-91
  concept, 57, 61-64
  with decimals, 195-196
  decomposition, 89-91, 96
  drill, 81, 92-93
  facts, 61-64, 79-81
  fractional numbers, 169-173
  manipulative materials, use of, 62-64, 80-84, 87-88
  mathematical sentence, 62-64
  meaning, 57, 61-64
  mental, 91-92
  in primary grades, 61-64
  problem solving, 93-94
  regrouping in, 89-91
  sets in, 61-64
  zero in, 90-91

Tangram, 52, 186, 221, 392
Teacher preparation, 386-388
Teacher's manual, 384-386
Tests and testing (*See* Evaluation)
Time learning of, 69-70
Triangle, 28, 50, 139-141, 145, 148, 158

Union of sets, 7, 8, 62, 64, 139

Visual aids in learning (*See* Manipulative materials)
Volume, 248-251, 258

Whole numbers, 5-6, 53-54
Word Problems (*See* Problem solving)

Zero, 43-44, 48, 57, 59, 60, 110-111